Edmund W. H. Holdsworth

Deep-Sea Fishing and Fishing Boats

An account of the practical working of the various fisheries around the British Islands

Edmund W. H. Holdsworth

Deep-Sea Fishing and Fishing Boats
An account of the practical working of the various fisheries around the British Islands

ISBN/EAN: 9783337193140

Printed in Europe, USA, Canada, Australia, Japan

Cover: Foto ©Andreas Hilbeck / pixelio.de

More available books at **www.hansebooks.com**

DEEP-SEA FISHING

AND

FISHING BOATS.

AN ACCOUNT OF

THE PRACTICAL WORKING OF THE VARIOUS FISHERIES
AROUND THE BRITISH ISLANDS,

WITH

ILLUSTRATIONS AND DESCRIPTIONS OF THE

BOATS, NETS, AND OTHER GEAR IN USE.

BY

EDMUND W. H. HOLDSWORTH, F.L.S., F.Z.S., &c.,

LATE SECRETARY TO THE ROYAL SEA FISHERIES COMMISSION.

LONDON:

EDWARD STANFORD, 6, 7, & 8, CHARING CROSS, S.W.

1874.

All rights reserved.

PREFACE.

Most of the materials for the following Account of the Deep Sea and general Coast Fisheries of the British Islands were collected by me whilst Secretary to the Royal Sea Fisheries Commission, whose Report was laid before Parliament early in 1866. My duties in that capacity obliged me in most cases twice to visit almost every fishing station of any importance in the United Kingdom, thus enabling me to make a personal examination of the various boats and appliances used in the fisheries at each place, and sometimes to take part with the fishermen in their work. Towards the end of 1865 the necessity for an official inquiry into the working of the pearl fisheries on the coast of Ceylon led to my being sent for a few years to that colony, and obliged me to postpone bringing these pages before the public; the delay, however, although a matter of some regret to me, has afforded me an opportunity of observing the changes which have since taken place, and of noting the progress or decline of particular fisheries since the removal of all restrictions on their working.

To do this at all effectively it has been necessary to revisit the more important stations in England; while for later information about more distant parts of the coast I have been to some extent dependent on the several Annual Reports of the Scotch Fishery Board and of the Inspectors of Irish Fisheries which have appeared since 1865. In addition to these resources, however, I am indebted to the Hon. B. F. Primrose, the experienced and obliging Secretary to the Board, for many interesting communications about the recent condition of the Scotch fisheries; and my acknowledgments are also due to the Irish Inspectors for their courteous replies to my inquiries about the fisheries under their charge.

Among the various kinds of fishery noticed in the following pages, beam-trawling, drift-fishing, seaning, and deep-sea line-fishing have been especially discussed; and under the head of Fishing Stations a general idea has been given of the nature and extent of the fisheries carried on from the principal places along the whole coast of the British Islands. The unusual opportunities which have fallen to my lot of acquiring direct information on the general subject have enabled me in almost every case to speak from personal knowledge of the various matters treated of; and although in dealing with the multitude of details involved in a description of the Sea Fisheries of the United Kingdom, I can scarcely hope to have escaped some errors, I trust they will be found to be those of omission rather than statements unsupported by fact. It has been my object to give within moderate compass an accurate sketch of the recognized methods by which our markets are supplied with sea fish (with the exception of shell-fish, which are only incidentally noticed), and of the general condition of the various fisheries at as late a period as the character and arrangement of the work permitted. Early acquaintance with many parts of the subject has materially aided me in the task; for it is not generally easy to obtain even a simple statement of facts from many of the best-intentioned fishermen; and without some practical knowledge of the fisheries the value of the often contradictory information given by those who are engaged in them cannot be properly estimated.

In the illustrations to this work I have endeavoured to represent the various minute details which, often trifling in themselves, are characteristic of the fishing boats and gear of particular parts of the coast; and to ensure as much accuracy as possible the drawings have in all cases been made on the wood or copper by myself. The engraving has been in the skilful hands of Mr. William Dickes and Mr. W. J. Smyth; and, considering the technical character of the subjects, I have good reason to congratulate myself on the result of the care they have bestowed on the work.

I should add that as most of the engravings were finished before the issue of the present regulations for lettering and numbering the fishing boats, the old system of marking is the one represented; it was practically the same as the new system, so far as it went, but it was applicable only to the larger class of boats.

E. W. H. H.

London, 1874.

CONTENTS.

INTRODUCTORY.

Fisheries a subject of interest and importance to this country — Fishermen commonly unacquainted with many of the habits of fish — Improvement in the appliances for fishing — Fisheries not a nursery for the Navy — Condition of the fisheries — Supply of fish to the markets — Impossibility of estimating it — Effect of the extension of railways and the use of ice on the development of the fisheries — Great increase of trawlers — Immense demand for fish — Prices — The fish trade — Salesmen and fishmongers

ERRATUM.

Page 389. Line 7 from foot, *for* "fathoms" *read* "yards."

— Size and description of trawl-smacks — Improved rig — Cost of vessels and gear — Barking sails — Working the trawl — Shooting the net — Towing — Action of the trawl — Ground-fish and floating fish — Resistance of the water — Heaving up — Hoisting in the fish — Varied contents of trawl — Suitable weather — Depth of water — Condition of trawl-fish — Classification of — "Prime and offal" — Abundance of certain kinds — Fishing grounds, continued supply from — Plymouth, Brixham, North Sea — Discovery of Silver Pit — Large number of trawlers 51

II.—DRIFT-NET FISHING.

Long practice of — How the fish are caught — Proper time for fishing — Description of drift-nets, materials, size — Yarmouth luggers, how fitted up — Herring fishing — Shooting the net — "Driving" — Interference by trawlers — Regulations to prevent it — Hauling the nets — Mackerel fishing — Pilchard fishing — Looking for herrings — "Appearances" — Phosphorescent water objectionable — Effect of sounds on fish — Regular appearance lettering and numbering the fishing boats, the old system of marking is the one represented; it was practically the same as the new system, so far as it went, but it was applicable only to the larger class of boats.

E. W. H. H.

London, 1874.

CONTENTS.

INTRODUCTORY.

Fisheries a subject of interest and importance to this country — Fishermen commonly unacquainted with many of the habits of fish — Improvement in the appliances for fishing — Fisheries not a nursery for the Navy — Condition of the fisheries — Supply of fish to the markets — Impossibility of estimating it — Effect of the extension of railways and the use of ice on the development of the fisheries — Great increase of trawlers — Immense demand for fish — Prices — The fish trade — Salesmen and fishmongers — Registration and classification of boats imperfect — Alleged scarcity of fish inshore — Supposed spawning habits of sea fish — Important discoveries by M. Sars — Floating spawn — Fish do not necessarily approach the land for the purpose of spawning — Destruction of small fish in bays probably of slight importance — Close-time unnecessary — Extent of ground trawled on and of ground undisturbed — General prospects of the sea fisheries
Page 1

I.—TRAWLING.

Uncertainty as to origin of — Various kinds of trawl — Supposed long use of — Principal trawling stations — Description of the beam-trawl — Beam, heads, net, ground-rope — Arrangement and use of pockets — Warp, bridles — Size and description of trawl-smacks — Improved rig — Cost of vessels and gear — Barking sails — Working the trawl — Shooting the net — Towing — Action of the trawl — Ground-fish and floating fish — Resistance of the water — Heaving up — Hoisting in the fish — Varied contents of trawl — Suitable weather — Depth of water — Condition of trawl-fish — Classification of — "Prime and offal" — Abundance of certain kinds — Fishing grounds, continued supply from — Plymouth, Brixham, North Sea — Discovery of Silver Pit — Large number of trawlers 51

II.—DRIFT-NET FISHING.

Long practice of — How the fish are caught — Proper time for fishing — Description of drift-nets, materials, size — Yarmouth luggers, how fitted up — Herring fishing — Shooting the net — "Driving" — Interference by trawlers — Regulations to prevent it — Hauling the nets — Mackerel fishing — Pilchard fishing — Looking for herrings — "Appearances" — Phosphorescent water objectionable — Effect of sounds on fish — Regular appearance of the herring — Different seasons at different places — Notice of the seasons at various localities — England, Scotland, Ireland — The herring a northern fish, but not a migrant from the Arctic Sea — "Whitebait" — Consideration of the question of its specific distinctness — Seasons for mackerel drift-fishing at various localities — Season for pilchard drift-fishing — Spawning of the pilchard — Season for sprats — Spawning time — Drift-fishing for sprats exceptional .. .. Page 97

III.—LINE-FISHING.

Universal practice of — Longlines and handlines — Longline, description of, length, number of hooks — Shooting the line — Buoys — Hauling in — Welled-smacks, description and cost of — Baits — Whelks, mode of collecting — Enemies of the cod fishermen — Seasons for cod fishing — Longlines and trawlers — Handlining for cod — Description of tackle — Capture of small fish — Variable seasons — Impossibility of catching more than part of the fish in the sea — Large breeding stock must always be left — Storing live cod — Cod-chests — Killing the cod for market — "Live cod" — Coast fishing — Small hookers — Dandy-line, description of — Herrings caught by it at spawning time — Only used in Scotland 136

IV.—SEAN-FISHING.

Antiquity of — Classification of seans — General description of — Pilchard-seaning — Herring-seaning or "trawling" in Scotland — Ground-sean — Kinds of fish caught by the sean 156

V.—BAG-NETS.

The stow-net — Description of and mode of working — Sprat season — Large takes of sprats by the stow-net — Trim-nets — Bag-nets in Waterford Harbour — Description of — Whitebait net in the Thames 161

VI.—KETTLE-NET AND WEIRS.

The kettle-net — Description of and localities for — Objections to on account of danger to navigation — Gradual reduction in their number — Weirs — Open to same objection — Description of weirs — Action of — Practically of little value for catching fish 167

VII.—TRAMMEL OR SET NETS.

Description of ordinary set-nets — Used for catching turbot, hake, &c., and crabs in Scotland — Description of the true trammel — Its peculiar action — Red mullet at Guernsey 173

FISHING STATIONS—ENGLAND.

Annual returns of the number of fishing boats — Registration imperfect — Present classification of boats useless for any practical purpose — Ports and Port Letters — **Carlisle to Runcorn**, number of boats — Character of the fisheries — Trawling at Fleetwood and Liverpool — Morecambe Bay shrimping — Description of boats — **Beaumaris to Cardiff** — Welsh fisheries unimportant — Trawling at Carnarvon and Tenby — Oyster fishing at Milford and Mumbles — Weirs — **Bristol to Padstow** — Bridgewater Bay — Bag-nets at Burnham — Flat-bottomed boats — Barnstaple Bay and Bideford — **Hayle to Fowey** — Cornish fisheries — St. Ives pilchard fishery — Pilchard seans — Mode of working — Regulated by Act of Parliament — Landing the fish, curing, packing — Annual exports — Mackerel drift-fishery — Mount's Bay luggers — Line-fishing — "Tumbling-nets" — Oyster fishing at Falmouth — **Plymouth to Weymouth** — Plymouth trawlers — Scarcity of fish in Plymouth market since the opening of the railway — Line and drift fisheries — Brixham long famous for its fisheries — Supposed to have originated beam-trawling — Want of evidence on the question — Mr. Froude's mention of Brixham trawlers in the time of Elizabeth — Inaccurate reports on the recent condition of Brixham trawling — Steady increase of the fishery — Continued supply of fish — Line, drift, and sean fisheries in Torbay — Mackerel fishing at the Chesil Beach — **Channel Islands** — Mackerel fishing — Guernsey fishing boats — Cessation of the herring fishery — Congers, red mullet — Trammels, sand-eel seans — Jersey — Crabs and lobsters — Grey mullet caught by hook — **Poole to Newhaven** — Various fisheries — Keer-drag — Stow-boating in the Solent — Brighton "hog-boat" — Drift and sean fisheries — **Rye to Ramsgate** — Inshore and deep-sea trawling — Kettle-nets, shrimping — Whiting fishing — **Faversham to Colchester** — Fisheries from the Thames — Trawlers and cod-smacks — Water carriage and land carriage of fish — Steam-vessels and sailing carriers — Barking formerly an important station — Leigh shrimpers — Description of shrimp-net — Oyster dredging and stow-boating .. .. Page 177

FISHING STATIONS—ENGLAND (*continued*).

Harwich to Boston — Decline of Harwich as a fishing station — Mr. Groom's account of the introduction of welled-vessels — Cod-chests at Harwich — Shrimp-trawling — Railway returns of fish traffic — Herring fishery from Lowestoft and Yarmouth — Comparative failure of the mackerel fishery — Great increase of fishing boats at Lowestoft and Yarmouth — Rise and long continuance of the Yarmouth herring fishery — Swinden and Manship's account of it — Yarmouth Haven often difficult to enter — Fish market — Landing fish on the beach — "Swills" — Mode of counting herrings — A "last" of fish — Curing red herrings and bloaters — Smoking, packing —

Yarmouth as a trawling station — Mr. Hewett's introduction of ice — Cromer crab and lobster fisheries — Local regulations for preserving them — Fisheries in the Wash — Leach's herring — **Grimsby to Whitby** — Rapid increase in the importance of Grimsby as a trawling station — Improvement in the size and style of fishing smacks — Grimsby Docks — Quantity of fish annually landed there — Fish market — Selling the fish — Packages formerly and now in use — Importation of ice — State of the trawling interests at Hull — Increased number of smacks — Collecting fish by the carriers — Present system of fishing — Fish put into ice as soon as caught — Bridlington and Flamborough — Description of cobles — Various fisheries on this coast — **Middlesboro' to Berwick-on-Tweed** — Line-fishing — Cod, haddock, and coalfish — Bratt-nets — Outcry against the trawlers — Inquiry by Royal Commission in 1863 — Herring fishing on the Northumberland coast — Cullercoats fishermen engaged in salmon fishing, but sea fish not diminished — "Keel-boats" — Fisheries at Holy Island and Berwick — Summary and relative importance of the English fisheries .. .. Page 230

FISHING STATIONS—SCOTLAND.

Methods of fishing in use — Partial change from open to decked fishing boats — Advantages of the latter — Fishery Board returns of boats and men in the herring and white fisheries — Board of Trade returns imperfect — **Leith to Kirkcaldy** — Fisheries in the Firth of Forth — Newhaven cod and haddock lines — Dandy-line fishing at Dunbar — Important herring fishery at Eyemouth, North Berwick, Anstruther, &c. — Winter fishery — Seaning for sprats — Beam-trawling — Mackerel fishing — Lobsters and crabs — **Dundee to Peterhead** — Herring fishing and longlining — "Finnan haddies" — Steam-tugs at Aberdeen for towing the fishing boats — Advantages of the system — **Banff to Wick** — Extensive drift and line fisheries — Sprat fishing in Beauly Firth — Scottish fishing boats, description of — Increased size and peculiar rig — "Scaith" on the Banff coast — Importance of Wick as a station — Measuring the herrings — Classification of the fish — Scottish Fishery Board — Curing, packing, branding, exportation — Immense number of herrings caught — Winter fishery — Exposed situation of Wick — Fishery harbours — Importance of — Difficulties in constructing them — Drift-nets — Sheep-skin buoys — **Kirkwall to Lerwick** — Orkney fisheries uncertain — Frequent bad weather — Line-fisheries — Dried fish for the Spanish market — Abundance of crabs and lobsters — Orkney fishing boats — Shetland fisheries — Importance of the line-fishery — Herring fishing uncertain — Longlines and handlines — Distant fishing grounds — Cod-smacks — Line-fish salted and dried — Grimsby smacks at Faroe — Discovery of Rockall — Difficulty in fishing there — Cod fishery at Davis' Straits — Shetland boats, Norway yawls — Taaf-net — Whales at Shetland — Industry and enterprise of the Shetlanders — Returns of Shetland cured fish — Markets 275

FISHING STATIONS—SCOTLAND (*continued*).

Stornoway — Fisheries at the Hebrides — Herring fishery in the Minch — Close-time for herrings — Bad effects of — Inquiry into, and consequent legislation — Curing herrings — Branding disregarded — Irish markets — Longlining — Line-fish generally cured dry — Lobster fishery — Trade in periwinkles — Fishing boats — Returns of cured fish — **Campbelton to Greenock** — Inshore beam-trawling — Lochfyne — Disputes between drift and sean ("trawl") fishermen — Alleged objections to sean-fishing — Prohibition of seaning — Inquiry into the subject by two Commissions, resulting in repeal of prohibition — Recent scarcity of herrings in Lochfyne — Various suggested explanations of it — Peculiar character of Lochfyne — Great depth of water — Situation of the loch favourable for the visits of the herring, but the object of those visits not easily explained — Lochfyne fishing boats — Returns of cured herrings — **Ardrossan to Dumfries** — Ballantrae banks formerly spawning ground for herrings — Set-nets for cod and turbot — Solway fisheries unimportant — Summary of Scotch fisheries and remarks on the fishermen .. .. Page 313

FISHING STATIONS—ISLE OF MAN.

Castletown, Douglas, and **Ramsey** — Herring fishery on the west, south, and east coasts — Large herrings near the Calf — Spawning ground in Douglas Bay — Mackerel fishery — Deep-sea trawling — Longlining, season for — Manx fishing boats — Number of crew — Shares — Industry of the Manxmen 338

FISHING STATIONS—IRELAND.

General decline in the number of fishing boats and fishermen — Discrepancy in the returns by different authorities — Small proportion of regular fishermen — Decline of the fisheries on the west and north coasts — East coast fisheries improving — General emigration from the west — Exposed coast and bad weather, obstacles to fishing there — Continued distress said to be the result of the famine in 1846 — Little apparent prospect of improvement — Loans recommended by the Fishery Inspectors — Questionable advantage of the system — Fishing only a small part of the occupation of many of the fishermen — Unwillingness of the thriving Irish people to help the fishermen — Mr. Whitworth's offer of help — **Dublin to Waterford** — Prosperity of the Dublin trawlers — Scarcity of crews — Agreements — Trawling grounds in the Irish Sea — Objection to the trawlers by line fishermen — Restrictions on trawling — Skerries wherry — Disappearance and temporary return of haddocks — Fishing yawls — Season for herring fishery — Fish mostly sent to England — Arklow fisheries — Wexford herring cots — Trawling at Waterford — Extraordinary regulations — Nymph Bank a productive fishing ground — Native fishermen and strangers — Frequent abundance of pilchards — Hake, sprats .. 341

CONTENTS.

FISHING STATIONS—IRELAND (*continued*).

Youghal to Tralee—Decline of the Dungarvan fisheries—Trammel-fishing at Ring—The hammer-trawl—The otter-trawl—Kinsale mackerel fishery—Idle habits of the Kinsale fishermen—Fishing Company unsuccessful—Transport of mackerel to England—French fishing boats—Attempted establishment of a pilchard fishery—Objections to it by the fishermen—Kinsale hookers—Bantry Bay a good trawling ground—General fisheries imperfectly worked—Dingle Bay very productive of fish—Royal Irish Fisheries Company formerly successful—Removal of restrictions on trawling—Line and drift fisheries—"Curraghs," or canvas canoes—Dingle fishermen generally industrious—**Limerick to Sligo**—Galway fisheries not fully worked—Difficulties caused by the Claddagh fishermen—Good trawling ground—Systematic search for spawn under the direction of the Fisheries Inspectors—Herring fishery—"Claddagh law"—Other fisheries—Galway hookers—Bofin Island—Fishing Company unsuccessful—Boat harbour now being constructed—Oyster fishery in Clew Bay—Line-fishing on the outer coast—Donegal Bay—Sprat fishery at Inver—Accidents from whales—Herring fishery only near the shore—Line, trawl, and trammel fisheries—Haddock plentiful off the coast, but scarce in the bay—Fisheries probably capable of extension, but fishermen generally very poor—**Londonderry to Drogheda**—Fisheries for the most part unimportant—Fishing boats, yawls—Line-fishing at Rush—Ardglass a large station—Summary and analysis of Irish fisheries—Their uncertain prospects

Page 369

FISHERY REGULATIONS	397
APPENDIX ..	405
INDEX	417

LIST OF ILLUSTRATIONS.

YARMOUTH LUGGERS ..	*Frontispiece.*
	PAGE
THE BEAM-TRAWL	55
TRAWL-HEADS	56
FRENCH TRAWL-HEADS	57
TOWING THE TRAWL ..	78
HOISTING IN THE FISH	80
YARMOUTH LUGGER—DRIFT-FISHING ..	107
BUOY TO LONGLINE	139
WELLED-SMACK	140
LEAD AND SPRAWL-WIRE OF COD-LINE ..	146
GRIMSBY COD-CHEST	149
DANDY-LINE	154
THE STOW-NET	161
MINGLE	164
THE KETTLE-NET	167
MORECAMBE BAY SHRIMPER	182
CLOVELLY AND TENBY FISHING BOATS	185
BURNHAM FISHING BOAT	186
MOUNT'S BAY LUGGERS ..	196
WINK IN DREDGING BOAT	198
TORBAY HOOKER	211
GUERNSEY FISHING BOATS	213
BRIGHTON HOG-BOAT	221
THE THAMES SHRIMP-NET	227
THAMES SHRIMPERS	228
HARWICH COD-CHEST	233
DRIFT-BOAT ENTERING YARMOUTH HAVEN	238
LANDING FISH ON YARMOUTH BEACH	240
COBLES	262
HERRING FISHING—NORTHUMBERLAND COAST	270
KEEL-BOATS—HOLY ISLAND	272

LIST OF ILLUSTRATIONS.

	PAGE
Scotch Fishing Boats	292
Orkney Fishing Boats	303
Shetland Yawl	309
Lochfyne Fishing Boats	332
Manx Fishing Boats	341
Skerries Wherry	361
Wexford Herring Cot—on shore	364
Wexford Herring Cot—under sail	365
The Hammer and Otter Trawls	371
Curragh, or Canvas Canoe	380
Curragh	381
Galway and Kinsale Hookers	387
Irish Fishing Yawl	393

DEEP-SEA FISHING.

INTRODUCTORY.

Fisheries a subject of interest and importance to this country — Fishermen commonly unacquainted with many of the habits of fish — Improvement in the appliances for fishing — Fisheries not a nursery for the Navy — Condition of the fisheries — Supply of fish to the markets — Impossibility of estimating it — Effect of the extension of railways and the use of ice on the development of the fisheries — Great increase of trawlers — Immense demand for fish — Prices — The fish trade — Salesmen and fishmongers — Registration and classification of boats imperfect — Alleged scarcity of fish inshore — Supposed spawning habits of sea fish — Important discoveries by M. Sars — Floating spawn — Fish do not necessarily approach the land for the purpose of spawning — Destruction of small fish in bays probably of slight importance — Close-time unnecessary — Extent of ground trawled on and of ground undisturbed — General prospects of the sea fisheries.

IF it were our desire to enter into the history of the rise and progress of the British Sea Fisheries, we should soon meet with a difficulty in the scarcity of trustworthy materials for the work, especially in all matters relating to the methods by which they were carried on; for even in the case of the great herring fisheries on particular coasts, local records of which go back for many centuries, there is very little information to be gathered except about charters and bounties, and regulations for the buying, selling, and curing of the fish. Of the practical part of the fisheries in general, the description of nets and lines in use, and, with rare exceptions, the kinds of fish taken, history tells us little or nothing, and we are compelled to fall back on the memory of old fishermen and the traditions which may have been handed down to them, for any knowledge of the subject in what by courtesy may be called olden times. Our purpose, however, is to speak of modern fisheries, and the few introductory remarks we shall offer relate to their condition at the present day, so far as they can be ascertained, and the influences which affect them; to the spawning habits of some of the sea fish; and to the question of what support recent investigations of that part of the subject give to the idea that unrestricted fishing is likely to result in a permanent decrease in the supply of fish.

Sea fisheries must always be regarded with considerable interest in a country like our own, of which no part is more than a very few hours' journey from the coast, where in some form or other they come under our notice. Independently of their economic value in furnishing a large supply of food to the people, they are justly regarded as of importance in fostering the national disposition for seafaring pursuits, in training a great number of the maritime population to a life in which hardship and danger are unavoidable elements, and in giving occupation to many thousands besides who are engaged in the trades and manufactures they directly encourage. There is also an idea of sport and of uncertainty, necessarily connected with genuine sport, which gives a charm, perhaps often unconsciously, to the pursuit of fishing, even when the fisherman is toiling for his daily bread; while to those who only take to it as an amusement, and do not require to consider the money value of their captures, the attractive nature of the occupation is especially evident. Almost all the attendant circumstances of his profession take the fisherman out of the category of ordinary workmen; his labour is not mechanical, and steam can only help him indirectly in his work. Unlike the farmer, experiments in fattening and judicious attempts at crossing form no part of his occupation; no gigantic turbot has yet brought a gold medal to the breeder, nor has a fresh Lochfyne herring or a Torbay sole received even "honourable mention" from any other body than the consuming public. The fisherman is in fact a professional sportsman, and his business is to entrap or entice into his hands the various kinds of fish which are likely to bring him the best return. But to do this effectually requires a long apprenticeship and continual observation in the wide field of Nature; the habits and migrations of fish should be studied, the influence of weather considered, and the nature of their food and the ground frequented by many fish at the several seasons of the year should be accurately noted and as carefully remembered. A knowledge of such matters is, however, more frequently the result of accident than of systematic inquiry; and we do not generally find much evidence of intelligent observation on some points with which it might be supposed every fisherman would strive to become acquainted. We naturally turn to the fishermen for information about the spawning habits of the different fishes they are year after year in the habit of catching; yet on this important subject it is difficult to obtain a concurrent opinion from the fishermen of adjoining stations, or even from those dwelling in the same village and working for years over the same ground. The food of fishes is another subject on which much might be learned if the fishermen were disposed to take a little more trouble for their own advantage. An examination of the contents of the stomachs of the fish when just caught would very probably lead to the use of a greater variety of bait than is now put on the hook; and the fishermen would doubtless be astonished to find how large a proportion of the diet of many fishes consists of different kinds of crustacea. It is rather remarkable that some of the baits in general use, and which are undoubtedly attractive—mussels and whelks for example—are just those particular kinds which can form but a very small or probably no portion of the natural food of the fishes which take them. Some fishes have teeth specially fitted for crushing the hard shells of mollusca, but that is not the case generally; and without the assisting hand of the fisherman few of our edible fishes would have an opportunity of tasting these particular delicacies. When the herrings are on the coast and are accompanied by a host of cod, coalfish, &c., then in many places the fishermen are careful to open these predaceous fishes for the sake of the herrings they have swallowed, and which afterwards may be usefully employed as bait; but there the examination ends, and at other seasons it matters little apparently in the estimation of most fishermen what the fish have been feeding on so long as some of the mussels or whelks provided for their entertainment meet with acceptance.

We presume there can hardly be a doubt that, except in the case of very small fish, there is a strong cannibal propensity among the finny tribes—that, in fact, fishes as a rule feed on fishes; this would seem to point to the advantage of a more general use of fish-bait—living, if possible; but of course in this there would be a frequent difficulty. The subject does not, however, appear to have received the attention it deserves; and although pieces of fish are commonly used at certain times and places, they are employed more with the idea of their being agreeable to any fish which may happen to wander near them, than to attract by any resemblance to the form and appearance of the living and natural prey. The principle of live-baiting, however, is recognized in some localities; and we may notice the fact that in the North Sea the hooks used on the longlines are of such a size as may be taken by comparatively small fish, which, when hooked and struggling to escape, become attractive baits to the larger cod. The Guernsey fishermen also have long been aware of the value of a living bait, and largely use the sand-eel for that purpose, as we shall hereafter have occasion to notice.

It may appear presumptuous on our part to talk of fishermen not knowing what is best for their own interest, but it is unfortunately a fact that the inhabitants of fishing villages are generally unwilling to make any change from what has been the practice there. We had many opportunities of observing this in the course of our wanderings round the coast; and in one dark corner on the eastern shores of England it was publicly stated by the fishermen that they would not think of trying any other mode of fishing than such as they were accustomed to, because they had been brought up to work in a particular manner, and no other kind of fishing had ever been attempted by their fathers. This was said at a time when complaints were being made by them against the trawlers from other parts of the coast for catching and carrying away fish which the line fishermen of the place looked upon as their exclusive property, although of kinds which they only occasionally caught. At the larger stations there is happily more disposition to adopt what appear to be improvements in working the fisheries; and the higher prices now given for fish stimulate the fishermen to increased exertion, and encourage them to make use of better kinds of boats and gear.

Fishermen are generally proud of their boats and of their professional knowledge. We were once told in Ireland that we should find every fisherman there insisting on the boats of his own locality being the best in the country; and if by any chance we could obtain his confidence, he would tell us that his own boat was the best in the place. This feeling, however, although common, was not universal, nor is it by any means confined to Ireland. We all have a natural disposition to think well of what has done us good service; and it is only when we have to compete with strangers that we fully realize the defects in our cherished property which throw us behind in the race. This is notably true of fishing boats; and the tendency in recent years among fishermen to visit parts of the coast at long distances from their own homes, so that boats of different styles and classes often fish in company, has led to many improvements being made, especially in regard to their size and for the comfort of the men. The result is that the boats can go farther to sea, and are more independent of weather. There is, of course, increased expense, but larger returns are made because the fishing is carried on with more regularity and system.

Since the recent great extension of net-making machinery fishermen have come to rely very much on manufacturers for their gear, and especially for drift-nets, which are now made of suitable lengths and sizes, requiring little trouble on the part of the fishermen to mount and fit them ready for use. It is but a few years ago that on very many parts of the coast almost the whole of the gear was prepared at home, the wife and daughters of the fishermen twisting lines and making nets with a rapidity almost incredible to those who had not seen the work going on. Trawl-nets are still made by hand, and the best Manilla hemp is now frequently used for them; but cotton is in favour for lighter nets, and has also been introduced for fishing lines. All the fisherman's appliances have undergone improvement; but machinery cannot do everything for him; he must still be able to fit out his boat and put his gear in working order; he must be a sailor and pilot at sea; and he must have the peculiar knowledge on which, of course, his success as a fisherman mainly depends. The thorough-going fisherman is therefore a man of many parts; and such men are increasing in number with the growth of regular deep-sea fishing, and the general tendency of the more strictly coast fishermen to go farther away from home.

While on the subject of fishermen, we may say a few words about our sea fisheries being what is popularly called a nursery for the Navy. The idea is a very old one, and perhaps at one time had a great deal of truth in it; but we believe it is a delusion to suppose that in modern times fishermen will readily give up their independent life for the strict discipline of a man-of-war. The result of our inquiries around the coast a few years ago, when fishing was not more profitable than it is now, if indeed as much so, was that, notwithstanding its many advantages, no service was so unpopular among fishermen as that in the Royal Navy. It must be remembered that although the fisherman goes to sea and learns to handle a boat or larger craft in almost any kind of weather, he, unlike the professed sailor, does so only as a means of enabling him to carry on another and totally distinct occupation. His legitimate business is fishing; that is the end and object of his going to sea; and it is the charm of that profession, which so long as it brings him in even scanty returns, prevents him from readily changing to another. Fishermen in slack times will sometimes ship for a coasting voyage or a trip up the Mediterranean, but this is done with the sole idea of employing their time till the herring or some other profitable fishing season returns. The voyage is begun with the comparative certainty that it will be completed in a few weeks or months, and then the attractions of their old pursuit will lead them back to their homes, and the profits to be derived from a steady prosecution of the fishery.

It may be said that the entry of fishermen in the Naval Reserve is opposed to the views we have put forward; but the number of thoroughbred fishermen who have enrolled themselves in that preliminary service is utterly insignificant compared with the vast body of men who are still unfettered by such an engagement. It is not difficult to discover why fishermen should have a dislike to the Navy. One cause for it is that whatever fishery regulations are enforced, such as marking and numbering boats, carrying lights, &c., the duty is very frequently performed by naval men in some shape or other—Coastguardsmen, or those from Admiralty cruisers. Thus the naval man comes to be regarded by the fisherman as a sort of natural enemy; not one, however, who can or will do him any serious harm, but who obliges him to conform to certain regulations, perhaps admitted by him to be possibly useful, but at the same time not productive of such obvious advantage to him as to compensate for the trouble and expense of attending to them. A second reason is that fishermen as a class are accustomed to a more independent life than other workers of the same rank. Fishermen are bred up to their business from infancy; their earliest recollections are of boats, nets, and fish, and by the time they are old enough for the Navy, or to choose their profession, they have begun to understand something of the attraction of a fisherman's life; there is the daily speculation as to what may be caught; the share or part share of the capture is of increasing interest; and the prospect rises before them of one day becoming master or even owner of a boat. These are considerations which are not easily lost sight of by the rising generation of fishermen. Older men are even less likely to give up their independent life; and, as we have frequently had opportunities of seeing, master and men when at sea work together with a heartiness and goodwill which show the common interest they feel in their occupation. It can hardly be a matter of surprise that men accustomed to such a life should decline to submit themselves to the necessary discipline of the Navy, although the present and prospective advantages of that service should in various shapes be pointed out to them.

Were England engaged in a naval war, and the seas around her threatened by the enemy so that the coasting trade was impeded and deep-sea fishing became a dangerous pursuit, then undoubtedly many fishermen would be eager to take part in defending their own; but those are times when patriotism and possible prize-money call upon everyone, and in such a contingency there would be no failing in the supply of men who are accustomed to the sea, either from merchant ships or fishing boats. Something more than this, however, is wanted for our modern navy, and considerable training is necessary to turn out the man-of-war's man of the present day. No doubt there is plenty of material for the purpose in the country, but we question if it must be looked for among the fishermen, or that they will be readily induced in times of peace to give up an occupation they have been familiar with from childhood, so long as it continues to provide them with moderate means of subsistence.

This brings us to a consideration of the present condition of the sea fisheries as compared with their state ten or twenty years ago.

Two methods naturally suggest themselves by which a conclusion on this subject might be arrived at; namely, a comparison of the quantity of fish now and formerly brought to market, and of the amount of capital at different times invested in the fisheries, as indicated by the number and size of the boats employed in them. The circumstances on which in ordinary times these questions would depend are the degree of abundance of fish on the coast, and the demand for them in the market. But other elements must be considered when we look into the state of the Irish sea fisheries, for there we find an almost continuous decline in the number of fishermen and boats, although fish are abundant and markets generally good. Emigration is year after year carrying away thousands of men who are unable to provide themselves with the necessary appliances for fishing, or who at the best of times worked at it in only a half-hearted manner. There are some thriving exceptions, however, and the decline of the fisheries on some parts of the Irish coast is due rather to the condition of the people there than to any particular scarcity of fish. We shall enter more into this subject in subsequent pages, and may now consider the question of the supply of fish to the English and Scotch markets in particular.

Direct means of ascertaining what quantity of fish is caught by any particular method of fishing or by all of them combined, at the present time or in former years, are unfortunately wanting. Ingenious newspaper correspondents have before now made estimates of the quantity or number of each kind of fish sold at Billingsgate in the course of a year; but the fact is, that unless every salesman in the market will take the trouble to make up under each head an account of his total sales for the twelve months, hardly an approximate idea of what is annually disposed of there can be obtained.

The amount of market tolls received by the City will not give much help, for they are paid on the conveyance, not on the weight of fish delivered; and whether the contents of a waggon be five or fifty packages, the dues are nearly the same. An increasing proportion of fish is now brought to Billingsgate by either sailing or steam carriers; but here again, whatever may be the size of the vessel, the toll is on either a full or a half cargo, and the quantity of fish is unknown except to those who are immediately concerned in its sale. Billingsgate, however, is only one of the important markets which are now supplied direct from the coast; and the quantity of fish annually carried by the great system of railways is only known to the several companies composing it; and, with few exceptions, they object to furnish information on the subject. Then there is the fish which is consumed where it is landed, and this is unquestionably a very large quantity, although probably much less than was the case twenty or thirty years ago on many parts of our extensive coast line. Whatever it may be, there are obviously no present means of getting an account of it. Even of cured fish our knowledge is very imperfect. It is true that the Scotch Fishery Board gives us an accurate return of the number of barrels of herrings cured *wet*, but it has nothing to do with any kind of smoked fish; and while the Cornish merchants send out their trade circulars with particulars of the annual export of pilchards, they can tell us little or nothing of the home consumption of these fish, for there is no record of the quantity caught. In fact, no means exist of making even a rough estimate of the produce of our sea fisheries at the present day.

But although we have no figures to show what is the actual quantity of fish now caught, or how much was taken twenty years ago, it is quite possible to form a decided opinion on the question of whether the supply of fish to the market has been increasing or diminishing. The evidence in favour of a large but gradual improvement in this respect cannot be mistaken; and it is to be found in the immense number of markets all over the country which now have their regular supplies of fish; in the much larger number and generally better class of fishing boats in use; and in the fact that, notwithstanding the greatly increased demand for fish in recent years, the prices obtained for it by the fishermen—the producers—have not advanced in the same proportion as those of beef and mutton. The price to the consumer is another question, of which we shall speak presently.

We need hardly say that the extension of railways all over the country has gradually opened up markets which were formerly inaccessible to fish salesmen, and has led to the increasing demand for fish of all kinds; for it is not merely the better sorts which are sent inland, but thousands of tons of plaice and haddocks, of which the trawlers appear to meet with an inexhaustible supply in the North Sea, find a ready market at a moderate price in the manufacturing districts, where not many years ago they were almost unheard of.

One of the unexpected results of railway extension has been to greatly diminish the supply of fish to the inhabitants of coast towns. When the proceeds of a day's fishing could only be disposed of within a comparatively short distance of home, fish was a common article of food with all classes in the place. They were the nearest and most desirable customers, and had their turn first. But now the facilities for transport and the demand at inland markets, as well as from the insatiable appetite of London, have made a fishing station one of the last places in which the consumer will find his wants provided for, unless, as is frequently the case, the local fishmonger be supplied from London or some other large market. The dearness and scarcity of fish are consequently matters of common complaint by people on the coast; and the conclusion is often arrived at that the fish have been destroyed or driven away, and the fisheries are on the high road to ruin. A little investigation of the subject, however, would in most cases lead to the discovery that since the time when fish was cheap and abundant in the local market, the number of fishing boats and fishermen had been gradually increasing at the place, and the fish traffic from the nearest railway station becoming annually more developed.

While making systematic inquiries all round the coast a few years ago, preparatory to the active work of the Royal Commissioners, we generally had reason to consider it a hopeful sign when we were told by the retail fishmongers at any place we visited that they were to a great extent dependent on the railways for their supply of fish. Nor is it surprising that such should be the case. The larger and more regular the quantity of fish brought in every day by the fishermen at any particular station, the more is it worth the while of the wholesale dealers or their agents to attend the arrival of the fishing boats, when they purchase often in large lots what each may have caught. The fishermen perhaps do not in such dealings obtain such good prices generally for their fish as they occasionally received when their wives used to retail it in the town and neighbourhood; but they have a certain market, and are saved the trouble and anxiety necessarily attending the hawking of their stock about the country, with the chance of part of it becoming spoilt before they have found customers for it. At that time fish formed a considerable portion of the diet of the fisherman and his family; it cost them little or nothing, or appeared to do so; for what is not directly paid for with hard money is frequently regarded as costing little. But now what the fisherman saves for his own use is very commonly of more recognized value, and part of what would be sure of a purchaser with the rest of his catch as soon as he brought it ashore. The money he might obtain for it would not go so far in buying beef or mutton; but meat of that description is now often a daily dish where formerly it was only thought of as a Sunday dinner. The times appear hard to him, for his living is more expensive; but he is apt to forget that his mode of living has somewhat changed.

It might naturally be supposed that fishermen would largely benefit by the great demand for fish at the present time; but there are reasons why this should not be the case. They may not be worse off than they were twenty years ago, as some of them think when they consider the higher prices they have to pay now for everything belonging to their fit out, for they unquestionably get a larger money return for their labour; but the fact must not be lost sight of that the persons who are actually engaged in catching the fish, and who often have to contend with difficulties, dangers, and losses of which the buyer is content to remain in real or assumed ignorance, are not the men who receive the largest share of the money for which the fish is ultimately sold to the consumer. The sale of fish is now organized into a regular trade; the wholesale dealers have agents in all directions; transport and even telegraph charges are heavy items in the salesman's expenses; and each person through whose hands the fish passes adds his percentage to the cost, until at last when it comes to the consumer, the price charged is frequently three or four times as much as the fishermen received for it. In London the West End fishmongers are the persons who manage to secure by far the largest proportion of profit from every fish which comes into their hands.

We will take the case of the trawlers, a class of fishermen which supplies, with the exception of cod, almost the whole of the most expensive and favourite kinds of fish brought to table. Trawled fish is divided for market purposes into two classes, distinguished by the names of "prime" and "offal"; the former consisting of turbot, brill, soles, and doreys, and the latter of plaice, haddocks, and other kinds of inferior fish, for which, many years ago, the demand did not nearly keep pace with the supply.

From the following abstract of a statement[1] fur-

---

[1] For details, see Trawling, page 88.

nished to the Royal Commissioners by Mr. Henry Knott, the owner of several trawlers at Great Grimsby, of the weight and value of fish taken by one of his vessels in each of five consecutive years, some interesting facts are arrived at :—

In the five years 1860–1864 :

Prime .. 86 tons sold for 1971*l*.=23*l*. per ton, or 2½*d*. per lb.
Offal .. 357   „   731*l*.= 2*l*.   „   or nearly ¼*d*. per lb.

Total 443   „   2702*l*.= 6*l*.   „   or averaging nearly ¾*d*. per lb.

At that time, then, the fisherman received only 2½*d*. per pound for the fish which brought the highest price in the London market, and barely a farthing per pound for the inferior kinds. Prices have risen considerably of late years; but it is doubtful whether the fishermen have benefited by the greater demand to anything like the extent that the fishmonger has by his increased charges to the consumer. Before the introduction of ice for preserving his stock of fish, the fishmonger had a risky trade; he could only buy what he thought would be sufficient to supply the general wants of his customers for the day, he was always liable to have some portion of his stock unsold, and the perishable nature of it would then most likely involve him in some loss. This was properly provided for by the price he fixed for what he was pretty sure of disposing of; and if he sold all, so much the better for him. His customers then had tolerably fresh fish for the good prices they paid him. But what is the case now? The trade has been revolutionized; a large proportion of the fish now brought to market, excluding herrings and sprats, is put into ice as soon as it is out of the water; it is brought on shore, sometimes after several days, and sold; it is then repacked in ice and forwarded to Billingsgate, or other large markets, where it is purchased by the fishmongers, who have a stock of ice at home ready to receive it; and there it remains till it is wanted, only a certain quantity, sufficient to make an attractive display, being laid out at one time for sale. The fishmonger is no longer disquieted by any doubts about the fish which is unsold to-day being sound and presentable to-morrow; if his cellar be in proper order, there need be no cause for anxiety. The use of ice, of course, adds to his expenses, which he makes the public pay for, but it is a real and great saving to him in fish; were it not so, we may be quite sure he would have little to do with it. The wholesale dealers benefit by the use of ice only so far as it brings a larger quantity of fish into their hands for sale. They cannot lay by what is not at once disposed of. Overburdened Billingsgate must be cleared out to-day, or there will be no room for what will certainly be brought there to-morrow; and if the supply be more than is required by regular London and country customers, the rest must be got rid of at a price which attracts another class of buyers—the costermongers. There is always a very large quantity of "offal" fish purchased by these itinerant dealers, and their business lies at the east end of the town, in poor districts, and back streets generally. Plaice are in particular request by their customers, and notwithstanding the immense supply of this fish daily sent or brought in by the trawlers, there appears to be always a sale for it. But it not unfrequently happens that there is a glut of some of the better kinds of fish, and, as we have said, the market must be cleared; then the costermongers may be seen going with their barrows into more select neighbourhoods than they usually visit, and hawking soles, haddock, and whiting fresh from the market, as well as their more general stock in trade. And they sell excellent fish at very low prices, while the fashionable world are paying fashionable rates for such fish as the ordinary purveyors may like to send them fresh from the ice. This no doubt is wholesome food; but it has commonly that absence of flavour and firmness which tells plainly that it is long since it was fresh from the sea.

There is no help for it, however; for were ice not used by the fish dealers and many of the fishermen, a much smaller supply of fish would be in a saleable condition when it reached the market, and the quantity sent would also be considerably diminished; at the same time the existing facilities of transport inland direct from the fishing stations would, as at present, certainly lead to a great demand for it in the country; competition between the buyers for the various markets would send up prices till they reached a point which would cut off hundreds of thousands of would-be consumers; and although fish would then be supplied in a fresher and better condition than is now generally the case—for it would be only recently out of the water—it would be only a luxury in very many houses where it is now a common article of food.

By opening up such numerous markets the railway system has created an immense increase in the demand for fish, and the use of ice alone has contributed materially to meet it by preserving in a wholesome condition a very large quantity of fish which would have been otherwise unsaleable. The result of the combination of these two influences has been a considerable development of the fisheries, and consequently an increase in the number of boats and men employed, especially in the deep-sea fishing.

We may notice one more point in connection with the supply of fish. In former years, when railways were in their infancy, most of the fish sold at Billingsgate was brought there by water carriage. It was the one great market, and London was the first place to have her wants supplied. At that time the salesmen forwarded to the country such fish as could be spared and was likely to reach its destination in proper order. Even after railways had been considerably extended, they were used more for distributing the fish to the country than for bringing it to London; for, excepting Yarmouth, the North Sea stations had not then attained very much importance, and both trawlers and liners mostly hailed from the Thames. As the coast lines of railway became completed, their convenience for sending the fish to London was soon recognized, and their fish traffic rapidly increased; for London was still the great wholesale market, and the salesmen supplied the country fishmongers according to the orders received by post. But as time went on, and the electric telegraph became generally established throughout the country, a great change took place in the mode of doing business. The agents at the different fishing stations received notices by "wire" from their principals in London of the country orders to be executed, and the fish was forwarded accordingly direct from the place where it was landed, thus saving both time and expense. This is the present practice, so far as it can be carried out; but there are many parts of England which can still be most conveniently supplied from Billingsgate. There is an immense business, however, done by "wire," and telegraph charges have become an important item in the salesman's accounts. It will, perhaps, be difficult to find stronger proof of the great increase in the supply of fish, and that the sea fisheries have not been going to ruin, as many people for several years past have believed to be the case, than the fact that although a great part of the fish now sent into the country is forwarded direct from the coast, instead of, as formerly, first coming to London, the business at Billingsgate has so completely outgrown the capacity of the market that the enlargement of the building is now being carried out by the Corporation.

Columbia Market was constructed partly with the view of relieving the pressure at Billingsgate, but it does not appear to be in favour. The situation contrasts unfavourably with that of the old market in being so far from the Thames, so that water-carriage would not be available for bringing in the fish; it would be entirely dependent on the railways, and the salesmen at Billingsgate have before now found the advantage of possessing other means of conveyance when railway rates have been advanced. Steam-vessels are now coming into regular use as fish carriers, and will probably, to a great extent, supersede the sailing cutters, which have been hitherto generally employed for that purpose.

The evidence of an increased supply of fish to the market afforded by the number and character of the fishing craft now in use also appears to be unmistakable. The actual increase in the number of boats within any definite period cannot be ascertained, as it is only since 1869 that the registration of all classes has been attempted, and the difficulties in carrying out that portion of the Sea Fisheries Act, 1868, have not yet been so far overcome as to ensure very accurate returns. We shall have occasion to discuss the subject more in detail when we notice the various fishing stations around the coast; and we need only say now that as every registered boat will require an annual endorsement of her certificate, each new boat, or old one on change of owner, a new registration, and that notice must be given by the fishermen of every boat sold, lost, or broken up, the difficulties which now exist in obtaining precise annual returns are not likely to diminish. They do not present themselves, however, so much on the thickly populated English coast as in many of the thinly inhabited parts of Scotland and Ireland, where the machinery for enforcing the regulations is less easily worked. Of the manner in which fishing boats are classified we shall only here observe that it is very complicated; and that when boats of the same size are placed in different classes according to whether they do or do not sometimes carry a sail—when craft ranging from 15 tons to 70 tons and upwards are all grouped together, and no distinction whatever is made between the boats engaged in the different methods of fishing, the returns must be practically useless for giving (as we presume was intended) any definite means of judging of the condition of our sea fisheries.

The evidence obtained, however, by the Royal Commissioners showed distinctly that for many years previous to their inquiry, there had been a gradual increase in the number of fishing boats at most places along the coast; and since the date of their Report, the improvement in this respect has been of a most decided character at some of the large stations. The trawlers, by adding largely to their fleet, spending more money on their vessels, and bringing in a steady supply of fish, have disappointed those who, in 1863–4, predicted their speedy ruin; the drift fishermen are not in a less thriving condition than they used to be, and their boats have shown an increase rather than a diminution in number and size; the deep-sea line fishermen have also added to their fleet; and we have no reason to think that, taking the coast generally, a smaller share of fish of all kinds falls to the lot of the individual fisherman than was the case ten or twenty years ago. We are quite willing to admit that there may be places on the coast where the takes of herrings or of line-fish are not always so good now as they have been; but if the fish are not caught there, it is not because they have disappeared from the sea, for the markets tell us that the general supply is larger than ever. Improved prices have no doubt helped to develop the fisheries; but it must be remembered that the fisherman has to pay more for almost everything he requires for his household and his business, so that his increased gains are not all profit to him. There has been a general tendency to increase the size of fishing boats, and this of course involves the expenditure of more money. Now nothing is more certain in connection with our sea fisheries than that, as a rule, the money invested in the means of carrying them on is obtained by fishing; advances, it is true, are frequently made to fishermen by the special tradesmen with whom they deal—that is, they are sometimes in part fitted out by them; but this is done in full confidence of being repaid, and till the debt is cleared off, some security is generally given on the property. The simple question in such cases is the character of the man, for no doubt is felt about his ability to free himself if he work steadily at his fishing and have ordinary success. If then we find the fisherman building larger boats and spending more money on his fit out, it is not unreasonable to suppose that fishing has been a profitable occupation to him, and that, in spite of all his grumbling about bad times, he expects to get a good return in fish for his increased outlay. In some cases, however, persons otherwise unconnected with fishing will invest their money in the trade and join those who have practical experience of it; others have been foolish enough to go into the business, knowing nothing of its working, and have paid some one to manage it for them; the result in the latter case has sooner or later been a heavy loss, as any master of a fishing boat could have told them would be the case. It must not be supposed, however, that everything goes smoothly with even the industrious fisherman; he has to contend with bad seasons, unfavourable weather, loss of, or damage to, both boats and gear, which often throw him back in the world and perhaps ruin his prospects for some time to come; but with ordinary "luck," as he would himself say, he has not much fear; and the present style and number of fishing boats appear to us strong evidence that he has good ground for his confidence.

What we have now said only partially applies to Ireland. The returns of fishing boats in that country show an almost continuous decrease in the aggregate; but that is not correct for all kinds of fishing, as deep-sea trawling is in a thriving condition there; and the fisheries on the east coast, where emigration is not carrying away the fishermen, are showing signs of improvement.

Before leaving the subject of the supply of fish, we may say a few words about the average takes by each boat. It is said by those who believe the fisheries are declining, that, although there may be an increase in the number of fishing boats, especially marked in the case of the trawlers, the takes of fish by each vessel are less than they used to be. It would be difficult to answer this if the argument were founded on the books of the smack-owner and not merely on opinion. It would necessarily follow that, although with a diminished yield of fish, about four-fifths of it being of the inferior kinds mostly consumed by the poorer classes, the price obtained for it by the fisherman had risen to such an extent as not only to cover the increased cost of all his ordinary necessities, but also to enable him to build new boats of a larger size, and in almost every particular of a more costly construction. We have no reason to believe that this is the case. The trawlers freely admit that the rise in price has been a great stimulus to their fishing during recent years, but there has been no complaint of any decrease in their takes of fish. We have inquired particularly on this point at Hull, Grimsby, Ramsgate, Brixham, and Dublin with the same result, and we have the authority of Mr. R. T. Vivian, the well-known smack-owner at Hull, for saying that the new smacks now in use, when they have large gear in proportion to their size (which is not always the case) catch *more* fish than was taken on an average by trawlers ten years ago. He adds in a communication made to us at the end of 1873:—" I have two new vessels that have done better for twelve months just expired than I remember any of mine ever doing before." This was in answer to a specific inquiry we made about the *quantity* of fish now caught by each vessel compared with what was taken in former years.

There seems little doubt, however, that inshore line-fishing has for some years past been less successful than was formerly the case. But this by no means applies to the whole of our coasts, or to all kinds of fish. The haddock on the north-east of England and the east of Scotland have been less abundant near the land, and on some parts of the coast are scarce within ordinary inshore fishing distances; but they are still plentiful in deep water, and the fisherman's chief complaint is that he must go farther to sea in order to catch them. That the scarcity is only local is evident from the fact that the deep-sea trawlers find no falling off in the numbers of this fish on the grounds where they have long been accustomed to find them at the proper season. We have yet to learn what influences the movements of this uncertain fish; and if we knew more about the state of our fisheries during the earlier part of the present century, it is quite possible that we should find there was the same variation formerly in the abundance of fish near the land that has been noticed in more modern times. Attention has been recently directed to the subject in consequence of the development of the trawl fishery in the North Sea. That appeared to the line fishermen on the north-east coast sufficient to account for the scarcity of this fish; the beam-trawl seemed to them especially suited to destroy the spawn, and it was therefore readily assumed that it did so; but we shall be able to show presently that the only way in which the trawlers can diminish the number of haddocks on our coasts is by catching them, and that is what the line fishermen themselves are so anxious to do. The disappearance of the haddock from Dublin Bay a few years ago was also attributed to the operations of the trawlers; but it is rumoured that they had long previously, for a time, forsaken the neighbourhood when no such reason for their doing so could be given. Last year these fish were again abundant on their old grounds; and, in 1872, plenty of these fish were caught there for about a week; then they disappeared as before.

The fact is that practically we know very little indeed about the habits of our commonest sea fish; and the sooner that is recognized, the better position we shall be in for making accurate observations on the subject.

The increase in the general size of fishing boats does not necessarily imply that fishermen are obliged to go farther to sea in order to obtain a living; that increase has taken place in boats of almost every kind, and is even more conspicuous among the trawlers which had long been accustomed to remain at sea for weeks at a time, than among drift and line boats which return home every day. Fishermen, however, are more enterprising than they used to be, and, with the increase in their numbers, are disposed to a wider range for their operations. Inshore fishing is giving place to more deep-sea work, and larger boats enable it to be carried on at distances from home which it was neither safe nor easy for the small ones to attempt. That the result has been satisfactory is manifest from the increasing tendency to continue the improvements in all that pertains to the fishing boat.

We now come to one of the most important questions in connection with the prosperity of the sea fisheries—that relating to the spawning habits of the several kinds of fish in request for the table. A knowledge of the habits of the salmon in this respect has been the basis of most of the legislation which has taken place for increasing the supply of that favourite fish; and although the protection of sea fish is far less within our power, an acquaintance with the localities in which their spawn is deposited and developed will enable us to ascertain whether any of the methods of fishing in use are likely to injure the germs of our future supply. For information on the subject we naturally turn to the fishermen, and a confident reply is usually ready for us. Rough ground or smooth ground—rocks, gravel, sand or mud, is pointed out as the haunt of particular species when ripe for spawning, and the conclusion is arrived at, perhaps not unnaturally, that such locality is the place selected for the future nursery. That spawn remains at the bottom, either free or attached to stones, seaweed, &c., or buried beneath the surface of the ground, is the universal belief among fishermen; and the probability of such being usually the case was strengthened by what was known not only of the places in which the spawn of the salmon and many entirely fresh-water fishes is deposited, but also by the well-ascertained fact that herring spawn is laid on the ground, to the rougher parts of which it firmly adheres. The herring is, however, the only one of our edible sea fish of whose spawning habits we have until recently had any very precise information.

The fact of fish ova being found floating at the surface of the sea was stated by both Professor Huxley and Professor Allman in 1867 before the Select Committee of the House of Commons on the Sea Coast Fisheries (Ireland) Bill, as within their knowledge and experience; and that the ova were in all cases alive, and some of them in an advanced state of development. Professor Huxley also referred in his evidence to observations then recently made by Norwegian naturalists on the spawning of sea fish, leading to the belief that the ova of the common cod naturally undergo their development while floating at the surface.

The subject is of great interest, especially in connection with the working of our sea fisheries, and we have accordingly taken some pains to ascertain the result of the investigations, so far as they have gone.

The observations referred to by Professor Huxley were apparently those made by Professor G. O. Sars of the Christiania University, the son and, we believe, successor in the Chair of Natural History, of the late Professor Sars,[1] whose name is held in reverence by every worker in marine zoology. The inquiry is still in progress, and the seas around the Loffoden Islands have been visited on several occasions for the purpose of making the requisite observations. Reports have been published from time to time, but they are in the Norse language, and their contents unfortunately inaccessible to most persons in this country. Professor G. O. Sars has, however, been good enough to communicate to us some of the more interesting results of his work, and we gladly take this opportunity of acknowledging his courtesy in furnishing the desired information in English for our use in these pages.

The following are some of the facts he has recorded: In 1864 he obtained by means of his surface-net—apparently the same kind of apparatus as is commonly used by naturalists for collecting minute floating forms of marine life—the ova of the common cod (*Gadus morrhua*) floating at the surface; examples in various stages of development were procured, the young fish hatched out, and the species identified beyond a doubt. In 1865 the same observations were made on the ova of the haddock (*Gadus æglefinus*), and it was satisfactorily determined that they went through all their

---

[1] The late Professor Edward Forbes spoke of this eminent Norwegian naturalist as "a philosopher who, pursuing his researches far away from the world, buried among the grand solitudes of his magnificent country, where the pursuit of science is his recreation, and the holy offices of religion his sacred duty, has nevertheless gained name and fame wherever the study of nature is followed. The unpretending writings of this parish priest have become models for the essays of learned professors in foreign lands, and his discoveries the texts of long commentaries by experienced physiologists."—*British Naked-eyed Medusæ*, p. 55 (Ray Society, 1848).

stages of development while floating at the surface, in the same manner as had been previously ascertained in the case of the cod. M. Sars writes to us that he was at first inclined to believe this development of the ova while floating was peculiar to the members of the Gadidæ or cod family, in its restricted sense; but in the summer of 1865 he visited the southern coast of Norway during the season for mackerel, and found abundant evidence of the same rule obtaining in the case of that widely distinct fish. There is, we believe, good reason for thinking that the actual spawning of the mackerel (*Scomber*) takes place at the surface, and that the ova do not rise from below, as may be the case with the spawn of fish which, like the cod and haddock, usually keep near the bottom; but in saying this we are only judging by the ordinary habits of the two last-mentioned species, and we have no special ground for assuming that those habits do not alter at the spawning season. It is not a very important question, however, for if the specific gravity of the ova be such as will keep them at the surface, it must be quite capable of bringing them there from any depth at which they may have been produced. Besides the ova of the mackerel, which were obtained in all stages and successfully hatched out—the young mackerel being easily recognized—the ova of at least four other kinds of fish were procured; "the ova being readily distinguished from each other both by size and by the colour and form of the embryo." M. Sars adds—"In some of them there was, as in the ova of the mackerel, a very discernible pellucid oil-globule at the upper pole, the magnitude and relative position of which to the embryo were characteristic of each sort. Of most of them I was able to get the young excluded, but they were still so imperfectly developed that it was hardly possible to determine the species." Earlier in the year also, at the Loffodens, he obtained several kinds of floating fish ova, some of which he succeeded in hatching; but he could not speak with certainty as to all the species. In his published reports, however, he mentions the gurnard (*Trigla*) as one of the fishes whose floating ova he had identified.

Entirely subversive as these discoveries of Professor Sars are of our popular notions about fish-spawning, it is even more unexpected to find that both he and M. A. W. Malm, of Gothenburg, have independently ascertained that the ova of the plaice (*Pleuronectes platessa*) follow this same rule of floating at the surface; and M. Sars adds that it undoubtedly applies also to the other Pleuronectidæ.

It is evident then that the floating of fish ova during the development of the embryo is not so exceptional as it appeared to be at the beginning of M. Sars' investigations; but that there is good reason for believing it to be the general rule in several distinct families of sea fish; whilst, as M. Sars points out, the development takes place at the bottom in the case of those fishes especially whose ova are cemented together by a glutinous secretion, or fastened in lumps to foreign bodies, such as Algæ, Hydroids, &c. He mentions as examples among others in which the latter mode is the rule, the herring (*Clupea*), the Capelan (*Osmerus*), the species of *Cottus*, *Liparis*, &c.

It is particularly worthy of notice that, according to these observations of the Norwegian naturalists, all the important kinds of fish taken by our line fishermen and trawlers, and the mackerel among such as are caught by the drift-nets, may be reasonably included—

and some of them are ascertained to be so—among the species whose spawn floats at the surface of the sea, and their ova cannot therefore be liable to the slightest injury by any method of fishing which is carried on upon or near the ground. For if that be the rule with the spawn of the cod and haddock, there can hardly be a doubt about its being so likewise with the ova of ling, coalfish, whiting, pollack, hake, and torsk (*Brosmius*)—all belonging to the same family. Again, turbot, holibut, brill, soles, plaice, dabs, and flounders are all closely allied, agreeing in certain obvious peculiarities of structure and in general habits. It has been ascertained by both M. Sars and M. Malm that the ova of the plaice, one of the most typical of this group of fishes, go through their several stages of development while floating at the surface; there is every reason to believe therefore that the ova of the other members of the family are subject to the same conditions. Mackerel and gurnards are known to belong also to this category; and the dorey, from its affinity to the mackerel, is likely to have the same habit in this respect as that fish. We can say nothing with certainty about bream (*Sparus*), red or grey mullet, or conger. On the other hand, we know that the herring spawn adheres to the bottom, and that of the pilchard and sprat, it might be anticipated, would be deposited in the same manner; but it has not yet been found there, so far as we are aware; and the late Mr. Jonathan Couch, who probably devoted more time to the study of the habits of the pilchard than any other ichthyologist, states[1] that he had reason to suppose that fish spawned at the surface, and the ova became mixed with a large quantity of tenacious mucus which spread out like a sheet on the

---

[1] *History of British Fishes*, vol. iv., p. 81 (1865).

water and kept them floating. If this should be confirmed, it will prove that even in the case of agglutinated masses of ova, development may naturally take place in them far away from the bottom.

The observations on spawning to which we have now called attention, startling as they may appear to us, are the result of a systematic inquiry into the subject by competent persons, and extending over several years. We have therefore no ground for not accepting the conclusions arrived at by Professor G. O. Sars, supported as they are in the very important instance of the plaice by the independent observations of M. Malm.

But what becomes then of the long-standing and widely-spread charge against the general body of trawlers of "annually destroying thousands of tons of spawn" of various kinds? It is strongly confirmatory of the accuracy of M. Sars' observations that no other deposited fish spawn than that of the herring has yet become really known to the fishermen; and we will undertake to say that the number of fishermen who have seen herring spawn *after* it has been taken up from the ground on which it was naturally deposited is exceedingly small, unless they have found it in the stomachs of haddock and several other fishes which are known to feed upon it.

Various marine substances well known to naturalists as being distinct forms of animal life, and whose structure is detailed in our text-books of zoology—sponges, zoophytes, ascidians, &c., for example—are grouped together by many of our fishermen under the single appellation of "spawn." Nothing has done more duty in this way than the common irregularly-shaped mass of invertebrate life called "thumbs," "teats," or "dead men's fingers" by the trawlers (who know it is not fish spawn).

and *Alcyonium digitatum* by naturalists. It is found on all parts of the coast, and it is rarely that a trawl is hauled up without some of this substance being among the contents of the net. The trawlers know very well that the variety of things called spawn by other fishermen are not so really; they cannot generally tell you what they are, and that is not very surprising; but we never met with a trawler who thought hermit crabs were young lobsters, as was distinctly stated by one of the witnesses before the Royal Commissioners at Galway, or who had any doubt about the spawn of the cuttle-fish. We have ourselves been with the trawlers on various parts of the coast, and have boarded them unexpectedly far out in the North Sea, and, officially and privately, have done our best to find fish spawn in the trawl; but we have never succeeded; and the conclusion we arrived at was that rough ground, on which the trawlers do not and cannot work, was the situation in which fishes, as a rule, deposited their spawn. This was, however, before M. Sars had begun his observations; and the negative results of our examinations on the ground have received a simple explanation by his inquiries at the surface.

It appears then there is little reason to believe in the possibility of destroying by any existing method of sea fishing the deposited spawn of any of our important edible fishes, with the exception of the herring; and we have no evidence that any injury is caused even in the case of that fish, for in the few places in which it is known that the spawn of the herring is deposited, trawling is rarely carried on. The subject may be looked at, however, from another point of view, and it is one worthy of the consideration of those who believe our fisheries are being ruined. We mean the literally enormous quantity of spawn annually consumed by the public all over the country. We need hardly say that there is a general demand for full-roed fish; roe of various kinds is considered a delicacy, and the fishmonger obtains a higher price for the sea fish which contains it than for one that is said to be "poor." The public are the persons in fault here; for the fishermen naturally look out for those fish which will bring them the highest price. Let us take the herring as a conspicuous example of this. It is the object of the curers to obtain "full fish" if possible; they will give the highest prices for them, because they know the public prefer and will pay more for them. It is true that "fat fish"—those with hardly any development of the roe—are also in favour; but they are less frequently caught, and must be eaten without delay, or their particular flavour is lost. It seems generally admitted that these fish will not cure so well as the others—a matter that yet requires explanation, since in the case of the closely-allied pilchard, the fat fish are those most in demand for salting. However, the nearer herrings are to the spawning time, the better, as a rule, is the market for them. When therefore the public decline to give the highest price for those fish which contain the largest quantity of roe—when the finest Yarmouth bloaters are unsaleable, and the " Full " Crown brand of the Scotch Board of Fisheries loses its value in the home and foreign markets, then our fishermen will perhaps not seek to catch more full-roed herrings than they can consume in their own families; but we cannot now well blame them for taking such fish, as everyone, from the highest to the lowest, is most anxious to purchase.

It might be imagined that if the millions of herrings which are annually caught just before the spawning time were permitted to deposit their ova, we should have an immense and obvious increase in the number of fish in following years; but such a supposition would be based on the idea that the millions now caught form a large proportion of the herrings on our coasts. There is no reason to believe, however, that they make up more than a very small percentage of the hosts in our seas. Those which are caught by drift-nets, which is the general method employed, may be said really to be taken by chance; they happen to come where the nets are floating, and in trying to pass through them they become meshed. But, as any fisherman will acknowledge, the fishery is a pure lottery, depending not only on the number of fish where he may have shot his nets, but also on whether or not the fish will rise far enough to come within their reach. Again, the extent of netting used in the herring fishery, immense as it appears to be when the number of square yards is calculated or estimated, is utterly insignificant when we consider what the superficial area of the sea occupied by it on any one night is to that in which the herrings are entirely unobstructed in their movements, even if we suppose them all to be within a moderate distance of the land. Reasonable calculations have been made of the number of herrings that no doubt are consumed during the season by the gannets at the island of St. Kilda alone—a number startling to those persons who believe our fishermen get the largest share of the fish in the sea; and Professor Huxley repeated before the Parliamentary Committee in 1867, the result of an investigation he made while at work on the Scotch Herring Commission a few years previously, to the effect that the number of herrings it might be expected would have been consumed by the cod and ling known to be taken in any one year on the Scotch coast, if they had not been caught, would, from the acknowledged voracity of those predaceous fishes, have exceeded the total number of herrings which ordinarily fall to the share of all the Scotch fishermen. Of course this is only an estimate, and we know that such calculations are liable to error; but from what fishermen tell us of the way in which cod attend on the shoals of herrings— from the manner in which the cod caught during the herring seasons are crammed with those fish, as we have ourselves had opportunities of seeing, and from the herring being one of the most killing baits for it, we cannot doubt that the estimate in this case (two herrings daily for seven months for each cod) is below rather than above the truth. But the cod and ling are only two of a host of enemies the herring has to escape from if it can. It is well known that during the herring season whales and porpoises are among the surest signs of there being plenty of these fish in the neighbourhood; and the gathering together of gulls and other sea birds is another of what is called the "appearances of fish." What may be the daily consumption by all these hungry mouths it is impossible to conceive, but we may feel assured that it is enormous; and we may add that, so far as we can judge from the behaviour of seals, sea birds, and sea fish in confinement, digestion in fish-eating vertebrates must go on with great rapidity, for their appetites appear to be insatiable. We have not mentioned the countless scattered sea birds or the several kinds of fish, besides the cod, which contribute to the destruction of the herring; but we think enough has been said to show that the fishermen's share of the spoil cannot be a large one. And when it is remembered that the herring fishery on our coasts has been carried on for centuries with an enormous destruction of spawn before it has been shed, and that, notwithstanding all this waste of reproductive power, the Yarmouth fishery, for example, and the oldest on record, has within the last very few years been more productive than it had ever been known before, the fear of injuring future fisheries by our eating full-roed herrings seems unlikely, and by any chance disturbance of spawning beds utterly unreasonable. The great enemies to spawn of all kinds are not the fishermen, but fish of various sorts, both round and flat; and floating spawn is doubtless largely devoured by sea birds and surface-swimming fishes.

The greatest destruction of young fish-life, however, probably takes place when the young animal assumes an independent existence and begins to swim about in the world of waters around it. As soon as it becomes capable of any active movement the great struggle for life commences; it has to eat, and to take care that it is not eaten; but in the war that is being incessantly carried on among the finny tribes—large fishes feeding on small ones, and small ones on smaller—the newly-hatched fry are heavily weighted, and myriads must be devoured before they have strength to turn upon their neighbours. Yet millions and millions of these little creatures must escape an early death, it may be, not many of them to attain anything like maturity, but still to live long enough to take an active part in the destruction of their smaller kindred and neighbours, and perhaps to become worthy of a humble position at the fishmonger's stall.

There is reason to think the limit of growth in some species of fish is not reached until after many years, and that only a few of them live long enough amidst the many dangers to which they are continually exposed to attain unusual dimensions. The cod among purely sea fish appears to be an example of this. It has been observed that when any newly-discovered cod-bank is first worked some fish of remarkable size are pretty sure to be caught. This was the case at Rockall, far out on the Atlantic side of the Outer Hebrides; and many years ago it was so on the Newfoundland banks. But monster cod five or six feet in length, as were at first frequently reported, are now very seldom met with. Their rarity at the present day appears capable of explanation without any necessity for supposing it to be an indication of the ground being overfished. As war is continually going on among fishes, and the larger ones as constantly devouring the smaller, the bigger a fish becomes the less danger it is in of being eaten by the others; it has fewer natural enemies to encounter, and its chance of life under these conditions is therefore better the longer it lives—of course, within the natural limits of a cod's healthy existence. But when the bank is visited by the fisherman a new danger arises, common to almost all sizes of fish, and to which the monster is perhaps more exposed than any of its smaller kindred. The fisherman's bait is likely to be attractive to fish of various sizes, but the presence of a big fish near it would most likely be sufficient to drive the smaller ones away, and to ensure its getting possession of the tempting morsel to its own ultimate sorrow. On the other hand, if the prize should be secured by one of the more numerous smaller ones, the struggling captive itself becomes a conspicuous attraction, and lures the patriarch to its fate. As already mentioned, hooks on longlines are commonly used of such a size as can be taken by small fish, and yet sufficiently strong to hold the larger fish, which frequently seize those already hooked. The big fish are thus generally among the first to be caught on ground that is newly worked; and there being reason to think cod require many years to attain unusual size, the chances of their escaping the bait long enough to do so become less in every year of the continuance of the fishery. As, however, the cod begins to spawn when it is of a very moderate size, the capture of the very large ones does not specially affect the increase, and there seems to be always a good supply of growing fish of various ages.

What we have already said about the situation of fish spawn while undergoing development materially lessens the interest in the question of where the fish are when the spawn is being shed. But it is not a subject that should be altogether passed over when discussing the habits of those fishes whose capture gives employment to so many thousands of our population, besides supplying the markets with an immense quantity of excellent food.

It will probably be difficult to find any matter relating to the sea fisheries on which people in general are better agreed than that it is a rule for fish to come in from deep water to shallow water for the purpose of spawning. It is a very old idea, and receives some support from the fact that fish of several kinds are observed near the land when they are ready to spawn, and the herring may be mentioned as an apparently notable example. There are some objections to it, however, which it will be desirable to consider; and in doing so we have no wish to dogmatize on the subject, but merely to point out that we all have a great deal more to learn before we can safely say whether or not any rule exists on the matter.

There is no question that vast numbers of herrings spawn near the coast, and in a very few cases the locality is known, but generally speaking we cannot say where it may or may not be; all we know is, that some of these fish are more or less near the land when they are ripe for spawning, and very probably in shallower water than they would be in 30 or 40 miles farther out. A glance at the charts, however, will be sufficient to show that the latter would not necessarily be the case in all places where herrings periodically appear. But if spawning be the sole, or even chief, object which brings the full herrings near the land, what is it leads those which have no appearance of the roe becoming developed to take precisely the same direction on several parts of the same coast? The Lowestoft boats begin the spring herring fishery 50 or 60 miles off the land, and carry it on with only a slight intermission in May until the close of the midsummer fishery in the middle of July. Now let us see what is the condition of these spring and summer fish. When they are first met with, at the *farthest* distance from the land, they are so young and small that nets with meshes below the ordinary herring size are required in order to catch them. Complaints, as is well known, are constantly being made of the destruction of these at first almost worthless fish; but as they come nearer the land they increase in size and quality, until at the later part of the fishery, when they are only a few miles from the shore, they are good fat fish, but still with very little appearance of roe in them. Then they disappear, and the fishing ceases till the autumn, when the spawning fish are looked after. It appears to us very unlikely that these young spring fish should have been produced from spawn deposited near the land by the autumn herrings, have made their way 50 or 60 miles out to sea, and then turned round and come back again. If not, we must conclude that they began life far away from where they should have been hatched, according to the common idea. Again, if spawning had nothing to do with the movement of these shoals from deep to shallow water, or, at all events, towards the land, have we any reason for supposing that such was the motive of those fish which came in at the autumn spawning time? Such evidence as we possess seems to point to there being more than one spawning season, and that the spawn is deposited wherever the fish may happen to be when it is ripe; but why the herrings should make periodical visits to the land, whether in spawn or not, has yet to be shown.

Precisely the same thing occurs with the mackerel; but M. Sars has ascertained that with that fish the spawn is frequently shed far out at sea, and in very deep water. As before mentioned, the ova of the mackerel float at the surface, and there is no occasion therefore to seek any suitable bed for them. Yet the mackerel gradually makes its way inshore in precisely the same manner as the herring does; and half-grown fish without any roe are often as numerous among the moving shoals as those which are full of spawn. The great body of pilchards appear on the Cornish coast after they have spawned in deep water; but a few, apparently of different shoals from the very large majority, are in spawn when near the land in autumn. We find the same thing happening in the case of sprats, fish of almost every size being caught in the same week—we might almost say on the same day—some with the roe in various stages of growth, and others with none to be seen. We might go through the whole list of our edible fishes without being able to find one which we could say with certainty spawns only inshore. We presume that no one who has given the slightest consideration to the subject will contend that the millions of plaice annually caught in the neighbourhood of the Doggerbank must be the produce of spawn shed by those fish which frequent our sandy bays. The plaice is a ubiquitous species, and we have no evidence whatever that it does not spawn in its usual haunts, wherever they may be, inshore or in deep water. The fact that plaice, soles, and many other kinds of fish are caught near the land when they are full of roe shows nothing more than that those individual fishes would probably have spawned in that neighbourhood; but the trawlers catch the same kind of fish in precisely the same condition far out at sea, and we may therefore as reasonably conclude that the latter would have shed their spawn in deep water. If it were the rule for fishes in general to spawn inshore, the immense multitudes of each kind which in their season would collect there for that purpose could hardly escape the notice of the fishermen; but we do not hear of very extraordinary numbers being observed at that time more than at any other.

It may be said, however, that the number of very young fish, particularly flat-fish, found in shallow sandy bays, is a strong argument in favour of inshore spawning. There is no doubt whatever that more very small flat-fish are *caught* in such situations than in deep water; but independently of the question of comparative numbers existing in the different localities, it is as well to remember that the young fry in the sandy bays are caught by shrimp-nets and small-meshed trawls which are never used in deep water, and that the fish so taken come under our notice by being brought on shore, or emptied out of the net and thrown away before our eyes.

We are, however, quite disposed to believe that the number of young fry frequenting these sandy bays, as well as those which are caught there, is much larger than would be found in an area of equal size in deep water. But we do not think it necessarily follows that they were all bred there. If it be true, as M. Sars has no doubt of its being, that the ova of all the Pleuronectidæ or flat-fish float at the surface, and there is very good reason to think the spawn of these fishes may be shed at all distances from the land, there can be little doubt that some of these floating ova in various stages of development are drifted close to and into the bays after having been for some time the sport of the tides. Many of them are no doubt washed on shore like other drifting objects and are destroyed, but others which then happen to be just at the point of hatching are precisely in the situation most favourable for the preservation of the young fish as soon as it leaves its prison-house; for it can reach the shelter of the sand without having very far to go. The probability—we are obliged to put it in that way, for direct evidence is wanting, but we think we are justified in using the word—is that those young fry which escape being eaten remain in the locality for some days or weeks, perhaps longer, and their numbers are daily recruited by additions from the same source, resulting in the abundance of which the small-meshed nets give us plenty of evidence. It seems most likely that all the ova produced by those fishes which actually spawn in these bays are either washed on shore or drifted away; for they must be incapable of resisting the action of the tides. This leads us to the perhaps unexpected conclusion that the millions of fry in any particular bay are most probably the produce of spawn shed in other localities. As these very young fishes increase in size they gradually make their way into deeper water, but apparently remain for some time not very far off.

The Brixham and Plymouth trawlers, whose usual fishing grounds are only a few miles from the land, find that the nearer they work inshore the larger is the number of young fish in their nets; but they always take some; and this is also the case with the North Sea trawlers. It cannot be avoided, for young fish are found everywhere; but they are probably nowhere so numerous in equal areas as along the shores of sandy bays; and there unfortunately the most effective means of destroying them can be and are employed. Incalculable numbers, however, after being hatched out at the surface, must certainly find a safe resting place on the ground in deep water, as proved by the immense and continuous catches there of plaice and soles of various sizes; and the destruction of small fish in the bays by shrimpers and others, however much it is to be regretted, has therefore not the importance which apparently attached to it when the parent fish were supposed generally to select those particular localities for the deposit of their spawn upon the ground.

The deep-sea trawlers catch a varying number of young fish wherever they work, but they are of a larger size generally than those taken in the shoal water of bays such as we have been speaking of. The quantity of entirely useless fish thus caught, thrown away, and probably wasted, if not eaten by other fish, is, however, very much less than is commonly supposed;

for a good deal of what is spoken of as small fish has some value, and finds purchasers, although at a low price. It would be better if they were not caught until larger, and the trawlers would willingly do without them, but they cannot help themselves. Fish of all sizes find their way into the net, and a moderate-sized sole will wriggle through a mesh that one might suppose would be much too small to allow it to pass; while very small soles are often unable to escape through meshes which are abundantly large for them, because they have not strength to open a passage through them when they are strained so much as to become closed; or they may be crowded with other fish in the pockets. We do not know how many escape at present; but the use of a larger mesh would certainly ensure the loss of a great many fair-sized fish which now are captured; and, for the reasons we have mentioned, more of the small ones would not necessarily escape.

There is no method of fishing which does not involve waste in some form, either by killing immature fish or destroying spawn in the adult. Even if we look at the salmon fishery, hedged about as it is by enactments, good, bad, or indifferent, according to the various opinions of the persons directly interested in its prosperity, we find the same thing going on; and we venture to think there are many people who now sigh over the capture of a two-pound codling which might have become a ten-pound cod, perhaps in a couple of years, but who would not hesitate to basket a three-pound grilse, although with two years' grace it would probably have become a twenty-pound salmon, if not more. If salmon, like herrings, were considered in their prime when just ready to spawn, very much higher penalties than those at present provided would be necessary to ensure such protection as they now properly receive at that season. A close-time is needed for salmon, because their only spawning grounds are high up in the rivers; and the opportunities and appliances for capturing the fish before they can reach those grounds are so many, that spawning might practically be prevented if no protection were given. It is entirely different in the case of sea fish, even if we suppose the common idea to be correct, that they all spawn in more or less shallow water near the land. It would be idle to imagine that our sea fisheries are now, or are ever likely to be, carried on in such a manner as to catch any large proportion of the fish before they could reach the supposed spawning beds; it would be equally incredible that it would pay our small inshore trawlers to continue working on these supposed spawning grounds, or, strictly speaking, on some of them— for the alleged destruction of spawning fish and of spawn is by no means general around the coast—so long as to catch most of the fish in the locality. No possible extent of fishing, therefore, can prevent a considerable number of fish from freely spawning when the proper season for it arrives. Nor is there the slightest evidence to show that if the spawn were deposited there, it would necessarily be injured by being disturbed. On the contrary, we know by the experiments of Professor Allman and others that, in the case of herring spawn, there is no difficulty in hatching the ova after it has been dredged up and kept under unfavourable conditions in the house. The statements which have before now been confidently made, that the spawn of sea fish is commonly buried in the ground, have no foundation on direct observation; it would, of course, be very difficult to ascertain that such was the case; and when those persons who assert it are pressed on the subject, they can only say they think so, perhaps because the ova of salmon are covered over.

Yet, with the great difference in the conditions affecting the spawning of salmon and sea fish, it is no uncommon thing to find it put forward as a logical argument that, if it be right to establish a close-time for the salmon during the spawning season, we should on the same principle have one for the fishes of the sea.

We may here observe that the extent of ground actually fished by the beam-trawl is much less than appears to be generally supposed; and the destructive effect in capturing fish, whether of marketable size or otherwise, of this method of working proportionately exaggerated. The nets used by the deep-sea trawlers range from about 36 to 50 feet wide at the mouth; or, to use the ordinary expression in describing them, that would be the length of the beam. Fifty feet is the outside length we have heard of, and it is only in the new class of vessels that it is so much; but we will take that as an example. Now, it would require 120 of such trawls, placed side by side, to fill up the breadth of a nautical mile of 2000 yards. The proportion of ground covered by a single trawl, of the size we have mentioned, will perhaps be better apprehended by reducing it to a small scale; if we take $\frac{1}{1200}$th, then the largest sized trawl would be represented by half an inch on a space five feet wide. The small inshore trawlers work with beams ranging from 15 to 25 feet in length, and the longest of these would occupy only a quarter of an inch on the reduced scale. We shall have occasion in subsequent pages to speak of the various grounds systematically trawled over in the course of the year. We may here mention, however, that in the North Sea they are of considerable extent, but of much less size in the English Channel; in both, however, they are small compared with the areas never touched by a trawl—not because there is any reason to believe no fish are to be found there, but in consequence of the depth of water, or the rough or muddy nature of the bottom.

In the hundreds or, we may say, thousands of square miles of trawling ground in the North Sea, there must be a great deal of the bottom which is very little disturbed; for if fifty large trawlers were to work abreast within a space of two miles, nearly four-fifths of the ground would be untouched by their nets. The harvest the trawlers are continually gathering in is a moving one, and the trawling grounds may be successfully worked over day after day, for there are no means of preventing the fish from coming upon them from other places in the neighbourhood. This is shown in an unmistakable manner in the case of the Brixham and Plymouth grounds; both of them being of very limited extent, and yet furnishing a supply of fish throughout the year, the number and description varying with the seasons.

In these introductory observations we have endeavoured to show, by well-ascertained facts, and, we believe, by reasonable deductions from them, that the supply of sea fish has not fallen off, but that, from the additional and regular distribution of it to the markets throughout the country, owing to the facility of transport provided by the great system of railways, it must have immensely increased for some years past; that there is no reason to believe any of our edible fishes specially seek the bays or neighbourhood of the land for the purpose of spawning; that the conclusions to be drawn from the investigations by Professors Sars and M. Malm are entirely opposed to the idea of the spawn of most of those fishes being at any time within reach of injury from trawling or any other method of fishing in use; and that the two last considerations tend greatly to diminish the importance of the destruction of young fish, which, however much it is to be regretted, takes place more or less wherever fishing is carried on.

We can see nothing to prevent our fisheries being increased beyond their present extent, so far as that increase may depend on the general supply of fish in our seas; but their development will be regulated, as in all other trades, by the cost of producing the article and the price obtained for it in the market. The increase or decrease, however, in the number of fishing boats, or even, if it were possible to obtain it, in the quantity of fish caught in two successive years, would be no certain indication of a general improvement or otherwise in the condition of the sea fisheries; longer periods must be compared in order to arrive at any just conclusion on the subject, for there are good and bad seasons for fishing, depending on various causes; and these and other circumstances may affect the number of fishermen from time to time, and their ability to keep up or add to their boats.

There may be occasion to return to some of the subjects we have now been discussing, but we shall only do so in the hope of making our account of some of the fisheries more complete and intelligible.

We shall now proceed with a description of the manner in which the several methods of sea fishing are carried on. They will come under the following heads :—

1. Trawling.
2. Drift-fishing.
3. Line-fishing.
4. Sean-fishing.
5. Bag-nets.
6. Kettle-net and Weirs.
7. Trammel or Set-nets.

I.—TRAWLING.

Uncertainty as to origin of — Various kinds of trawl — Supposed long use of — Principal trawling stations — Description of the beam-trawl — Beam, heads, net, ground-rope — Arrangement and use of pockets — Warp, bridles — Size and description of trawl-smacks — Improved rig — Cost of vessels and gear — Barking sails — Working the trawl — Shooting the net — Towing — Action of the trawl — Ground fish and floating fish — Resistance of the water — Heaving up — Hoisting in the fish — Varied contents of trawl — Suitable weather — Depth of water — Condition of trawl-fish — Classification of — "Prime and offal" — Abundance of certain kinds — Fishing grounds, continued supply from — Plymouth, Brixham, North Sea — Discovery of Silver Pit — Large number of trawlers.

THE most important method of fishing by which a regular supply of the best and most varied kinds of sea fish is obtained for the market is that commonly known as "trawling"—a name evidently derived from trailing or dragging; the trawl being a bag-net, which is towed, trailed, or trawled along the bottom; and it is so constructed as to capture those fish especially which naturally keep upon or near the ground. There are several varieties of the trawl, but the differences between them relate to the appliances in use for its effective working rather than to the principle of its construction or the object for which it is to be employed. In all cases[1] it has the general form of a triangular bag

[1] The term "trawl" belongs properly to the bag-net which is towed or trailed along the bottom; but on the west coast of Scotland the name is systematically applied to the sean or circle net used for catching herrings. The herring-trawl in Scotland is therefore the same kind of net as the sean employed for catching pilchards, herrings, and mackerel on the English coasts. The unfortunate misuse of the name "trawl" in Scotland has led to a great deal of misapprehension on the part of writers on the sea fisheries; and even Mr. Couch, the well-known author of the *Fishes of the British Islands*, appears to have been misled by it, as, when speaking of the various methods of catching herrings, he says (vol. iv., p. 105), "We believe also that not long since ingenuity has contrived to render the trawl effective in the fishery for

or purse, and the variations in shape or fittings are due to the different plans adopted for ensuring the mouth of the bag being kept open, so that the fish may enter whilst the net or bag itself is towed along out of sight at the bottom.

The origin of the trawl-net appears to be unknown, but an eminently primitive method of working it is still in use on the Atlantic and Mediterranean coasts of Spain. The Spanish trawl differs but little in shape from the English net, except in having the cod or last part of it in the form of a short broad receptacle for the fish instead of a long and narrow one. Its chief feature is that, in order to keep the mouth of the net open so as to work efficiently, two vessels are employed. They are termed "Parejas," signifying pairs or couples, and they sail together at a certain distance apart, towing the net between them. An improvement on this plan, although very far from being satisfactory, is the hammer or pole trawl, still used on some parts of the south and south-west coasts of Ireland. Only one vessel is required to work it, and the mouth of the net is extended by ropes leading from wings of netting on both sides of it to poles projecting one on each side of the vessel. It is but a clumsy contrivance, and only suited to smooth and shallow water. It will be further described when the Irish fisheries are spoken of.[1] The otter-trawl is the same kind of net as the one just noticed, but otter-boards are fastened to the end of the wings, and by their peculiar and kite-like action cause

---

herrings, by using it somewhat on the principle of a moving stow-net. The gaping and enormous bag is sunk to the proper depth by a rope, and in this condition is carried along among the hosts of fish by the moving vessel." Mr. Couch makes no mention of the sean being, in Scotland, called a trawl, and there is no evidence of his having been aware of the fact. We have never heard of the beam-trawl being used in the manner described.

[1] Page 371.

the extension of the mouth of the net without any necessity for poles. The otter-trawl is much used on board yachts, but does not meet with much favour from professional fishermen. Their preference is given entirely to the beam-trawl, which has been in use for many years, and, notwithstanding some disadvantages, has on the whole proved to be a productive and useful implement of fishing. There is nothing to show when the addition of the beam was first made to the trawl, nor is it certainly known whence the idea originated. There is some reason to think, however, that to Brixham is due the credit of having first adopted it in this country for deep-sea fishing, and possibly of having introduced it, although we believe Barking also puts in a claim to it. The commencement of the system probably dates from some period in the last century. Old fishermen at Brixham remember their grandfathers being trawlers; but the number of vessels and their size were then small compared with those of the present day, and we can obtain no further information on the subject than that beam-trawling had been carried on for a long time, or, as was said by one old fisherman, whose chronological ideas were perhaps not very clear, "may be from the time of Moses,"—a possibility not quite consistent with the general idea at Brixham, that beam-trawling originated in that long-famous fishing port.

The same method of fishing is general on the coasts of Holland, Belgium, and France; but the Dutch are peculiar in using two trawls at once, one being towed from the bow and the other from the stern of the vessel. It is a question whether, taking the year through, much advantage is gained from this system, although undoubtedly large catches are made by it at times.

The principal stations in England for deep-sea trawlers are Plymouth, Brixham, Dover, and Ramsgate, south of the Thames; London, Lowestoft, Yarmouth, Grimsby, Hull, and Scarborough on the east coast; and Fleetwood and Liverpool on the west; with Carnarvon and Tenby on the coast of Wales.

There is no beam-trawling station of any importance on the coast of Scotland.

In Ireland the trawling stations for large vessels are Dublin, Waterford, Dingle, and Galway.

Inshore trawling is carried on by small craft on several parts of the coast of the three countries, but much less in Scotland than elsewhere.

The Beam-trawl.

(*Plate II.*)

The beam-trawl may be simply described as a triangular, flat, purse-shaped net with the mouth extended by a horizontal wooden beam, which is raised a short distance from the ground by means of two iron supports or heads, the upper part of the mouth being fastened to the beam, and the under portion dragging on the ground as the net is towed over the bottom.

In describing it in detail, such a net as is used by the Brixham men in their own waters, or by their descendants or followers on other parts of the coast, may be taken as a fair example.

The beam (*a*) is made of various lengths, according to the size of the nets, and to a great extent to the length and power of the vessel which is to tow it. In the large trawl-smacks now in general use for deep-sea fishing it varies from about 36 feet to 50 feet; in small

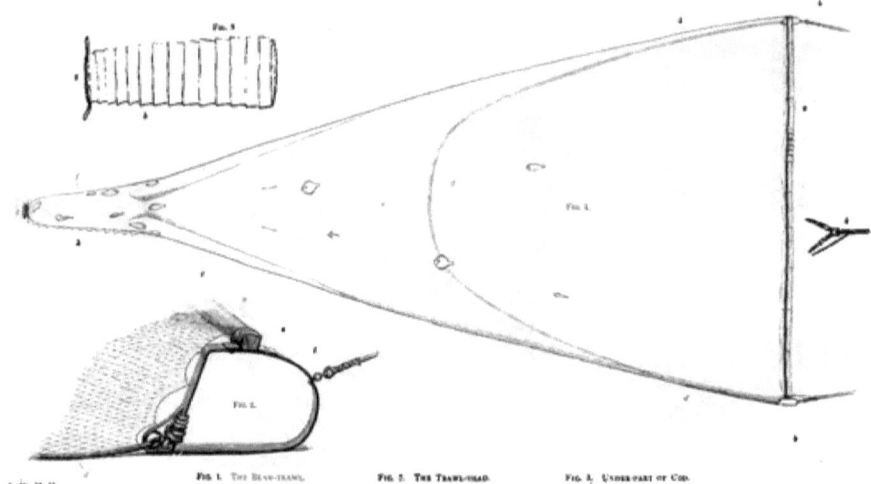

Fig. 1. The Beam-Trawl.   Fig. 2. The Trawl-Head.   Fig. 3. Under part of Cod.

craft for inshore work the length is very much less. The beam is usually made of elm, but sometimes of ash or beech, the timber selected being such as can be found naturally grown of the proper thickness; but as it is difficult to meet with a straight piece of sufficient length and size for an ordinary large trawl-beam, two or more pieces are usually scarved together, and the joints firmly secured by iron bands. The whole is roughly trimmed, and the strength of the timber is not impaired by more chipping and finishing than necessary. The length of the beam for each vessel is mainly determined by the distance between the taffrail and the after shroud, convenience and security both making it desirable to carry the beam, when not in use, hoisted up alongside, with one end projecting just beyond the stern of the vessel, where it is made fast by a special rope or chain, and the other coming in front of the after shroud or shrouds. The advantage of this arrangement is obvious, as it is generally the case that the beam has to be hoisted up whilst the vessel is rolling and pitching about in a seaway. The after end of the beam is first got into its place, and the fore part is then hoisted up until level with the top of the bulwark, over which and between two of the shrouds the iron head at the end of the beam finds a snug berth, and all danger of the heavy and somewhat unmanageable spar swinging on board as the vessel lurches is avoided. It would be often difficult to prevent this if the beam were not long enough to overlap the after shrouds.

Head-irons.—The object or use of the beam is to extend the mouth of the net; but in order to keep the mouth open so as to allow the fish to enter, it is further necessary to raise the beam, and with it the back of the net fastened to it, a certain distance from the ground.

This is effected by two iron frames placed one at each end of the beam, and called "trawl-heads" or "head-irons" (Fig. 1 *b, b*, Fig. 2). Each end of the beam is fixed at right angles into a socket or "joggle" (Fig. 2 *c*), either above or below the upper part of the head-iron, the shape of which varies within certain limits on different parts of the coast, or in the several countries whence trawling is carried on.

Fig. 2 represents the form in use by the Brixham trawlers, and the one largely adopted on our coasts. It is of wrought iron, and the lower part or "shoe," which works over the ground, and is consequently exposed to a great deal of wear, is made of extra thickness. The weight of the two irons ranges on different parts of the coast from 230 lbs. to 360 lbs., and varies generally with the size of the net and beam as they do with the size of the vessel; but in some parts of the North Sea where the tides are very strong, moderate-sized trawls require a great deal of weight in the head-irons to keep them on the ground. It is not to the interest of the fisherman, however, to weight his trawl-beam more than enough to keep his gear at

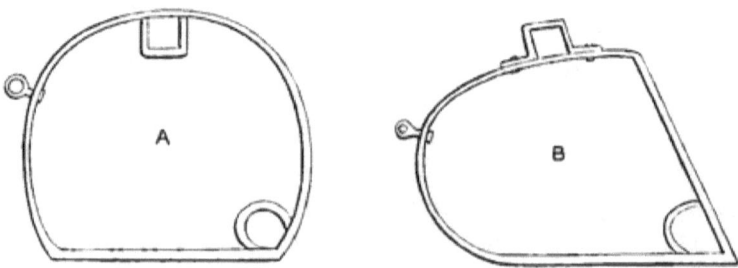

TRAWL-HEADS.

the bottom under the ordinary conditions of working. The stirrup-shaped Barking pattern (A) is peculiar, and has been a long time in use by vessels belonging to the Thames. It is now also generally adopted by the Yarmouth smacks, having been introduced by the Barking vessels, many of which find it convenient to make that port their station. Another form (B) is used on many parts of the coast by the small inshore trawlers, and is but a very slight modification of that employed by the Brixham men, the difference consisting in the iron loop through which the ground-rope passes before it is made fast being inside instead of outside the frame. Among other varieties of trawl-head may be mentioned those we have found used by some of the French trawlers (C, D), and the noticeable

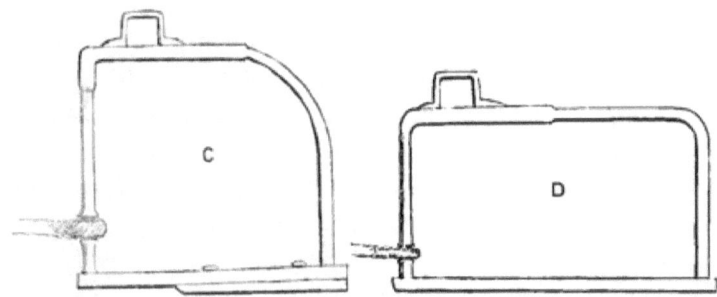

FRENCH TRAWL-HEADS.

feature in them is that the beam is placed so near the front of the head as to require the tow-rope to be fixed very low to prevent the fore part of the shoe burying itself in the ground. This is further guarded against in one variety by the additional length of the frame behind the beam. There appears to be a want of balance in these French irons which is not the case in those used by our own fishermen. No doubt there is some degree of fancy in the shapes adopted; but the English irons strike one as better adapted for their work, and the Brixham pattern is now being much used by the French trawlers. By means of these irons the trawl-beam is kept nearly three feet above the ground, so that it neither touches nor causes any disturbance of the bottom whatever; its sole use is to extend the mouth of the net, and if it were to touch the ground, as many persons believe it does, it would effectually frighten away the fish and prevent their going into the net.

The trawl itself (Plate II., Fig. 1) is, as we have mentioned, a triangular purse-shaped net, and consists of several portions, each having its own name. An old-fashioned bed watch-pocket laid on its face will perhaps give as intelligible an idea of the shape of a trawl-net as anything else. The upper part or surface of the net is termed the "back," and the under portion the "belly." The front straight edge of the back, or the "square" of the net, is fastened to the beam, and is therefore raised some distance from the ground. The corresponding lower part is cut away in such a manner that the margin forms a deep curve below, extending from one trawl-head to the other, close to the ground, and with the centre of the curve or "bosom" at some distance behind the beam and front of the net. The usual rule for the depth of the curve is that the distance from the beam to the bosom should be equal to the length of the beam. In French trawls it is very much less. There is, however, in all cases a considerable space of ground over which the beam and back of the net must pass before the fish lying on the bottom are disturbed by the under part of the net. The curved lower margin of the mouth of the trawl is fastened to and protected by the "ground-rope" (Figs. 1, 2 *d*). This is a piece of old hawser which has done its legitimate work, but now, "rounded" or covered with small rope to protect it from chafing and to make it heavier, answers the useful purpose of keeping the edge of the net on the ground so as to sweep the surface and disturb the fish, which passing over it then find their way into the narrow closed extremity of the trawl. The Yarmouth trawlers use a beam of about 36 feet in length, and a much shorter ground-rope in proportion than is employed by the Brixham and Grimsby fishermen; there being an idea on their part that when working in strong tides on the Doggerbank the large-mouthed nets are liable to close up—a difficulty, however, which does not appear to have been discovered by the fishermen from other ports. The ends of the ground-rope are made fast on each side by a few turns round the back of the trawl-head, just above the shoe, and the rope rests on the ground throughout the entire curve; the fish therefore have no chance of escape at either the sides or bosom of the net, and their only outlet when once the beam has passed over them is in front, so that they must dart forward in the direction in which the net is moving to enable them to get clear of it. The object of making the ground-rope of old material is that it may break in case of getting foul of rocks or any chance obstruction which may be met with on the generally smooth ground where a trawl can only be worked with advantage. If in such a contingency the ground-rope were strong and good, the least mischief likely to ensue would be the anchoring of the vessel by her trawl, involving great loss of time in clearing it, and resulting, probably, in breaking the beam and other damage; but as these nets are used in deep water where there is always more or less sea or swell, the great danger to be feared when the net gets foul is the parting of the warp by which the trawl is towed, and the consequent loss of the whole gear. If, however, the ground-rope give way, the only damage likely to result is in the under part of the net behind it being torn open; the whole apparatus then comes away clear, when it can be hoisted up, overhauled, and the netting and rope repaired. It was formerly the custom to weight the ground-rope to ensure its close working over the bottom, and it is still sometimes the practice at Yarmouth to use short lengths of chain for that purpose, secured at each end by ropeyarns to the ground-rope, so as to be easily torn away in case of getting foul. The French trawlers also use chain on the ground-rope, but in those we have examined a great length of chain has been suspended in short festoons and secured by iron rings over the rope, and therefore not easily detached. Our west-country fishermen find that by giving a larger sweep to the ground-rope an old hawser is heavy enough without other addition than the small rope with which it is covered or rounded.

The narrow straight sides of the net between the back and the ground-rope, and extending from the trawl-heads to nearly on a level with the bosom, are called the "wings" or "gorings"; they are generally made of separate pieces of net, and are inserted when the several parts composing the trawl are put together.

From the bosom the whole net, now forming a complete bag (Fig. 1 e), tapers to the cod or purse, a length equal to about two-thirds of that of the beam. The cod (Fig. 1 f) is a narrow bag about one-seventh of the entire length of the trawl; it is that part of the net into which all the fish which pass over the ground-rope sooner or later find their way, and in which most of them are collected when the net is hauled in. The extremity, or "cod-end" (Figs. 1, 3 *g*), is closed by the draw-rope or "cod-line," which gathers the end of the net together and prevents the escape of the fish until it is got on board, when the rope is cast off, the cod-end opened, and the fish fall out. The under part of the cod having a good deal of the weight of the fish on it, is of course exposed to a great deal of wear and tear as it is dragged over the ground, so, to protect it from chafing and being destroyed, pieces of old net termed "rubbing pieces" or "false bellies" (Figs. 1, 3 *h*) are fastened across it in such a manner as to overlap one another successively from one end of the cod to the other, and thus to relieve the strain on the net itself. In the French trawls the net is very much shorter in proportion to the length of the beam; it tapers regularly to the end, has no distinct cod, as in the English nets, and the rubbing pieces extend across the under side of the trawl for some distance from the end, which is specially protected from chafing by having a stout hide underneath.

Just above the entrance to the cod the "pockets" (Fig. 1 *i, i*) are placed, one on each side of the interior of the main portion of the net. They are not separate parts of the net, but are made by simply lacing together the back and belly for a length of about 16 feet, in a line from the outer edge of the bag downwards and inwards to its small end and the commencement of the cod. This part of the bag is therefore divided into three spaces, and of nearly equal breadth at the lower end, those at the sides being the pockets, and the central space that through which the fish must pass on their way from the entrance of the net to the cod or general receptacle. This passage between the pockets is guarded by a veil of netting called the "flapper,"[1] fastened to the upper part or back, and with its free edge directed towards the cod, so that the fish can easily make their way under it into that part of the net, but cannot so readily return. The mouths of the pockets face and open into the cod or end of the net where the fish are collected, and there being no means of escape for the fish at the cod-end, many of them, and especially the soles, work their way along the sides of the cod into the pockets, continuing their progress in that direction till they are stopped by the gradual narrowing and termination of these long funnel-shaped enclosures.

It does not appear very difficult to understand why soles especially should generally be found in the pockets of a trawl. Soles are naturally quiet fish, and bury themselves more completely than any of the other kinds which keep on the ground, excepting perhaps some of the rays. In an aquarium they will remain for hours in the same place during the day, and so much covered by the sand as to make it often difficult to discover them. Their general feeding time is at night, and then of course they are more on the move and out of the ground, which will explain what the trawlers have long since found out by experience, namely, that heavier catches of these fish are always made by night than by day fishing, except sometimes in very deep water. But when soles are disturbed, their first impulse is to hide themselves in the sand after darting a very short distance from the place where they were lying. Having once crossed the ground-rope of the trawl, however, and entered the net, they cannot bury themselves, because the net is between them and the ground; moreover, it is constantly dragging over the bottom as the trawl

---

[1] The position of the flapper is marked by a dotted line in Fig. 1.

moves forward, so that the fish can get no rest on any part of it. Sooner or later the soles find their way into the "cod," where still further disturbance is no doubt caused by the crowd of other fish. The endeavours they all of course make to escape will bring them sooner or later to one side or other of the cod, and by following that part of the net backwards, and so getting out of the crowd, they soon come to the mouth of the pockets. Now the pressure of the water which enters the mouth of the trawl expands the general body of the net as it is being towed over the ground, tending to keep open the passage between the pockets into the cod, and which, as has been mentioned, is guarded by a valve of netting to prevent the return of the fish. But the pressure of this enclosed water would have no such effect on the pockets, because they are virtually outside the bag; the boundaries of the actual cavity of the net being at the inner margins of the pockets. The backward pressure of the water on them is therefore only on their outer surface, from their narrow closed ends downwards, and tends to flatten them throughout their entire length. Theoretically, then, the mouth of the pockets should be closed with the rest, so far as bringing the upper and under surfaces together would do so; and probably few fish would find their way inside. But some of the soles, in their endeavours to hide, and with their natural habit of running themselves, if possible, below the surface, might even under these conditions discover the entrance. The construction of the net, however, is such that the mouths of the pockets are always kept open; for the cod of the net being made with a small mesh offers great resistance to the escape of the water flowing into it, and is accordingly much expanded; and the mouths of the pockets facing that part of the net must necessarily be opened by this expansion. It is also the case that the water flowing into the cod, and being unable to escape readily through its walls, forms return or eddy currents along the sides into the pockets, keeping them open more or less throughout their length, according to the extent of pressure, and so helps to move the fish in that direction. Several kinds of fish are often found in the pockets; but the special advantage of these parts of the trawl is in securing the soles, which in their endeavours to find some quiet resting-place try every means of escape from the net. When the fish have once entered the pockets they move on to the end, where they are powerless, and the successive additions from the "cod" often result in the pockets being well packed with fish.

It has been objected that pockets are useless, and that they only hold a certain number of fish, which would otherwise be found in the cod. But it is believed by professional fishermen, and we think with reason, that, independently of the fish being practically secured by the pockets, the whole contents of the net are turned out in better condition from the weight of the fish being distributed over a larger space, and not subjected so much to the irregular knocking about to which they are more or less liable when there is a heavy load at the end of the net. They also escape being crushed when, as sometimes happens, large stones find their way into the cod. These points are not of so much consequence when the trawl is only worked for an hour or two at a time; but as the deep-sea trawlers habitually keep their nets down for five or six hours continuously, considerations of this kind should not be lost sight of.

The proportions we have given for the different parts

of the beam-trawl may be taken as those generally adopted in the construction of the large deep-sea nets, but they vary somewhat in different localities and in different vessels; some trawlers make the cod of the net longer than others, and in some of the small trawls used by inshore fishermen we have seen the number of pockets increased to six. In the large trawl-nets the meshes are of four sizes, diminishing from 4 inches square in the back to $1\frac{1}{2}$ inch in the cod; and the twine used for the under part of the net is usually a size larger than that for the back.

The trawl is towed over the ground by means of the trawl-warp, generally a 6-inch rope, 150 fathoms long, and made up of two lengths of 75 fathoms spliced together. The end of this warp (Fig. 1 k) is shackled to two other pieces of 15 fathoms each, termed the "spans" or "bridles," which lead one to each end of the beam and shackle on to swivel-bolts (Fig. 2 l) in the front of the head-irons. Another rope, of much smaller size, but a little longer than the bridle, and called the "dandy bridle," is made fast to that end of the beam which comes astern when it is hoisted on board, and the other end of this rope is hitched round the trawl-warp just above the shackle when the net is in the water. The use of this rope will be explained when the mode of working the trawl is described.

The vessels used for trawling are commonly called smacks. During the last twenty years great improvement has been made in their design with the object of making them faster; and in some few cases it may be a question whether by the adoption of very fine lines sea-going qualities have not been to some extent sacrificed to the desire for increased speed. Formerly the smacks were much smaller than at the present time, and ranged from 23 to 36 tons N.M. They were built with the principal object of living through anything, and rarely failed to make good weather of it at all times. Many of these strong well-built vessels are still at work, and would be likely to hold their own for many more years, were it not that sea-going qualities are not the only ones required at the present day. Now, the greater demand for fish and the increased number of smacks have led to more competition among the fishermen, and time has become more valuable; for the first boats in are likely to get the best price for their fish. Most of the modern trawl-vessels are of a large size, running up to 70 tons N.M., and are fine powerful craft of upwards of 60 feet keel and good beam. They are, as formerly, built high at the bow and with plenty of sheer, making them easy and comfortable sea boats; and whilst their increase in size enables them to use longer trawl-beams and larger nets, the general improvement in the knowledge of ship-building has led to the adoption of easier lines in their construction, resulting in the much better sailing qualities which are now required to meet the demands of the trade. The quick delivery of the fish is every day becoming a more important object, as the demand for it increases all over the country; and the smacks may daily be seen racing back to the great trawling stations to land their fish, each one endeavouring, often with the help of balloon canvas, to bring her catch early to market, where the buyers are waiting with orders to purchase for all parts of the country.

The vessels regularly employed in trawling are, as we have said, called "smacks," a term which appears to have been long applied to fishing boats rigged as sloops or cutters. In these smacks the mast is stepped well forward so as to allow of a large and powerful mainsail, at the same time giving plenty of room for the stowage of a long trawl-beam and large net when not at work. The rigging of these vessels was formerly rough and simple, and a long head to the mast to support the short topmast was all that was necessary when only a small topsail was to be set; but the larger light sails now carried commonly require the addition of crosstrees and backstays to secure the spar under the strain it has to bear. In the west country the bowsprit is without any rigging as the head sails are small, and it is desirable to have no bobstay in the way of the trawl-warp, which there being always hauled in over the bow, has to be led thence outside clear of the rigging to one side or other of the vessel, according to which tack she is on when at work, and to be brought on board again amidships, where it is made fast to the pump-head. A large winch is fitted just before the mast for heaving in the trawl, and there is a small windlass astern, called the "dandy wink,"[1] shipped between the head of the companion and the bulwark, for hoisting up the after end of the beam when the trawl is got on board. In the North Sea trawlers the trawl-warp is worked and got in over the side by means of a patent capstan shipped near the centre of the vessel. This excellent contrivance is worked by two ordinary winch-handles acting on an arrangement of rack and pinion fitted either to the top of the spindle round which the capstan turns, or to an iron standard by the side of the capstan.

The large trawl-vessels now in use from Grimsby and Hull, and recently built, are rigged in a different manner from that which has long been the general

---

[1] "Dandy" signifies small, and "wink" is the name applied to a windlass worked by short fixed levers instead of by movable handspikes.

custom with the smaller craft. It was found that the increased size of the mainsail and heavy main-boom necessary for these larger vessels required more hands to manage them; and as the quantity of fish taken by these vessels did not increase in proportion to the greater size—the nets used by them being only slightly enlarged—economy and convenience were both in favour of reducing the large mainsail if it could be done without seriously diminishing the working power of the vessel. The new trawlers were therefore built of considerable length, so as to give plenty of room for a good mizenmast; the mast being stepped well forward to allow sufficient steering room abaft, the large unmanageable mainsail was got rid of, and the reduction in its size made up by a good-sized gaff mizen. These vessels can now be worked economically, and the sails, being in comparatively small pieces, are managed with only one hand more than in much smaller craft. Although these large trawlers do not bring in much more fish than vessels perhaps 15 or 20 tons smaller—for the longest trawl-beams now in use do not exceed 50 feet—it is believed that their greater cost is compensated for by the additional accommodation provided. The crew have more room and increased cooking conveniences, and there is much better stowage for the ice and fish; and it speaks well both for the owners and the prosperity of the fishing trade that the men who are exposed to the hardships and dangers of the deep-sea fisheries are taken good care of by those who, having in most cases themselves gone through the practical part of the work, are now in the happy position of owners, and can remain comfortably on shore.

At Yarmouth, and some other places on the North

Sea coast, the luggers, when not employed in herring fishing, are in some cases converted into trawlers; and as the lug-rig is not very suitable for that mode of fishing, a temporary change is made, and they are fitted out with a different set of masts and sails; the dandy, or perhaps speaking more correctly, the ketch rig with gaff sails being the one adopted, the same as just described in the large modern-built trawlers at Grimsby and Hull. Some of the Ramsgate and Brixham vessels are now rigged in the same manner, and we have no doubt that it will be very generally adopted for the new vessels on various parts of the coast where deep-sea trawling is carried on, although, as a rule, fishermen are not fond of giving up what they have been long accustomed to.

The cost of trawl-smacks has largely increased during the last ten years, in consequence of their much greater size; and the capital invested in this part of the fishing trade is added to yearly by the substitution of larger vessels for those previously employed. In 1862 a new trawler ready for sea, and what was then considered one of the larger class, could be built and fitted out for 700*l*. or 800*l*.; but the vessels before mentioned as having recently come into use at Hull and Grimsby cannot be turned out ready for work for much less than 1200*l*. each. This includes a fit out of all that is required for fishing, and costing about 70*l*. or 80*l*. A fit out consists of a double set of almost every part of the gear, to provide against accidents, and generally to save the time which would be lost if the smack were obliged to return to port before she had done a fair quantity of work. A trawl-net will perhaps last from two to four months, according to the nature of the ground worked on; but during that time parts of it will have to be renewed. The back of the net, being exposed to the least wear, lasts the longest; the under part will generally require renewing twice, and the cod five or six times before the net is finally condemned. The cost of a new net is about 9*l*. when made of ordinary hemp; but Manilla is coming into use for this purpose, as it is very much stronger, although more costly. It is dressed with coal-tar, which preserves the material better than either Stockholm tar or tan. One of the large nets now used, and measuring about 50 feet across the square, cannot be made for much less than 16*l*.

"Barking" the sails of fishing craft is almost universal in this country. It consists in mopping them over with a solution of oak-bark, tar, grease, and ochre, which acts as a good preservative to the canvas; this is done every six or eight weeks, and a yard is prepared and kept for the purpose at all the important fishing stations.

Working the Trawl.

Among the conditions desirable for successful trawling is a favourable tide—one of only moderate strength, as the trawl, which is always towed in the same general direction as, but a little faster than, the stream, then works steadily and is easily kept on the ground. When the vessel has arrived on her fishing ground the first part of the tide is chosen for beginning work in, as she can then tow for several hours in the same direction, and the usual practice is to keep the trawl down till the tide has done—about five or six hours. The vessel is first put under easy sail in the direction in which she is going to tow, depending on the wind suiting the tide, as a tolerably straight course must be kept, and this can only be done when the wind is generally fair, or more or less abaft the beam. The net is then thrown overboard or "shot," beginning at the cod, until the whole trawl is clear of the vessel and hanging from the beam, which is still in its place, hoisted up alongside. The end of the trawl-warp is previously passed outside from the bow, in the Brixham vessels, and being brought round clear of the shrouds is shackled to the two ends of the bridle, two or three turns of which are taken round the pump-head just abaft the main hatchway. In the North Sea trawlers, where the trawl is hauled up over the side, the warp is already in its place, and only requires being made fast to the bridle. Everything is now ready for lowering; and that part of the proceeding, simple as it may appear, is really one requiring considerable care; for unless properly managed the net and beam will not reach the bottom in the right position for working—that is, with the trawl-heads downward and the mouth of the net open below; for if the trawl were to turn over and fall on its back, the beam would be on the ground and the ground-rope above it; the entrance to the net would therefore be closed. The lowering is thus managed:—The fore bridle is first slacked away until that end of the beam is well clear and stands out at a considerable angle from the vessel, the after part being still kept in its place by the dandy bridle, which comes in over the taffrail to the small stern windlass or dandy wink by which it is worked. This rope is then slacked away till the whole beam is in the water, and the inner end of the rope is brought forward to be made fast to the warp, just above the shackle, till it is again wanted when the beam has to be hoisted up. The beam is now held by the two parts of the main bridle, and they are slowly paid out till it hangs evenly from them; if the whole gear be then in a proper position more way is got on the vessel and the warp given out so as to allow the trawl to sink to the bottom, which, as the vessel is under way, it will do at some distance astern. After that the quantity of extra warp allowed is determined by the judgment of the master, according to the various circumstances of weather, tide, and description of fish expected to be caught. It will be obvious that if the trawl were allowed to sink perpendicularly, which would be the case if the vessel had no way on her whilst the gear was being lowered, it would be liable to turn round with any twisting there might be in the warp, and it would be very much a matter of chance whether the trawl came to the ground on its back or otherwise. With all the precautions taken it sometimes happens that a mistake is made. When this is the case the irregular jerking of the warp as the trawl is towed along shows something is wrong, and then there is nothing to be done but to heave up and shoot the net again.

If all appear to be going right the warp is finally made fast by a small rope called the "stopper," a couple of turns of which are taken round the pump-head, and the ends laid round the warp in opposite directions, so as to overlap and cross at each turn, and thus to ensure a good hold; they are then secured. The object of the stopper is to save the warp in case of the trawl getting foul; for being a small rope it would, under any sudden strain, snap or part before the warp, and the trawl would not be lost. More warp can then be paid out, and the vessel sailed in such a direction as perhaps to clear the obstruction; if not, the next thing to be done is to try and heave up, and as the warp is got on board and the strain becomes more perpendicular, the trawl generally comes away clear, perhaps with only the net damaged.

Supposing the trawl to have reached the bottom and to be working properly, the only thing remaining is to keep the warp at such an angle with the length of the vessel as to make her steer herself in the desired course. The large mainsail in these smacks being the great driving power, they have always a strong tendency to fly up in the wind. This can of course be counteracted by the ordinary mode of steering; but that is unnecessary when the trawl itself can be made to do the work. If, for example, the wind be so fair that the vessel can run nearly before it, the warp is led over the stern or, more commonly, over the weather quarter close to the taffrail, and is prevented from slipping forward by a stout thole-pin inserted in one of the many holes bored for that purpose along the gunwale. Then if the pressure on the after sail tend to carry the stern round, it is opposed by the heavy drag or resistance of the trawl, which pulls it back and keeps the vessel straight. This resistance, it must be understood, is so great as to reduce the speed of the vessel from perhaps eight or nine knots to one and a half or two, so that, when trawling, she cannot sail fast enough to go much out of her course, even under any sudden pressure of wind, before her head is again brought to the right direction. Should the wind be more on the beam, the warp is carried farther forward, and its position adjusted according to a sort of rule of thumb and observation of the course made; allowance being given for a good deal of lee-way by heading the vessel nearer the wind—making her look higher, as it is called, than her proper course. In this manner the vessel is made to steer herself, and practically keeps the desired course within the not very precise limits necessary for working with the tide over her fishing ground.

One hand stays on deck to look out for any change of wind, to trim sails, and, by occasionally feeling the warp, to ascertain if the trawl be working properly. Feeling the warp is a very simple but effective test, for when all is going right a slight but regular vibration is felt on the hand being firmly pressed down on that part of the rope which is outside the vessel; whilst an irregular jerking action is evident if the trawl be going over rough ground or not keeping steadily at the bottom. The rest of the crew go below and turn in, or employ themselves in some other more or less profitable occupation till the watch has to be relieved or it is time to get the trawl up.

We may now say a few words about the action of the beam-trawl when at work. This net is specially constructed for catching what are called ground-fish—those which not only as a rule keep at the bottom, but also naturally hide below the surface of the sand or mud, as the case may be. With rare exceptions all the soles, turbot, and plaice brought to market are caught by the trawl; the various kinds of skate or ray are also obtained by the same means; and notwithstanding the peculiar habits of all of these fish there is very little chance of their escaping when once the trawl-beam has passed over their heads. It is well known that fish in general, when at rest, lie with their heads to the stream or tide; it is the only position in which they can keep their places by a slight action of the tail and other fins, and it is one which facilitates the process of respiration by allowing the water to pass in a natural direction through the mouth and out at the gill openings. Those fish which bury themselves, or, to speak more correctly, cover themselves with sand or mud by a peculiar action of the fins, and which from the shape of their bodies are not much exposed to the effect of the current, nevertheless follow the same rule more or less; and although, when on the move, fish of course swim in various directions, and in quiet water may rest without much regard to position, they practically lie head to stream in a tideway. The ground which flat-fish especially frequent is that with a smooth surface, and it will be evident from what has been said of the construction of the trawl that it can only be effectively worked over such a bottom. Rocky or rough ground is destructive to the net, and therefore fatal to this method of fishing. The trawl is always towed with the tide, but a little faster than it is running; were it otherwise, the net being lighter than the beam, loaded as it is with the iron heads, would be liable to be drifted forwards and to prevent the entrance of the fish. The slight excess of speed in the trawl over the tide, varying according to circumstances from half a knot to about a knot and a half in the hour, keeps the net in a state of expansion, and in a proper position on the bottom; the ground-rope can then do its duty.

The proper working of the ground-rope—its biting action or close pressure on the ground over which it is dragged is of the greatest importance when soles, turbot, and their kindred are worked for, as these fish when disturbed do not rise from the ground as is the habit with "round-fish," such as haddocks, gurnards, &c., but seek safety in the sand. When, therefore, as the trawl is slowly towed along, the ground-rope disturbs the flat-fish which, as has been mentioned, are lying more or less head to the stream—they lie exceedingly close, as is the habit with all animals which hide themselves—their first impulse is to dart forwards and again bury themselves; but the rope pressing closely on the ground in front of them prevents this, and the sand, being disturbed by the rope and the net immediately following it, is raised in a sort of cloud which hides the slight obstruction, so that the fish pass over the ground-rope unwittingly, and once within the net they gradually find their way to the small end of it. Should the fish, however, by any chance turn round and dart towards the mouth of the net, there would probably be a considerable distance to go before they would be clear, for the ground-rope sweeps the bottom from the foot of the two head-irons to a distance of 40 or 50 feet backwards to the bosom of the net, and this whole space is enclosed above by the back, and at the sides by the wings, so that there is no possible escape in any direction above ground but at the entrance under the beam. The trawl is moreover moving forwards all the time, and as flat-fish when disturbed only swim a short distance before they again try to hide themselves, it almost amounts to a certainty that, if they do not bury themselves deeply, they will sooner or later pass over the ground-rope into the net. In the case of such round-fish as keep close to the bottom, haddocks, for example, the result is very much the same, for when they are disturbed by the ground-rope they naturally rise and pass the slight obstacle without knowing it; if, on the contrary, they dart towards the mouth of the net, they may escape in that direction; but they also will probably have some distance to go before they can get clear, and the upper part or back of the net is an effectual barrier to their escape upwards.

The great resistance offered by the trawl to the forward movement of the vessel towing it—a resistance sufficient to reduce her speed from, say, eight knots to one knot—is very commonly ascribed to the supposed great pressure of the beam and net on the bottom, and to their not being towed lightly over the ground, but dragged through it. This is the foundation of most of the arguments used by the opponents of trawling— persons who never can have sought to ascertain the real action of the trawl, and who talk of the destruction of spawn, &c., by the heavy beam, apparently unaware that the beam is raised nearly three feet from the ground, and that were its position reversed not a fish could enter the net. It must not be forgotten that the weight of the whole gear is very considerably diminished by its immersion in the water, so much so that the loading of the ends of the beam by the head-irons and the occasional use of chains on the ground-rope are necessary to keep the trawl at the bottom and to counteract the tendency it has to rise owing to the resistance of the water to the beam and the upward pull of the trawl-warp leading to the vessel. The great drag is unquestionably due to the pressure of the water inside the net. Anyone who has been looking on when a sean or circle net has been at work must have observed the labour required to drag the net through the water, and that the fact of the foot of the net touching the bottom or not hardly affects the proceeding. The great difficulty is evidently due to the resistance of the water inside the net, as shown by the meshes being fully spread open. The same action must be familiar to many persons in the case of landing-nets, shrimp-nets, &c.; and it would be hardly needed to mention the subject if the enormous resistance there must necessarily be to a bag-net of the dimensions of an ordinary deep-sea trawl, when towed through the water at even moderate speed, were not so commonly overlooked. But a proof of the great resistance to the trawl being from the water and not from dragging over the ground may be easily given. In the early part of the year the Brixham and Plymouth trawlers catch a great number of hake in their nets, but they have to work in a particular manner to do so. Hake generally keep very near the bottom; they are active and restless fish, and would be likely to dart forwards and escape from the net if it were moving at only the usual rate of from half a knot to a knot and a half faster than the tide. To catch these fish it is necessary to keep the net almost clear of the ground, or barely skimming it, and to tow the trawl at the rate of two or two and a half knots. But to obtain this increased speed, and although favoured by the net hardly touching the ground, every sail that can be put on the vessel is often required; a half square-sail or sort of lower studding-sail is frequently rigged up to a yard-arm on the weather side, in addition to the ordinary sails, if the wind be sufficiently aft for it to stand, and the curious appearance is often presented of the vessel laying over to the breeze and apparently rushing through the water (Plate III.) when in reality, with all the help of a great spread of canvas and a favourable tide, she is not going more than five knots over the ground. The resistance here must evidently be caused by the water inside the net, and not by the friction of the net on the bottom. It is of course considerably increased by the more rapid movement of the trawl through the water; but the slowest rate of trawling practised must be fast enough to expand the net behind the ground-rope, or the fish would not enter it, although it is in the very slow trawling, when working for soles especially, there is the greatest pressure on the bottom from the ground-rope.

TOWING THE TRAWL.

The next thing to be noticed is the heaving up of the trawl. When the tide has done, or the limits of the fishing ground have been reached, the hands are turned up, the stopper of the trawl-warp is cast off, the slack of the warp goes overboard, and the vessel swings round with her head to the trawl, and very soon also head to wind. This is the case with the Brixham trawlers, which, as before mentioned, get in the warp over the bow by a large winch. In the North Sea smacks the warp comes in over the side, a large semi-circular opening in some vessels, or a square gangway in others, with a roller fitted in it, being made for that purpose opposite the capstan. We are now speaking, however, of the west-country vessels. The foresail and any light sails being got in, the boy is sent below to the rope-room just abaft the mast, and two hands go to the winch to heave in the warp. This last is a tedious process at the best of times, seldom occupying less than three-quarters of an hour, and in bad weather sometimes taking two or three hours, the vessel rolling and pitching heavily all the time. As the warp is brought on board by the winch it is coiled away below by the boy, so as to be ready when the net is to be again shot. As soon as the shackle joining the warp to the main bridles comes in, the end of the dandy bridle, which was temporarily made fast above the shackle when the net was lowered, is cast off, taken aft, and brought in over the stern to the dandy wink or small windlass; the men at the winch meanwhile go on heaving till the beam appears at the surface; it having been swung alongside, the after end is hoisted up astern by the dandy bridle and secured; a tackle is then hooked on to the fore end of the beam and hauled upon till the head-iron is got over the gunwale and made fast between two of the shrouds. Nothing now remains but to gather in the net; this is done by hand, and it is stowed away on the top of the beam and the gunwale till only the cod is left, the various fish which congregate in and crowd the pockets being shaken from their hiding-place as the net is hauled in, so that the whole catch is in the cod or end of the trawl when it comes on board. Eager looks are cast over the side to see what sort of a haul has been made, and it is a bad sign when nothing is said and the bag is got on board without a word. Should the haul be a tolerably good one, however—perhaps from half to three-quarters of a ton of fish—it is a different matter; a selvagee strop is passed round the upper part of the bag, the fore halyards are hooked on to it, and the winch is again put into requisition to hoist up the result of the day's work, two of the hands standing ready to receive the bag as it comes on board (Plate IV.), and to cast off the cod-line which closes the end of the net. This being done, the whole mass of fish falls on deck. The scene is a remarkable one, and such as can be met with nowhere else. The contents of the net are of course frequently of a most varied description, and they differ according to season and locality. The first to separate themselves from the quivering mass on deck are the fishermen's great and ever-present enemies, the dog-fish—"dogs," as they are usually called, lashing their tails and snapping their jaws, ferocious to the last, as they wriggle about the deck in everybody's way, till they are sooner or later quieted with a blow on the head and once more consigned to the deep. Turbot and brill expend their last energies in convulsive flappings; but the soles, plaice, and skate take things more quietly, whilst some of the various species of gurnard erect their

Trawling.—Hoisting in the Fish.

fins and display life tints of the most delicate beauty, but of which only faint traces will remain by the time they are laid out for sale on the fishmonger's board. Whiting form a considerable item at certain seasons in the catches of the Devonshire trawlers, as haddock do among the hauls made in the North Sea. A few cod of various sizes are frequently taken; and hakes, as already referred to, are specially fished for during the early part of the year. These last, in accordance with their restless habits, often find their way into the pockets, and the silvery sheen of their scales makes the net conspicuous at some distance as it is being hoisted on board.

Among the variety of animal life brought up by the trawl, especially on the Devonshire coast, where many parts of the bottom are shingly, but not too rough to work upon, crustacea are frequently abundant, and whilst the fishermen are busy picking out the prime fish and separating the different kinds for packing, a lobster will perhaps suddenly flap its way out from among the slippery crowd; edible and long-legged spider crabs stalk forth with solemn and ridiculous gravity, and hermit crabs in dozens rattle their shelly domiciles about the deck with their accustomed business-like air, seeking to anticipate the happy time when, the marketable portion of the catch having been set aside, they, with starfishes, zoophytes, cuttle spawn, and other marine productions coming under the heads of "sculsh" and "scruff," and of no value to the fishermen, are returned to their native element.

To the naturalist the contents of the trawl are generally of unbounded interest, not only on account of their varied character, but because of the natural appearance and living beauty of the animals. It is a tempting subject to dwell on, but it does not legitimately come under the head of sea fisheries.

Among the circumstances which affect the supply of fish brought to market the weather is by far the most important; in fact, as regards those kinds which are the particular produce of the trawl, it is, taking one year with another, the only thing which causes any material fluctuation; for there is no reason whatever for believing that the fishing grounds are becoming exhausted, or that many more smacks might not be as profitably employed in trawling as those which are now afloat. The hot summer months are those in which the least work is done, because then there is very often not enough wind to enable the vessels to tow the trawl. In light weather the quantity of extra warp allowed after the net has reached the ground is much less than with ordinary working winds, so as to give the trawl a help by taking off some of the dead weight of the beam and head-irons on the ground and lessening the friction over the bottom. Any strain on the warp then tends to lift the beam slightly, and as the rope is always at an angle with the ground the weight of the beam helps to bring it forward and towards the perpendicular. It is, however, a matter requiring nice adjustment, and after all is frequently of little practical advantage, for the resistance of the water within the trawl, as soon as the net begins to move, can only be overcome by strong pressure on the sails or by some other mechanical driving power. What the trawlers like is a fresh steady breeze—one that would enable them to do eight or nine knots off the wind when the trawl is not overboard; they can then afford to lose six or seven knots by the resistance of the net, and yet move fast enough to enable it to do its work properly.

Winter is the great trawling time, because then there is pretty sure to be plenty of wind, and if too much, sail can always be reduced; but, unfortunately, strong winds are generally accompanied by a good deal of sea; and when that is the case, although a great deal of extra warp be allowed in order to equalize the strain and prevent jerking, it is difficult to keep the trawl steadily moving over the ground. There is always a danger in such cases of breaking the warp, and almost a certainty of doing so and of losing the whole gear if the net should then get foul; besides this, the difficulty of heaving up the trawl is greatly increased, two or three hours are often spent in the operation, and the fish are liable to be killed and very much knocked about before they can be got on board. All these circumstances combine to induce the fishermen to wait for more moderate weather, it may be for only a day or two, or perhaps more, but in any case the supply of fish sent to market is lessened for the time; the weather which puts a stop to the work of one vessel having probably the same effect on most of those fishing in the same district. The Plymouth trawlers are especially subject to loss of time from bad weather in winter, as at that season south-westerly winds prevail at the mouth of the Channel, and there is commonly a good deal of sea setting in over their very limited fishing ground, only a few miles from the land. Although they can and do work when it blows very fresh, a succession of heavy gales almost puts a stop to trawling there, and the supply of fish landed at Plymouth fluctuates more than on any other part of the coast.

In the North Sea each smack when fishing with the fleet remains at sea for six weeks or two months at a time, and frequently at so long a distance from land that there is little hope for her if she cannot face the terrific gales which sometimes blow there. Good craft as they are, and with stout hearts on board, the weather sometimes overpowers them, and a winter rarely passes without bringing news of some smack being missing, with trouble and mourning for the survivors of those hardy fishermen who have perished with her. In the disastrous gale of the 26th of November, 1863, no less than seven trawlers belonging to Hull alone, and each with a crew of five hands, were totally lost, and nearly twenty others were afterwards towed into harbour disabled.

But if they have sometimes more wind there than they want, they are rarely compelled by a continuance of calms to remain very long idle. There is generally wind enough for them to work with, especially as soles or other kindred fish, abundant on those grounds, do not require any great speed in the vessel. The supply of fish from the North Sea, therefore, is in general tolerably steady, unless during the prevalence of unusually bad weather; and a large proportion of the trawl-fish regularly brought to market is now caught north of the Thames.

The depth of water in which the trawlers work when on the usual off-shore grounds is very rarely so much as 50 fathoms; and taking the various fishing grounds around the coast most of the trawling is done in between 20 and 30 fathoms. There are some exceptions, however, and notably among them are the famous Silver Pits in the North Sea, in a depth of 50 fathoms; but fishing is not carried on there constantly, as the productiveness of the locality is dependent on the coldness of the season, which drives fish of all kinds, and especially the soles, into the deep water.

We have often found a remarkable discrepancy in the soundings given by the fishermen for any particular locality and those marked on the Admiralty charts. For example, in the Great Silver Pit, the trawlers will tell you that they work in 50 fathoms, particularly about the middle and near its western end; yet there is nothing over 40 fathoms marked in the charts. Again, we have been told of heavy catches of fish being made in 50 fathoms near the Wolf Rock, on the Cornish coast; but there are no soundings of that depth marked within many miles of that locality. The use of charts is understood by many of the deep-sea fishermen, and they have told us over and over again that they often cannot make their soundings agree with those of the Admiralty. It might be supposed that the fishermen on these occasions were not on the right ground; but the position of the Silver Pit is very well known to them, and there are no chart soundings coming near 50 fathoms within a long distance of that particular locality. The difference between high and low water will not account for anything like 10 fathoms; yet we can hardly suppose the charts are wrong; and it is almost as difficult to believe that the fishermen, who are constantly using the lead, should be so far out.

The condition of the trawl-fish when brought up in the net depends very much on the state of the weather, the length of the haul—that is, the time during which the net has been at work—and the quantity and kinds of fish which have been caught. The weather affects the condition of the fish, because if there be much sea on the trawl does not work steadily over the ground, and the fish collected at the cod-end are jolted and jerked with every sudden strain on the trawl-warp; this continues whilst the slack of the warp is being hauled in;

and when once the net is clear of the ground the fish are often heaped together at the end of the bag, although not necessarily so, and this may tend to crush and kill some of them. This result, however, only follows to any extent when, in consequence of the bad weather, it requires two or three hours' work to get the trawl on board. The length of the haul of course affects the condition of the fish more or less, because the longer they are confined in the net whilst it is dragged over the ground, the more they are likely to suffer from the crowding and knocking about; and the quantity of fish tells in the same way. Round-fish at all times suffer more than flat-fish; but when fish of any kind are killed they become so much dead weight pressed against the net, and accordingly are especially liable to damage, having lost their elasticity and power of movement. To these causes of injury may be added the occasional admission of large stones to the net, but this is not a very frequent one, and when it occurs leads perhaps as often to the net being torn as to injury to the fish.

These difficulties in trawling, however, are to a great extent exceptional; and although much has been said at various times by the agitators against this method of fishing, for the purpose of showing that trawl-fish must necessarily be " mangled and unfit for food," it is nevertheless the fact, that practically all the turbot, brill, soles, and doreys which come into the market – fish which fetch the highest price, and of which hundreds of tons are consumed every year by the richer classes — are caught by the trawl; whilst thousands of tons of plaice and haddocks, with other kinds of so-called inferior fish, are procured by the same method, and are eagerly bought, not only by that large proportion of the population whose necessities oblige them to seek for nutritious food at the lowest possible price, but also by vast numbers of people who can afford to make an addition to their ordinary diet of beef and mutton. It will be evident that as the profitable working of the trawl depends on the fish caught by it being sent to market in good condition, there would be no ready sale for it were it not the rule that a very large proportion of the catch was alive when brought on board; for there is a great difference in the appearance of fish which have died after they are taken out of the water and those which have been washed about in the net for some time after they are killed.

In the many opportunities we have had of seeing the beam-trawl worked and of examining the fish as soon as they were out of the net, the proportion of dead fish has been utterly insignificant; and those which had suffered were usually among the small ones, some of which are sure to be caught on all fishing grounds. Gurnards, whiting, and haddock, when very small, seem especially liable to suffer, and are apparently killed at the end of the net by the pressure of the larger fish above them.

We have previously mentioned that trawl-fish are classified under the names of "prime" and "offal," or coarse fish; the former including turbot, brill, soles, and doreys; offal comprising plaice, haddocks, gurnards, skate, and such other kinds as are occasionally caught in the trawl. Red mullet must be excepted, however, for although not strictly coming under the head of "prime," they are what the Billingsgate salesmen look upon as "West End" fish. The proportion of prime to offal fish taken by the trawlers varies with the season, and also depends very much on the particular banks or grounds worked over.

The following return[1] of the actual produce of one of the Grimsby smacks during each of the five years 1860-4 was furnished by Mr. Henry Knott, of Grimsby, to the Royal Sea Fisheries Commissioners, and was published in the Appendix to their Report in 1866. It was represented as giving a fair idea of what had been done during the time by trawlers properly worked and with average success; and is valuable as affording some data for estimating the quantity of fish supplied to the markets by this method of fishing. It also shows how much the prices obtained by the fishermen fluctuated; although there is no reason to think the consumers derived very much benefit from the low prices often paid by the fishmongers.

Years	Weight of Fish									Amount Realized								
	Prime			Offal			Total			Prime			Offal			Total		
	tons	cwt	qrs	tons	cwt	qrs	tons	cwt	qrs	£	s	d	£	s	d	£	s	d
1860	18	19	2	66	4	3	85	4	1	320	7	9	114	0	6	434	8	3
1861	13	1	3	69	16	2	82	18	1	392	11	6	177	16	5	570	7	11
1862	12	19	1	52	14	2	65	13	3	360	4	8	105	13	1	465	17	9
1863	18	4	0	74	9	2	92	13	2	455	0	0	145	0	0	600	0	0
1864	22	18	2	94	7	3	117	6	1	443	6	0	189	7	6	632	13	6
	86	3	0	357	13	0	443	16	0	1971	9	11	731	17	6	2703	7	5

In the North Sea, at some distance from the land, enormous catches of plaice and haddocks are sometimes made, and the quantities of these fish which are still daily landed at Hull and Grimsby from grounds which have been regularly worked over for many years would appear incredible to most persons who had not attended the arrival of the trawlers, and gained some knowledge of the extent of the interests largely dependent on the continuous supply of these "offal fish."

---

[1] Referred to at page 15.

Haddocks were at one time almost worthless to the trawlers from the want of a market for the enormous number of these fish which were caught; and it was then no uncommon occurrence for the bulk of this part of the catch to be thrown overboard, the men having orders not to bring on shore more than were likely to be disposed of. The idea of drying and smoking them, as had long been done on the Scotch coast, was then carried out at Hull, and afterwards at Grimsby, and proved so successful that, to quote the words of one of the fish dealers, "not a fish's eye is now thrown away." The demand for fresh fish generally has, however, increased so much of late years, that a much smaller number of the trawled haddocks is now smoked than formerly, and many of the best fish are sent, packed in ice, to the fresh market, where they readily sell at good prices, although they may not have quite so bright an appearance as those obtained by the hook. The number of line haddocks sent to market is trifling, however, compared with those caught by the trawl; they are not taken on the ground where the trawlers work, and are said by them to be "hungry" fish, which are not in good condition, and will bite at anything; whilst those frequenting the trawling grounds are stated to be well-fed fish which will not readily take a bait. On this point we can offer no opinion. The prejudice existing in some quarters against trawled haddocks is no doubt principally due to their generally less inviting appearance, owing to their having been gutted as soon as caught; and because, from the large numbers taken at once, less care is bestowed on their packing than is desirable to make them look well on being landed. Practically, the great markets are supplied with haddocks by the trawlers in the North Sea.

On the south and south-west coasts, on the contrary, haddocks are met with in such small numbers that the Brixham and Plymouth trawlers do not specially look for them. Whiting take their place there. The catches on that part of the coast are usually more varied in their character than in the more distant parts of the North Sea, and the hake is a fish taken there in large numbers during part of the year.

Soles are generally distributed wherever there is clean sandy ground; but they are not found so much in very deep water, except during cold weather. The London market is principally supplied with this fish from the banks off the Norfolk coast and from the Channel; and a large proportion of the soles which are captured by any of the trawlers is sent to that market, whence they are distributed over the country. It is rarely that any number of soles is landed at Hull, and the Grimsby shops are often supplied from London.

Turbot are found more or less on all parts of the coast; the North Sea has long been famous for these fish, especially along the Dutch shore, where, during warm weather, they are caught in very shallow water. Large supplies of turbot were formerly sent by the Dutch fishermen to the London market long before our own trawlers had established themselves on our eastern coast, or had found out how much was to be done in the North Sea. There are many of these fish also caught in the Channel, wherever there is trawling ground, and no doubt they are numerous in many places where, on account either of the depth of water or the nature of the bottom, no trawl has ever been worked. We have heard of extraordinary catches of turbot having been made in the neighbourhood of the Wolf Rock, near the Land's End; but the depth of water there and the frequent heavy sea make it difficult to trawl successfully on that ground.

Plaice, another of the fishes caught in countless numbers by the North Sea trawlers, are also generally distributed around our coast, and some of them are usually obtained by the trawl wherever it is worked. They are in great demand among the poorer classes in London and the large manufacturing towns, and make an important contribution towards the supply of cheap and wholesome food. Formerly they were in particular request and fetched a high price from a class of consumers in London who now perhaps have little to do with them; the fish were known as "live plaice" from their being brought alive to the market, and the vessels employed in catching them were welled-smacks, such as are used for the North Sea cod fishery; but there is now such a large supply of fish of various kinds and in fine condition sent to London that "live-plaiceing," as it is called, has gone very much out of fashion; and the welled-smacks are used almost entirely for their original purpose of bringing in live cod. A description of these vessels will be given in our account of deep-sea line-fishing.

The deep-sea fishing grounds systematically trawled over are very small compared with the extent of sea bottom which, from its unsuitable character or the depth of water over it, has rarely or never been disturbed by a net; and no stronger argument can be needed to show that the supply of fish has not fallen off than the fact that no trawling ground which in past years was regularly fished and found generally productive, has yet been abandoned, or even worked on by fewer vessels than formerly. For many years there has been a general and gradual increase in the size and number of the smacks; and the addition of new and larger vessels at some of the stations during the last few years has far exceeded anything that could have been anticipated. This large increase in the number of trawlers has not been in consequence of any discovery of new fishing grounds, but is due to the greater demand for fish; and this appears likely to increase rather than to diminish. Trawl-fishing is a fairly profitable business when managed by practical men; and as the master and men are not paid fixed wages, except in the London vessels, but have their shares in the proceeds of the fishing, it is their interest to work only where they know they can find plenty of fish. This they do regularly on the old grounds; and no greater fluctuation in the supply of fish from them by each vessel has been observed recently than in former times.

In order to show how much may be done on any particular trawling ground, we may say a few words about the condition of the fishery at Brixham; and a knowledge of the facts may possibly reassure those who think the supply of sea fish is rapidly diminishing and the fishermen as rapidly being ruined. Brixham has long been famous as a fishing town; it is essentially a trawling station, and has been so beyond the memory of anyone now living there. We may safely say that trawling has been carried on from that town for at least a hundred years; and although the trawl-smacks were much smaller thirty or forty years ago than at the present time, the fishing has always been in the deep water a few miles from the land except in very bad weather, when some of the vessels would work inside the headland; and the smacks employed in it were intended to face any kind of weather. The ground on which the Brixham men habitually fish lies between the Start Point and a little to the northeast of Torbay, a distance altogether not exceeding 20 miles, and of variable width, but mostly from 3 to 8 miles off the land. This ground has always been more or less productive, and continues so at the present time. There were nearly a hundred smacks regularly fishing over this ground in 1872, a larger number than had ever worked there before; and we hear from several independent sources that the fishing trade at Brixham was never more prosperous than it has been of late.

The Plymouth trawlers also have their own ground, and rarely leave it; they like to keep within sight of the Eddystone; and work over an area about 21 miles long, and not exceeding 9 miles at its widest part, including some very productive ground not very far from the land. Bad weather often interferes with their working steadily in winter; but the smacks have gradually increased in size as at other places, and also in number up to a certain point, from which there has been only a slight variation during the last ten years. There were sixty-six smacks fishing from Plymouth in 1872 over the same ground as has been constantly worked for considerably more than fifty years.

Of other important fishing banks, the Inner and Outer Diamond Grounds, off Hastings, and the Varne and the Ridge in mid-channel, farther to the eastward, have long been famous for the better kinds of flat-fish; whilst from the North Foreland far into the North Sea, there is a great range containing numerous banks apparently inexhaustible in their supply of fish. Many of these fishing grounds lie off the coasts of Norfolk and Lincolnshire, and produce vast numbers of soles and other prime fish; among those most favoured by the fishermen are the Swarte Bank, Inner Well Bank, Inner Silver Pit, Sole Pit, Leman, Smith's Knoll, and the Dowsings; whilst farther north and more off the land, there are the Dogger, Outer Well Bank, Great Silver Pit, and Botany Gut. What the trawlers call the real Well Bank is south of the Great Silver Pit, and they consider that marked "Outer Well Bank" on the Admiralty charts as merely part of the Dogger. Botany Gut runs along the eastern side of the Well Bank nearly up to the Silver Pit, but does not actually join it. These are grounds systematically trawled over at some part or other throughout the year, according to season and weather; for it is found that, year after year, fish of various kinds congregate for a time in particular places, and then move off to other quarters. If the fishermen do not find them in one place, they look for them in another, and they have no fear of being very long without getting a supply. Haddocks, plaice, and turbot are the fish principally obtained from the Dogger and neighbouring banks, and soles in the colder weather.

The Great Silver Pit was first worked over during a very severe winter (about 1843). The Well Bank and Botany Gut had been explored and discovered to be very productive grounds; and between them and the Dogger, and bearing nearly true east from Flamborough Head, the Admiralty chart showed a bed of deeper soundings, ranging in some parts of it from 30 to 40 fathoms—the whole extending for about 60 miles east and west, and from 6 to 10 miles wide. This patch was marked the "Outer Silver Pit," and on trying it with the trawl, in the deeper parts at the western end and near the middle soles were found during that very cold season in almost incredible numbers; the nets were hauled up bristling with fish trying to escape through the meshes, and such catches were made as the most experienced fishermen had never before dreamed of. The discovery soon got wind, and a migration of trawlers from Ramsgate and Brixham took place; but although with the breaking up of the cold weather this extraordinary congregation of soles became dispersed, more attention was henceforth directed to the North Sea fishing generally; and in subsequent years the Silver Pit has again been found very productive whenever the winter has been very severe, or, as the trawlers call it, in " Pit seasons."

At the time of the discovery of this ground the number of North Sea trawlers was very small; they were then only of about half the size of the majority of the smacks at the present day; and not enough was known of the fishing grounds to tempt the fishermen far from the land in vessels of such little power, either to face the weather they would be likely to encounter, or to seek for fish at a long distance from the market. The first objection has been fairly met by the large increase in the size of the smacks; and the second has been practically removed by the great extension of railways along the coast, the employment of large fast-sailing cutters or steamers as " carriers" to collect and bring in the fish from the smacks, and especially by the introduction of ice for preserving the fish. As the advantages of the North Sea fishery became better known, Hull rapidly assumed importance as a trawling station; and in subsequent years Yarmouth, Grimsby, and a few other places along that coast became at first the resort, and then the head-quarters of hundreds of smacks.

Cod fishing by hook and line had long been carried on in the North Sea, as it is at present; but the vessels employed in that fishery were of a larger class than the older trawlers, and they had wells for the purpose of keeping their fish alive, involving an additional expense in their construction, which, although justified by the high prices the live cod obtained in the market, would not be generally met by a corresponding advantage in the case of trawled fish.

There cannot be less than 1000 sea-going trawlers of various sizes now systematically working in the North Sea, besides nearly 300 fishing in and near the English Channel; and more than 100 on the Lancashire and Welsh coasts.

II.—DRIFT-NET FISHING.

Long practice of — How the fish are caught — Proper time for fishing — Description of drift-nets, materials, size — Yarmouth luggers, how fitted up — Herring fishing — Shooting the net — "Driving" — Interference by trawlers — Regulations to prevent it — Hauling the nets — Mackerel fishing — Pilchard fishing — Looking for herrings — "Appearances" — Phosphorescent water objectionable — Effect of sounds on fish — Regular appearance of the herring — Different seasons at different places — Notice of the seasons at various localities — England, Scotland, Ireland — The herring a northern fish, but not a migrant from the Arctic Sea — "Whitebait" — Consideration of the question of its specific distinctness — Seasons for mackerel drift-fishing at various localities — Season for pilchard drift-fishing — Spawning of the pilchard — Season for sprats — Spawning time — Drift-fishing for sprats exceptional.

ALTHOUGH nothing is known of the origin or introduction into Britain of the method of fishing by drift-nets, there is reason to think it has been practised by our fishermen for many hundred years; and it is certainly no modern invention, although probably not dating so far back as the sean or the casting net. The ground on which now stands the thriving town of Great Yarmouth is said to have been a place of resort for fishermen during the herring season as early as the sixth century, and there is no reason for believing that the long-standing Yarmouth fishery was ever carried on by any other method than that of drift-nets, as at the present time. We may conclude therefore that, wherever the system originated, it has long been in use, and that drift-nets have been more or less worked ever since that remote and uncertain period when herrings were first fished for in the open sea. They are the only nets by which fish like the herring, pilchard, and mackerel, which come much to the surface, and at the same time are in deep water far from the land, can be caught in large numbers; for although these fish are of course taken in abundance by seans when they come close enough inshore, yet, for many weeks previously, drift-fishing is the only method by which the large supplies are obtained for the market.

The term "drift-net" is derived from the manner in which the nets are worked; they are neither fixed, towed, nor hauled within any precise limits of water; but are cast out or "shot" at any distance from the land where there are signs of fish, and are allowed to drift in any direction the tide may happen to take them, until it is thought desirable to haul them in. When at work they are extended in a long single line, their upper edge being supported at or near the surface by means of floats, the nets hanging perpendicularly in the water, and forming, as it were, a perforated wall or barrier many hundred yards long and several yards in depth. The shoals of fish, in their endeavours to pass through this barrier, force their heads into the meshes, the size of the mesh used depending on whether herrings, pilchards, or mackerel are expected to be caught, and being such as to allow the head and gill-covers to enter, but not to permit the thicker body of the fish to go through. When the fish has forced its way through the net beyond the gill-covers it may generally be considered as effectually meshed; there is, indeed, little chance of its escape, for the mesh is only large enough for a fish of average size to push its way so far when the gill-covers are laid close; but it is necessary for them to open again that the fish may breathe; that the water which brings air to the gills may pass out through the gill-openings; and as this is taking place, and the fish is struggling to get clear from the net, the mesh slips forward and catches in the gill-openings, from which it cannot easily be cleared without more or less injury to the fish. In drift-net fishing, then, the nets act as barriers to intercept the moving shoals, and the fish become meshed in their attempts to pass through.

This method of fishing is, with very rare exceptions, carried on only at night;[1] and it is found that just after sunset and before sunrise, when the change from light to darkness, or the reverse, is taking place, the fish are especially likely to "strike" the net; they appear to be then particularly on the move, the change of light affecting them in some manner which is but little understood. That the fish are really impelled to "move," as it is called—that is, to become more active or to rise to the surface, when there is a change of light—appears tolerably certain, at all events, in the case of the herring; it often happening, as is well known to the fishermen, that when the nets have sometimes been in the water during many hours of darkness, without signs of fish, there has been a heavy strike just as the moon has risen; although the continued brightness of a moonlight night is generally considered unfavourable for fishing, especially if the water be tolerably clear. Indeed, one of the conditions of successful drift-fishing is that the nets should not be easily discernible; and on the rare occasions when it is attempted by daylight, discoloured water is essential to success. Good hauls have sometimes been made under such circumstances both at Yarmouth and on the coast of Scotland.

[1] In Waterford Harbour we have seen drift-nets worked during the day for catching salmon; but for the ordinary purposes of open-sea fishing they are seldom used except at night.

DRIFT-NETS.

For a description of drift-nets, and the mode of working them on a large scale, we cannot do better than give some account of the method by which the Yarmouth herring fishery has long been carried on. Drift-fishing, or "driving," as it is generally called, is there worked with fine decked boats, larger in every way than on other parts of the coast, and the fishermen consequently can venture farther to sea and run the chance of worse weather than most of the smaller fishing boats are capable of with a due regard to security.

The nets used for herring driving are made either of cotton or hemp—"twine," as the latter is called; some fishermen preferring the one material, some the other, and it is not unusual for the two kinds to be placed alternately in the same train of nets. Cotton nets are finer in the line and more flexible than those of twine, and they are generally believed to be more effective from these qualities. Machinery of a very beautiful and ingenious character is employed in making them, and large supplies are turned out from the factories at Bridport and many other places. Cotton nets when new are first saturated with linseed oil, and then boiled for two or three days in bark liquor, a preparation now consisting principally of catechu, which for the preservation of nets has practically superseded the oak-bark formerly used. In some cases they are dressed with coal-tar instead of being barked. These nets come from the factory in "pieces" 60 yards long and 9 or 10 yards deep, the depth of the net containing two hundred meshes; and it is the custom of the fishermen, when speaking of the size of a net, to say it is so many yards long and so many meshes deep, as the case may be. Each piece is divided into two nets 30 yards long. When a net is prepared for use it is mounted or fastened to a small line only 18 or 20 yards long, that length of line being appropriated to the 30 yards of net, so that the "lint" or netting is set slack, and gives way a little when the fish strike it, and from its flexibility holds the fish better than would be the case if the net were fully stretched. The ends of the net are called the "heads," the upper edge of the length the "back," and the lower one the "foot," or sometimes the "sole." The heads are roped as well as the back, but the foot is usually left free, so that the net is less likely to hitch in anything at the bottom when used in rather shoal water or near the ground. The back of the net is fastened at intervals of a few inches by very short lines termed "norsals" or "nossles" to the cork-rope, a small double rope enclosing at various distances pieces of cork as floats to keep that part of the net uppermost. The number of such nets used by each vessel depends very much on her size, and ranges from 80 to 130. They are fastened together end to end, and, thus united, form what is called a "train, fleet, or drift of nets," often extending to a length of more than a mile and a quarter. The mesh is about an inch and a quarter square, equivalent to thirty or thirty-two meshes to the yard,[1]

---

[1] The size of the mesh, or the number of meshes to a yard, which is the fairest way of judging of the average dimensions, is easily ascertained by a simple method of counting in use among fishermen: the ends of four or five rows of meshes are brought together in the hand and the net stretched tight; the result is transverse parallel rows of knots, the spaces between the rows being the length of one of the four sides of the square or diamond, and which is taken as the size of the mesh; thus, an inch mesh is one whose four sides are each an inch long, and not, as was sometimes supposed, a mesh an inch long between opposite knots when it is pulled straight. Counting the rows of knots therefore within a certain fixed length gives the average size of the meshes. When the inch mesh, or thirty-six to a yard, was the minimum size allowed

when the net is new; but after long use and frequent barking or tarring it becomes contracted to an inch or less.

Twine nets are of stouter material and more lasting than those made of cotton, but they are much stiffer and heavier to work. They are usually made in several narrow pieces called "deepings," which are laced together, one below the other, there being three or four deepings in the depth of a net, according to the fancy of the fishermen. These nets are generally barked once or twice in the season, but are never tarred. There is still some diversity of opinion about the comparative durability of the two kinds of material; but there is no question that the finer the net is, if it has sufficient strength for its purpose, the less likely the fish are to be alarmed by its appearance, and cotton is every day coming in more use on that account.

Each drift-boat is supplied with two sets of nets; one having a much larger number of floats on the cork-rope than the other, so as to keep it quite at the surface when there is evidence of the fish being generally near the top of the water. The other net, and the one most frequently used, has only a sufficient number of corks to keep the back of the net uppermost, and is supported at the proper depth by means of ropes fastened to small kegs or buoys, technically known as "bowls."

It might be supposed that when it was desirable to keep the nets at the surface it would be only necessary to shorten the buoy-ropes; but that has proved not to

by law for herring nets, there was frequent occasion to measure them, as the size of the mesh was constantly diminishing by the contraction of the twine; but since the passing of the Sea Fisheries Act, 1868, removing all restrictions from fishing gear, the fishermen are left to their own devices, and have only to take care that their nets are suitable for the kind of fish they desire to catch.

be sufficient, as unless the whole back of the nets be well corked, the lengths between the buoys are liable to sink in the centre by their own weight if the strain at the end of the fleet of nets is not great enough to keep them well extended, and so only those parts remain at the surface which are directly supported by the bowls. This is not of so much consequence when the fish are swimming at some depth, as the shoals are then more dispersed, and it is difficult to say how deep they may be; but when they are swimming high and playing at the top it will not do to give them a chance of passing over any part of the nets.

The bowls are distributed at regular distances along the whole train of nets, each net having one of these buoys to support it; and certain divisions of the train are distinguished by bowls of different colours. The first net is marked by a small white bowl called the "puppy," and at the end of four nets is a dan or buoy with a staff or pole bearing a small flag. The rest of the nets are marked in four divisions; at the first quarter from the pole is a bowl painted one quarter red and three quarters white; the next is half red and half white, and at the commencement of the last division the bowl is three quarters red and one quarter white. The intermediate bowls are all black. The whole fleet or train of nets is made fast to the vessel by a warp of three and a half or four inch rope to which all the nets are fastened by small ropes called "seizings," two to each, and long enough to allow the warp to hang down at their foot. The object of having this warp is to facilitate the hauling in of the nets, to take off the direct strain from them when this is being done, and to prevent any of them being lost in case of their being cut by accident. Drift-nets being used almost entirely at night, and often extending for a long distance across the course of vessels passing up and down the coast, are sometimes liable to be damaged by vessels running over or through them; and if by chance the nets are cut, the warp which hangs below and is fastened to every one, holds the train together and prevents any serious mischief.

All the vessels used in the Yarmouth herring fishery are decked; the largest of them, about 36 tons N.M., being 52 feet on the keel, with 17 feet beam, and 7 feet depth of hold (Frontispiece). They are lugger rigged, with two masts only, and carry a jib when necessary, a large dipping fore-lugsail with the tack hooking on to an iron bumkin outside the stem, and a working mizen and topsail. The mizenmast is stepped a little on the port side to allow room for steering, as there would not be sufficient play for the tiller if it were quite amidship, unless placed farther forward. The larger boats are generally built with a counter and square stern, which give more room on deck; but many of the smaller boats have an upright round stern, and this is advantageous when running before a sea, and often prevents disaster from broaching-to. The mizenmast is always kept standing; but to enable the boat to ride easier when drifting, the foremast is made to lower backwards on the same principle as is adopted in barges and vessels which have to pass under bridges in inland navigation. It may be seen any day in operation on the Thames. An open space is left in the deck immediately behind the mast-hole, and the mast falls back into this as it is lowered by means of a burton tackle from the mast-head to the stem of the vessel; the heel of the mast being the pivot on which it moves. In the centre of the vessel is fixed a broad upright piece of timber, about

12 feet high, fitting into a case of hard wood at the deck; this upright is called the "mitch-board" (probably a corruption of "midship-board," from its position), and the top of it forms a crutch for the mast to rest upon when lowered. By this arrangement the advantage of a lowered mast is obtained without interfering with the deck room required when the nets are being hauled in. The arm of the crutch on the port side was made longer than the other, and before 1868 was used as a standard on which a lantern was fixed when the vessel was engaged in fishing. The Yarmouth boats now carry the two regulation "driving" lights on the mizen-stay.

On the quarters of the vessel the oars or sweeps are secured in iron frames, called "lumber-irons," out of the way, till they happen to be wanted.

The internal fittings are in accordance with the requirements of the work to be done, and the hold is divided into compartments for the fish, nets, warp, &c. Immediately in front of the mitch-board on deck is the hatchway leading to the net-room, and along the sides or "wings" of this compartment the fish are stowed away as they are sent below. Abaft the mitch-board is the rope-room, in the wings of which the salt is kept, 5 or 6 tons of this necessary material being the quantity usually carried; and between the rope-room and the mizenmast stands the capstan, of a conical shape, and worked by bars in the ordinary manner; by means of this the warp and nets are hauled in.

The number of men in the larger vessels ranges from nine to eleven, or in a few cases to twelve; this being determined by the size of the boat and the proportionate length and weight of the nets. Time is valuable in drift-fishing; for if the fish are abundant the nets are not allowed to remain very long in the water, but are hauled in and shot again, and these processes are very laborious. The fish also are all the better for reaching the market early, so that everything is in favour of doing the work smartly. The principal part of the labour in these drift-boats is not of a kind requiring much experience in the men either as fishermen or sailors; more than half the number of hands taken are therefore composed of shore-going men at other times than during the regular fishery season. Strong arms are the principal things wanted for heaving in the nets, and the "capstan-men" are made up from countrymen and idlers, who soon get their sea-legs, and learn to do such work as is required from them, whilst the management of the vessel, the selection of the fishing ground, and other professional duties are all done by or under the direction of the master, mate, and two or three other experienced fishermen.

We now come to the operation of "shooting the nets"; and we may here mention that the expression "shooting" is in use on all parts of the coast for throwing or paying out longlines and nets of every description; it does not seem to be applied to handlines; but the trawlers, the seaners, the drift fishermen, and the longliners, all speak of "shooting their gear" or "making a shot" when beginning to fish after their respective methods.

Shooting the nets as done from the Yarmouth luggers —the operation is practically the same in all cases, differing only in some of its details—is thus managed:— The time universally fixed upon for commencing work is just about sunset, and when the fishermen have reason to think they have arrived in the proper place for herrings, or they observe the "appearance of fish"—of

Pl. V.

Yarmouth Lugger—Drift Fishing.

which we shall speak subsequently—the vessel is put before the wind, and shooting the nets over the quarter of the vessel is begun. The nets are all stowed in regular order in the net-room, and to prevent any danger of their hitching whilst passing over the deck, a "bank-board" is placed between the hatchway and the top of the bulwark, over which they are hauled, a roller at the edge of the hatchway taking off the strain there would otherwise be in getting up the nets from below. Two hands shoot the nets, one taking charge of the corks and bowls, and the other looking after the netting or "lint"; one of the capstan-men looks out for the seizings as the nets come on deck, and runs aft with them to the mate near the taffrail, who makes them fast to the warp. This goes on till the long train of nets with the corresponding length of warp are all overboard; 15 or 20 fathoms more warp, as a "swing rope," are then paid out, and the vessel is brought round head to wind, the sails are taken in, the mast lowered till it rests on the mitch-board, a small mizen, called the "drift-mizen," is set to keep the vessel head to wind, and the regulation lights are put up to show that the vessel is fishing (Plate V.); the watch is then set, and the nets and vessel drift with the tide.

It is very rarely that there is an absolute calm; and as the faintest breath of air is felt by the vessel, she of course drifts away under its influence faster than the nets, which being under water do not feel it; a strain is consequently put upon the nets and keeps them extended, whilst both nets and vessel are carried along bodily by the tide. In bad weather more swing rope is allowed that the vessel may not have too great a drag on the nets, and she sometimes rides with as much as 100 fathoms of warp out.

In Plate V., representing one of the Yarmouth luggers when "driving" or drifting, the single lantern she has fixed on the top of the mitch-board shows the manner in which the light was carried by these vessels before the passing of the Sea Fisheries Act of 1868. According to the Act passed in 1843 for carrying into effect the Fishery Convention concluded in 1839 between Great Britain and France, it was ordered that all boats engaged in drift-fishing should hoist on one of their masts two lights, one over the other, and three feet apart; but very few of its provisions were ever enforced, and drift-boats practically carried just what lights they pleased, and placed them where they liked. The complaints laid before the Royal Sea Fisheries Commissioners in 1863–4 of the damage occasionally done by trawlers when working where drift-fishing was going on led to the discovery of the fact that drift fishermen very rarely carried the two lights ordered by the Convention Act for the purpose of showing that they had their nets in the water. This would of course dispose of any legal claim for damages against the trawlers; as, however great their carelessness might have been in coming among the drift-boats, their answer to the charge was reasonable enough, that they had no means of distinguishing a drift-fishing vessel from any other at a moderate distance. The complaint and reply to it were sometimes made in amusing ignorance by both sets of fishermen of there being any regulations requiring the drift-boats to carry two lights, or forbidding the trawlers to come within three miles of any drift-boat engaged in fishing. The trawlers in fact brought a counter charge that the drift-nets were on some occasions shot across their course where they were towing the trawl, and that they could not avoid the risk of cutting through the nets without slipping their trawlwarp and probably losing their gear altogether. The interests of the two sets of fishermen unfortunately clash, as often happens in other cases, but neither of them would willingly get their nets fouled and lose their chance of fishing if it were easy to avoid doing so. The above regulations are also inserted in the recent Sea Fisheries Act, 1868, and are more strictly enforced than formerly; and although it may appear somewhat hard on the trawlers to oblige them to keep at least three miles from any drift-fishing, it is perhaps not altogether unreasonable, seeing that the great herring harvest only lasts for a comparatively short time, and the produce of it is very valuable. The trawlers in the North Sea have a wide range of ground to work over; but they allege, with some justice, that as the herrings shift about, the hundreds of drift-boats are constantly changing their ground, and it is difficult to say where they are not likely to be met with, particularly in the early part of the season, when they fish at a long distance from land. In the western part of the Channel cases of great hardship might easily occur, for the trawling grounds are very limited in extent, and it would be no very difficult matter under this regulation for the drift-boats to put a stop altogether to trawling at night during the drift season.

Whilst the drift-nets are in the water the warp is occasionally hauled in till the first net is reached; this is called the " look on " net, and by examining it some idea may generally be formed of whether many herrings are about, or the dogfish are numerous. The latter are at times very mischievous, and do a great deal of damage to both the fish and the nets if they are left long in the water.

When it is thought desirable to haul in the whole fleet of nets the warp is led through a snatch-block fixed near the mast-hole, to the capstan, passing under a roller just in front of it, and which keeps the warp low down when it makes its first turn, the conical shape of the capstan preventing any overlapping of the turns of the warp afterwards, and ensuring its free delivery over the roller into the rope-room, where a boy coils it down so as to be ready for running when it is again wanted. One hand, who from his particular duty is called "cast off seizings," disconnects the nets from the warp as it comes on board; the mate and another man are stationed at the nets, one of them at the corks, the other at the lint, and get them in; and two more, of whom the master is generally one, pass them over the "scudding pole," which is fixed fore and aft between the mitch-board and the mast. "Scudding the fish," as it is termed, enables them to be easily shaken out of the net, whence they fall on the deck and then through temporary openings into the well or hold. The nets having been cleared of fish are then sent down to the net-room, where they are taken charge of by the net-stower. Everything is thus done in a systematic manner, and the nets and warp are all clear for making a second shot as soon as the first haul has been completed. As soon as the fish are all out of the nets they are sprinkled with salt ("ronsed" or "roosed") and stowed away in their proper compartments, the "wings" of the hold. If, however, the haul of fish be a heavy one, only part of the nets are got on board at first, and the fish from them salted and stowed away; then the remaining nets are got in and the work completed.

When the night's fishing is over, the mast is got into place again, sail made, and the vessel either returns to port or, if fish are scarce, shifts to a fresh berth for the next night's work.

If for any reason the nets are not used for two or three days, they are taken up and wetted to prevent their heating, which would soon rot and destroy them.

Drift-nets for mackerel are worked on precisely the same principle; but as these fish generally keep near the top of the water, the nets are well corked so as to make them float quite at the surface; and there is no occasion for such a depth of netting as is used for herrings. A fleet of mackerel nets as used by the Yarmouth boats is, however, of very great length, and is made up of eleven or twelve score of nets, extending to as much as $2\frac{1}{2}$ miles, or double that of a herring fleet. The meshes are about twenty-two or twenty-three to the yard, and the nets have hitherto been generally made of twine; but if there were a prospect of improvement in the Yarmouth mackerel fishery the new nets would probably be made of cotton. The mackerel "voyages," however, have been so unprofitable during the last few years that there is little inducement to invest very largely in new gear for that fishery.

Pilchard drift-nets, as used on the coast of Cornwall, are about the size of those for herrings, but with a smaller mesh, one not exceeding thirty-six to the yard. Shrunk herring-nets are frequently employed for catching pilchards when the meshes have become too small for their original purpose.

The number of nets carried by drift-boats of the various classes in use on different parts of the coast depends of course mainly on the size of the boat, but the weather to some extent affects the question of how many of those carried should be used on any particular occasion. If a fleet of nets were shot in the usual manner, as nearly as possible in a straight line, and left to itself, the tide would soon throw it into irregular curves and folds, leading to entanglement and waste of net surface; and one good purpose served by the vessel or boat in holding on, or swinging to the end of the train is, that she prevents this by getting a strain on the whole warp, and keeping the nets extended very nearly in a straight line. If there happened to be much of a breeze and the nets were few, the vessel would have too much power and would drag them after her; and any decided movement of the nets in the direction of their length would be likely to alarm the fish and prevent their striking. On the other hand, when the nights are very calm it is difficult to get strain enough on a long fleet; and under such circumstances we have seen the nets belonging to different boats overlapping and confounded together. Wind enough to ruffle the surface is always desirable for drift-fishing, as it not only enables the boat to keep the nets well extended, but by darkening the water it prevents the nets being readily seen by the fish.

The circumstances which guide the drift fishermen in their selection of any particular spot for fishing are often of a very uncertain character, and frequently there is nothing more to influence them than their knowledge that the fish were in some particular neighbourhood or at a certain distance from the land at a corresponding period in former seasons. At the commencement of the fishing season they can only be guided by such considerations; but when the fish are becoming more abundant and occasionally showing themselves at the surface, what is called the "appearance of fish," that is, large collections of sea birds and the presence of whales and the smaller cetacea, is a tolerably sure indication of there being plenty of fish in the neighbourhood. We cannot agree with Mr. Mitchell when he remarks, that the fishermen "trust too much to the appearance of waterfowl, the larger fishes (cetacea?), &c.; and although there may be great abundance of herrings in one place, they may be misled by these appearances, and go to another place, when the sole circumstance of a few sickly herrings swimming near the surface takes them from the proper fishing ground."[1] The fact of herrings swimming near the surface is surely no sign of their being sickly, if indeed such a term can be commonly applied to shoals, however small, of these fish, unless after being possibly exhausted by spawning, towards the end of the season. Good herrings often come to the surface, as is well known to all fishermen, and they do so at any time in the season, depending probably more on conditions of weather than anything else. Gannets and other sea birds would be considerably at fault if their instincts led them day after day and week after week to trust to the chance of getting only a few sickly fish; and the presence of porpoises and the larger cetacea is certainly a sign of there being an attraction in the shape of plenty of food. The shoals of fish may be large or small, but it is contrary to very long experience that such "appearances" are not well deserving of attention. Herrings do not remain long in one place, and it is the object of the fisherman to keep as much as possible with the general body of fish gradually working towards the shore. The boats may make a good fishing one night, and in the absence during the following day of any particular indications of fish they may remain about the same place for the next night; but they are not likely to make a mistake if they follow

[1] *History of the Herring*, pp. 82, 83 (1864).

any appearance they may have observed in the day at a few miles distance, although it may be quite possible that there are plenty of fish close by, but out of sight. There must necessarily be a great deal of uncertainty in a fishery of this description, for there is very little known of the causes which influence the fish in their daily movements, although it is probable that the greater or less abundance of food is an important one.

The phosphorescent light produced at times by myriads of minute medusæ and other marine animals when disturbed, especially in fine calm weather, is sometimes made use of by fishermen in their search for herrings, and often leads to the discovery of fish when other indications are wanting. The fishermen call it by the names of "brimming," "waterburn," or "marfire";[1] the last term we have found especially in use on the coast of Northumberland. When the water is in this condition the slightest agitation, as is well known, produces sparks and flashes of light; and the presence of fish is often indicated by the streaks of light which are caused by their suddenly darting through the water, and even when stationary, by the luminous patches which then result, we are inclined to believe, from the constant movements of their fins. We have seen the fishermen take advantage of this when looking for a desirable place for shooting their nets: a man leaning over the bow of the boat and occasionally rapping with a piece of wood against the planks close to the water. Now and then a fish betrayed itself by the line of light it produced as it darted away, and when these indications became more numerous it was decided to shoot the nets. This luminous condition of the water, however,

---

[1] Mar-fire = sea-fire; the prefix apparently one of the numerous derivations from *mare*, the sea.

is generally very unfavourable for fishing, although we have seen moderate hauls made under such circumstances. The water is then usually too clear and the nets are too distinct for the fish to strike freely; and beautiful as is the appearance of the illuminated nets as they are drawn through the water, the fishermen generally have good reason to expect the result of their night's labour under such conditions will not be very large.

The effect produced on the fish by the noise caused by rapping on the boat in the instance we have just mentioned may appear to have some bearing on the question of whether fish at some little distance below the surface are likely to be disturbed by general noises above it; but it really has little to do with it. We have good authority for saying that, in such a case as this, the vibration would be transmitted directly through the boat to the water, and thence to the fish; for it is produced by something in immediate contact with the water, and on a substance whose power of conducting sound is considerable. A general opinion prevails, however, among fishermen that sounds produced even on the land will reach fish in some depth of water; and complaints have sometimes been made of fish having been frightened away from their feeding by the noise of artillery practice on the adjoining shore half a mile, or even very much more, distant. But fishermen are apt to forget that the fish when below the surface of the water are not under the same conditions for hearing such sounds as they themselves are when above it; and they may well be excused if they are ignorant of the fact that the sound from gun-firing, which strikes so loudly on their own ears, is to a great extent reflected from the surface of the water, and what passes through it is lessened in proportion. It is unlikely, therefore, that the slight noise produced by striking on the bow of the herring boat would have been audible at the depth of one or two fathoms, after simply passing through the air to the water; but the effect of the rapping was evident, and is clearly explicable on the hypothesis of the direct transmission of the sound through the boat.

There appears to be very little doubt, however, that fish at or near the surface may be alarmed, or, in the case of some pond fish, even attracted, by sounds more or less distant and above it. Mr Couch,[1] in his account of the pilchard, says:—The fish are alarmed at noise; and the firing of a heavy cannon at a distance of 20 miles has been known to cause the fish to sink;" but we believe that in many instances the movement is induced more by what is seen than what is heard by the fish. The disturbing effect of heavy firing on shore upon fish in a depth of 10 or 15 fathoms, and at a distance of half a mile or a mile at sea, is a matter on which good evidence is required; and the testimony of fishermen, who generally clamour against everything they fancy in some way interferes with their interests, is not the most trustworthy on this subject.

The seasons for drift-fishing depend on the kind of fish which is to be sought for, whether herrings, pilchards, mackerel, or sprats; for although the last-mentioned fish is principally caught in the stow-net and the sean, it is also taken by drift-nets on certain parts of the coast.

There is considerable diversity in the times at which the same kind of fish is found on various parts of our coasts; and this difference in the seasons leads to much larger captures in the course of the year than would

---

[1] *History of British Fishes*, vol. iv., p. 89 (1865).

otherwise be the case, for the boats from several districts are enabled to unite in working successively on different stations, instead of being confined to their own. This is especially the case with regard to the herring and mackerel fisheries. The old theory of the migration of the herring from the Arctic Ocean is now out of date; and such evidence as has been obtained of the habits of this fish leads to the belief that the only definite changes of locality it makes are from deep water more or less distant from the land to shoaler water near the shore, or the reverse. The object of these movements has yet to be explained. Where there is deep water not very far from the land, herrings are likely to be found more or less at all times of the year, as seems to be particularly the case at the Outer Hebrides. There are certain months, however, in which they regularly make their appearance, and are successfully fished for on a great part of the coast of the British Islands. The fishery season, although not at the same period in all parts, is tolerably regular for each district; and this, taken in conjunction with the fact that certain districts are commonly visited by fish having particular characters of size or appearance, sufficient to enable the salesmen or curers to speak with some confidence as to where they were caught, confirms the growing opinion that herrings do not move very far from their native waters.

Enough is known of their movements to justify the belief in two very distinct arrivals of these fish on many parts of our coast, producing the summer or autumn and the winter fisheries. In some districts the winter herrings are not observed; in others they are seen but not fished for, as the bad weather at that time often interferes materially with systematic work, or other and perhaps more profitable fisheries may be engaging the attention of the fishermen. But the subject is receiving more consideration than it did a few years ago, and a winter herring fishery is now regularly carried on from Wick, the largest station on the east coast of Scotland, as well as at the entrance to the Firth of Forth, and on the west coast.

The great herring harvest is everywhere gathered in during the second half of the year, and it may be useful to give a short notice of the seasons at which the fishery is worked on different parts of the coast. The months to be mentioned are those in which the herrings are looked for; but the catches are generally small at first, and sometimes the shoals remain a long time at a considerable distance from the land.

The herring fishery is carried on at the Shetlands and Orkneys from July to September, but it is not of great importance at the former group of islands. The tides run with great strength there, and make drift-fishing hazardous and uncertain. It is continued during the same months with more or less success along the eastern coasts of Scotland and England nearly down to the Humber, but about Flamborough Head the fish are later than farther north; and the home fishery at Yarmouth and Lowestoft is from September to the end of November. In the Channel the general fishery is still later, although small fat herrings are often taken by the Hastings boats during the mackerel season in June; at Ramsgate it is during October and November, but in the far west it lasts till the end of the year, or even to January or the beginning of February, running into the period when the regular winter fishery, as distinct from the autumn one, takes place on both coasts of Scotland.

It might be supposed that as the herrings appear on

our extreme northern coasts at the beginning of the general fishing season, and are gradually later as we proceed south, there was some truth in the old theory of migration, and that the fish caught in the Channel in December are the remains of the shoals which were on the coast of Scotland in August; but the condition of the fish at the different places is opposed to such an idea. In the north the herrings are "full" at the end of August and in September; then they spawn and disappear. Those caught in the neighbourhood of Yarmouth are not in the best condition—nearly ready to spawn—till October and November. They cannot, therefore, belong to the great shoals which were spawning two months earlier in the north. Again, at the eastern end of the Channel the fish are full in November; but about Penzance, and in the west generally, they do not spawn till December, or even a month later. These differences appear to point to the shoals being distinct and somewhat local, and are quite inconsistent with any general theory of migration from the Arctic Sea.

At the Outer Hebrides and on the west coast of Scotland the herring fishery begins in some places as early as April, and goes on continuously till nearly the end of September, when the herrings spawn; and a separate winter fishery takes place in January and February. The fishermen say the herrings are always on the west coast, but of course are out of condition at certain times. The spawning seasons appear to be in September and February or March.

The great fishery in the Firth of Clyde, Lochfyne, and the Kyles of Bute, is from June to September; but here again the herrings never seem to be entirely absent, and some may be caught in parts of Lochfyne throughout the year. There is no apparent reason why the herrings taken there should be of better flavour than those caught elsewhere, but there is a general idea that the west coast fish are more delicate than those on the other side. As the fishery on the west begins very early, the explanation may be that there is a larger proportion of fat fish or maties than of those which are approaching spawning condition.

The Isle of Man fishery begins in June on the western side of the island, and finishes in October on the east side, where the fish most probably deposit their spawn.

On the north of Ireland the herrings are found from July to September, becoming rather later on the east coast; but it is difficult to fix on any very precise periods, as the local fishing is not carried on very systematically, and the principal catches are commonly made at some distance from the land, and by boats from distant districts, working between Howth and the neighbourhood of the Isle of Man; the fish being landed for the most part at the former important station and at Ardglass. There is a fishery at Arklow during a great part of June, the fish being fat and with no appearance of roe. After that month the herrings almost disappear, and nothing more is generally done there till October, when a somewhat different class of fish is met with, also without roe, but not so fat as those caught in June. This second fishery is continued till nearly Christmas.

On the south and south-west of Ireland there appear to be two seasons; the summer fishery, beginning in May or June, and lasting till September or October, when spawning takes place; and the winter fishery, from Christmas to the beginning of March, which also is a spawning month. On the Atlantic side, however, the herring fishery is very uncertain, as the coast is too much exposed for regular deep-sea fishing to be carried on at night without considerable risk; and the fish do not always come far enough into the bays to be caught in large numbers. Galway Bay, however, has generally been an exception; and the herring fishery has been carried on there regularly with varying, but often considerable success, from the end of June to December.

We may now turn again to England, in order to notice a special fishery carried on principally by the Lowestoft fishermen. Three distinct fisheries are recognized and worked by these men and by the fishermen from Gorleston, adjoining Great Yarmouth. They are known as the spring, the midsummer, and the Michaelmas or autumn fisheries. The spring fishery was not much attended to until about 1850 or 1852, but it soon grew into some importance, and has been continued with varying success in subsequent years. It is commenced about the middle of March in deep water, 50 or 60 miles from the land; the fish are then small; there is little to recommend them either in size or quality for the market, and they sell at very low prices, sometimes not fetching more than a few pence per hundred, to be employed only for manure. The mesh used for catching them is below that of the ordinary herring size, and runs up to thirty-nine or forty to the yard. As the season advances the fish gradually come nearer the land, put on fat, and become more marketable. The spring fishery continues till the first week in May, when the herrings appear to become scarce, and the fishermen then get their nets ready for the summer fishery, which requires a larger mesh. The interval between the two fisheries is of very short duration, often only a week; and on resuming work, the summer fish are found at only a few miles from the shore. The condition of these fish leads to the belief that they are only the remains of the spring shoals, as they are of the same description as those previously caught, and without any roes; but they are rather fatter. The midsummer herrings are always more valuable than those taken in the spring; and it is thought by many fishermen and others interested in the supply of marketable produce that great injury is done to the later fishery by so many fish being taken early in the year. A short supply of summer herrings has therefore been frequently accounted for by the preceding fishery having been largely worked. On the other hand, it has been contended that the summer fish are often as abundant as they ever were before the spring fishery came into fashion. Recent experience, however, does not support this statement, as with a more or less successful series of spring fisheries, the summer herrings have been exceedingly scarce for the last seven years.

The second, or midsummer fishery, is continued till about the middle of July; and no herrings are afterwards caught by these fishermen until the great autumn fishing begins about the first week in September. It will be seen from the above sketch of the general seasons for herring fishing, the particulars of which are the result of our personal inquiries at the several localities, that the shoals are on some part or other of our coasts almost throughout the year; and it agrees with the statement of the Billingsgate salesmen, that there are herrings in the market nearly all the year round, but in much greater abundance during particular seasons.

Although shoals of maties or fat herrings appear on many parts of the coast, either by themselves or in company with full fish, we have abundant evidence that a large proportion of the herrings which approach the shore from deep water during the fishing seasons are getting into spawning condition; and that the spawning takes place before they return to the open sea. They are then said to be "shotten," and are considered of comparatively little value for the table; in some places they are called "razor fish" from their thin, sharp appearance. After spawning they gradually disperse, and apparently return to deep water, although examples may not unfrequently be met with inshore long after the usual herring season is past; in fact, in some localities herrings of one kind or another may be found at all times of the year. The spawn is known to be deposited on the ground, and sometimes in comparatively shallow water; but it does not necessarily follow that the process should always take place near the shore. There is no doubt, however, about that being frequently the case; as, on the coast of Scotland particularly, herrings are successfully fished for with hook and line whilst they are on the ground at the spawning time. The very young herrings are abundant along many parts of the coasts where spawning and spawned fish were previously found in large numbers; and older fish in various stages of growth are met with on some part or other of the coast throughout the year. It appears unnecessary, therefore, to resort to any theory of migration to explain the presence of herrings at any particular time on the coasts of the British Islands. Everything is in favour of their being a resident species, and there is some evidence to show that the fishes of a district do not range far away.

Our herring is, undoubtedly, a northern fish,[1] but it is most common in the cooler parts of the temperate region in our hemisphere, and more abundant on our own coasts throughout the year than it has ever been known in the Arctic Ocean.

Before concluding our remarks on the herring we may say a few words about the "whitebait"—a fish which has for many years provided materials for controversy among a few naturalists and a great many writers on fishes. It is hardly necessary to say that the fishes which are sold as "whitebait" in the shops are mixed with many kinds of small fry which, if they were called by their right names, would never be allowed to pollute the refined palates of epicures of the present day; but cooks are not expected to be naturalists, and even if they were, their triumphs consist as much in making palatable dishes from unpromising as from promising materials. However, among the so-called "whitebait" there are plenty which may bear that honourable title; but the question is, whether the fishes to which it should be given are young herrings below a certain size, or others which can be distinguished from them by sufficiently well-marked and constant characters. As there is no doubt of the "whitebait" belonging to the same genus (*Clupea*) as our herring, it is only necessary to look for specific distinctions between them; and these should be found

---

[1] It is by no means certain that the herrings found in the Black and Caspian Seas are of the same kind as those frequenting the western coasts of Europe. There are no specimens in the British Museum from the former localities; but *Clupea pontica* has been described from the Black Sea, and *C. caspia* from the Caspian; the first, according to Dr. Günther, appearing to be closely allied to our herring, and the second to be intermediate between the herrings and the shads (*Cat. Fishes Brit. Mus.*, vol. vii., pp. 418, 419). These are probably the species characteristic of those seas, and in that case may be the herrings referred to by Mr. Mitchell in his account of the various localities in which herring fishing is carried on.

either in the number of fin-rays, the position of the fins, the number of vertebræ, or the arrangement in certain groups of teeth, if present. If no distinction can be found in these characters, then we venture to think there will be no solid foundation for specifically separating the one from the other.

Yarrell[1] and Couch[2] are the two last English ichthyologists who have given independent figures and descriptions of the whitebait; and in a matter involving the discrimination of a species from another which is very well known, we might expect an agreement between those authors on the points which they considered important. We will therefore compare the number of fin-rays as given by Yarrell and Couch:—

WHITEBAIT (*Clupea alba*).

	Dors.	Vent.	Caud.	Pect.	An.	Vert.
Yarrell	17	9	20	15	15	56
Couch	17	8	19	17	..	..

In three out of the four fins mentioned by both authors there is a difference in the number of rays; and we should not like to say that in any case they were probably incorrectly counted; although only eight ventral rays, as given by Couch, is open to strong doubt.

We will now compare these characters with the corresponding ones in the herring, and will add the number of fin-rays given by Günther[3]:—

HERRING (*Clupea harengus*).

	Dors.	Vent.	Caud.	Pect.	An.	Vert.
Yarrell	17–19	9	18–20	15–17	14–16	56
Couch	19	9	..	15	16	56
Günther	17–20	9	..	..	16–18	56

---

[1] *British Fishes*, 2nd edition, vol. ii., p. 207 (1841).
[2] *Fishes of the British Islands*, vol. iii., p. 114, pl. cciii. (1841).
[3] *Cat. Fishes Brit. Mus.*, vol. vii., p. 416 (1868).

Of the three fins mentioned by Günther, he considers the number of rays in the ventral to be of generic importance, and the number in the dorsal and anal fins generally to have specific value.

Here, then, we find considerable variation in the number of fin-rays as given by two of the three authorities; and there is no doubt that herrings differ very much in this character in some of their fins, as can be easily recognized in moderate-sized specimens; but it also varies in the "whitebait," and within nearly the same limits.

One very distinctive character in our herring is, according to Günther, an *ovate* patch of vomerine teeth; this is found in both the "whitebait" and the herring down to a certain size, in the specimens in the British Museum, where there is a large collection of herrings and reputed whitebait from different localities. These specimens in spirit, although on some points not so good for comparison as freshly-caught fish, are very valuable for other reasons, as many of them belonged to Yarrell, Parnell, and other naturalists, and were intended as representatives of the supposed two species.

We now come to two characters believed by many people to be very distinctive of the whitebait, namely, the large proportionate length of the head to the body, and the more uniform silvery appearance of the fish. Of the first, we may say that among both the true herrings and the reputed whitebait these proportions vary, and especially in the smaller specimens—whether very silvery or not; and the shape of the head is also subject to some variation. With regard to the second point, we cannot safely speak from the Museum specimens, as they are all more or less affected in colour by the spirit in which they are preserved; but we think that *if* reputed whitebait differ in any respect whatever from true herrings, it may be in having a more silvery coat, or, strictly speaking, in having less colour on the back and a more bleached appearance. If this be so, the fact of such fish having frequented comparatively brackish water, and therefore obtained food probably different from what they would have met with in the sea, may go far to explain the difference in appearance; but degrees of colour alone, we need hardly say, are utterly worthless for the purpose of distinguishing species. No reputed whitebait containing spawn has been met with; there is very strong reason, therefore, for believing them all to be immature fish; and as they have not a single specific character to distinguish them from herrings, it appears to us to require no very great stretch of imagination to conclude that when they leave the brackish water and grow large enough to breed, they do so under the guise of the ordinary herring. If the whitebait be really a distinct species, we have yet to discover by what tangible and constant character it can be distinguished; and if there be no character of any recognized specific value which is not found in both the herring and the reputed whitebait, and the immaturity of the latter be invariably indicated by the undeveloped condition of the reproductive organs, the grounds for separating them are not very obvious.

The drift-fishery for mackerel is principally on the coasts of England and Ireland. These fish appear at first in deep water south and south-west of the British Islands, and are caught sometimes as early as January 60 miles west of the Land's End. The Cornish fishery, however, does not generally begin till towards the end of February, and it extends into June. May, June, and

July are the months in which most of these fish are caught by drift-nets in the English Channel and the North Sea; and they are often abundant in August or even later, but the full-grown fish are not then in such good condition as they were a few weeks earlier. Mackerel without any roe in them are found off Hastings in January, but being in deep water, are not then fished for. In October and November, after the close of the regular season, they are again caught by the Hastings fishermen in the herring nets; and these fish are short and fat, and without any roe. The spawning season appears to vary within certain limits, but June is about the general time for it; and it has been already mentioned that mackerel do not go to the ground, like the herrings, for the purpose of depositing their spawn, but shed it quite at the surface, and at varying distances from the land. According to our observations on the Devonshire coast, mackerel remain in shoals or " schools" until after they have spawned, and while thus congregated they do not very readily take a bait; but after this process has taken place, towards the middle of July, the shoals become dispersed, and the fish, instead of then making their way to deep water, as appears to be the general habit of the herrings under like circumstances, draw nearer the land and even enter the harbours, where they afford excellent sport with the hook and line. Mackerel do not lose condition so much as the herrings by the act of spawning, and they soon recover after feeding voraciously on the young sprats and other small fry which abound at that time near the land. Half-grown mackerel, with no appearance of roe in them, are more or less abundant on the coast at the same time as the large ones, or in some localities preceding, in others following, them; and it must be within the experience of most persons who have been engaged in mackerel fishing, that both large and small fish are frequently caught in the same waters and on the same day. It seems quite clear that both kinds cannot make their approach to the land for the purpose of spawning; in fact, as the spawn floats, there is no apparent reason why the mackerel should come inshore at all with that object; some other motive must be sought for these periodical visits, and it appears likely that an abundant supply of food is the main attraction to both old and half-grown fish, and that they instinctively seek it among the myriads of young surface-swimming fry which frequent the shoaler water. We know little of what many kinds of fish feed on; but there can be little doubt that the search for food is one of the principal causes of their migrations; and to this we are disposed to look for an explanation of the movements of those species which periodically visit our coasts.

The mackerel fishery at the Isle of Man is from June to August, but it is not of much importance; and in the latter month they are also caught in Lochfyne, but only by the sean; this fishery either there or on any other part of the coast of Scotland not being of sufficient consequence to justify the expense of regular drift-nets for the purpose.

Kinsale has been for some time the head-quarters of the mackerel fishery in Ireland, and large numbers of these fish are landed there during March, April, May, and June, by Manx boats and others, besides those belonging to the place. On the west coast the visits of the mackerel, like those of the herring, are very uncertain, and the sean instead of the drift-net is frequently brought into requisition when the fish come close enough inshore. Galway, however, has a more or less regular fishery for mackerel from June to November, and they are found at times in Donegal Bay during the same period.

Pilchard fishing by drift-nets begins on the Cornish coast in July, and is carried on till December; but during the later months the fish come near the shore, within reach of the seans; and the drift-boats are forbidden by law to fish within half a mile of where those nets are being used. Pilchards may be regarded as essentially west-country fish, as the great fishery for them is on the coast of Cornwall, and they are to be found in that neighbourhood throughout the year. They are also fished for to some extent on the south coast of Devon, and are occasionally met with farther up Channel, and even in the North Sea. In the south and south-west of Ireland they are so frequently abundant that it may be hoped the attempts lately made to work for them systematically will lead to the establishment of a regular fishery.

The distance from the land and the direction in which the pilchards are first met with on the Cornish coast appear to vary to a considerable extent; but we shall perhaps not be far wrong in saying that few pilchards are taken during the season farther at sea than 10 or 12 miles, and that they are found south rather than west of the Land's End. On the south coast some of the shoals soon come in near the land, and the fish are taken at the same time by both drift-nets and seans. They make an early appearance also on the Irish coast, whence it is believed they come in October and November to the north shore of Cornwall. It is during those months that the important sean-fishery at St. Ives is expected to take place; but the pilchard is capricious in its movements, and these fish sometimes pass along the coast out of reach of the seans. There seems no doubt that the great shoals which visit St. Ives strike the coast not far north of that place; and although a few pilchards are sometimes caught at Tenby, they do not appear generally to enter the Bristol Channel. It is only towards the end of the season that they come very near the north coast of Cornwall, and they are then going in a southerly direction, to be seen no more till the following year.

A great deal has been written at various times about the pilchard, and, from its comparative localization and abundance on our south-western coasts, it might be expected that the regular habits of the fish would be tolerably well understood; there are many points in its economy, however, still requiring investigation, and among them the spawning habits may be specially mentioned. Where and when does spawning take place? It is a process which we might reasonably anticipate would be carried out according to some definite rule of season and locality; but apparently this is not altogether the case, and the capricious movements of the pilchard are to some extent paralleled by the variation in its spawning habits, so far as they are known. It appears pretty certain that the bulk of the pilchards caught on the Cornish coasts are fat fish and with undeveloped roes. They will not cure or "save" well if they are not in this condition; and cured pilchards have been an important article of export to the Italian states for very many years. The pilchard fishery lasts from July to December; but in April and May these fish are met with by the mackerel "drivers" at a long distance from the land, and they are then ready for spawning. This might be expected from the fact of most of the fish caught in autumn being without roe. As mentioned in our introductory observations, Mr. Couch was disposed to believe from such evidence as he possessed that the pilchard spawned at the surface, and that the ova were enveloped in a sheet of tenacious jelly which enabled them to float. Many miles of water far away from the land had been observed covered with this spawn, but the development of the ova had not been traced. That pilchards commonly spawn far out at sea, whether at the surface or not, is evident from the fact of their being taken there by the mackerel nets, the mesh of which is sufficiently large to allow a pilchard to pass through if it be not in spawning condition; but Mr. Couch tells us that on some parts of the Cornish coast, the pilchards are ready to spawn in October, and that spawning then takes place near the land. From our inquiries among the fishermen we learnt that this October spawning was not very general, and it occurred mostly among the fish on the eastern part of the coast. We have distinct evidence, however, of more than one spawning season, as in the case of the herring; but there is nothing to show that any particular locality is frequented by the pilchards for the special purpose of depositing their spawn. The fact of the bulk of these fish shedding their ova in deep water is favourable to the idea of the floating of the ova during development, and the occasional spawning near the land appears to us to point to the same conclusion as we arrived at in the case of the herring—that the process takes place independently of locality, and has no obvious connection with the periodical movements of the fish. Feeding and reproduction are the two great motive instincts of all animals, and it is evident that the latter does not impel the bulk of the pilchards to come inshore.

The periodical appearance of immense shoals of sprats in our bays and estuaries during winter is another instance of a great movement towards the land, but not obviously for spawning purposes. Cold weather drives many of our fishes into deep water, but in this case the habit appears to be reversed; for although young sprats are also abundant on many parts of the coast during summer, and particularly so in some of our southern harbours, the old ones are rarely numerous inshore except in winter.

There has been some doubt as to the regular spawning time of this fish, and it is still unknown whether the process takes place at the surface of the water or on the ground—in deep or shallow water. Some information has been gained, however, about the time of spawning; and so far as it goes it points to there being two seasons, as in the case of the herring and pilchard. Yarrell[1] mentions having taken them full of roe on the Dorsetshire coast in June; and Couch[2] speaks of the spawning season being in summer, and probably late in autumn also; but neither of those authorities appeared to have been aware of the abundant evidence there is of a regular winter spawning on some parts of the coast. It is stated by the fishermen in Torbay that the sprats are full of roe in November and December—the time at which large captures are made there by means of the sean. Farther eastward the sprat fishing is worked on a much larger scale than on the Devonshire coast, and we have very precise information about the condition of the fish taken there. The season for sprat fishing by the stow-net lasts from early in November to some time in February; and in the Solent the fish are

[1] *Brit. Fishes*, vol. ii., 2nd edition, p. 198.
[2] *Fishes Brit. Islands*, vol. iv., p. 110.

at first mostly small, but at the end of December and beginning of January a great many large ones are mixed with the others, and these are approaching spawn condition. Ramsgate is one of the few places were sprats are caught by drift-nets, and consequently only the larger fish are taken. These are so nearly ready for spawning at the end of December and beginning of January that the fish with hard roes can be readily distinguished from those with soft ones—the females from the males—by the ordinary mode of handling them; and most of those taken in January have spawned before the middle of the month. The largest fishery for sprats is at the mouth of the Thames; and the fish caught there generally agree in size with those taken in the Solent at the same periods, the full-roed fish being most abundant at the beginning of the year, which is confirmed by the Billingsgate salesmen, who say that January is the spawning month. Now, as the large and full-roed fish form but a very small proportion of the thousands of tons of sprats caught every year close to the land, it cannot be supposed that spawning is the general object of the visits of these great shoals to the bays and estuaries along the coast; and the question becomes more perplexing, if it be true, as stated by Parnell, that the sprat is very sensitive to cold; for, whatever may be the case in the Firth of Forth, there is no doubt that the sprats, young and old, are most abundant in shallow water along the English coast at the coldest time of the year. Although these fish have been taken in spawning condition in summer on certain parts of the coasts, there is no reason to believe they are ever very numerous at that time near the land; and negative evidence would lead us to expect the breeding habits of the sprat to be more akin to what is said of the pilchard than what we know of the herring—namely, that it not improbably spawns at the surface, in summer generally in deep water, but in winter nearer the shore. If any drift-fishery were carried on in summer with meshes small enough to catch the larger-sized sprats, we might obtain more information about the probable localities and actual time of the summer spawning, but we are not likely to get any help in this matter from professional fishermen; and little as we have been able to say about the breeding habits of this very common fish, we believe it embodies most of what is really known on the subject at the present time.

Sprat fishing on the English and Scotch coasts, whatever may be the method employed, is always carried on in winter, but on the south-west of Ireland and in Donegal Bay it is earlier, and lasts from August to nearly Christmas.

Drift-fishing for sprats is quite an exceptional method of catching them; it is adopted, however, about Ramsgate, Deal, and Hastings; a short train of untanned nets being used from small boats worked by a couple of men, and the produce consisting only of the larger and more valuable fish.

We believe there are still some persons in existence who persist in the belief that sprats are nothing but young herrings; but we trust they are not very numerous in these enlightened times.

III.—LINE-FISHING.

Universal practice of — Longlines and handlines — Longline, description of, length, number of hooks — Shooting the line — Buoys — Hauling in — Welled-smacks, description and cost of — Baits — Whelks, mode of collecting — Enemies of the cod fishermen — Seasons for cod fishing — Longlines and trawlers — Handlining for cod — Description of tackle — Capture of small fish — Variable seasons — Impossibility of catching more than part of the fish in the sea — Large breeding stock must always be left — Storing live cod — Cod chests — Killing the cod for market — "Live cod" — Coast fishing — Small hookers — Dandy-line, description of — Herrings caught by it at spawning time — Only used in Scotland.

This is probably the oldest method of fishing, with the exception of that by the primitive fish spear, and, not only on our own coasts, but throughout the world, is the one most generally carried on. In one form or other it comes within the reach of all classes, and the scale on which it is worked by our sea fishermen depends more on capital and locality than on any essential difference in the kind of gear or the manner of using it.

Line-fishing at sea is comparatively simple work, requiring but little of the skill so often needed for the more delicate operations in fresh water; and although in many cases greater success undoubtedly follows the use of finer tackle and more varied baits than tradition and example have led most of the professional fishermen to adopt, a knowledge of the localities frequented by the different kinds of fishes at the various seasons is generally the most important part of the sea fisherman's education.

There are two principal methods by which our line fisheries are carried on, namely, by longlines and handlines. Both are very simple in their character, and a short description of each, as practised on a large scale, will probably be sufficient for their explanation, as the general subject must be more or less familiar to all who have visited or resided on the coast.

The longline, spilliard, spiller, bulter, or trot, all of them names given to the same kind of line, according to locality, size, or the purpose for which it is used, is a very general means of fishing, as many kinds of valuable fish are caught with it, and any length of line may be worked. It is extensively used in the North Sea for the capture of cod, ling, holibut, and haddocks; and some of these fish when taken by hook and line have often a better appearance and command higher prices in the market than when caught by the trawl.

Great Grimsby has taken an important position with respect to this kind of fishing, and no better idea of it can be obtained than by examining the method by which it is carried on from that port.

Longlining is there worked by means of smacks, mostly of the size of the larger class of trawl-vessels previously described. They carry from nine to eleven hands each, and remain at sea until they have a fair cargo of fish, which are kept alive as long as possible in a well built in the vessel; the construction of this well will be explained after we have spoken of the lines and the manner of working them.

A complete set of longlines, as used in one of these vessels, consists of about fifteen dozen, or 180 lines 40 fathoms in length, each supporting twenty-six hooks on smaller short lines called " snoods," which are fastened to the main line at a fathom and a half apart, that distance being sufficient to prevent the snoods fouling one another and the hooks becoming entangled. A " string" of this description, made up of the 180 lines of 40 fathoms each fastened together into one, is 7200 fathoms long, equal to more than seven nautical miles, or about eight ordinary ones, and has 4680 hooks. These are baited with the common large whelk, which, owing to its toughness and substance, is not easily washed off the hook, and is besides an attractive bait for cod and ling. The operation of baiting these hooks of course takes up a good deal of time, and gives plenty of employment to the numerous hands on board before the line can be shot. Longlining by these smacks is only carried on during the day, as light is desirable for the men to see what they are about when hauling in. The lines are shot about sunrise, or earlier if the weather be fine, and sometimes a second shot is made if time will permit, but they are always hauled up before night; they are laid across the tide so that the snoods may drift clear of the main line. When a "shot" is to be made, the smack is put under easy sail, and kept as much as possible with the wind free, so as to make a fair straight course whilst the line is being paid out. The lines are neatly coiled, and with the baited hooks are laid in trays all ready for running, each tray containing from twelve to sixteen pieces, and they are paid out one after another until the whole length of line is overboard. No corks or floats of any kind are used to raise it off the ground, but the line is kept steady at every 40 fathoms by a very small anchor, and its position at the two ends and at every intermediate mile is marked by a hooped buoy or "dan" of a conical shape, with a pole or staff passed through it and carrying a small flag. The line is usually shot at about halftide, and when the operation has been completed the smack heaves-to in the neighbourhood till the tide has nearly done. Then the hauling up begins. The foresail of the smack is lowered, and the end buoy being taken on board, the vessel makes short tacks along the course of the line, which is shown by the buoys at every mile; the line is hauled in as the vessel goes along, and the fish are taken off the hooks. Sometimes the line is hauled into the smack's boat, which is about 18 feet long, and very roomy; in this a water-tight space is set apart for the fish to be kept alive in till the boat returns to the smack; but this plan is only adopted when there is special occasion for it, as the water in the North Sea is rarely smooth enough for it to be carried out satisfactorily. As cod are not only the most valuable fish taken by these lines, but command a specially high price, everything is done to ensure their reaching the market in the finest possible condition, and this can be best accomplished by keeping them alive. They are accordingly placed in the vessel's well as soon as they are taken off the hook, having first undergone the operation of puncturing the air bladder or "sound," which, apparently from the long struggles of the fish to get clear of the hook, becomes unusually inflated, and would keep it floating in an unnatural position at the surface if put into the well in the condition in which it came off the hook.

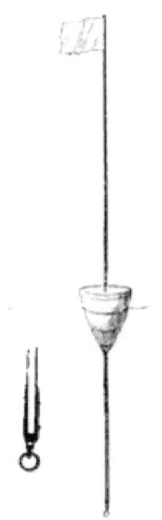

BUOY TO LONGLINE.

The use of wells for keeping the cod alive was first tried in 1712, at Harwich, a port for many years famous as the head-quarters of the home cod fishery, and still used as a station. The "welled-smacks," as they are called, are specially constructed for the purpose; the well not being a tank fitted into the vessel, but a part of the smack itself. Two strong water-tight bulkheads are built entirely across the vessel from keelson to deck, enclosing a large space in the centre of the vessel; this

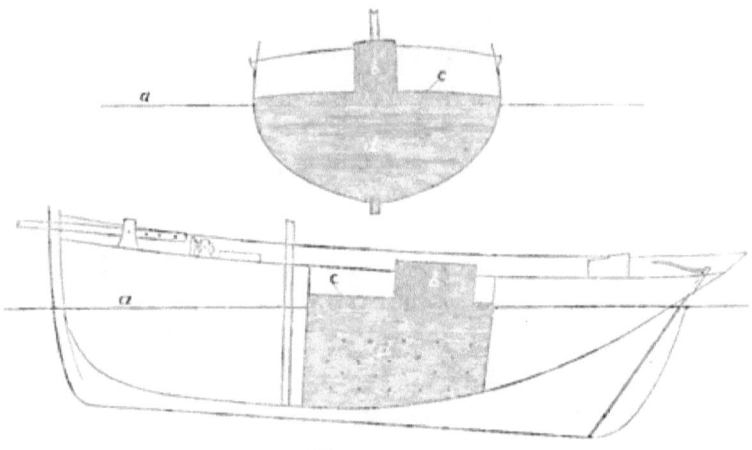

WELLED-SMACK.

is the "well," and a constant supply and circulation of water from the sea is kept up within it through large auger holes bored in the bottom of the vessel at various distances below the water line. The entrance to the well is on deck, through a hatchway (*b*); and in front and on each side of it runs what is called the "well-deck" (*c*), which keeps the level of the water (*a*) within certain limits when the smack is rolling about or pressed down under sail. Cod are the principal fish put into the well, and when they have been caught in a moderate depth of water, they will live a long time without deterioration under such circumstances. Ling, however, which are generally caught in deep water, and cod from like situations, do not thrive in the vessel's well. There is some mortality also among the healthy fish, arising from their being knocked about in the vessel during bad weather. This cannot be avoided, when there are many fish on board; but they are taken out at once and packed in ice; and each line-smack on returning to port, generally has a number of such fish preserved in that manner, including also cod, ling, and haddock which were not considered lively enough to put into the well when they were taken off the hook. It is no uncommon thing, however, for a smack to return from the Dogger with from twenty to twenty-five score of fine live cod, besides perhaps two-thirds of that number of fish in ice. Holibuts are commonly taken by these longlines, and they are easily kept alive in the well, and fetch a good price in the Grimsby market, where they are known by the familiar abbreviation of "buts."

The cost of these welled-smacks is considerably greater than that of "dry-bottomed" vessels of the same size; and although it is difficult to understand why the construction of the well should be so expensive, there is nevertheless a difference of about 300*l.* between the first cost of a welled-smack and of a trawler of the larger class—about 68 tons N.M.; the former amounting to 1500*l.*, and the latter to 1200*l.* The working expenses of the line vessel are also heavier than those of the trawlers. Each cod-smack carries from nine to eleven hands, of whom six or seven are apprentices of different ages. The principle of paying by shares, so general among the trawlers, except in the case of the Barking men, is only adopted by the owners of line vessels for the payment of the captain. He receives nine per cent. of the proceeds of the "voyage"; but weekly wages are paid to the others, the mate getting 22*s.* and the men 20*s.* each; the apprentices receive from 4*l.* to 10*l.* a year according to their length of service. Provisions for all hands are found by the owner, without deduction for them from the wages.

Bait is an important item in the expenses of a cod-smack; it comes next on the list after wages, provisions, and depreciation of vessel, and costs more than the wear and tear of sails and rigging. Whelks or "buckies," as they are called in Scotland, are exclusively used as bait on the longlines by the cod-smacks, on account of their toughness and the good hold they consequently give to the hook. It is a curious circumstance that although mussels, which are such an excellent bait for almost all kinds of fish, are in general use with longlines when worked from small boats; they are said not to answer for the smacks, notwithstanding that the lines are on the same principle and commonly catch the same kinds of fish. The explanation given of this is that the smack works in rougher water and is under less control than the boats—that as the line runs out very fast, and has a rapid drag through the water on its way to the bottom, soft bait like mussels is very likely to be washed off the hook; but small boats are under the command of the oars, and the line goes overboard slowly, each hook entering the water and sinking without more resistance than there would be to a handline in a tideway.

The procuring of whelk-bait is a regular trade, in which many small craft from 12 to 15 tons are constantly employed. Large quantities of these shell-fish are obtained from Boston and Lynn Deeps, but they are also fished for along the Kentish shore and on other parts of the coast.

Of the methods in use for catching whelks the one adopted about Harwich is that called "trotting." The trot is only another name for a longline of small dimensions; but instead of having baited hooks, common shore crabs are threaded on the snoods, about twenty on each; and the whelks, which are carnivorous in their habits, seize and keep as firm hold, whilst devouring them, as if they were hooked. When the line is hauled up the snoods are found covered with whelks. This fishing for whelks, besides contributing so largely to the capture of cod and other fish, results in the diminution of one of the most inveterate enemies of the oyster and mussel, and thus performs a double service.

Another mode of obtaining whelks is by means of baskets baited inside with pieces of fish, and having a net stretched over the end with an opening in the centre for the admission of the whelks. It is something on the principle of the crab-pot, and is said to be efficient, but it is not in very general use.

The plan adopted by the Grimsby whelk fishermen is by shallow hoop-nets baited with refuse fish and sunk to the bottom; in these the whelks collect in large numbers, and are caught without any difficulty. The supply is generally well kept up, and should there be any scarcity during the cod season the deficiency is made up from the London market. A good many whelks are also obtained by the oyster dredgers.

Each smack takes with her as bait for the voyage during the regular longline season about forty wash of whelks; the "wash" being a stamped measure capable of holding twenty-one quarts and a pint of water; but in March, towards the end of the season on the Dogger, not more than from fifteen to twenty-five wash are required. The whelks are preserved alive in bags made of netting, and are kept in the well until wanted, when the shells are broken and the animals extracted. The smacks remain at sea for a few days only, rarely as long as a fortnight at a time, depending on the number of fish they have caught, or the demand there is likely to be for them.

The great enemies the cod fishermen have when longlining are the dogfish, which at certain seasons, but fortunately not every year, commit great havoc among the cod which have become hooked. One case is recorded of nearly every fish on the line having been more or less eaten by the "dogs," and the smack returned to harbour with her rigging covered with skeletons. Of six and a half score of cod on the line only six fish were found alive. The clearer the water the more danger there is from "dogs," as the cod can then be seen for some distance when struggling on the hook, and once having attracted attention there is little hope of escaping their enemies.

The season for longlining is during the winter months, and the fishing is carried on at that time on two widely separated grounds—on the Dogger from November to March or April, and on Cromer Knoll from November to February. The latter ground, although comparatively small, has been a favourite place of resort for many years, and still shows no signs of becoming exhausted during the proper season. Longlines are set on rather rough ground, usually where the trawlers cannot work; but the deep-sea liners sometimes fish in the same neighbourhood, and without making any complaint of the trawlers carrying away their gear. Considering that Grimsby is such a large station for both liners and trawlers, the fact that the two classes of fishermen work harmoniously not far from one another, and sometimes over the same ground without more injury being done to the lines than the

admitted damage of occasionally carrying away a few
hooks, is strong evidence in favour of the statement
that if the trawler keep clear of the buoys used with
the longline, the trawl can pass over the intermediate
spaces without doing more than the most insignificant
injury. That it is not always possible for the trawlers
to avoid the line will be evident when it is remembered
that the lines are set across the tide for a distance of
many miles, with only a buoy at every mile to mark
them; and that the course of the trawler, there working down with the tide, must take her over them; for
although it may be easy enough for the liners to see
the nearest buoys, knowing the direction in which they
should be, the trawler is not likely to observe them
until they are so close that she has only time to alter
her course sufficiently to give them a tolerably wide
berth, and to take the trawl over the lines where the
least damage is likely to be done. The great outcry
against the trawlers a few years ago for carrying away
longlines, as was alleged, was raised by fishermen on
the north-east coast, who did not like to see fishing
boats from ports farther south catching fish which they
considered belonged to themselves; although in many
cases the local fishermen did not adopt the most effective
means of catching them. In March or April longlining
is put a stop to, and but few line-cod are caught in
the North Sea for the next three months, except sometimes on the Dutch coast. Many of the cod-smacks go
away to Iceland and the Faroe Islands, where a somewhat fluctuating fishery for cod has been carried on for
many years. Handlines are there used, and the fish are
always salted.

In July handline fishing for cod commences in the
home waters, and is continued till near the end of

October. This fishing is mostly carried on at from 10 to 30 miles from the coast, as the herrings at that time are approaching the shore, and the cod follow them closely. The same welled-smacks are used for handline fishing as for longlining, and they carry the same number of hands; in fact, the only difference is in the fishing grounds and the kind of line employed. The handline is about 45 fathoms long, having at the end a sinker of lead of from $5\frac{1}{2}$ to 7 pounds weight, with a

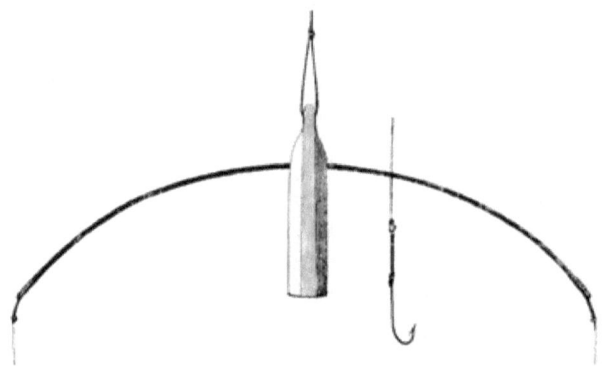

LEAD AND SPRAWL-WIRE OF COD-LINE.

stout iron wire called the "sprawl-wire" fixed in it near the top, at right angles to the body of the sinker, and slightly curved downwards at the ends; to each of these is fastened a snood of smaller line six feet long, supporting a single large cod-hook twice the size of those used on the longline, as with these handlines no fish but cod are taken. We have seen the hook sometimes fastened to the snood by a number of open strands of soft twine about three inches long, so that the fish cannot bite through the line and carry off the hook, the teeth passing between the strands without injuring them. This plan answers all the purpose of wire, and is more easily applied to hooks with the ordinary form of shank. It is not so much in use now, however, as formerly, and the snood is now generally fastened directly to the hook. When fish are very abundant as many as five or six hooks are put on each snood, but on ordinary occasions there are only two hooks to a line. Whelk-bait is here used as with the longlines.

Whilst handline fishing, the smack is hove-to, and each of the hands works one line, keeping the baits a few inches from the bottom, unless the herrings are about, when the cod come very near the surface, and it is only necessary to put one or two fathoms of line overboard. It is found that the fish do not bite very freely during a great part of the day, so that it is not necessary for everyone to be at work till towards sunset; then all hands are kept fully employed. The fish are put into the well as soon as caught. A considerable number of the cod taken within a few miles of the shore are only half-grown fish; there being a marked difference in size generally between those caught 10 or even 15 miles from the land and those brought from the Dogger. They are not caught at the two localities at the same season, however; but when the inshore fishing ceases, and the herring season is pretty well over, the young cod then having attained a considerable size, and become fat on the abundance of food provided for them in the shoals of herrings, appear gradually to work their way off the land, and are looked for on the Dogger by the longline fishermen. It has been charged against the handliners, fishing inshore, that two-thirds of the cod they bring in are not more than half-grown. There can be no doubt of the truth of the charge; but it is replied by the fishermen that, comparatively small as the fish are, they readily sell at a good price, and there are not enough cod at that season in the distant grounds to pay for catching them. Cod fishing is so far peculiar that it is only the fact of the fish commanding a high price that induces men to incur the heavy expenditure necessary for building and equipping vessels for the purpose; and as the same smacks and fishermen work both the inshore and offshore fisheries, any undue destruction of cod at the former should become apparent to the men when they change their ground. The margin of profit for the owner of a cod-smack is not so large but that any serious diminution in the catch for the year would soon be felt; but although the charge of taking small cod is of many years' standing, and is as well founded now as it ever was, it is difficult to believe that the consequences have been so disastrous as the prophets told us would be the case; for instead of the smacks diminishing in number, and the owners becoming ruined, there has been a large increase of vessels during the last ten years, many of them are of a larger class than formerly, and therefore more costly, and the number of fish brought to market has averaged about the same as before for each smack. There are good years and bad ones with fishermen of all classes, however; and some of the liners complain of the last two or three years not having been so productive as usual. Should there be any sensible diminution in the supply of cod in future years, as the result of *over-fishing*, a very simple remedy will certainly be applied: in all open-sea fisheries, such as that for cod, a time must come, long before the fish are nearly exterminated (if that be possible) or even reduced to small numbers, when it will be unprofitable to fish for them; the smack-owners, having a due regard for their own interests, will then withdraw many of their vessels from the fishery; less ground will be worked over, fewer tempting baits will be held out to the unwary, and many fish which might otherwise have been caught will have an opportunity of spawning and helping to restock the haunts of their ancestors. But when it is remembered that cod are only caught by hook and line—for the very few taken by the trawl are hardly worth consideration—and that their capture depends entirely on their being tempted by the baits, it is difficult to believe in the possibility of their numbers being so far reduced in the open sea as to cause any diminution which would not be made up yearly by a very small proportion of the spawn that would be produced by the survivors. It is not a question of spawning beds being destroyed, or of the fish being unable to get access to them, for it has been ascertained that the ova float and are developed at the surface of the water; but it is whether the cod can be so tempted to their destruction as to materially diminish their numbers for any time. This appears most improbable.

When the smacks arrive with their cargoes of live and dead fish at Grimsby the cod are taken out of the wells by means of long-handled landing nets, and are placed in wooden boxes or chests, which are kept floating in the dock; and there the fish are stored till they are wanted for the market.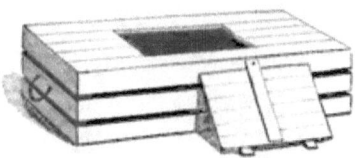

Grimsby Cod-chest.

Each chest is 7 feet long, 4 feet wide, and 2 feet deep; the bottom is made of stout battens a short distance apart to allow free admission to the water, which also has access through the sides and ends between the planks of which they are constructed. The top is wholly planked over, except in the centre, where there is an oblong opening for putting in and taking out the fish, and which is closed by a cover when the chest is afloat and in use. Two rope or chain handles are fixed in the ends of the chest, for convenience in moving it about and hoisting it up from the water. Each chest will hold forty good-sized cod, or nearly a hundred smaller ones, and the fish will keep alive in them without any material falling off in their condition for about a fortnight. The cod is the only fish stored in this manner, except on rare occasions, when a cargo of live haddocks is brought in. The chests belong to the smack-owners individually, or to a small number of them who have formed an association for their own benefit, or for the purpose of letting them to those owners who may want additional storage room. A charge of ninepence is made for each chest every time it is stored. There are usually about 400[1] of these chests in the Grimsby fish-dock, sometimes all in use, and containing from 15,000 to 20,000 live cod.

Every day during the cod season a certain number of these stored fish, according to the demand, are taken out of the chests and sent off by rail to London and other markets. A remarkable scene is then presented, and one peculiar to Grimsby and Harwich, the places

---

[1] A paragraph appeared in one of the morning papers in March, 1872, stating that there had been large arrivals of cod and ling at Grimsby, and that "these chests, a thousand in number, were all full, and smacks had to keep their fish on board. There were not less than 50,000 live ling and cod in the tanks." We happened to be at Grimsby at the time when these large arrivals were said to have taken place, and on inquiring into the truth of the above statement, found that the number of chests used for storing cod was about 400, and one vessel had been delayed for a few hours on account of all the chests being in use. Ling will not live in these tanks, and consequently are never put into them.

where live cod are kept in store. It is well known that as a rule fish are firmer and better for the table if they are killed as soon as taken out of the water, instead of being allowed to die slowly by suffocation, as the gills become dry and incapable of performing their proper functions. This is especially the case with the cod; and as a matter of humanity it may be a question whether there is much to choose between the sudden and violent death to which they have now to submit and the slower and, it may be called, more natural process of dying from want of water. The interests of the fish dealers and the gastronomic taste of the consumers have, however, settled the question in favour of violence; and the proceeding no doubt derives a great deal of its appearance of inhumanity from being conducted on a large scale, as at Grimsby, where hundreds of fish are sometimes killed in the course of a day.

When the time arrives for preparing the fish for market a chest of cod is brought alongside a hulk kept for the purpose and moored in the dock near the market-place; tackles from a couple of davits are then hooked on to the handles, and the chest is hoisted up till nearly clear of the water, which drains through the bottom and leaves the fish dry. The cover is then taken off, and a man gets into the opening and takes out the fish, seizing them by the head and tail. The commotion among perhaps forty or fifty cod just out of the water is of course very great, and it is often no easy matter to get a good hold of them; but, one after the other, they are lifted out and thrown up to the deck of the hulk, where they are taken in hand by another man, who performs the duties of executioner; he grasps the fish tightly behind the head with his left hand, holds it firmly on the deck, and giving a few heavy blows on the nose with a short bludgeon, kills it at once. With a large and lively fish it is sometimes as much as can be done to hold it down with one hand on the slippery deck whilst giving it the *coup de grâce;* but the work is generally skilfully performed, and the dead fish rapidly accumulate into a large heap, whence they are taken on shore to be packed in bulk in the railway trucks waiting close by to receive them. Each truck will hold about twelve score of good-sized fish, or a proportionately larger number of smaller ones. The fish thus killed and packed reach Billingsgate in time for the market early the next morning, and are known in the trade by the name of "live cod," as they are quite fit for crimping on their arrival, some hours after having been killed in the manner described. These cod command the highest price, and are looked upon as essentially " West End" fish.

The advantage of being able to store the cod alive is of course a general one; for not only is the market more regularly supplied than would otherwise be the case, owing to small catches during bad weather or delays from calms or adverse winds, but the fish themselves come into the hands of the fishmongers in a fresher state than almost any other kinds supplied to them.

Line-fishing by the two methods just described is carried on more or less on all parts of the coast, with various modifications in the size of the hooks, the kind of bait, the form of leaden sinker, and the length and size of the lines, dependent mainly on the kind of fish worked for. Excepting in the case of large cod, ling, holibut, and skate, and haddock at certain times of the year, line-fish are mostly caught within a few miles of the shore; and the boats employed, either rowing or sailing, are of small size, ranging from five or six tons downwards, and undecked, or at most with a covered forecastle. In the Channel ports small sailing "hookers" are very numerous, and great numbers of whiting, bream, and various other fish are caught by them, especially during the summer months. They are commonly either smack or dandy rigged; the latter being a very convenient fashion for fishing craft of all sizes, and, as before mentioned, a modification of it now becoming generally adopted for the large class of trawl and line vessels. In the herring and mackerel seasons the small sailing hookers are in some places used for working the drift-nets; but hooking is the principal purpose for which they are employed and generally are best adapted.

On parts of the coast of Scotland larger boats are used for line-fishing, and many of them are decked. The same boats are also used for drift-fishing, and they will be further noticed when the Scottish fisheries are spoken of.

One other method of line-fishing — that by the "dandy-line" or "jigger"— deserves to be noticed, although it appears to be in use at only a few places, among which we may mention Wick, the fishing stations at the entrance to the Firth of Forth, and Tarbert on the west coast; and for a very short period in each year. The line has a leaden sinker or plummet (B) about four pounds weight at one end, and above it, at intervals of eight inches, the line is fastened by an ordinary clove-hitch (C) to the centre of pieces of whalebone or stout wire nine inches long, having a very short line at each end supporting a bright tinned hook. Eight or ten of these spreaders are thus fastened at right angles to the line (A), and the whole apparatus is

154   DEEP-SEA FISHING.

lowered to the bottom, and then moved gently up and down. No bait is used; the bright shining hooks

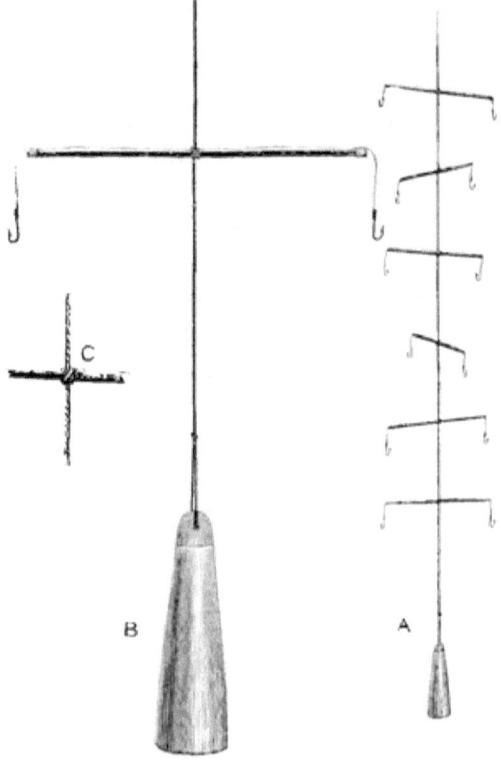

DANDY-LINE.

offering sufficient attraction to the fish. This line is employed for catching herrings to be used as bait for the cod-lines, and appears to be effective only when the herrings are tolerably numerous close to the ground about the spawning season. It is probable that not much direct advantage is derived from this method of fishing as it is not in very general use.

The name "dandy"-line is not very intelligible;

and, as is so commonly the case with technical terms used in connection with fishing gear, no help can be given by the fishermen as to its meaning or derivation. The manner in which the line is worked by moving it gently up and down points strongly, however, to "dandle" as the real name; and "dandle-line" is not improbably the correct reading, if, as we believe to be the case, the word have the same signification in England and Scotland.

IV.—SEAN-FISHING.

Antiquity of — Classification of seans — General description of — Pilchard-seaning — Herring-seaning or "trawling" in Scotland — Ground-sean — Kinds of fish caught by the sean.

The sweep-net, commonly known in this country as the sean or seine, is one of the oldest implements of fishing of which there is any record; and may be recognized under various names from almost the earliest times to the present day. Mr. Couch, in his notice of the thunny fishery,[1] enters at some length into the history of this net, and thus concludes his remarks on the probable antiquity of its use in this country:—"As we have seen that the Phœnicians in the earliest ages were accustomed to use the sean, and it is known that they traded to the county of Cornwall before the days of Moses, it is a reasonable guess that this sort of net was introduced among our ancestors by that people."

Whatever may have been the date of its introduction here, whether before or after the time of Moses, it appears to have always retained the same essential character; and the principal alteration either in its construction or in the manner in which it is worked probably consists only in the addition of a pocket to the middle or bunt, and perhaps in using one net for the purpose of enclosing the fish, as is the practice at St. Ives, and another for completing the capture and removing them from the water. These points will be noticed in the course of our description of the nets.

Seans may be divided into three classes, namely, the

[1] *Fishes of the British Islands*, vol. ii., pp. 91-94.

sean proper—sometimes also called the "stop-sean"—the "tuck-sean," and the "ground or foot-sean." All these nets have the same general character, and are used for surrounding or encircling the fish; but they differ slightly in the manner in which they are employed. They consist of a long train of netting varying considerably in dimensions, but are always of greater depth at the middle or "bunt" than at the ends, which are called the "sleeves" or "wings"; and are shot either in a circle if the net is to be worked entirely from the boat, or in a semicircle if it is to be hauled on shore. The back or upper edge of the net is buoyed up by corks to keep it at the surface, a matter of great importance, as the net is principally used for catching surface-swimming fishes; and the foot is weighted with lead to keep it down, so that the net may hang perpendicularly in the water.

Seaning is conducted on a large scale at St. Ives for the capture of pilchards, and we may here give a short notice of the nets used for that purpose, deferring the more detailed account of pilchard-seaning till we speak of the Cornish fisheries generally. Two, or sometimes three, nets are employed there for enclosing a shoal of fish, or as much of it as can be managed at the time. The first or principal net, there called the "sean," is about 200 fathoms long and 10 fathoms at its greatest depth; to this another net of the same kind, called the "stop-sean," and 100 fathoms long, is united; and the two are shot together, the boats with each net starting from the same place, rather on the outside of the shoal if it be not very large, but moving in different directions, although with the intention of ultimately reuniting. The sean is at first carried along outside, parallel to the shore, and brought round towards it, thus cutting off a portion of the shoal, whilst the stop-net is shot at a right angle to the other and towards the land, across the course of the fish, so as to stop them. If one stop-net be not long enough for the purpose, a second is joined to it, and the end of this and of the large sean are hauled towards each other till they meet and the fish are entirely surrounded. The circle is then gradually contracted by taking out the stop-nets, till the whole catch is enclosed within the single large sean, the ends of which are at once fastened together. The whole concern is then slowly hauled towards the shore into some quiet part, if possible, where there is not much tide, till the foot of the net grounds, or touches the bottom; and there it is securely moored. The fish are taken out of this net by the tuck-sean, which is 70 or 80 fathoms long, 8 fathoms deep at the sleeves, and 10 at the bunt. It is shot inside the large sean, and as it is hauled in the foot of the bunt is raised so as to get the net under the fish and bring them to the surface, when they are taken out in baskets and put into the boats to be carried on shore.

In many places where only one net is used for the whole process, and the enclosed fish are at once "tucked" into the boat, the net is called, according to fancy, either a stop-sean or a tuck-sean. The catches of pilchards at St. Ives, however, are so large at times that several days may be required for landing the fish, and it would be impossible to use one net for all purposes. In Lochfyne and on some other parts of the coast of Scotland where seaning is carried on, it is called "circle-net" fishing or "trawling," the latter being a term which, out of Scotland, is applied to an entirely different kind of fishing, as we have before pointed out.[1]

[1] Trawling, p. 51, *note*.

Theoretically this kind of net might be used anywhere for catching surface-swimming fishes; but in deep water there is a probability of the fish escaping below the net, and the necessity for employing rowing boats also interferes with its successful use except very near the land or in the smooth water of sheltered bays or lochs.

The ground-sean or foot-sean, sometimes called a seringe-net, is always hauled in on the shore; it is constructed on much the same principle as other seans, but is not nearly so deep at the two wings, and the meshes there are generally much larger than in the bunt. Each wing terminates in a pole fastened to the back and foot ropes; and to this pole a long drag-rope is attached by a short bridle, and is used in hauling in the net. When the sean is to be shot the end of one of the drag-ropes is left on shore in charge of some of the fishermen, and the other rope and the whole of the net are put into the stern of the sean-boat, which is then rowed out from and back to the shore, the boat making a large or small sweep according to the length of the sean, which is thrown over as the boat is rowed along. When this is completed the end of the second drag-rope is landed, and the fishermen, divided into two parties, one at each rope, slowly haul in the net, working the two sides evenly and gradually approaching each other as the net comes in, till at last they meet, and the bunt or middle of the net, in which all the fish are collected, is then drawn on shore.

The ground-sean is a very convenient kind of net, as it may be used of almost any size wherever the bottom is tolerably smooth and there is a beach on which it can be landed. It is much used at Brighton for catching mackerel, and also along the Chesil Beach, near Portland, for the same purpose. At the latter place the bunt of the sean opens into a long pocket made with a very small mesh, and the fish collect in this as the net is being hauled in, so that there is less chance of their escaping than there is with the more simple form of sean, which requires careful management of the back and foot ropes when a large body of fish is enclosed. The same plan is sometimes adopted at other places, but we have not found it in very general use among professional fishermen. Seans are worked on a large scale for catching mackerel, pilchards, herrings, and sprats; and smaller ones are employed for sand-eels, smelts, or flat-fish. Various kinds of fish are frequently taken by them at the same time, and they are often shot without there being any very definite idea of what they may bring in. Such kind of scaning is known in Cornwall by the very expressive name of "blind-hauling."

The meshes of seans are in all cases made rather small, particularly in the bunt; as the object in using these nets is to enclose the fish, and not to mesh them as with drift-nets.

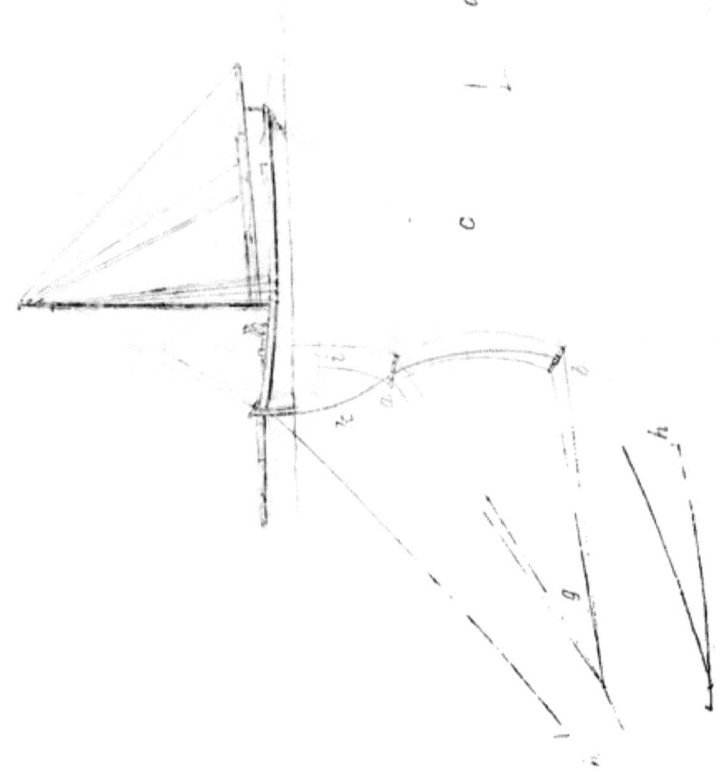

THE STOW-NET

V.—BAG-NETS.

The stow-net — Description of and mode of working — Sprat season — Large takes of sprats by the stow-net — Trim-nets — Bag-nets in Waterford Harbour — Description of — Whitebait net in the Thames.

THE STOW-NET.

(Plate VI.)

This gigantic bag-net, exceeding in length the largest trawl, is exclusively employed for catching sprats, and is regularly used for that purpose in winter at the mouth of the Thames, in the Solent, and the Lynn and Boston Deeps.

The stow-net, as generally used at the mouth of the Thames, where the principal fishing by this method is carried on, is a conical bag, about 60 yards long, and is made up of from four to six portions or lengths, according to the expected scarcity or abundance of fish. The mouth or entrance of the net is 30 feet deep on each side, and is fastened above and below to two stout pieces of wood called "balks"; the upper balk (a) being 21 feet long and the lower one (b) 22. The latter is sometimes made of iron for the sake of the weight, which, as will be presently shown, is necessary in order to keep the mouth of the net open; but to avoid the risk of the stout but long iron rod bending or breaking, it is thickly cased with wood in the centre for more than half its length; if it is made entirely of wood, additional weight is given to it by loading it with lead. The form of the mouth is therefore nearly rectangular, but deeper than it is broad; this difference, however, is lessened when the net is at work, as the manner in which it is moored tends to bring the two balks together, although this is guarded against as much as possible. The first portion of the net, called the "quarters" (*c*) from being made up of four pieces or sides, is 15 or 16 yards long, and each quarter tapers from fifteen score meshes $1\frac{2}{3}$ inch square at the "wide," to five score meshes $1\frac{1}{4}$ inch at the other end. The next portion is called the "enter" (*d*); it is 12 or 13 yards long, with a mesh a little more than half an inch square throughout, and diminishes from eight score to forty-five meshes on each side; but this part of the net is frequently made in one piece, and with of course four times the above number of meshes all round. Next to the enter come the "sleeves" (*e, e*), of which sometimes, when there is an abundance of fish, as many as three are used. They are each generally about 10 yards long, with nine score half-inch meshes all round. The last portion of the net is called the "cod," "dock-hose," or "wash-hose" (*f*), and runs to a length of five or six yards; the mesh here is rather larger than in the sleeves, being three-quarters of an inch square, and eight score meshes go to the circumference of this part of the net. There is some little variation in the proportions of the several parts of the stow-net as used in different places, but such as we have given above may be taken as fairly representing those generally adopted. The boats employed in this fishery are very commonly those used at other times for deep-sea oyster dredging, and the shrimping boats on the Thames also take part in it.

The net is moored by a double bridle, one from each balk, the four ropes composing them, and called "hand-fleets" (*g*), being united at some distance in front of the net to the "string" (*h*), the other end of which is fastened to an anchor of about four hundredweight. The vessel is held by the same anchor, so that in any case of dragging, owing to the great pressure of the tide against the net, the vessel and net move together and keep the same relative positions. The lower balk is weighted either with lead or iron to keep it down, and two ropes called "templines" (*i*) lead from the ends of the upper balk to each side of the vessel; by these the balk is raised and the mouth of the net kept open. One important part of the gear remaining to be noticed is the "wind-chain" (*k*); it is made fast to the middle of the lower balk, and leads through an iron strop or loop on the upper one to the bow of the vessel, where it comes on board through a short davit close to the bowsprit. By heaving on this chain the mouth of the net is closed, and the two balks with the net are raised to the surface. Lastly, a rope called the pinion (*l*) leads from the end of the net to the stern of the vessel; this is brought into use when the fish are to be taken out of the net.

When the stow-net is to be used the vessel takes up a position at the beginning of the tide where there are signs of fish, or in localities where the sprats are likely to be found; she then anchors, and at the same time the net is shot, and streams away below and astern of the vessel; the sails are stowed and no special attention is required till the tide has nearly finished, only one hand remaining on watch to see when it is getting slack water and to keep a general look-out; for the fishing is carried on in some of the numerous channels at the entrance of the river, and often close to the track of vessels going up or down.

As soon as the tide is becoming slack the wind-chain is hove in and the net brought alongside. It is then got in amidships by a long-handled iron hook called the "net-hook," and overhauled till the cod is reached; the end of this is hauled in by the pinion, which is then cast off, and the fish are measured into the vessel's hold in quantities of about three bushels at a time; the master using a wooden instrument called a "mingle" to hold the net so that only a certain quantity of fish shall pass out at once. In this manner the whole catch is worked through the end of the cod or wash-hose into the vessel's hold, the body of the net being at the time secured alongside by means of ropes called "girdlines." Such a net will cost between 30l. and 40l.

MINGLE.

"Stow-boating" is carried on both by day and night, and, as might be expected, the state of the weather makes very little difference in the catch if the sprats are on the coast. The fishing generally begins early in November, and is carried on with more or less success till about the middle of February. At the early part of the season the fish are mostly small, but towards the end of December they vary a good deal in size, and include a great many full-grown fish nearly or quite ready to spawn; at the later part of the sprat season fewer large fish are caught. When the shoals are of considerable size, and the captures are proportionately great, very few fish besides sprats are taken; but at other times young herrings and other small fishes of many kinds are frequently mixed with them. Sprats are sold wholesale by the bushel, and are generally purchased out of the stow-boats by various dealers who supply the markets. The takes are sometimes enormous; and when the fish cannot be got to market in proper time, or the demand there is slack, they are sold for manure, for which purpose they are at times in great request. No approximate estimate of the vast quantity of sprats taken every winter by the stow-nets can be made. The supply fluctuates from year to year; but the scarcity or abundance in any one season has no apparent connection with the extent of the fishery in the previous one.

The Trim-net.

This net is constructed on the same principle and worked in the same manner as the stow-net, but is very much smaller. It was originally used in fresh water, but has found its way to the entrance of certain rivers running into the Wash; and is employed for catching smelts, eels, and flounders, fishes which are found more or less where the water is partly tidal, and therefore brackish. The main points of difference between the trim-net and the stow-net are in size and in the shape of the mouth. Instead of having a nearly square entrance as in the stow-net, the trim-net has a triangular mouth; the lower part being fastened to a beam 22 feet in length, and the two sides each to a pole 18 feet long, so that the mouth of the net is always kept open by this wooden frame. The net itself is only about 30 feet long, and can be worked with much smaller boats than are required for the gigantic stow-net. It is set facing the stream in precisely the same manner as the other net, and of course catches an immense quantity of small fish at times, besides those kinds for which it is professedly employed.

Near Passage, at the inner part of Waterford Harbour, sprats are taken in long bag-nets suspended between stakes, the remains, we believe, of old disused salmon weirs. These nets are 14 feet wide, and 8 feet deep at the mouth, tapering for a length of 14 fathoms to the end. They are placed in rows across the course of the tide, and act precisely in the same manner as the stow-net, but their successful working of course entirely depends on whether the sprats come within their reach, as they cannot be moved from place to place where the fish may chance to be, as is done in the case of a stow-net worked from a vessel.

The net used in the Thames for catching whitebait is essentially the same as a stow-net, but on a very much smaller scale.

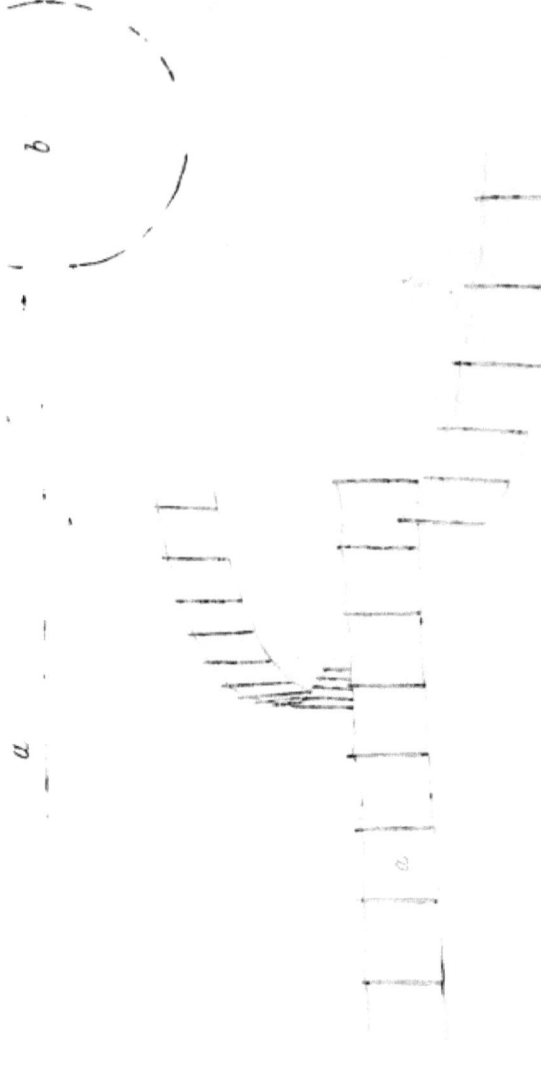

THE KETTLE-NET.

VI.—KETTLE-NET AND WEIRS.

The kettle-net — Description of and localities for — Objections to on account of danger to navigation — Gradual reduction in their number — Weirs — Open to same objection — Description of weirs — Action of — Practically of little value for catching fish.

THE KETTLE-NET.

(*Plate VII.*)

THIS is a method of fishing which is only adopted on the line of coast between Beachy Head and Folkestone, and for the purpose of catching mackerel when they come very near the land. It is used to most advantage where the shore slopes very gradually, and a great deal of ground is consequently laid bare between high and low water marks. Its principle is much the same as that of the fishing weir, although the arrangement of the apparatus differs considerably; both contrivances, however, are such as to turn the fish in a particular direction, and to lead them into an enclosure where they are ultimately captured. The kettle-net is divided into two portions, consisting of a long straight barrier (*a*), and a circular enclosure or "pound" (*b*), both being constructed of similar materials. The barrier has a framework or skeleton of stakes 11 feet high and 8 feet apart; these are fixed in the ground in a straight line, extending from high-water mark to near the limit of ordinary low tides; the length of the barrier varying of course in different localities with the flatness of the shore and the extent of ground laid bare; in some cases the distance is not more than 200 yards, in others it may be 500 or 600. Along the whole length of this row of stakes a train of netting is fixed, reaching from the top of the stakes to the ground, old herring-nets being generally used for this purpose, as their meshes are too small to catch the mackerel, and therefore do very well to turn them. A wall or barrier is thus made running at a right angle from the shore. At the lower end of this barrier is the pound (*b*), a circular enclosure usually about 200 yards in circumference, and constructed in precisely the same manner as the barrier. The entrance to the pound is on the land side, and about 35 feet wide; and the barrier terminates near the middle of, and rather within, the opening, leaving a passage 15 feet wide on one side and 20 feet on the other; the latter is made on that side of the barrier which the mackerel are most likely to strike in the course of their movements along the shore.

The manner in which the kettle-net works is obviously very simple. At the latter part of the mackerel season the fish often come close inshore with the rising tide, and as the stakes are rarely covered by the water the mackerel cannot pass the barrier; and being unable to go round it on the land side their course is turned outwards until they arrive at the other end, where they apparently find themselves in open water, but are really within the pound. Having once entered this enclosure, there they are likely to remain, unless they can escape over the top during the short time any part of it may chance to be covered; but as the tide falls the top of the pound shows more and more above water; and the enclosed fish seek the deepest part of their prison, where they are ultimately collected in what little water may be left when the tide has finished ebbing. The fishermen then have nothing to do but to go with a horse and cart into the pound and take out the fish before they are left quite dry, as may happen with certain tides. Where the shore is very flat, and much more ground is exposed at spring tides than at neap tides, it was formerly the practice to set up a second arrangement of stakes and nets beyond the first; the inner end of the second barrier was joined to the outer side of the first pound, and a second and smaller enclosure made at the other end, at extreme low-water mark. By this plan the kettle-net could be worked with almost any tide; and if either of the pounds did not ebb nearly dry the enclosed fish could always be taken out by means of a small sean. The additional barrier and pound, however, have been forbidden in some cases, and are now generally done away with; and the prohibition is a first step towards the gradual suppression of these nets; for if no serious objection could be made to them on the ground of their capturing very small fish—indeed less on that score than the ground-seans are open to—other complaints of a more tangible character have led the Board of Trade to discourage their employment. It is found that these stake-nets, scores of which are placed at short intervals along a line of beach, and extending for various distances from the shore, are very dangerous to boat navigation; besides this, a monopoly of the shore fishing has been sometimes acquired by one or two persons who have fixed their kettle-nets along perhaps a mile or two of coast to the complete exclusion of the seaners; and although heavy catches of mackerel are occasionally made by these nets, the supply from the seans is generally more certain and profitable to both the fishermen and the public when there is a clear space for working them where the fish may happen to be. The objection to kettle-nets on account of their obstructing the navigation is, however, the principal reason, as we understand, for the interference of the Board of Trade; and we believe that no new kettle-nets are to be fixed, or old ones renewed, without permission from the authorities.

WEIRS.

These contrivances are not much used along the coast, and might be done away with advantage to navigation, and but very trifling loss in the supply of fish to the local market. We have had opportunities of closely examining the construction and action of these weirs in Swansea Bay, where they have long been in use; and although they have been the subject of much local complaint on account of their destroying small fish, it is a question whether the evil is of sufficient magnitude to call for their suppression for that reason alone. They are constructed of stakes driven into the sand, and wattled so as to form a fence through which the water easily passes, but sufficiently close to detain any fish which may come inside when the tide flows over or round them; for, unlike the kettle-net, the weir is always covered at high water. The two arms of the weir extend for a distance of sometimes 200 yards each, and terminate near low-water mark, at very nearly a right angle to one another, in a closely-woven conical basket, having a mousetrap entrance facing the inner side of the weir. For about 40 or 50 yards from the basket the two arms are padded close to the ground, with a "cramming" of bushes and matting, in order to retain some of the water, so that when the tide has ebbed beyond the weir, which happens at spring tides, there is a certain space inside which is never left quite dry. Several of these weirs are constructed in a continuous line, and some are united at the inner extremities of the arms, so that a more or less continuous zigzag barrier is formed by them, extending for a distance, perhaps, of two or three miles along the shore, at a little above ordinary low-water mark. The action of these weirs is more simple and certain even than that of the kettle-net. The fish pass either over the weir when the tide is well in, or round the ends of it; and all which are inside the barrier when the tide has ebbed sufficiently to expose the top or leave the ends dry have no means of escape, but are obliged to seek temporary safety, as the tide continues falling, in the shallow pool remaining in each of the lower angles. Some of them find their way into the basket trap, and are taken out dead when the basket has been left dry; and those which are in the pool are landed by means of a small net.

Although at first sight these weirs may appear to be effectively constructed for catching fish, it is clear that none can enter them until the tide has risen sufficiently to flow either over the top, which is nearly six feet high, or around the extremities of the arms; and, for some hours afterwards, before the tide has ebbed to the same point, there is nothing to prevent the fish which have come inside the zigzag line from escaping. Mackerel, herrings, and sprats are said to be occasionally taken in these weirs, and great numbers of very young fish of various kinds, including flat-fish; but we question whether a great deal that has been said on this subject is correct. Young flat-fish are not very active swimmers, and at spring tides they would have a long distance to travel from beyond low-water mark to be able to get round the arms of the weirs. The result of an examination we made of the fish caught on such an occasion was that nine-tenths of the small fish taken—and the catch of all kinds was trifling—were round-fish, including diminutive cod, whiting, and many kinds which never come into the market. At neap tides the case may be different, as for several tides the water may never leave the weirs. In some instances nets have been substituted for the wattled fence, and fewer small fish are said to be caught by them; but as a great many sprats are taken in this manner, the meshes must necessarily be very small; and we should think there was not much difference between them as regards their capacity for capturing small fish.

VII.—TRAMMEL OR SET NETS.

Description of ordinary set-nets — Used for catching turbot, hake, &c., and crabs in Scotland — Description of the true trammel — Its peculiar action — Red mullet at Guernsey.

UNDER this head we include all those nets which are set or fixed whilst they are at work; and in which the fish are caught by becoming entangled or "trammeled" in the meshes. Two kinds of net are, however, commonly spoken of under the name of "trammel"; and these, whilst agreeing in the manner in which they are set, differ considerably in their principle of construction and the mode in which they secure the fish.

The net generally called the trammel, especially in the south of Ireland, but a set-net on most parts of the coast of Great Britain, is of a very simple character, having much the form of the ordinary drift-net already described, and ranging, according to circumstances, from 20 or 30 yards to as much as 300 yards in length; the depth also varies, but never exceeds a very few yards. It is shot in the direction of the tide, and is anchored and buoyed at each end; the intermediate portion being supported by small cork floats placed at intervals along the back-rope, and the foot-rope is weighted with lead, or in some places with a simple and inexpensive substitute in the shape of stones sewn up in canvas. The size of the mesh varies according to the kind of fish the net is intended to catch; and as it is important that there should be a good deal of slack net so that the fish may be more easily meshed, the netting is shortened up and gathered into puckers along the edges where it is fastened to the ropes. It is easy to understand that round-fish like hake might be readily caught in such nets; and they are taken in large numbers by this method in the south of Ireland; but it would appear more difficult to capture flat-fish in the same manner. These nets, however, are successfully used for that purpose, especially on the coast of Yorkshire and Northumberland, for taking turbot; and under the name of "bratt-nets"[1] were formerly subject to special regulations as to the size of mesh and the length of time they were to remain in the water. Skate and other kinds of fish are also taken by these nets, and they are even used by some of the fishermen in the Firth of Forth for catching crabs or "partons," as they are there called. On the same and some other parts of the coast when the herrings are spawning, and consequently keeping very much at the bottom, it is the custom to "ground" the nets ordinarily used for drifting, and by anchoring them to convert them for a time into set-nets. In this manner large numbers of herrings are sometimes taken when none can be caught near the surface; and this mode of fishing for them is usually carried on during the day. Herring-nets are also occasionally set between stakes driven into the ground; but in such cases the nets are so placed as to intercept the fish when they are swimming near the surface. This plan, however, is seldom adopted except in localities where the poverty of the fishermen or the scarcity of fish prevents the ordinary methods of fishing being carried on.

The net to which the name of "trammel" is properly applied is not much used, except in particular localities,

---

[1] "Bratt" is the name commonly given by the fishermen along the north-east coast to the true turbot, and "turbot" is there applied to the holibut.

and is perhaps more commonly employed by the fishermen at the Channel Islands and in the south-west of England than elsewhere. We will take one of the Cornish nets for description, as it will fairly represent the principle on which they are all made. The trammel is composed of three long nets[1] placed side by side, and fastened together at the back, foot, and ends. Each outer net or "walling," as it is generally called, has a depth of five meshes 10 inches square, and is 40 or 50 fathoms in length. These wallings are mounted so that the meshes of both exactly correspond in position, and a fish might pass through them as if they were only a single net. The third net, however, is placed between the other two, and has a mesh only two inches square; but it is twice as long and as deep as the outer ones, the excess being gathered in at short intervals along the edges where the three nets are united. The result is a large quantity of slack netting through the whole extent of the trammel. Thus prepared, it is set in the usual manner in the direction of the tide, and anchored and buoyed at each end, the back of the net being corked, and the foot weighted as in the set-nets previously described.

The action of the trammel is peculiar. The outer nets or wallings stand with their meshes fully open and exactly opposite each other, with the small-meshed net between them; and a fish, in trying to pass through

---

[1] The word Trammel comes from the low Latin *tramallum* or *tramela*, which is derived from *tres macula*, i.e. three meshes; whence also *tramaglio*, Ital.; and *tremail*, *tramail*, Fr., more directly from *trois mailles* with the same signification as in the Latin.

Du Cange, in his Glossary, says, "TRAMALLUM, *Tramela*, Species retis ad capiendos pisces. Gallis, *Tremail* (spelt *Tramail* in modern French), Italis, *Tramaglio*, sic dicta, quod tribus *maculis*, vel triplice *macularum* ordine, quas *mailles* nostri dicunt, confecta sit."

It is a question, however, whether the trammel was first used for catching birds or fishes; it has long been employed for both purposes.

the first one, meets the second, which is very slack, and carries a portion of it through the third net, thus producing a bag or pocket beyond it. The more the fish struggles the more it becomes "trammeled"; and sometimes, in its efforts to escape, it carries the pocket back through the adjoining large mesh, making its case still more hopeless. The advantage of a walling on each side of the slack net is twofold: it obliges the fish to strike it just where it can be forced through the large mesh beyond it, and it makes the trammel equally effective if the fish strike it on one side or the other. In Cornwall the trammel is called a "tumbling-net."

It is very much used at Guernsey for catching the red mullet for which that island is celebrated; and it might be employed with advantage on many parts of our own coast, but its apparently complicated nature is against its being generally adopted by the ordinary class of fishermen.

FISHING STATIONS.

ENGLAND.

Annual returns of the number of fishing boats — Registration imperfect — Present classification of boats useless for any practical purpose — Ports and Port Letters — **Carlisle to Runcorn,** number of boats — Character of the fisheries — Trawling at Fleetwood and Liverpool — Morecambe Bay shrimping — Description of boats — **Beaumaris to Cardiff** — Welsh fisheries unimportant — Trawling at Carnarvon and Tenby — Oyster fishing at Milford and Mumbles — Weirs — **Bristol to Padstow** — Bridgewater Bay — Bag-nets at Burnham — Flat-bottomed boats — Barnstaple Bay and Bideford — **Hayle to Fowey** — Cornish fisheries — St. Ives pilchard fishery — Pilchard seans — Mode of working — Regulated by Act of Parliament — Landing the fish, curing, packing — Annual exports — Mackerel drift-fishery — Mount's Bay luggers — Line-fishing — "Tumbling-nets" — Oyster fishing at Falmouth — **Plymouth to Weymouth** — Plymouth trawlers — Scarcity of fish in Plymouth market since the opening of the railway — Line and drift fisheries — Brixham long famous for its fisheries — Supposed to have originated beam-trawling — Want of evidence on the question — Mr. Froude's mention of Brixham trawlers in the time of Elizabeth — Inaccurate reports on the recent condition of Brixham trawling — Steady increase of the fishery — Continued supply of fish — Line, drift, and sean fisheries in Torbay — Mackerel fishing at the Chesil Beach — **Channel Islands** — Mackerel fishing — Guernsey fishing boats — Cessation of the herring fishery — Congers, red mullet — Trammels, sand-eel seans — Jersey — Crabs and lobsters — Grey mullet caught by hook — **Poole to Newhaven** — Various fisheries — Keer-drag — Stow-boating in the Solent — Brighton "hog-boat" — Drift and sean fisheries — **Rye to Ramsgate** — Inshore and deep-sea trawling — Kettle-nets, shrimping — Whiting fishing — **Faversham to Colchester** — Fisheries from the Thames — Trawlers and cod-smacks — Water carriage and land carriage of fish — Steam-vessels and sailing carriers — Barking formerly an important station — Leigh shrimpers — Description of shrimp-net — Oyster dredging and stow-boating.

HAVING described the methods of sea fishing which are more or less in use around the British Islands, we propose now to give a general sketch of the character of the fisheries in the different districts, and to notice the principal stations which provide the means by which the larger supplies of fish are daily obtained for the market. To enter into many details on these subjects would involve a great deal of wearisome repetition; and, except in the case of the larger stations, it will be unnecessary to do more than indicate the general kinds of fishing in which the fishermen of the several districts are employed. The extent of the fisheries can be only approximately ascertained, as nothing less than an intimate acquaintance with every fishing town and village along the coast will enable one to understand how much is being done. The Annual Returns published by the Board of Trade of the number of fishing boats registered under the Sea Fisheries Act, 1868, promised materials for ascertaining the progress or otherwise of the fisheries during the last three years, so far as the mere number of boats in the three classes was any indication of the extent and character of the fishing. But the form in which the returns are given makes it impossible, even with a considerable knowledge of the localities, to say which boats or how many of them are engaged in any particular work. The number of boats given is also only approximately correct. In the first year of registration under the Act it was understood that boats of every description which under any circumstances were employed in fishing, whether for the purposes of sale or not, were to be included in the returns, and numbers of small private boats and a good many yachts of various sizes were consequently registered; but since the exemption, by a subsequent Order in Council,[1] of all boats not actually employed in the fishing trade, hundreds of craft have been taken off the register, and we understand that a further reduction will probably be necessary. It is also quite possible that many

[1] See Appendix.

boats in thinly-populated districts in Scotland and Ireland have not been enumerated; whilst, on the other hand, boats which have been broken up or sold will remain on the register unless notice be given for their removal. Considering the general class of persons to be dealt with, it is therefore not surprising that great difficulties should be found in obtaining perfectly accurate returns from year to year. However useful these returns may be in future, if prepared on an intelligible system of classification, the latest and most correct publication, that for 1872, gives nothing of practical value as regards the size of the boats, or anything by which the fisheries they are used for can be guessed. The number of First Class boats, those of 15 tons and upwards, is probably near the truth, and they will include trawl, drift, line, stow-net, and dredging boats up to the largest size. The Second Class boats are also employed for these purposes as well as for any other kind of fishing except, perhaps, in some cases, for seaning; for no matter how small a boat may be, so long as she sometimes carries a sail and is under 15 tons, she would go into the Second Class, unless the registering officers exercise the discretionary power given them to put small boats which sometimes carry a sail, into the Third Class. How often this is done it is impossible to say, but in the returns of English boats we find some under 10 feet keel in the Second Class, and many over 20 feet, and a few over 30 feet, keel in the Third Class. According to the present classification the Third Class boats may be such as are used for anything with the exception of trawling and stow-net fishing. More than half the fishing boats in Ireland are placed in this class; a large proportion of them probably under the discretionary power we have mentioned, as we can hardly believe there are as many as 4000 fishing boats there which never hoist a sail.

The returns are obtained through the Custom House, and each collectorship includes all the boats within its district, and has certain distinguishing letters with which all the fishing boats belonging to it are required to be marked.

Although these returns are by no means trustworthy, particularly those previous to 1872, it will not be desirable to omit all reference to them; we shall therefore give the number of registered boats for each Port according to the last return, and prefix the Port Letters by which all the boats belonging to it are distinguished. Some little idea may then be gained of the localities in which the fishing interests are strongest, and from which the larger supplies of fish are obtained for the market.

It will be convenient to take the three countries in succession, beginning with the north-west of England, and following the line of coast round to Berwick on the north-east; then taking Scotland and Ireland; and illustrations will be given of such kinds of fishing boats as are peculiar to the different parts of the coast.

CARLISLE TO RUNCORN—NUMBER OF BOATS.

Port Letters.	Port.	Year.	1st Class.	2nd Class.	3rd Class.
C.L.	Carlisle	1872	—	18	1
M.T.	Maryport	,,	1	48	2
W.O.	Workington	,,	—	14	—
W.A.	Whitehaven	,,	17	15	34
L.R.	Lancaster	,,	5	122	101
F.D.	Fleetwood	,,	53	27	—
P.N.	Preston	,,	3	46	—
L.L.	Liverpool	,,	35	137	10
R.N.	Runcorn	,,	3	35	17

The fisheries along the north-west coast of England are of a very varied character. Drift-fishing is neither important nor regular, as the herrings are uncertain in their visits; and when they make their appearance in the bays, where the fishing mostly takes place, a great many of the boats are not well provided with suitable nets for catching them. Trawling is carried on to a considerable extent, both inshore and off the land, and shrimping is an important fishery in many districts. Liverpool is the oldest of the deep-sea trawling stations on this part of the coast, but this fishery appears never to have been prosecuted with much energy, and the number of smacks there has been for many years subject to great fluctuation. Fleetwood has of late become the principal station, and the smacks sailing from that port have largely increased in size and number during the last twenty years. Whitehaven, Blackpool, and Southport, are also interested in deep-sea trawling, and the extension of railways along the coast has helped to develop this particular industry. The trawling grounds lie between the English coast and the Isle of Man, and some of the vessels, those belonging to Liverpool especially, work a good deal in Carnarvon and Cardigan Bays.

Inshore trawling by the smaller boats is very general in all the rivers and bays, both for flat-fish and shrimps, and the latter fishery is very productive. Morecambe Bay has long been famous for its shrimps, the fishery for which has been carried on there for a great number of years. The ground consists of a large extent of sandbanks, which for the most part are laid bare at low water, leaving innumerable channels between them; and in these the shrimps are found in myriads. The ordinary beam-trawl, but with a very short ground-rope and a half-inch mesh, is used for catching them; the boats engaged in this work being mostly half-decked, and cutter-rigged, and about five or six tons measurement; they carry a boom mainsail, gaff topsail, and large jib, and have each only one man, or sometimes a man and a boy, to work them.

Morecambe Bay Shrimper.

The shrimps are riddled as there may be time to do it between the hauls, and the small ones are thrown overboard with any young fish which may be taken with them. At times the sifting cannot be completely done on board, and the smaller shrimps are then taken on shore with the others and used for potting. From twenty-five to thirty quarts a day are considered a fair catch for a boat; and the shrimps have a large sale in the manufacturing districts, and are also well known in the London market. Longlines come into use in the latter part of the year, and besides more valuable fish taken in this way are considerable numbers of dogfish. It appears strange to hear a good word said of the mischievous and predatory "dogs"—the dread of most fishermen around the coast; nevertheless, they seem to be in request in certain parts of Lancashire, where they are sold under the name of "Darwen salmon!"

There is also a good mussel fishery on this part of the English coast.

BEAUMARIS TO CARDIFF—NUMBER OF BOATS.

Port Letters.	Port.	Year.	1st Class.	2nd Class.	3rd Class.
B.S.	Beaumaris	1872	2	58	68
C.O.	Carnarvon	,,	14	115	36
A.B.	Aberystwith		2	6	75
C.A.	Cardigan	,,	—	54	35
M.	Milford	,,	13	159	112
L.A.	Llanelly		2	—	—
S.A.	Swansea		3	184	—
C.F.	Cardiff	,,	—	1	—

The Welsh fisheries, so far as they depend on the native population, are quite unimportant, except with respect to oysters. There are a few large trawlers at Carnarvon and Tenby; but the Tenby ground and, as we have already mentioned, Carnarvon and Cardigan Bays are principally fished by trawlers from English stations. Line-fishing and a little drifting are carried on along the coast, but the boats in use are generally small and the supply of fish is barely sufficient for local demands. Oyster dredging is the principal work at Milford and Swansea on the natural beds in the neighbourhood; but at Beaumaris and Carnarvon there is very little done in that way except in connection with oysters brought from Ireland, and laid down to fatten for the market. The lazy methods of fishing by weirs and set-nets for herrings and chance fish are adopted in some places with occasional success; but, apart from what may be a question as to the abundance or scarcity of fish on the Welsh coast generally, the great development of the mining and quarrying industries in the Principality will always be likely to interfere with much local attention being given to a systematic prosecution of the sea fisheries, with their attendant uncertainties.

Tenby is the only really important place as a fishing station; and besides the trawl-smacks belonging to it, some of the Brixham vessels work on the Tenby ground every summer, which is the only time the fish are found there. The regular trawling season lasts from April to September; after that the Brixham men leave, and the smacks belonging to Tenby mostly lay up for the winter; a little trawling only going on at that season in Carmarthen Bay. The fishing ground lies between Lundy Island and Carmarthen Bay; and the general scarcity of trawl-fish in winter is believed to be owing to the disturbance of the ground by the heavy Atlantic swell setting into the funnel-shaped entrance of the Bristol Channel. In winter line-fishing and oyster dredging are especially carried on; and in the regular seasons mackerel, pilchards, herrings, and sprats are taken either by seans or fixed nets; but these fisheries are more or less uncertain. The boats used for dredging and line-fishing are large open ones, with a crew of three men in each; and carry a fore-lugsail and sprit mizen.

The principal fishery about Swansea is in connection

with Mumbles, or Oystermouth, as it is frequently called, and a considerable number of large open boats is employed from there in dredging for oysters along the

CLOVELLY AND TENBY FISHING BOATS.

coast and off the land. These oysters are brought in and laid down on " perches " or spaces between tide-marks, the boundaries between them being marked by lines of stones. Each fisherman, or those who work together, have their own perch, for which a small rent is paid to the owner of the foreshore, and the oysters are kept there until they are wanted for the market. Along the Swansea beach are placed the weirs and stop-nets previously noticed,[1] and in which sprats and other fish are occasionally taken. Line-fishing and a little inshore trawling are also carried on in this neighbourhood.

BRISTOL TO PADSTOW—NUMBER OF BOATS.

Port Letters.	Port.	Year.	1st Class.	2nd Class.	3rd Class.
B.L.	Bristol	1872	1	3	42
B.R.	Bridgewater	,,	—	69	25
B.E.	Barnstaple	,,	1	76	35
B.D.	Bideford	,,	8	117	11
P.W.	Padstow	,,	—	83	36

[1] See Weirs, p. 170.

On the southern side of the Bristol Channel we come to Bridgewater Bay, which is worked by a number of boats for both fish and shrimps; and, as in all large bays with only a slight depth of water, the fish found there are for the most part of small size. The sandbanks, however, are the haunts of immense numbers of shrimps, and the Burnham fishermen catch them in bag-nets set close to the ground, and suspended between stakes driven into the sand. As the tide leaves the banks dry the shrimps and small fish find their way into the bags, which have a funnel-shaped valve of netting inside, like the entrance to a mousetrap, not far from the end; so that the shrimps having once passed through are not well able to return. Numbers of fish too small to be of any use are caught in these nets, and at times there is said to be great destruction of small fry in consequence. This unfortunately is more or less the result with all the devices in use for catching shrimps. The boats used by the Burnham fishermen are flat-bottomed and sharp at both ends; they carry a small spritsail and foresail, and are worked by a couple of men.

BURNHAM FISHING BOAT.

Barnstaple Bay and the ground between that and Lundy Island are successfully fished by small trawlers from Barnstaple, Bideford, and Clovelly. Ground-seans are much used at Bideford for catching various kinds of fish; and, in the conflicting interests of sea fishing and salmon fishing, were, and probably still are, objects of terror and suspicion to the conservators of the neighbouring salmon streams. Drift-fishing is carried on by the inhabitants of the romantic little village of Clovelly, but the herring fishery has been for many years subject to great fluctuation. Longlines or spillers are in general use along this part of the coast, and a fair supply of good fish is procured by them.

At St. Agnes and Newquay, in the Padstow district, there is a commencement of the pilchard sean-fishery, which may be considered as almost peculiar to the coast of Cornwall; but as it is unimportant except south of Trevose Head, we shall defer our notice of it until we speak of St. Ives and the Cornish fisheries generally.

HAYLE TO FOWEY—NUMBER OF BOATS.

Port Letters.	Port.	Year.	1st Class.	2nd Class.	3rd Class.
H.E. or S.S.	Hayle	1872	56	162	91
P.Z.	Penzance	,,	41	166	73
F.H.	Falmouth	,,	8	280	165
T.O.	Truro	,,	—	28	111
F.Y.	Fowey	,,	16	324	118

The above five ports include all the fishing stations on the Cornish coast, except the few small ones in the Padstow district. The Cornish fisheries are very important, as is evident from the number of registered fishing boats engaged in them, and their produce is in great demand in the general, local, and foreign markets. The fisheries include drifting and seaning for mackerel, pilchards, and herrings, line-fishing, a little trawling, and general crab and lobster fishing. Oyster dredging employs a good many people at Falmouth, but there is not much work of this kind done on the other parts of the coast. The two principal fishing stations are Penzance, or Mount's Bay, as it might be more properly described, and St. Ives, which although, strictly speaking, coming within the port of Hayle, has the privilege of carrying the distinctive letters "S.S." on its boats. These two stations possess a fleet of fishing boats whose good qualities have long made them famous; and the enterprise and daring of their hardy crews have made Cornish fishermen respected wherever they have gone. St. Ives is especially famous for the extent of its sean-fishery, carried on more or less from September to November for pilchards; and this essentially Cornish fish then occupies the attention of everyone in the place. Under the head of "Seaning" a short and general account has been given of the manner in which this fishery is conducted, and we will now speak of it more in detail, and notice the regulations by which the numerous seans are worked within the limited space available for them. These regulations are for the most part embodied in a local Act of Parliament;[1] and as the working of the Act has met with general approval from those who are immediately affected by it, no change has been made, and it is not included among the numerous enactments repealed by the Sea Fisheries Act, 1868.

The pilchards strike the northern coast of Cornwall to the eastward of St. Ives, and the fishermen at Newquay and St. Agnes sometimes have a chance of using their seans; but the fish do not generally come in any numbers close to the land on their passage westward

[1] 4 & 5 Vict., c. 57.

until they are near St. Ives, when, in following the line of coast, they in some years enter and work round the bay in enormous shoals. Then is the seaner's opportunity; and the ground in some parts of the bay is so favourable for his work that very large captures of pilchards are sometimes made if the fish come within proper distance. The seaning ground is on the western side of the bay and extends southwards for about three miles from the bar. It is divided into six stations or "stems" by marks or boundaries on the land, in positions fixed by the local Act. These stations are known as the Carrick Gladden, the Poll, the Leigh, Porthminster, Pedn Olver, and Carrick Leggoe, or Carn Crowze; and no fishing boats besides those employed in the sean-fishery are allowed to fish or anchor within a certain distance of these stems between an hour before sunrise and the same period after sunset, from the 25th of July to the 25th of December; whilst any chance boats which may have occasion to pass within the limits of the stems must do so at not more than 20 fathoms from the shore. This fishery is rather uncertain, depending as it does on the fish coming well into the bay; but under favourable circumstances it is likely to be so valuable that it is for the general interest that everything else should give way to it. For this reason also no seans below a certain size are allowed to be used, so that the danger of disturbing a large body of fish and perhaps frightening them away without having secured a good haul may be as much as possible avoided. The smallest dimensions of a legal sean at St. Ives are 160 fathoms along the cork-rope, with a depth of 8 fathoms at the middle or bunt, and 6 fathoms at the end of the sleeves or wings. A certain length of tow-rope and warp to enable the net to be shot at a considerable distance from the shore is also required. It may appear remarkable to many persons that the Act should expressly state that the fathoms by which the nets and gear are to be measured are to be fathoms of six feet each; but there is a reason for it, inasmuch as the "fisherman's fathom" in the west of Cornwall usually consists of only five feet. We do not remember hearing of this short fathom on any other part of our coasts.

The above dimensions are the smallest allowed for these seans, but there is no limit in the other direction, except that imposed by the difficulty of working much larger nets. Those in use at St. Ives vary from 160 to 200 fathoms in length, and are from 8 to 10 fathoms deep; the meshes being from 18 to 20 to the foot, or about three-quarters of an inch square, and of the same size throughout. The back of the net is supported by a well-corked rope above, and the foot is weighted with leads a little over two pounds each. The quantity of netting in one of these seans is enormous, and the extent of it far exceeds the dimensions of the sean as prepared ready for use; for 18 feet of netting or "twine" are mounted on every 11 feet of back rope, and the same quantity of netting on 10 feet of rope at the foot. There is consequently a great deal of elasticity in the net between the back and foot ropes to meet the varying pressure of the fish when large numbers have been surrounded, and the two ends of the sean are brought together.

Besides the sean, but only in conjunction with it, one or two stop-nets, each not exceeding 120 fathoms in length, are used when first surrounding the fish, so that altogether about 400 fathoms of net are employed in one operation of seaning at St. Ives.

As there are nearly 250 seans there and only six

stations from which they can be worked, some arrangement is necessary to prevent confusion and interference, and to enable each sean to have its turn if possible. Some of the stations also are more favourable for working in than others; and the regulations in the Act specially relate to the manner in which the stems are to be taken possession of, and the length of time they are to be held. The seans are all registered, and many of them belong to companies. In practice it is found generally convenient for individual owners to unite into associations; and at a meeting of the sean-owners, held previous to the fishing season, it is usual to arrange all the seans in a certain number of groups as can best be managed, each group having so many turns according to its size, and then the order in which they are to work is decided on. It will be unnecessary to describe the minute details for which the regulations provide, as they are only of local interest; and we will now say a few words about the boats and method of working.

The "sean-boat" is about 32 feet on the keel, and with plenty of room for carrying the net; it has a crew of eight men, six of them for rowing and two for shooting the sean. Two "tow-boats," about 24 feet long, and each carrying a stop-net, with a crew of six men, make up the working party; but besides these there is a small boat, called the "lurker" or "volyer," from which the master of the sean directs all the proceedings. The position of the shoals is pointed out by men called "huers," who are selected from the sharpest and cleverest of the fishermen. There are generally two of them on the look-out on shore above each station, and they signal with a large white ball to the boats waiting below to take their turns. These men remain on duty for three hours at a time, and receive 3*l.* a month and one hogshead out of every hundred hogsheads of fish taken. We have already[1] given some account of the mode in which the nets are shot, and need here only repeat that the sean and stop-net are united, and the boats from which they are thrown out start from the same point, but at a right angle to each other, and ultimately meet again after enclosing as much of the shoal as they can manage to surround. When the circle has been contracted to the limits of the sean without the stop-net, the fish, if few, are taken out at once; but if the catch be considerable, the sean is hauled in towards the land by a warp and berthed in some convenient place, as much as possible out of the way of the tide, which is one of the great difficulties to be contended with in these large seaning operations. It is then securely moored, and if desirable additional support is given to the cork-rope by means of kegs. The fish are now practically secure and cannot escape below, as the foot of the net everywhere touches the ground, and the back-rope is well buoyed up. At low water the fish are taken out by means of the tuck-sean which is shot within the other net, and as it is hauled in the foot is raised and the fish are brought to the surface. They are then baled out in large oval baskets, well known in the West of England under the name of "flaskets," and taken on shore. The operation of landing and carrying the fish to the curing houses, as well as of hauling the sean towards the shore, is performed by a number of men termed "blowsers"; and it appears likely that the heaving in of the sean-warp, by means of a capstan on the beach, work in which everyone lends a hand, has given rise to the expression "*heav-ah, heav-ah*," which is heard on all sides when seaning is in

[1] Sean-fishing, p. 157.

progress, and the meaning of which has been the cause of much disquietude to the numerous persons who have endeavoured to fathom the mystery. We do not presume to speak authoritatively on the question, but it seems not unlikely that the explanation may be more simple than has often been imagined. The men employed in the various sean-boats receive 45s. a month each, and one-ninth of the fish between them; the division of the fish is made as soon as they are brought on shore, and every household does a little curing on its own account, for a Cornishman is not happy in his own county unless he have a stock of pilchards for his use in winter. The blowsers are paid in proportion to the catch of fish.

Curing is done generally, but there are some establishments in which the operation is carried out on a large scale, and the fish when properly prepared are exported to the Mediterranean, the Italian ports being the general destination. The curing is the especial work of the women, who pack the pilchards in alternate layers of coarse salt and fish on the stone floor of the curing house until the "bulk" has reached a height of 5 or 6 feet. Here the fish remain for a month, and the oil and brine draining from them are carried off by gutters in the floor to a cistern. When the fish have been sufficiently salted they are washed and packed in hogsheads with the heads outwards and a rosette of fish in the centre; a circular piece of wood called a "buckler," rather smaller than the head of the cask, is then placed on the top of the fish, and strong but gradual pressure is applied by means of a lever, until the mass of fish is reduced one-third in bulk, and a great quantity of oil squeezed from them; this drains through the sides and bottom of the cask, and is collected as before. The cask is filled three times before the pressing is finished, which is not until after eight or nine days, and then the hogshead of fish should be four hundredweight gross. The quantity of oil obtained from the pilchards depends on the season, but at least two gallons per hogshead are expected, the early fish—those obtained by the drift-nets—producing the most. It is much used by leather-dressers, and, like other kinds of fish oil, is probably employed for a variety of purposes. The average number of fish packed in a hogshead is about 2500; and although the pilchard fishery fluctuates a good deal from year to year, the variation depends more on the success or otherwise of the seans than anything else, as they cannot be worked unless the fish come within a certain distance of the land. In some years hardly anything has been done with these nets; whilst, on the other hand, as many as 5500 hogsheads were once actually saved from the part of a shoal enclosed by a single sean. This catch, we were told at St. Ives, was the largest on record, and far greater than what the fishermen are generally disposed to regard as a very successful haul.

Pilchard-seaning is carried on more regularly on the southern coast; but the nets are fewer, and as there is a larger choice of ground, there is not so much occasion for the various regulations which are almost a matter of necessity at St. Ives; many of them exist, however, as a matter of custom, and are generally approved of. Seans of very different sizes are in use; some of them equal to the largest at St. Ives, and others so small as to give rise to the complaint that many fish are lost because of their inability to enclose as many as might be taken if one of the larger nets were in possession of the ground. On the other hand, the obstruction the owners of small seans meet with from the larger men causes much complaint. Additional nets are not so much used on the south coast as at St. Ives, and the takes of fish by them are rarely so large as those on the northern shore.

Drift-fishing is largely carried on all round the coast, and is in great favour, the produce for the most part being taken for home consumption, whilst that of the large seans, belonging generally to wealthy proprietors, is cured for exportation.

Interference by the drift-boats with the proper working of the seans when the fish are very near the land was such a frequent cause of complaint that some restrictions were thought desirable by the Government when framing the Sea Fisheries Act, 1868; and the following regulations are now in force:—

31 & 32 Vict., cap. 45, sect. 68.

"On the coast of Cornwall, except so much of the north coast as lies east of Trevose Head, no person between the twenty-fifth of July and the twenty-fifth of November in any year—

"(a) shall, from sunrise to sunset, within the distance of two miles from the coast, measured from low-water mark (whether in bays or not), use a drift-net or trawl-net; or (b) shall, within half a mile of any sea-fishing boat stationed for seine-fishing, anchor any sea-fishing or other boat (not being a boat engaged in seine-fishing), or lay, set, or use any net, boulter, or implement of sea fishing (except for the purpose of seine-fishing);

"Any person who acts in contravention of this section shall be liable on summary conviction to a penalty not exceeding twenty pounds."

For the following table of the annual export of pilchards we are indebted to Messrs. G. C. Fox and Co., of Falmouth; it shows how great have been the fluctuations in this particular trade—one mainly dependent on the successful working of the sean-fishery:—

Year.	Hhds.	Year.	Hhds.	Year.	Hhds.	Year.	Hhds.
1815	15,000	1830	22,040	1845	30,807	1860	4,984
1816	20,000	1831	26,648	1846	34,137	1861	11,078
1817	21,000	1832	31,930	1847	11,623	1862	17,854
1818	1,700	1833	10,637	1848	7,594	1863	25,677
1819	2,900	1834	25,295	1849	25,588	1864	22,139
1820	800	1835	23,833	1850	25,530	1865	9,929
1821	2,000	1836	18,762	1851	26,736	1866	11,294
1822	9,123	1837	15,349	1852	15,283	1867	15,832
1823	21,109	1838	7,580	1853	21,276	1868	19,993
1824	7,611	1839	12,856	1854	6,815	1869	15,113
1825	12,651	1840	23,372	1855	6,103	1870	6,048
1826	10,670	1841	9,605	1856	18,833	1871	15,683
1827	5,238	1842	20,735	1857	15,921	1872	{ 1,138[1] / 18,406 }
1828	26,018	1843	8,859	1858	18,179		
1829	700	1844	13,976	1859	3,289	1873	31,019

The mackerel drift-fishery,[2] as well as that for pilchards, is very general on the Cornish coast, and the finest boats from Newlyn and Mousehole, in Mount's Bay, and other stations, are regularly employed in it during several months in the year. These boats run from 30 to 40 feet on the keel, with from 11 to 13 feet beam; they have a depth of 6 feet inside, and a good keel. The larger ones are decked, and the others, locally called "hatched boats," are partly decked, and have a large hatchway which can be closed in when necessary. They are all built with sharp sterns (Plate VIII.), and are remarkable for their good sailing and weatherly qualities. The lug-rig is universally adopted, only two masts being carried—a foremast and a mizen, the latter stepped well forward out of the way of the

---

[1] Previous season's fish.
[2] See Drift-fishing, p. 127.

Pl. VIII.

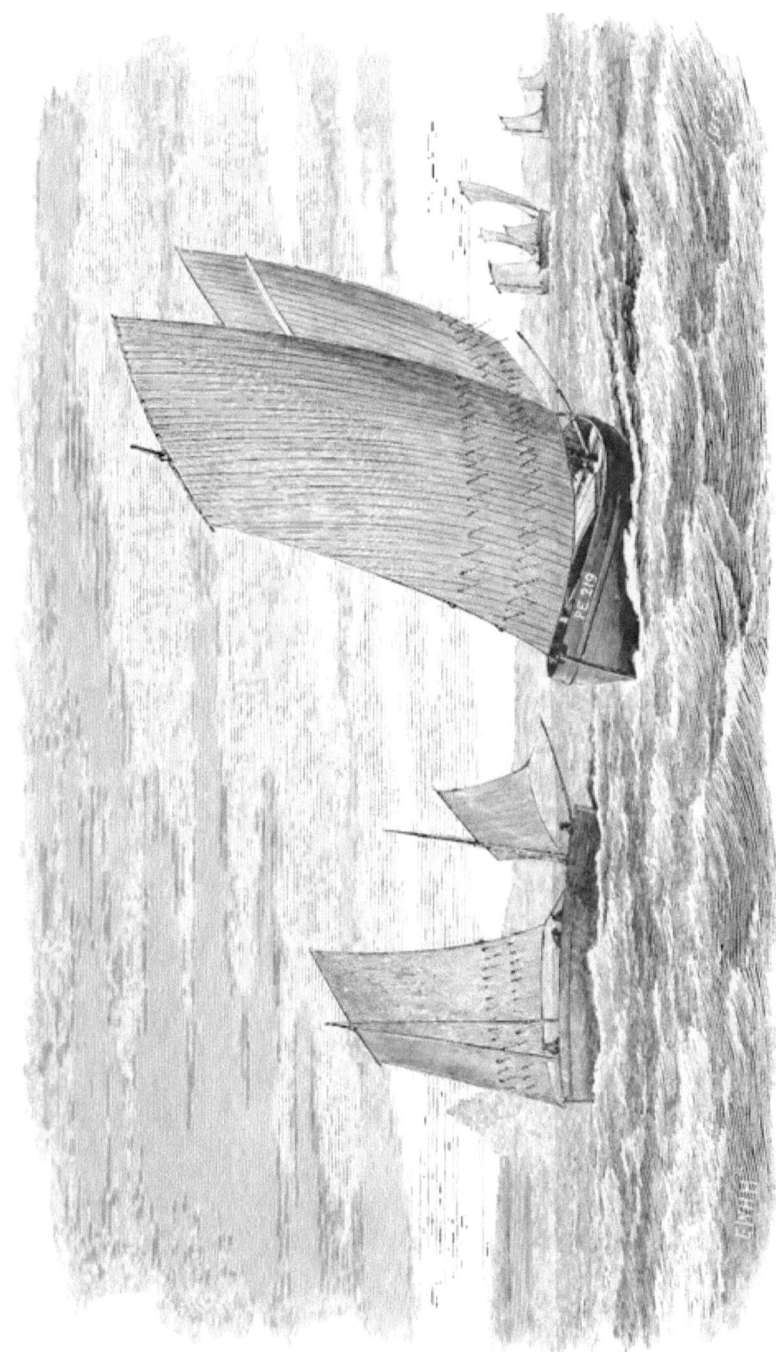

Mount's Bay Luggers.

tiller. In winter a stump mizenmast is used, but is shifted in summer for one with a standing topmast, so that a topsail may be carried. It is the custom to have several lugs of different size, the smaller ones being set on either mast, according to the weather; this is preferred to the ordinary practice of reefing, which, however, can also be done if necessary. Different classes of boats are professedly used for mackerel, herrings, and pilchards; but the largest boats are fitted out with nets for the three kinds of fish, and the herring boats have both herring and pilchard gear; the regular pilchard boats are the smallest, and have only their proper nets. The number of hands carried by each boat depends partly on her size and partly on the kind of fishing she is engaged in; the smallest boats have three men and a boy; the herring boats have an extra man; and the mackerel boats, when engaged in herring fishing, carry five men and a boy, their full complement being seven hands, which all the larger fishing boats take when they go after herrings to the Irish and North Sea fisheries. The first cost of the three classes of boats properly fitted out with nets ranges from about 120*l.* to nearly 600*l.*

Line-fishing is very general along the coast, but it is mostly by handlines; the boats coming to anchor at some miles off the land, and the distance at which they fish varying with the season. Whiting, bream, gurnards, and many other kinds of fish are taken in this manner. Trammels, in some places called "tumbling-nets,"[1] are also sometimes used; and the rocky western coast harbours a great many crabs and lobsters, which are taken in the well-known circular "pots," or baskets, with the entrance at the top.

[1] See Trammels, p. 175.

The oyster fishery at Falmouth has not escaped the depression which has been felt for some years past in the trade generally; but the ground on which they are found is very extensive. The oysters are collected by the dredgers, and sold to the merchants or dealers, who lay them down on parts of the shore which have been used for that purpose for a great number of years.

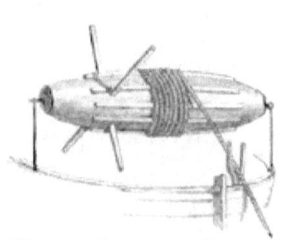

WINK IN DREDGING BOAT.

Most of the dredging is done by rowing boats; a small anchor or grapnel is let go, and 50 or 60 fathoms of rope paid out as the boat is rowed astern; the dredge is then put over, and the boat towing the dredge is hauled up to the anchor by means of a small wink fixed in the bow, and round which the rope passes. This is a very old method with the Falmouth dredgers.

PLYMOUTH TO WEYMOUTH—NUMBER OF BOATS.

Port Letters.	Port.	Year.	1st Class.	2nd Class.	3rd Class.
P.H.	Plymouth	1872	66	290	16
D.H.	Dartmouth	,,	136	270	93
T.H.	Teignmouth	,,	1	108	172
E.	Exeter	,,	—	210	103
L.E.	Lyme (Dorset)	,,	1	37	119
B.T.	Bridport		—	24	54
W.H.	Weymouth	,,	3	83	253

The section of the coast we now have to notice includes two stations which have long been famous as the head-quarters of beam-trawling in the West. These are Plymouth and Brixham; the latter belonging to the port of Dartmouth. Trawling no doubt was carried on from Plymouth before the beginning of the present century, as fifty years ago there were thirty smacks belonging to the port, but they were only of half the size of most of the fine vessels now at work there. In those times the supply of fish must have been generally sufficient, and often more so than, to meet the demand for the town and those parts of the neighbourhood within reach of the hawkers; and we have often heard of the abundance of fish there used to be in the local market, and the low prices at which it could be purchased. The population was then comparatively small, and they had the full benefit of most of the fish brought in, for there were no means of sending away more than a very small quantity. By the last return there were sixty-six trawl-smacks belonging to Plymouth, averaging 34 tons N.M., which, for this style and class of vessel, would be equivalent to nearly double the tonnage by builder's measurement. The present smacks are not only more than double the number of those at work fifty years ago, but they are of twice the size; yet fish is now often scarce in the Plymouth market, and high prices must generally be paid for it. These facts are sometimes considered as quite sufficient to prove that the sea fisheries have very greatly declined and are rapidly going to ruin. But it must not be forgotten that the vast increase in the local population has caused a very much greater demand for the fish— that the railway has for the last thirteen or fourteen years carried away hundreds of tons of fish annually to parts of the country where, in the old times of abundance at Plymouth, such an article of food was scarcely seen from one year's end to another; and, lastly, that even with the present higher prices, the Plymouth trawlers must catch a very large quantity of fish, or they would not be able to build and keep up a fleet of such costly vessels as they have had in use for some years past. The conclusion that the fisheries are declining does not appear therefore to be well founded.

The trawling ground off Plymouth is, as we have before mentioned, of very limited extent, being about 21 miles in length and 9 miles in its greatest breadth; the larger portion of it is west of the Eddystone, and inside that well-known mark. The frequent bad weather in winter often puts a stop to all kinds of fishing outside the Breakwater, and the consequent fluctuation in the success of the deep-sea fishery has at times checked the development of the trawling interests. The Plymouth men keep almost entirely on their own ground, and except at certain times when they work specially for soles, all their fishing is done by daylight. Their general practice is to go out early in the morning, and to return in the afternoon. Besides trawling there is hooking, both by hand and longlines; and drift-fishing for mackerel, herrings, and pilchards is also carried on; but the drift-boats which work from Plymouth belong to a large extent to other ports, the direct railway communication from the town giving them great facilities for sending away their fish. There is also a sprat fishery by seans in winter. It is believed that the deposit of mud in the Sound, due to the erection of the Breakwater, has destroyed many of the feeding grounds of fish which are said to have been at one time plentiful inshore.

Brixham, situated on the south side of Torbay, has long been famous for its connection with the sea fisheries; and has good grounds for disputing with Barking the honour of being considered the mother-port of our deep-sea beam-trawlers. The commencement of this method of fishing cannot now be traced; it is quite possible, however, that it was in use in bays and sheltered places, where small craft could be employed, long before it was attempted in the open sea. There is plenty of evidence that at the beginning of the present century trawl-boats and the nets they used were very much smaller than those now employed; and it appears likely that, as we have suggested, the advantages of the beam-trawl were first ascertained by working with small nets in shoal water. It is worthy of notice that on the many parts of the coast of the United Kingdom where this method of fishing is carried on by small craft inshore, the same general triangular form of trawl-head is adopted; and this, with a few modifications, is used by all the deep-sea trawlers from Brixham and the stations colonized by men from that town. Barking, on the other hand, has a pattern[1] of its own; and it was only used by vessels from the Thames until they adopted Great Yarmouth as a fishing station; since that time trawling has been rapidly gaining favour with the Yarmouth and Lowestoft men, and the Barking pattern is now more or less in use at those ports, both by native and London smacks. From its localization, and its peculiar and more symmetrical shape, it appears likely to have been intended as an improvement on the pattern in general use on other parts of the coast; and therefore does not afford any evidence as to when trawling was begun by the Barking fishermen.

We are not disposed to think deep-sea trawling has been carried on for any very long period, either from Brixham or Barking; it is true that there is not much evidence to be obtained on the point; but Barking

[1] See Trawl-head, A, p. 56.

appears to have first become famous as a fishing station on account of its welled-smacks which were used for the North Sea cod fishery, as is the case now; and we know that at the beginning of the present century the Brixham trawlers were of small size. But if we may rely on Mr. Froude in this matter, Brixham had seagoing trawlers in the time of Elizabeth and the Spanish Armada, which will take us back to 1588—nearly three hundred years ago. In his description[1] of the English attack on the Spanish fleet, he says :—" Drake returning from the chase, came up with her (the *Capitana*, the Admiral's disabled ship.) in the morning. She struck her flag, and he took her with him to Torbay, where he left her to the care of the Brixham fishermen, and himself hastened after the Admiral. . . . . . The prize proved of unexpected value. Many casks of reals were found in her, and, infinitely more important, some tons of gunpowder, with which the *Roebuck*, the swiftest trawler in the harbour, flew in pursuit of the fleet."

In the course of a search for more information on this trawling question, we found the same vessel referred to in the ponderous work by " Mr. Oldmixon,"[2] who says—"At which instant a great galeon (the Admiral's ship) lost her foremast, and Sir Francis Drake in the *Revenge* took her . . . . and Sir Francis sent the *Roebuck* with her into Dartmouth."

He gives the names of the 88 ships composing the English fleet then in the Channel, only 35 of them apparently belonging to the Royal Navy; but the rest are described as " Other Ships of the best Sort"; and as they formed part of the English fleet, they were

---

[1] *History of England*, vol. xii., p. 397, Cabinet Edition (1870).
[2] *History of England* (Henry VIII.—Elizabeth), p. 588 (1730).

undoubtedly armed vessels. Among the first six of these stands the "*Roebuck, Sir Walter Raleigh.*" The remaining ships, forming more than half the fleet, are given under the heading of the towns by which they were provided.

The Roebuck is evidently spoken of as one of the armed ships, and not a mere fishing vessel; but although we will not venture to say the two versions are incapable of reconciliation, we should have been glad if comparing them had lessened our first doubt about there having been trawlers at Brixham so long ago as 1588.

We will now turn to modern Brixham, and say a few words about what has been the condition of the trawl-fishery there in recent years. The subject has some interest in connection with the allegation that beam-trawling not only causes a wasteful destruction of fish, but leads to a permanent exhaustion of the fishing grounds. The conclusions arrived at by the Royal Sea Fisheries Commissioners after an exhaustive inquiry into the subject in 1863–5 were to the effect that whilst trawling, like almost every other method of sea fishing, caused the destruction of a certain number of young fish, there was not the slightest appearance of the trawling grounds having become exhausted; but, on the contrary, the continual increase in the number of trawl-smacks was strong evidence that the supply of fish to be obtained from the grounds was greater than had ever been believed; for it seemed impossible to suppose that men would year after year invest their savings in vessels for the purpose of carrying on this particular method of fishing, if the supply of fish were year after year becoming less. Yet there are many people at the present time who adhere to the belief that the trawling grounds are becoming exhausted; and considering how much has been written on the subject by persons who were imperfectly acquainted with its merits, it is not surprising that the effects of beam-trawling should have been often misrepresented. We shall only notice, however, two reports on the state of the Brixham fisheries which have been published as official documents, and have therefore some claim to be regarded as authoritative.

In October, 1852, Mr. J. R. Barry, then Inspecting Commissioner of Irish Sea Fisheries, was deputed by his colleagues to visit Brixham for the purpose of ascertaining the condition of its trawl-fishery; and his report on the subject was published in the Appendix to the Commissioners' general Report for that year.

In May, 1863, Mr. Barry was again sent to Brixham with the same object, and his second report was published in the same form as the first; but as in this second report he quotes largely from that for 1852, it will be sufficient if we consider the quotations and statements in the last publication.[1]

At page 11 he says, referring to his report of 1852: "At that time I stated, 'Lieutenant Hoblyn, R.N., Chief Officer of Coastguards, from whom I received every assistance, states that there are now 224 trawling vessels marked and numbered out of the port, ranging from 25 to 45 tons, all cutter-rigged. They are called sloops, carvel built, and all exclusively beam-trawlers.'"

Now at the end of 1852, according to the Parliamentary Return of British Shipping, there were only 172 sailing vessels of 50 tons and under on the register

[1] *Report of the Deep-Sea and Coast Fishery Commissioners, Ireland*, for 1863, Appendix, pp. 11-14.

at Dartmouth, which is the port of Brixham. These would include all the Brixham "smacks" (as they are always called), besides pilot boats and a few other vessels. It is difficult to account for the mistake in the number of trawlers said to have been given by Lieutenant Hoblyn, unless he took the highest figures on the register as representing the number of smacks then existing; he perhaps not having been aware that the cancelled numbers of vessels lost or otherwise removed were not again used. Mr. Barry appears, however, to have been content with this information, and to have understood the figures as referring to the number of smacks actually working from Brixham, which a very little inquiry would have shown to be incorrect. Brixham has long been sending her men and fishing vessels to other stations, where many of them have permanently settled. Ramsgate, Dublin, Hull, and other places have thus been colonized, but those vessels have for many years afterwards remained on the original register at Dartmouth. The number of trawlers regularly working on the Brixham ground in 1852 has been inquired into at Brixham, at our request, with the result that at that time there were only about 70 smacks, ranging from 23 to 35 tons, instead of 221.

When Mr. Barry made his second visit to the town, in May, 1863, he reported having been struck with the same appearance of prosperity which he observed in it in 1852; but he explained this as being due to "its progressive state of transition from a prosperous fishing town to an important seaport," for he had heard at the Custom House that the number of trawlers on the register were then only 167. These he appears to have again understood as all working from Brixham.

In October in that year the Royal Sea Fisheries Commissioners held their public inquiry at Brixham into the condition of the trawl and other fisheries carried on from that town, and it was part of our duty as Secretary to that Commission to seek for evidence on the subject from all classes who were acquainted with it. The conflicting interests of the different kinds of fishermen led to a great deal of contradictory statement on many points; but it was unanimously agreed that the trawlers had been increasing in size and number for some time, particularly during the previous seven years. The President of the Fishing Club stated in his evidence that 95 smacks then belonged to Brixham, of which 85 regularly fished from that town, and the others did so during part of the year. One hundred and fifty-two vessels were insured by the Club, the only condition being that they belonged to Brixham men, but 57 of those vessels were permanently settled at other ports.

The Brixham trawlers, which according to Mr. Barry had decreased from 221 to 167 between 1852 and 1863, had really increased from about 70 to 85 during that interval.

Mr. Barry's belief in the decline of the fisheries at Brixham was confirmed, however, by observing that, at the census of 1861, the population of the town of Brixham had decreased by 1237, or nearly *one-fourth*, since the census of 1851; but startling as this great falling off at first appeared to him, he found a ready explanation of it, and said (page 14) :—"This extraordinary decrease may be accounted for in a great degree by the diminished number of fishing vessels."

The census return for 1861, which showed so great a decrease in the town population, gave, however, a slight increase in that of the whole parish, which Mr. Barry does not mention, and probably did not observe; and the discrepancy has been explained by the Registrar-General in a very simple manner, namely, that the limits of the *town* were first defined in 1851, and only about 300 of the population of the *parish* were then excluded; but in 1861, when more correct boundaries were fixed, about 1600 were excluded from the town. The apparent decrease was therefore solely due to the alteration of the *town* boundaries.

In the census of 1871, the town population of Brixham is that included within the Local Board District Boundaries, which are not quite the same as those fixed in 1861. But the census returns for fishing towns like Brixham are really of little value, as the number of fishermen on shore on any particular day is subject to variation. For example, the last enumeration took place on a Sunday, when most of the smacks were in port, and a large portion of their crews sleeping on shore; and the return shows a considerable increase in the population, partly from this cause; but although these fishermen may be legitimately included among the inhabitants of the town, their exclusion on former occasions by the mere accident of the day on which the census was taken, makes a comparison of the returns useless for judging of the increase or decrease of the local fisheries.

The number of fishing smacks on the Dartmouth register at the end of 1872 was 136; and with one or two exceptions they all belonged to Brixham men, either living at home or settled at other stations. There was a slight increase between 1863 and 1872 in the number of smacks regularly working from Brixham, nearly 100 vessels having been thus engaged in 1872; and the trawl-fishery has never been more prosperous than in recent years. This no doubt has been partly owing to the increased demand for fish and the higher prices obtained for it; but it clearly points to the fact that the Brixham fishing ground has not yet been exhausted, although it has been regularly and systematically trawled over by an increasing number of smacks for probably a hundred years. If Mr. Froude may be relied on, we may nearly treble that time, but we are content with the shorter period, about which there appears to be little question. We have already mentioned the extent of the regular Brixham trawling ground, but it may be desirable to speak of it again in this place. It lies between the neighbourhood of Start Point and a little to the north-east of Torbay, and is about 20 miles in length and of variable width, but mostly from 3 to 8 miles off the land. Some of the smacks occasionally go a little farther eastward or westward; in the summer a few visit Tenby, and in the winter about a dozen fish in the North Sea, but nine-tenths of the work is done on the home ground, and all the year round.

It will be unnecessary to say more about this last report, the general tenor of which is strongly adverse to fishing with the trawl, which, after having been carried on for nearly a century, was then more thriving and more extensively worked than had ever been known; and we should not have noticed either of the reports if Mr. Barry had not been known for so many years as the Inspecting Commissioner of Irish Sea Fisheries, and the chief adviser in all cases involving the making of regulations for their management previous to the appointment of the present three inspectors of the general fisheries of the sister country.

It must be remembered, moreover, that these reports were specially made to satisfy the desire of the Irish Commissioners for trustworthy information about the effects of trawl-fishing where it had been carried on for a great number of years on the same ground; they have been widely circulated and frequently quoted; it is therefore impossible to avoid some reference to their contents, especially as they are so little in harmony with what we have found it necessary to record as the real facts of the case.[1]

Before the extension of the railway to Brixham the fish landed from the trawlers was sent away by light carts to the nearest station; the smacks usually came in with their fish in the afternoon, and a large display was made in the market as the proceeds of the day's work were brought on shore. But a great change has taken place in this respect. The fish is now forwarded by fast passenger trains several times in the day, and the smacks come in at all hours, the majority of them in the morning, so that the fish is sent off to many parts of the country early enough to reach the consumer on the same day. The sales are made by the old-fashioned Dutch auction, beginning at a high price and reducing it until within the value set upon it by the would-be buyers. In the wholesale fish trade at Brixham, women as well as men are engaged as auctioneers—a custom not much in vogue at other large markets. A great deal of the fish is sent to Bristol, whence it is distributed to various parts of the country according to instructions telegraphed from Brixham, orders being frequently received for it by

---

[1] Our comments on these reports were submitted last year to the Inspectors of Irish Fisheries, but as we were subsequently informed that Mr. Barry had retired from the service, we sent a copy of them early in January last direct to that gentleman.

P

"wire" some time after the trains have departed with their freights. Ice is largely used in packing the fish, but none is taken to sea by these trawlers, as their fishing ground is only a few miles distant, and they land their fish every day. When this has been done, the smacks generally go off again, except on Saturdays, it having been always the practice of the fishermen to remain at home from that day till Monday morning, when the whole fleet again goes to sea. The trawlers work on the share system—undoubtedly the best for all parties. The master has generally some interest in the vessel, and he takes care that she is worked with due regard to economy, and that whilst no necessary expense is spared in keeping her sails and gear in proper order, everything is made to last as long as possible. This is one of the secrets of profitable sea fishing; and the absence of the constant interested supervision of the owner or part-owner of a fishing vessel is a principal cause of the failure of most joint-stock fishing companies.

The smacks which have been built of late years, either at home or at Dartmouth, for the Brixham men, have cost from 900*l*. to 1000*l*. each. They carry from four to five hands, of whom one or two are apprentices.

Besides trawlers there are a good many small hookers of four or five tons each, which work from Brixham and Torquay. They are used for handline, and quite recently longline, fishing for whiting, bream, cod, and other kinds of fish which are obtained at ten or twelve miles off the land, or at a less distance according to the time of year. In the summer when the mackerel come into the bay, these boats are often busily employed in catching them, and short poles are rigged out on each side, to which extra lines are attached, as, when the mackerel are biting freely, it is as well to use as many lines as can be conveniently managed.

Torbay Hooker.

Herrings, and sometimes pilchards, are caught by the Torbay boats, but the drift-fishing is not important. Seans are used principally on the Torquay side of the bay for mackerel and other kinds of surface-swimming fish, and large quantities of sprats are often taken in winter by these nets.

In Start Bay there are several small villages from which the fishermen work with ground-seans for various kinds of fish, the long sweep of sandy beach on that part of the coast being very favourable for such kind of fishing. Many years ago pilchards were regularly

p 2

taken there, and some buildings on the beach, well known by the name of Slapton Cellars, were, we believe, erected for the purpose of curing the fish in; but pilchards do not now regularly appear in any numbers much to the eastward of the Start. Fishing by handlines and longlines, or bulters, as they are generally called in the West of England, is also carried on; and there are many localities along this part of the coast in which crabs and lobsters are numerous.

The fisheries to the east of Torbay are mostly by line and seans; the latter are much used between Teignmouth and Exmouth for mackerel, herrings, and occasionally for pilchards. Drift-fishing is carried on to some extent from Beer, in the Lyme district, and small luggers — an unusual rig for fishing boats between Cornwall and Sussex — are used for the purpose. We need only further notice on this line of coast the somewhat extensive mackerel fishery by seans along the Chesil Beach, chiefly between Bridport and Portland. These seans are about 150 fathoms long and 10 fathoms at the greatest depth, with a small-meshed bag or pocket in the middle of the bunt. They are worked as ground-seans, and hauled in on the beach. The mackerel season lasts from about April to October.

There is also a little trawling in Weymouth Bay.

CHANNEL ISLANDS.

It will be convenient to say a few words here about the Channel Islands, as their geographical position and the character of their fisheries connect them with the part of the English coast we have just been considering.

GUERNSEY FISHING BOATS.

The following is the number of fishing boats which were on the register in 1872:—

Port Letters	Port.	Year.	1st Class.	2nd Class.	3rd Class.
J.	Jersey	1872	72	583	147
G.U.	Guernsey				

Guernsey is the only one of the islands whose fisheries require particular notice, as it not only provides for its own necessities, but helps to supply the Jersey and London markets. The fisheries are of a varied description and include those by drift-net, sean, trawl, trammel, and line. One of the most important is the drift-fishery for mackerel. It begins at about the middle or end of May, and lasts for ten or twelve weeks. It is mostly carried on to the west of the island, and at from 10 to 30 miles from the land; but in the later part of the summer the mackerel appear nearer home, and are then taken by the hook, very large ones being frequently caught at that time—some of them, it is said, weighing as much as two pounds and a half. A fleet of mackerel-nets as used by the Guernsey fishermen is from 1200 to 1500 fathoms long, but there is a considerable additional length of netting included in this measurement, as it is set slack on the back-rope or "rawling" in the proportion of 135 fathoms of netting to 100 fathoms of rope.

There is a fine class of boats used for this drift-fishery, and they are peculiar in both their build and style of rig. They run from 27 to 36 feet on the keel, the largest boats having 12 feet beam and drawing over 6 feet water aft, with less than half that draught forward.

The rig of these boats (Plate IX.) is that of a fore-

and-aft schooner, but with the addition of a mizen lug, which, however, is not always carried; topsails are set in light weather. A regular deck is laid as far aft as the mainmast, but beyond that the boat is open, and both masts can be lowered when fishing is going on. The smaller boats, used for more inshore fishing, have the same general character of build. A few years ago they were rigged with a jib, fore and main spritsails, and occasionally a mizen, either a small triangular sail or a spritsail; but more recently the gaff-sails have been gaining favour, and most of the small boats are now rigged in the same way as the large ones. The rapid tides and innumerable scattered rocks along the coast of the Channel Islands make the navigation there very dangerous at most times, and all the skill of the fishermen would avail them but little if they had not boats which sailed as well and were as easily handled as those which are characteristic of the islands.

The large mackerel boats carry five hands, and each man receives one share of the produce of the fishing, the boat takes another, and a seventh goes to the salesman. The small boats usually have two men in them.

Pilchard fishing is of comparatively recent introduction at Guernsey; it is carried on with small seans from June to November.

The sometimes capricious movements of the herrings have been well illustrated by the sudden disappearance of these fish from the Guernsey waters, as has before now been the case at other localities; but there is a story current in the island, which in this instance offers a remarkably simple explanation of the matter. We give it in substance as it was told to us:—

"There used to be a good fishery for herrings at Guernsey till 1830, when it suddenly came to an end.

On the evening of Easter Day in that year some boats, contrary to the usual custom of not fishing on a Sunday, went out with their drift-nets in pursuit of the herrings, and succeeded in catching some thousands of these fish. The herrings were brought on shore and sold readily in the market; but as the fishermen were bringing their captures to the market-place they were met by an old man whose many years had been spent on the stormy seas which wash the rocky shores of the island, and who, throughout his long career, had been accustomed to regard Sunday as a day of rest alike for fishes and fishermen. He inquired of the fishermen, now heavily laden with their spoil, 'When did you catch these fish?' 'Last night—Sunday night,' was the reply. 'Sunday night!' said he; 'then we shall have no more herrings.' There has been no herring fishery at Guernsey since that year!"

Herrings used also to be caught there by seans.

Guernsey is particularly famous for its congers; the rocky character of the coast there being well suited to the habits of this fish. Trots or longlines are employed for catching it, and squid is considered the best sort of bait from September to February; afterwards fish-bait of certain kinds is more generally used. Very large congers are sometimes caught there, and the museum at St. Peter's Port contains an example taken at the end of 1844, which measured 7 feet 6 inches in length and scaled 96 lbs. Guernsey weight, equal to more than 100 lbs. English. Conger is the important ingredient in the white soup so much in favour in the island.

Among the fish taken with handlines pollock, there

[1] The Guernsey fish evidently must have had much greater respect for the ordinances of the Church than those herrings which were said to have forsaken some other coast as soon as the newly-appointed vicar of the parish intimated his intention of taking tithe of the fish.

called "whiting," deserve notice, as they are abundant and of large size; but the true whiting is a very scarce fish on the Guernsey coast, although so numerous on the English side of the Channel.

Fishing with trammels is very general at Guernsey and the other islands, and one of the most profitable methods in use there. The true trammel, made up of three nets,[1] is the one employed, and the usual length of the outer nets or "walling" is 50 fathoms, the central net or "lint" being twice as long, although contracted to the limits of the others. Trammels are worked from July to the end of the year, and with most advantage about dusk and daybreak. The evening is the time generally chosen; in the summer the nets are set about 6 P.M. and taken up at 9, and in the shorter days of winter the fishermen are on the ground as early as 3 o'clock in the afternoon, and the nets are hauled in after being a couple of hours in the water. They are set in places where the tide is not very strong, and in the direction of the stream—not across it. It is in these nets that the red mullet for which Guernsey has such a name are taken. These fish are found there of a considerable size, $2\frac{1}{2}$ lbs. being no unusual weight for them; they rank high among "prime" fish, and the London market is always a safe one to send them to. Mullet will not take the net well in the dark, and in this respect differ remarkably from those kinds of fish which are generally taken by drift-nets, and which it is well known are caught in the largest numbers during dark nights, or when the water is discoloured. Of the other fisheries there is not very much requiring notice. A little trawling is carried on all the year round with nets having beams 18 feet to 20 feet long, but the nets

[1] See Trammel, p. 175.

differ from those in general use elsewhere in the number of the pockets, two, or even three, of them being made along each side. The advantage of these additional receptacles is not very obvious to us, but we have had no opportunity of using nets fitted in this manner.

Seans are employed for taking sand-smelt and sand-eels; the latter, when used alive, being a most killing bait for almost every kind of line-fish. We are informed by Mr. J. C. Wilcocks, who has been for many years intimately acquainted with the Guernsey fisheries, that the advantages of the living sand-eel as a bait have been recognized in the islands from time immemorial; and its use on our own coasts is strongly advocated by that gentleman in his thoroughly practical work on sea fishing[1]—written especially for the benefit of amateurs, but from which very many professional fishermen may obtain hints likely to be profitable to them. The sand-eel sean—also an old institution—is peculiar in having the bunt made of unbleached calico, with vertical gorings of fine netting inserted for the more easy passage of the water through it.

The Jersey fisheries, although of much the same character as those at Guernsey, are on a considerably smaller scale, not so much from any particular scarcity of fish, but because the Jersey men give their time to other occupations. The oyster fishery there, which for many years was of great importance, has very much fallen off, and now provides employment for only a few boats.

As might be expected from the rocky nature of the coast and the extent of suitable ground among the islands generally, lobsters and crabs are abundant, and a considerable fishery for them is carried on. The

[1] *The Sea-Fisherman*, Longmans and Co., 2nd edition (1868).

Minquiers rocks are among the most productive localities. The "pots" or basket traps in use are of the same hemispherical shape as in the West of England, and from fifty to ninety of them are worked by a boat with a couple of men. The largest lobsters and crabs are taken in deep water, but it has been found that those from shallower places are more capable of living through a long journey to market. As many as a hundred dozen of lobsters are often taken in a week during July by the Jersey fishermen, and large numbers are also captured at the other islands. Crawfish are also numerous at several localities, including Sark and the western side of Guernsey; and very fine prawns are occasionally caught by the same method as is employed for the larger crustacea, but with pots of a much smaller size. Shrimps are fished for with the common hand or "shove"-net.

On some parts of the Jersey coast grey mullet are taken in some numbers by the hook, and the plan there adopted, although now doubtless more widely known, was a few years ago apparently confined to the island. The fisherman having selected a station on some point of land with deep quiet water close to it, proceeds to bait the place by throwing in the soft bodies of prawns which have been removed from their outer casing and pounded to a pulp. This ground-baiting gradually collects the mullet; and after an hour or two the fisherman returns to his station, and with a stout rough rod and line, and a hook baited with a solid piece of the soft prawn, begins his fishing, and frequently succeeds in making a very good catch, at the same time keeping up the attraction by occasionally throwing in a little of the paste.

The number of Jersey men who regularly devote

themselves to the home fisheries is comparatively small; but some hundreds go away to the Newfoundland cod fishery for the season, and on their return many of them ship as sailors instead of taking to such fisheries as may then be in progress at home.

POOLE TO NEWHAVEN—NUMBER OF BOATS.

Port Letters.	Port.	Year.	1st Class.	2nd Class.	3rd Class.
P.E.	Poole (Dorset)	1872		61	16
S.U.	Southampton ..	,,	17	111	102
C.S.	Cowes (I.W.) ..	,,	5	182	101
P.	Portsmouth ..	,,	18	217	21
L.I.	Littlehampton	,,	2	156	36
S.M.	Shoreham	,,	18	171	132
N.N.	Newhaven (Sussex)	,,	8	52	97

Almost every kind of fishing is carried on within the limits of the above range of stations, and we now for the first time meet with sprat fishing by the stow-net. As we have already fully described[1] this net, and the manner in which it is worked, it will be unnecessary to say more now than that it is used in the Solent from November to February by fishermen from Itchen Ferry, Cowes, and Portsmouth. Several kinds of fishing on a small scale are carried on in the extensive sheet of water known as Poole Harbour, and among them we may notice shrimping with a net called the keer-drag—a flat conical bag of very fine mesh fastened to a narrow oblong frame, of which the sides and foot are made of iron and the back of wood. It is in fact very like an oyster-dredge, without any scraper, and works well over smooth ground. Spritsail boats, about 18 feet long, are in general use in Poole Harbour. Oyster dredging in the Solent

[1] The Stow-net, p. 161.

employs a great many boats from the adjoining shores; and the drift, line, and sean fisheries are worked according to season and locality on various parts of the coast of Hampshire, Sussex, and the Isle of Wight. Brighton, in the Shoreham district, is the best known among the regular fishing stations, and employs a large number of men with the drift and sean nets. The almost continuous line of beach on the Sussex coast requires a particular style of fishing boat for convenience in launching and hauling up where there is no harbour; they are accordingly built with very flat floors and large bilge-pieces to keep them upright when they are out of the water. Brighton once had a name for a class of boats in which these peculiarities were carried to excess, and there are still a few left of the old style—"hog-boats," as they are called, the representatives of what many years ago was the typical form of Brighton fishing boat. They are not without their admirers at the present day. These boats are rigged with two spritsails, a foresail, and jib, and are now mostly used for trawling.

The more modern boats, which are used for drift-fishing, are much finer craft, although retaining a good deal of the old style of build; they are longer boats, however, and sail faster, but without any loss of sea-going qualities; and are all rigged as luggers—the most convenient style for drift-fishing. The general tendency around the coast towards an increase in the size of fishing boats, so as to make them more suitable for regular deep-sea work, is shown at Brighton as well as at other places; and we hear that the smaller drift-boats are being got rid of and larger ones taking their places as fast as they can be turned out by the regular builders. The large class of boats are used for the mackerel fishery, and go as far away as the Land's End at the beginning of the season. The other

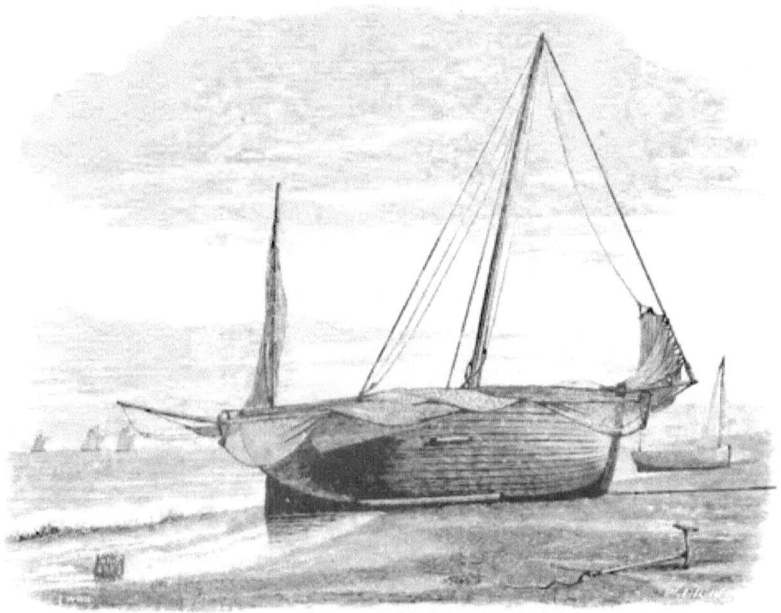

BRIGHTON HOG-BOAT.

drift-boats work after herrings in the latter part of the year; and when not so employed, many of them are used for trawling. The sean-fishery for mackerel is carried on all through the summer with varying success.

RYE TO RAMSGATE.—NUMBER OF BOATS.

Port Letters.	Port.	Year.	1st Class.	2nd Class.	3rd Class.
R.X.	Rye (Sussex) ..	1872	28	97	73
F.E.	Folkestone	,,	9	89	72
D.R.	Dover	,,	21	36	60
D.L.	Deal..	,,	8	79	27
R., or R.E.	Ramsgate	,,	139	43	—

In this section of the coast trawling and drifting are the important methods of fishing. The latter is principally carried on from Hastings, in the Rye district, and includes the fishery for mackerel, herrings, and sprats. Rye Bay is a locality of some little interest in connection with inshore trawling, as the ground has been systematically worked over by small trawlers from Hastings or Rye for a period beyond the recollection of anyone now living; and although great numbers of very small fish have been taken there year after year, there has been no failure in the supply of marketable fish up to the present time. Deep-sea trawling is carried on more or less from Folkestone, Dover, and Ramsgate, and the last has gradually become a very important station. It is a question whether the Barking or the Brixham men first colonized the place, but from its closeness to the Thames it is probable that the idea of deep-sea trawling was first derived from the former station. It has been unquestionably developed, however, by the Brixham fishermen, many of whose vessels have for about the last forty years either fished from or been settled at the port. Early in the present century there were only three or four small inshore trawlers at Ramsgate; there are now 139 smacks, averaging 37 tons each; and in June, 1873, about 100 of them were fishing from the station. The home ground is from north to east of the North Foreland, but in winter many of the smacks go into the North Sea and land their fish at other ports, as the neighbourhood of Ramsgate is dangerous in bad weather, and the trawlers like to have plenty of searoom. We may here mention that kettle-nets[1] are only used along this line of coast, and

[1] See Kettle-net, p. 167.

that nowhere else have we heard of drift-fishing[1] for sprats. The shrimp fishery, for which Pegwell Bay, near Ramsgate, has so long been famous, is still successfully worked; but it is carried on entirely by men who wade through the shallow water near the shore, pushing before them a wide-mouthed shrimp-net, fastened to a light semicircular frame.

The line-fishing along this coast is not very important. Inshore trawling is carried on eastward of Dungeness, as well as in Rye Bay; and we have recently seen the Folkestone luggers, which trawl after the drift season is over, bring in large numbers of marketable whiting —from eight to sixteen baskets to a boat—which had been taken within three miles of the shore.

FAVERSHAM TO COLCHESTER—NUMBER OF BOATS.

Port Letters.	Port.	Year.	1st Class.	2nd Class.	3rd Class.
F.M., or F.	Faversham	1872	28	201	30
R.R.	Rochester	,,	9	124	1
L.O.	London	,,	149	56	—
M.N.	Maldon (Essex)	,,	16	261	127
C.K.	Colchester	,,	132	250	40

With the exception of the London First Class vessels, many of the fishing boats belonging to the estuary of the Thames are employed during a great part of the year in the oyster and shrimp fisheries. In winter the larger of these craft go "stow-boating," as it is called; and plenty of occupation is given to the smaller ones at the different seasons in the whitebait and other river fisheries. The large London vessels, now 149 in number, consist of 110 trawlers and 39 cod-smacks; but beyond

[1] See Drift-fishing, p. 135.

belonging to the port, and being owned by London and Barking men, they have little to do with the Thames, and nothing with its fisheries. They all work in the North Sea, and their fish is landed at various ports—the cod at Grimsby or Harwich, and the trawl-fish is sent either direct to Billingsgate by steam or sailing carriers, or to some railway station on the coast, as may be most convenient at the time. Gravesend and Greenwich, once storing places for live cod, have been compelled to give up that connection with the deep-sea line-fishery, it having been found impossible to keep the North Sea cod alive for any time in the sewage-laden waters of the Thames. This portion of the fishing trade is being gradually concentrated at Grimsby, where the fish can be landed soon after they are caught, and whence they can be readily forwarded by rail according to the demand in the market.

The trawl-fish sent to Billingsgate are forwarded either by rail or water carriage, depending to a great extent on the part of the coast on which the fish are caught, but also on the facilities afforded by favourable winds for bringing the fish direct to London. At some ports on the east coast—Grimsby and Hull, for example—the quantity of fish landed there and sent away by rail has been steadily increasing. A great deal of this fish is forwarded to the inland markets, and the Hull and Grimsby smacks, which work largely for plaice and haddocks, do not regularly come to the Thames. London, however, is the great market for soles, and a very large proportion of these fish is sent to Billingsgate. Although vessels belonging to all the northern stations come to London, there is no positive rule for their doing so; but within the last twelvemonths (1873–4) carriage by water has been in increasing favour. The higher rates charged in 1873 by the railways from Yarmouth and Lowestoft have resulted in diverting a good deal of the trawl-fish traffic from those towns; and water carriage, which had previously been falling off, is now again increasing, that mode of transport being much facilitated by the present abundant supply of ice for packing the fish in as soon as they are caught.

Four steam carrying-vessels belonging to Messrs. Hewett and Co., and each bringing on an average about 2800 packages of fish, are constantly employed in this branch of the London fish trade; and numerous sailing carriers belonging to various ports, and averaging about 1000 packages each, also bring their cargoes direct from the North Sea to Billingsgate. The employment of steamers for bringing the fish to market had been talked of for many years, and, we believe, has been attempted before now, but without the success which, we understand, has been attained by Messrs. Hewett and Co. Their large experience of the fish trade, and the employment of several vessels built for the purpose, have no doubt enabled them to work the system to advantage; and under proper management it is likely to bear considerable development for the transport of fish from the more distant fishing grounds. It is yet a question whether it will *pay* to apply steam to the actual trawlers;[1] but we had an opportunity in 1872 of observing in an experimental vessel the practical advantage gained by its use, both when fishing, and going to and returning from the fishing ground.

Of the early history of Barking as a fishing station, or when its connection with trawling began, we have

[1] A Steam Cutter Fish-carrying Company have just begun working from Great Yarmouth. It is intended to use their vessels either for trawling or carrying, as may be from time to time desirable.

been able to obtain very little definite information. The town is said to have been interested in the sea fisheries for about 150 years; but the first precise account of it that has come under our notice relates to the year 1798, when, according to a statement[1] prepared by the late Mr. Groom, of Harwich, giving particulars of the introduction of welled-smacks at that port, some attempts were made at Gravesend, Greenwich, and Barking to construct smacks of a similar description, to be employed in the North Sea fishery. Barking appears to have greatly increased in importance during the following fifty years, as Mr. Groom states that, in 1852, she had as many as 134 trawlers, besides 46 smacks engaged in the cod and haddock line-fishery. But since that date a change in an opposite direction has been taking place, and the Barking fleet is now reduced to about 120 vessels, of which only three are engaged in the cod fishery. This, we believe, is the number owned at and reputedly sailing from Barking, but they may not all be on the London register; for, as we have before mentioned, local registration is a very uncertain guide to the number of fishing boats owned at or fishing from the port. As a station, Barking is undoubtedly declining; no smacks are built there now; and the advantages of the North Sea ports are gradually telling against the less convenient but once important stations on the Thames.

Leigh, a few miles above Southend, and in the Maldon district, has long been famous for its shrimp fishery, the proceeds of which are sent in large quantities to the London market; and as the fishery is carried on in tolerably salt water, although within the mouth of the Thames, we may as well give a short account of

---

[1] Sea Fisheries Commission, Minutes of Evidence, p. 456 (1864).

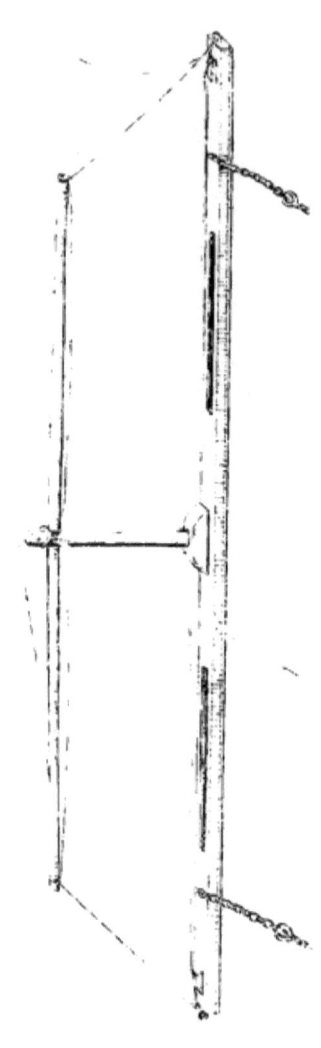

the manner in which it is conducted. The shrimp-net (Plate X.) used here for catching the brown or true shrimp, is peculiar to the Thames and its immediate neighbourhood, and is practically a beam-trawl with a second beam below instead of a ground-rope. This lower beam is made of a stout piece of oak 9 feet long, $2\frac{1}{2}$ inches thick, and $3\frac{1}{2}$ wide, flat above and below; it is weighted with about 25 lbs. of lead run into two spaces excavated on the upper side, and the under side of the beam is sometimes shod with iron. A stout stick, about $1\frac{1}{2}$ foot long, is fixed upright in a chock on the centre of the beam, and supports a pole 6 feet long, and parallel to the lower part of the frame. To these two beams the mouth of the net is fastened, and tightly strained at their ends. The net itself is about 12 feet in length, and tapers rapidly to the cod-end. The meshes are necessarily very small, in order to retain the shrimps, and are made of three sizes, ranging from half an inch square at the mouth of the net to a quarter inch at the small end. A simple but ingenious plan is adopted to prevent stones and small rubbish entering the net whilst it is being towed over the ground, and at the same time not to interfere with the capture of the shrimps. It is founded on the observed habit of these animals to rise a few inches from the ground when they are disturbed, and consists in leaving an open space of two or three inches between the lower edge of the mouth of the net and the beam to which it is fastened. Through this opening, sand, seaweed, and such small rubbish as is likely to be met with on the shrimping ground, easily pass, whilst the shrimps spring above the gap and find their way into the net. A three-span bridle from the lower beam and the top of the central stick is made fast to the warp by which the shrimp-net is towed. The shrimping boats are small decked smacks, about 32 feet over all; they carry a great deal of lofty sail, but for the sake of convenience have no main-boom, the main-sheet block working on a horse across the square and upright stern. The Thames Peter-boat differs from the regular shrimp-boat only in having a round stern, and is frequently used for the same purpose, although it is usually of a smaller size.

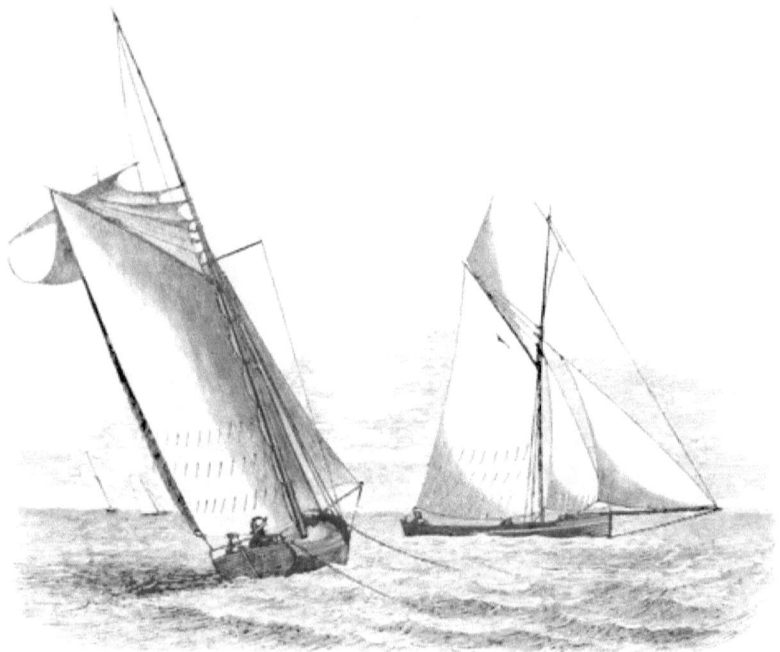

THAMES SHRIMPERS.

The usual shrimping ground is from Sea Reach to near the Nore, and the fishery is carried on by some of the boats throughout the year; but the best fishing is in the early part of the summer. From two to four nets are used by each boat, according to circumstances, and they are kept down from a quarter of an hour to an hour or more at a time, depending on the extent of ground they have been over. They are worked with the tide, as in ordinary beam-trawling. A man and a boy in each boat are sufficient for managing the full number of nets, as they are hauled in one at a time; the shrimps are immediately sifted, the small ones being returned to the water, and those of the size permitted by the regulations of the Thames Conservancy are put into the boat's well, to be kept alive until they are taken on shore in the afternoon. They are then boiled and sent by train in time for the London market the next morning. As in all other fisheries, there are good and bad seasons for shrimping, but there are no signs of any permanent decrease in the supply, and for several years past as many as 2000 gallons of shrimps have not unfrequently been sent to London as the joint produce of a day's fishing by the shrimpers from Leigh.

There is some trawling carried on at the mouth of the Thames both for flat-fish and prawns, or "red shrimps"; but these fisheries are not very extensive. The trawls used there are of the ordinary construction, and have a beam 16 or 18 feet long.

The boats belonging to the Colchester district are principally engaged in the oyster fisheries; but in winter stow-boating is extensively worked by the Brightlingsea men. The mode of fishing with the stow-net has been already described.[1]

[1] Page 161.

FISHING STATIONS.

ENGLAND (continued).

Harwich to Boston—Decline of Harwich as a fishing station — Mr. Groom's account of the introduction of welled-vessels — Cod-chests at Harwich — Shrimp-trawling — Railway returns of fish traffic — Herring fishery from Lowestoft and Yarmouth — Comparative failure of the mackerel fishery — Great increase of fishing boats at Lowestoft and Yarmouth — Rise and long continuance of the Yarmouth herring fishery — Swinden and Manship's account of it — Yarmouth Haven often difficult to enter — Fish market — Landing fish on the beach — "Swills" — Mode of counting herrings — A "last" of fish — Curing red herrings and bloaters — Smoking, packing — Yarmouth as a trawling station — Mr. Hewett's introduction of ice — Cromer crab and lobster fisheries — Local regulations for preserving them — Fisheries in the Wash — Leach's herring — **Grimsby to Whitby**— Rapid increase in the importance of Grimsby as a trawling station — Improvement in the size and style of fishing smacks — Grimsby Docks — Quantity of fish annually landed there — Fish market — Selling the fish — Packages formerly and now in use — Importation of ice — State of the trawling interests at Hull — Increased number of smacks — Collecting fish by the carriers — Present system of fishing — Fish put into ice as soon as caught — Bridlington and Flamborough — Description of cobles — Various fisheries on this coast — **Middlesboro' to Berwick-on-Tweed** — Line-fishing — Cod, haddock, and coalfish — Bratt-nets — Outcry against the trawlers — Inquiry by Royal Commission in 1863 — Herring fishing on the Northumberland coast — Cullercoats fishermen engaged in salmon fishing, but sea fish not diminished — "Keel-boats" — Fisheries at Holy Island and Berwick — Summary and relative importance of the English fisheries.

HARWICH TO BOSTON—NUMBER OF BOATS.

Port Letters.	Port.	Year.	1st Class.	2nd Class.	3rd Class.
H.H.	Harwich ..	1872	17	60	49
I.H.	Ipswich ..	,,	6	36	1
W.E.	Woodbridge ..	,,	15	99	51
L.T.	Lowestoft	,,	269	258	15
Y.H.	Yarmouth (Norfolk)	,,	493	462	47
W.S.	Wells (Norfolk) ..	,,	14	66	5
L.N.	Lynn (Norfolk) ..	,,	11	100	—
W.I.	Wisbeach			16	—
B.N.	Boston (Lincolnshire)	,,	5	89	7

The history of Harwich as a fishing station is somewhat remarkable, for it exhibits a rise to a position of the first importance in connection with a particular kind of fishery, and then a gradual decline to insignificance; not because of its particular trade ceasing to exist, but from its transfer to other ports. As a station for the North Sea cod fishery, Harwich has now entirely lost its importance, and there is but little prospect of its ever regaining the name it once deservedly possessed. To Harwich is due the introduction of welled-smacks,[1] by means of which the London markets have been for the last hundred and fifty years supplied with "live cod"; and the vessels were at one time also largely used by the Barking men in the trawl-fishery; but their employment for this purpose has been given up as the greater cost of such vessels is not generally met by any corresponding advantage.

In Mr. Groom's statement, previously referred to,[2] it is said that "In the year 1712, at Harwich, a seaport in Essex, welled-smacks were first constructed, suitable for fishing in the North Sea for cod-fish, &c.; and between that year and 1715 three vessels of that description were built, but very inferior to those which were afterwards constructed. In the year 1720 the number had increased to 12, and in 1735 to 30. Of that number Mr. Nathaniel Saunders (the progenitor of the three generations of the celebrated fish factors and salesmen at Billingsgate) had six, and with four of these, which were very superior to the other two, he visited the coast of Scotland in the course of his fishing expeditions, and was at that time the chief medium for conveying goods to

[1] After the Dutch method, according to Mr. Robert Fraser in his *Review of the Domestic Fisheries of Great Britain and Ireland*, p. 5 (1818).
[2] Page 226.

and from the north of Scotland. In the year 1745 his four smacks were engaged by the Government to carry the loyalist troops across the Moray Firth from Mickle Ferry to Inverness, from which place they proceeded to the memorable battle of Culloden. In 1766 a Mr. Olibar, a fishing smack owner at Harwich, made the first attempt to fish for cod with longlines on the Dogger Bank, but although he was very unsuccessful, he still persevered, and was so fortunate that in 1774 the number of smacks had increased to 62, of which 40 went regularly to the Dogger Bank to fish with longlines. In 1788 there were 78 smacks, and in 1798 the number had increased to 96. About this period a few attempts were made at "Gravesend, Greenwich, and Barking to construct smacks of a similar description, and the Harwich fishery gradually declined."

In 1852 there were only five cod smacks belonging to Harwich, and there has been very little change for the last twenty years.

It is difficult to understand why Harwich has not kept the position it formerly held; for although Grimsby has now become the leading station for cod vessels, and is not unlikely one day to monopolize the trade, Harwich has continued in favour as a storing place for live cod for many years since it ceased to have a large fleet of its own. When the Greenwich and other Thames smack-owners were obliged to give up the hope of keeping the cod alive in their own river, they transferred their store-chests to Harwich, and up to the present time cargoes of live cod have been delivered there regularly by the welled-smacks belonging to other places as well as by the few hailing from Harwich itself. The store-chests at Harwich are moored in the tideway, and are constructed on the same principle as those we have described as being in use at Grimsby,[1] but in order that they may offer less resistance to the stream their ends are rounded off, giving them a somewhat boat-shaped appearance. The chests at Grimsby being kept in the quiet water of the fish dock, the oblong shape is adopted as being more convenient for stowing a number of them together, besides providing more space inside and entailing less expense in their construction.

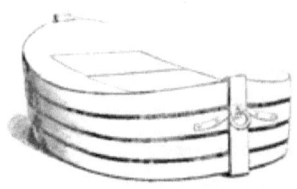

Harwich Cod-chest

A few deep-sea trawlers occasionally work from Harwich; and there are a good many small trawlers engaged in the fishery for prawns or "red shrimps" along the coast between Harwich and Orford. Trawling is also carried on in the river, and a net called "a Trim-tram" is likewise in use there. This net is essentially the same as the shrimp-net used by the Leigh fishermen for catching the brown shrimp; but it has a flat triangular frame fixed in front of the lower beam and resting on the ground, so that the mouth of the net is not likely to fall back and cannot fall forward with this projecting shoe. The point of this angular frame is slightly turned up to prevent it from running into the ground, and the tow-rope is made fast to it instead of to the beam, as in the shrimp-net. The contrivance strikes one as particularly clumsy, and the projecting frame must certainly interfere with the entry of the fish into the net, although complaints have been made of the destruction of small fish by its use. The mis-

[1] See Line-fishing, p. 149.

chievous effect is probably due more to the abundance of small fish in the locality where it is used than to the construction of the frame of the net.

Many of the First Class fishing vessels on the Harwich register are engaged in bringing lobsters from Norway—a trade with which one firm at Harwich has been connected for nearly fifty years.

The following is a return of the quantity of fish, principally consisting of cod, carried by the Great Eastern Railway from Harwich during the under-mentioned years:—

	Tons.		Tons.
1860	1507	1869	2011
1861	1830	1870	1644
1862	1690	1871	1741
1863	2071	1872	2643
1864	1931		

The fisheries carried on from Lowestoft and Yarmouth are of much the same character, and these towns may be regarded as the centres of the great herring fishery on the eastern coast of England, and holding an important position also as trawling stations. It is for the herring and mackerel fisheries by drift-nets, however, that Yarmouth has long been especially famous. The construction of a harbour at Lowestoft and the opening of a railway to the town have led to a very great development of the fishing trade there within the last few years; and the increase is especially remarkable in the number of trawlers which now sail from and belong to the port. In the drift-fishery also more capital has been put into the trade, and there has been an increase not only in the number, but also in the size of the fishing boats employed. In our general account of the drift-fishing[1] we have noticed the particular

[1] See Drift-fishing, p. 121.

seasons at which the herrings are fished for by the Lowestoft men; and we need not do more here than repeat that they regularly work the spring, summer, and autumn herring fisheries.

The mackerel fishery, carried on from May to July, has been very fluctuating for some years, and the mackerel "voyages" have been generally less successful than the other fisheries. This comparative failure has been accounted for by many people by the great development of the spring herring fishery, in which the small-meshed nets are said to frighten the mackerel then on the coast, without being large enough to catch them. It is one of the plausible explanations which, in our real ignorance of what causes the movements of mackerel on the various parts of the coast, may be accepted for what it is worth; but it is obviously quite hypothetical, and is unsupported by any known facts.

The drift-boats at Lowestoft are of the same build and rig as those at Yarmouth, but there is a larger proportion of small craft.

In the return of the number of fishing boats belonging to Lowestoft, furnished to the Sea Fisheries Commissioners, it is stated that in 1854 there were only 32, and in 1863 they had increased to 166, besides eight trawlers. By the last return, as given above, there were in 1872 as many as 269 boats, including trawlers, averaging 27 tons, and 258 of less than 15 tons.

No idea of the quantity of fish caught by these boats can be arrived at, as only part of it is landed at the port, and of this portion a good deal is cured, and is not included in the ordinary fish traffic of the railway. Of the mode of curing the herrings we may more legitimately speak in our notice of Yarmouth.

The connection of Yarmouth with the herring fishery

dates from the time when the first houses of the town were built, if we may credit the traditions and records on the subject. Indeed the site of the town appears to have been the resort of fishermen for some time previously.

Swinden,[1] in his account of the probable origin of Yarmouth, speaks of Saxon adventurers landing in Britain after the retreat of the Romans, and says, "Among the rest came Cerdick, the tenth in descent from Woden, with his son Cenrick, and as many men as he could transport in five ships. These landed at a place which, from their leader, was called Cerdickshore; now, according to Brompton, Yarmouth in Norfolk."

In a note, at page 15, he then quotes the conclusions of Manship (who wrote in 1619) about the origin of Yarmouth:—'And now by pregnant probabilities, it is my opinion very clear, that from the landing of Cerdick in anno 495, now 1124 years past, this sand, by the defluxion of tides, did by little and little lift its head above the waters; and so in short time after, sundry fishermen, as well of this kingdom, viz. of the Five Ports (being then the principal fishermen of England), as also of France, Flanders, and the Low Countries, yearly about the feast of St. Michael the Archangel, resorted thither, where they continued in tents made for the purpose by the space of forty days, about the killing, trimming, salting and selling of herrings, to all that thither came for that purpose; whereunto did resort the merchants of London, Norwich, and other places to buy herrings during the season, and then departed; as those fishermen who kill fish at Wardhouse use to do at this present. So in short time after,

[1] *History and Antiquities of Great Yarmouth*, p. 5 (1772).

as that sand became firm land, and that thereby traffic began more and more to be increased, men finding the same to be a commodious place to dwell and inhabit in, did for that purpose gather themselves together, to have a continual residence therein; and began to build houses, of which came streets, and of those streets this flourishing township.'

Considerable interest attaches to the history of Yarmouth from its undoubted connection with the herring fishery for at least many centuries; for although historians are not quite agreed about Cerdick landing in Norfolk, there is no doubt that the Yarmouth herring fishery was well established when Henry I. granted a charter to the town in 1108. The incidental mention by Manship that the fishermen and buyers assembled about the feast of St. Michael (the 29th of September) at the place where Yarmouth is now said to stand, is also worthy of notice; as it shows that, in the earliest times of the fishery, the Yarmouth herring season was at much the same time of the year as it is at present. For although Yarmouth boats now generally begin fishing in July, they then go some distance north, and the home fishery is only carried on from September to November.

As a description[1] has already been given of the boats and nets used by the Yarmouth drift fishermen, we will only now say a few words about landing the fish, and the manner in which they are converted into bloaters and red herrings.

Yarmouth once stood on an island, there having been two entrances to the river Yare, one on each side of the town. The northern entrance, however, has long been closed; and the river now runs along the back of

[1] See Drift-fishing, p. 100.

the town, and enters the sea on the south side, forming what is called the Haven. This entrance, although protected by two long and costly piers, is often difficult and dangerous for vessels to pass through, owing to the rapid stream setting out of the river at ebb tide; and if, at the same time, the wind be blowing strongly in, a heavy sea frequently breaks on the bar just where the edge of the river water is felt as it turns off northward, and escapes under the wooden pier on that side. In attempting to enter the haven under these circumstances the greatest care is necessary, therefore, to avoid being caught by the stream and carried away against the piles; and on such occasions a man is stationed at the end of the south pier, and signals with a black ball to the fishing boats which may be coming in (Plate XI.), directing them how to steer so as to run in on the safe side of the entrance, where there is more or less slack water. All precautions, however, are sometimes unavailing, and we have seen one of the luggers struck by a heavy breaker, making her broach-to, and sending her flying across the entrance apparently to inevitable destruction against the piles. The coolness of her master and her quick obedience to the helm saved her, however, by a few inches from the expected crash; and although much knocked about as she wildly dashed alongside the pier, and half filled with water by the tide pressing her against the piles, and nearly capsizing her, she was soon securely made fast, and ultimately warped off to a place of safety without having sustained very serious damage. We have previously mentioned that the crews of these drift-boats are largely made up of men who are not professional sailors or fishermen; and in this instance the alacrity with which the evident landsmen climbed

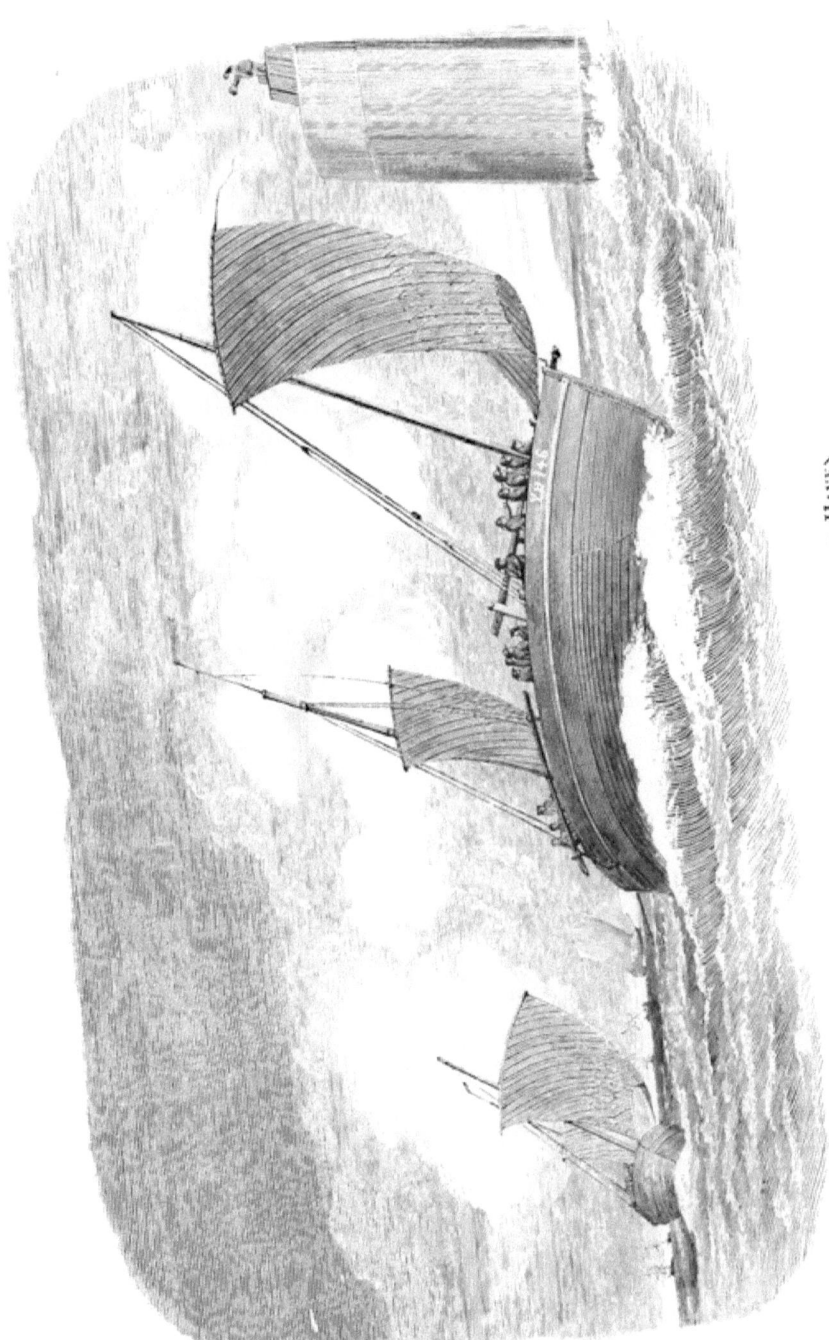

Boat entering Yarmouth Haven.

up the piles and left the apparently sinking lugger was conspicuous, and perhaps, under the circumstances, not altogether inexcusable.

The fishing boats, having once entered the haven, proceed upwards for nearly half a mile to the wholesale fish-market, which is a long covered structure facing the river. It has been erected during the last few years, and is conveniently situated for its purpose, as the fishing boats can lie alongside and discharge their cargoes into the market without the necessity for any land carriage. There is also plenty of unoccupied room along the bank of the haven for the extension of the market if it should be required.

When it is not convenient or practicable for the luggers to enter the haven, they come to anchor off the beach in front of the town, and the fish are landed in "ferry boats." This used at one time to be the regular practice. These ferry boats are large open boats, strongly built, and with plenty of room in them; they are worked by a class of persons well known there as "beachmen," who, besides being employed in landing the fish, have the more exciting occupation of manning the famous Yarmouth yawls to give assistance to the many vessels which make too close an acquaintance with the Scroby Sands and other dangerous shoals in the neighbourhood. The ferry boat takes off with her a considerable number of baskets called "swills," which are peculiar to Yarmouth, and are capable of holding about 500 fair-sized fish each. These baskets are broad and deep at the ends, and are tied in at the centre by a straight wicker-work handle running from one side to the other, making them look very much like two basket panniers joined together. As soon as the ferry boat has received her cargo from the lugger, the fish having been all counted into the baskets, she returns to land, and is placed broadside to the beach for the greater convenience of the men who have to take the fish on shore. A swill of fish is then raised to the gunwale of the boat, and a couple of beachmen take the basket between them in their arms, forming a bed for it by clasping each other by the hand—the right-hand man with his left and the other with his right hand—the other hands being brought round in front. In this way the swills are carried up the beach, and then placed in rows, two deep, ready for the sale, which takes place as soon as the cargo is landed.

LANDING FISH ON YARMOUTH BEACH.

On the eastern coast of England, excepting that part in the immediate neighbourhood of Scotland, herrings are commonly reckoned by the "last,"[1] nomi-

---

[1] "The Saxon *last*—a burden in general, as also particularly, a certain weight or measure; for as we say a last of herrings, so they say ein last corns, &c."—(Swinden, p. 39, *note*.)

nally consisting of 10,000 fish, but actually of 13,200. The following is the mode of computation:—

  4 herrings = 1 warp,
  33 warps = 1 hundred = 132 fish,
  10 hundred = 1 thousand = 1320 fish,
  10 thousand = 1 last = 13,200 fish.

A "hundred" of mackerel, however, only contains 30 warps, or 120 fish.

The herrings in the wholesale market are sold by the last, and are disposed of by ordinary auction, the salesman often expatiating on the good qualities of the fish in language worthy of a more suggestive subject than the one before him. It is the practice with most of the curers to make an arrangement at the beginning of the season with their own crews to pay them a fixed price for every last of fish they bring in. This is instead of paying a regular sum of money monthly as wages; and it induces the men to do their best, as a considerable catch of fish is necessary to enable the curers to pay the expenses of their vessels and establishments before they can make any profit. In very abundant seasons, however, the market for cured fish is so overdone that prices fall very low, and then heavy losses may be incurred. We believe that this was the case in 1871, and a large stock of that season's fish remained unsold for many months afterwards. The prices in the fresh market fluctuate very much from day to day, depending not only on the abundance or otherwise of the herrings, but also on the state of the weather allowing the fishing to be carried on with regularity, or causing interruptions.

On the arrival of the herrings at the curing house they are all washed to get rid of the salt put upon them on board ship as soon as they are caught; and then, without being gutted or any other preparation, they are again put into salt, that brought from Liverpool being the kind generally used. Their subsequent treatment depends on whether they are to be made into bloaters or red herrings. Bloaters are generally selected fish, full-roed, and of the best quality. The finest are made in October and part of November; but as any herring can be made into a bloater, and there being always a demand for them, their manufacture is carried on throughout the season with the best fish that can be obtained. Strictly speaking, a bloater is nothing more than a herring very slightly cured; it is kept from twelve to eighteen hours in salt, and then smoked for about twenty-four hours. At the end of that time it is fit for market, and the sooner it appears on the breakfast table the better it is likely to be. Red, well-cured, or high-dried herrings, as they are variously called, are kept in salt for fourteen days, then washed and hung in wood-smoke for another fortnight. Women are employed in the curing, and the fish, after being washed, are "rived" or strung on "spits"—thin sticks about $4\frac{1}{2}$ feet long, which are thrust under one gill-cover and out at the mouth. Twenty-five fish are put on each stick. The spits are then taken to the smoke-room, a lofty room, perhaps about 16 feet square, having a series of wooden frames reaching from floor to roof, with small transverse beams, called "loves," running from one side of the room to the other. These frames are 4 feet apart and the spits are placed in rows, one above another, between them, the ends of the spits resting on the loves. The roof is covered with tiles, uncemented, so as to allow a good draught through the room, which when filled contains three lasts of fish. On the stone floor of this room about sixteen fires are made, the fuel as a rule being oak billets, as the smoke from this wood gives a high colour to the fish. Ash timber, however, is sometimes used when a particular colour is required for some of the foreign markets. The spits of fish having been placed on the loves until all the space is occupied, the fires are lighted and kept burning for two days. They are then let out, and the fish allowed to drain or drip for a day; the fires are again lighted for two days more, and this process of alternately drying and dripping is continued for a fortnight; at the end of that time the herrings, then thoroughly cured, are called " high dried," and are fit for packing. This is done in barrels, two men being engaged in the operation; one standing with the spit in his hand, tells them off into the barrel, sliding them from the spit four at a time; these are for convenience counted as two, and the packing is done as rapidly as the teller counts the 2, 4, 6, 8, 10, 12, which would represent 24 fish. When the barrel is filled to the head, a screw press is brought to bear on the fish, and they are tightly flattened down so as to allow an additional number to be stowed away, 650 full-sized fish being about the number packed in each barrel, or a larger number of small fish, according to their size. The manufacturer's name and the number of fish are marked on each barrel; and it is one of the strong arguments brought against the system of Government brands, so commonly used and paid for by the curers of " white herrings" in Scotland, that the names and marks on the casks of Yarmouth herrings and Cornish pilchards are a sufficient guarantee of the quality of the fish in the large trade carried on with them to the Mediterranean.

The Yarmouth fish are sent to Italy, the Greek Islands, and the Levant.

For the home market the herrings are packed in boxes; and both boxes and barrels are usually made on the premises.

The mackerel fishery is carried on from the middle of May to the middle of July, but has not been so successful in recent years as formerly. The same boats and men are employed in it as in the herring fishery, and the mode of working is much the same in both. Twine nets have been used hitherto, but cotton will probably be substituted as new ones are required.

Trawling has been carried on from Yarmouth for nearly thirty years, but its importance as a trawling station dates from the time, about ten years later, when the vessels belonging to the late Mr. Samuel Hewett first sailed from the port. The convenience of the locality for landing the fish and refitting the smacks soon became evident, and for several years there was a busy time at his establishment at Gorleston, nearly opposite the present wholesale fish-market by the side of the haven at Yarmouth. The smacks rapidly increased, and at the present moment there are several hundred vessels engaged in this fishery, either belonging to the port or using it as a station. Since the death of Mr. Samuel Hewett (who rose from an apprentice) his large fleet of smacks has, we believe, been dispersed; and the firm of Hewett and Co. which succeeded him is now understood to confine its operations to carrying the fish to market, and the wholesale trade generally. Some of the family, however, still keep up the name as smack-owners. To Mr. Hewett is due the credit of introducing ice for preserving the fish on board ship; and nothing has tended so much to the development of deep-sea trawling, and therefore to the large increase there has been in the supply of fish, as the adoption, now almost universal with the trawlers, of the icing system. The bulk of the ice used for this purpose is imported from Norway, but a great deal is also procured in this country, Norfolk and Lincolnshire especially furnishing a considerable quantity every winter. An ice-house is now one of the most important requisites at a trawling station.

Each vessel takes a certain quantity of ice to sea with her, and those which remain out for several weeks fishing with the fleet are further supplied if necessary by the carriers when they go to collect the fish. The system of carrying by special vessels has long been at work in connection with the Thames and Yarmouth smacks, as their fish as a rule comes to the London market. Mr. Hewett had as many as eighteen carriers in almost constant work—smart powerful cutters with plenty of canvas and able to contend with any kind of weather except the trawler's great enemy—a calm. The system is still in force, and the carriers fill up from the vessels in the fleet of trawlers generally working in the same neighbourhood at particular seasons, giving a receipt to each smack for the number of packages she sends. Before the general use of ice everything depended on making a quick passage; sail was put on to the utmost extent the vessel would bear; and it used to be said that the lee-rail of a carrier was never to be seen when she was on her way to market. A mainsail rarely lasted more than one season, and the vessels were subject to the various additional expenses of wear and tear incidental to racing. The captain received a percentage on the price obtained for the fish, and as the value depended principally on its quick delivery, he had every inducement to press his vessel to her utmost. Time is of course important still, but the loss of a day or two is not of so much consequence as formerly; for the fish will keep in good order for a long time while packed in the ice. The danger now is after the fish has arrived, for it will not keep long after it has been taken out of the ice, if it happens to have been packed for some time. Regularity in the supply is therefore what is desired, so that there may be no glut in the market. This has been so far accomplished that the waste of fish from its being unfit for the table has enormously decreased, although from the circumstances just mentioned it cannot always be avoided. How far icing the fish destroys its flavour is another question; there seems to be no reason to think it makes it less wholesome, and happily for the fishmongers the large majority of fish consumers do not know what it is to have their fish cooked as soon as it comes out of the water.

The number of hands carried by the Yarmouth trawlers varies from five to ten; the London fashion of having a good many apprentices being continued in the Thames vessels when sailing from Yarmouth; and a smaller number of boys in the smacks belonging to the port. With the latter the share system of payment is the usual one; but in the Thames vessels, many of which perhaps belong to the same owner, the hands are paid regular wages according to custom; the master alone receiving an extra commission on the proceeds of the catch. These men sign articles for six weeks when sailing from Yarmouth, and for eight weeks from London.

Besides the regular trawlers which are employed all the year round, many of the drift-boats engage in that fishery when there is no drift-fishing going on; and as the lug-rig is not convenient for trawl-boats, a different set of masts and sails is then used, and the lugger is converted into a ketch. This rig we have before noticed[1] as coming into fashion with the regular trawlers at other ports, especially with the large ones recently built. The Barking pattern of trawl-iron is the one most commonly used at Yarmouth.

Between Yarmouth and the Wash there are a few small fishing villages, of which Cromer and Sherringham are the most important. The bottom along this coast is rocky, and the characteristic fisheries are those for crabs and lobsters; there is also some line-fishing, but the herring boats are few. The boats used by the crabbers are of a rather peculiar build—short and roomy, although sharp at both ends; their usual size is about 15 feet long and 5 feet beam; no thole-pins are used, but the oars are worked through holes cut in the gunwale plank. These boats carry a single large lug, with which they do pretty good work, and they have a crew of two, or sometimes three men. The crab season lasts from the 1st of April to the 20th of June, and the lobster fishery is systematically carried on from the middle of July till Michaelmas. The lobsters are in great demand for the numerous visitors to Cromer, but the crabs are generally sent inland. Ten years ago we found the great complaint of the Cromer fishermen was the absence of railway communication with the markets, and the uncertainty attending the sale of their crabs, as they were almost entirely dependent on two or three buyers from Norwich; and when none of these happened to come down they were obliged to get rid of their catches in the best way they could at home,

[1] See Trawling, p. 67.

and often for a mere trifle. 5000*l.* or 6000*l.* worth of crabs were sometimes taken in a season, and the fishermen had agreed among themselves that no crab measuring less than $4\frac{1}{2}$ inches across the shell should be brought on shore under a penalty of one pound. There was also a heavy fine for bringing in a "berry" lobster; and so convinced were the fishermen of the necessity for these restrictions that they kept a sharp look-out on one another, and informed against anyone they caught offending.

The protection thus voluntarily given by the fishermen to the crabs and lobsters was a matter of considerable interest to many more persons than the industrious inhabitants of Cromer; for its principle was that which had been and still is so frequently recommended for adoption to improve the supply from the other sea fisheries, and which is apparently based on the idea that when the young fish in any particular district or locality are left unmolested there must necessarily be a larger supply of old ones there in future. Now, however plausible this may appear, it is certainly at present no more than a theory, so far as it can be applied to the inhabitants of the sea; for we know nothing of what influences their movements, why they should visit or remain on any particular part of the coast, or whether the young fish we spare (as at Cromer) form anything more than the most insignificant item compared with the numbers which never come under our eye, or within our reach. However, the regulations we have mentioned have been for many years in force at Cromer, and they are so at the present time; but the result is not very encouraging: recent accounts describe both crab and lobster fisheries as steadily declining. As a test of the advantage of protecting the young fish, this experiment can hardly be considered a fair one, however; for it may reasonably be said that much benefit could not be expected from regulations at Cromer when indiscriminate fishing was carried on at Sherringham and other neighbouring villages; and this appears to have been the case.

The fisheries in the Wash are of several kinds, but, except in the case of mussels and shrimps, they are not very important. Jurisdiction is claimed by the corporations of Lynn and Boston over the fisheries carried on respectively on the Lynn and Boston Deeps; but, as the power of enforcing penalties for disobedience is questionable, the fishermen practically are left to their own devices. Stow-nets are used here in winter for the capture of sprats, and there is some fishing carried on at the same time for a small variety of the common herring, which appears in December and spawns in February or March. Before it was known that a winter spawning of the herring took place on many parts of our coasts, the fact of some of these fish regularly appearing about December near the Thames, having some little peculiarities in shape and size, and being ready to spawn in February, led Yarrell to consider them as specifically distinct from the ordinary kind; and he described the fish under the name of *Clupea Leachii*, or Leach's herring. He was further led to believe in its distinctness by finding the number of vertebræ apparently less than in the common herring. There is some doubt, however, whether this variation exists; and a more extensive examination of the supposed new species has resulted in ranking it as only one of the numerous races of the common herring. It is this particular variety which is found in the Wash during winter. Shrimping is carried on with the trawl, and soles are taken by the same means. There is also some smelt fishing by the trim-net, a description of which has been previously given.¹ The mussel "scorps" give plenty of employment, but have been the cause of much complaint, owing to the large use that has been made of the young mussels for manure. It does not appear, however, that the mussels on some of the scorps would ever be likely to grow large enough to be useful for bait; but where they will do so, due protection can hardly be a bad policy, for their value to the fisherman far exceeds any peculiar advantage they may have as manure. The scarcity of bait has been the great difficulty of the fishermen on the east coast during the last year, for the complaint with them has not been that fish are scarce, but that they could not procure enough mussel bait to catch them with.

GRIMSBY TO WHITBY—NUMBER OF BOATS.

Port Letters.	Port.	Year.	1st Class.	2nd Class.	3rd Class.
G.Y.	Grimsby	1872	330	16	25
G.E.	Goole	,,	6	1	—
H.	Hull	,,	313	340	1
S.H.	Scarborough	,,	109	153	—
W.Y.	Whitby	,,	20	277	4

In the section of coast extending from Grimsby to Whitby we find some of the most important fishing stations in the kingdom. Trawling has here its largest development, and also nearly its northern limit so far as the regular deep-sea fishery is concerned.

The important places are Grimsby and Hull. The situation of Grimsby at the entrance to the Humber, and the advantage it consequently has in that respect

¹ Trim-net, p. 165.

over Hull, were to a great extent lost sight of by the trawlers whilst the railway from the more important town provided the only convenient means of sending away their fish. The greater purity of the water at Grimsby had, however, led to its adoption as a storing place for live cod; and we believe it had been connected with the deep-sea line-fishery for several years before the first trawlers made it their head-quarters. This occurred in 1858, when four or five smacks migrated thither from Hull. Since that time Grimsby has been steadily growing in importance; and its development both as a trading port and a fishing station is mainly due to the Manchester, Sheffield, and Lincolnshire Railway Company, which have constructed extensive docks there and carried their line to the waterside.

The fisheries of which Grimsby is an important centre are the deep-sea trawling and cod-fishing. We have already fully described[1] the various incidents connected with the latter fishery, and need only add that the number of cod-smacks belonging to Grimsby has increased from 42 in 1863 to 82 in 1872, and that the increase has been in size as well as number. Besides these many liners from other ports land their fish here, and there is every reason to think that most of the cod-smacks will ultimately make Grimsby their head-quarters. There is not so much room, however, for development in this particular trade as in trawling; for the cost and working expenses of a welled-smack for the cod fishery are so great that they can only be met by obtaining a good price for the average catch of fish, and this will depend on the supply not being from too many vessels. The produce of fifty additional smacks would undoubtedly lower the general market consider-

[1] Line-fishing, p. 137.

ably, but the expenses of each smack would remain the same as at present. The demand for "live cod" is principally in London, where it is looked upon as "West End" fish.

With the trawlers it is a different matter, for they supply all classes; and both prime and offal fish are in constant and increasing request all over the country. Hull and Grimsby are both conveniently situated for supplying the manufacturing districts, and the ready sale there for the lower class of fish, such as plaice and haddock—the latter both fresh and smoked—has led to the great development of those two ports as trawling stations. The railway was completed to Grimsby in 1859; and, as we have mentioned, the first trawlers settled at that port in 1858, five smacks having come there from Hull. The advantages of the place soon became evident, and in 1863 the number of trawl-vessels had increased to 70. Since that date the additions to the fleet have been numerous, a stimulus having been given to the trade by the higher price paid for fish in common with other kinds of provisions; and in 1872 there were 248 trawlers and 82 cod-smacks belonging to and fishing from the port. The new vessels for both fisheries are considerably larger than those formerly built, and they are all of them ketch-rigged. The large additional capital put into the trade has, we understand, been partly the proceeds of successful fishing, and the rest has been provided by private persons who have joined some of the smack-owners in what has been proved to be a profitable investment.

Besides the regular Grimsby vessels, a large number from other places, varying at different seasons, fish from the port, using it as a temporary station; so that the quantity of fish landed there has enormously increased during the last few years. In 1872, it averaged 600 tons a week, or more than 31,000 tons for the whole year. This included fish of all kinds, but a very large proportion of it came from the trawlers.

By the courtesy of Mr. Reed, the dock-master at Grimsby, we are enabled to give the following return of the quantity of fish landed at the docks in each of the seventeen years, 1856–72; and although this does not represent the whole proceeds of the Grimsby fisheries, a great quantity of fish being sent by carriers direct to London, it gives some idea of the growth of the local fish traffic during the period. It must be remembered that the rise of Grimsby as a fishing station has not been at the expense of Hull and other places; for the increase of the trawlers has been general at all the regular stations on the east and south coasts within the last twenty years.

RETURN OF THE QUANTITY OF FISH LANDED AT GRIMSBY FROM 1856 TO 1872.

Year	Tons	Year	Tons
1856	1,511	1865	13,368
1857	3,135	1866	15,692
1858	4,314	1867	19,116
1859	4,712	1868	21,621
1860	4,842	1869	24,140
1861	5,371	1870	26,324
1862	8,521	1871	30,857
1863	9,408	1872	31,193
1864	11,198		

There is a separate dock at Grimsby for the fishing vessels, and that one proving not to be large enough for the increasing trade, a second is now in course of construction. The dock now in use has a covered landing wharf 882 feet long and 48 feet wide, with small offices upon it for the use of the various salesmen; and a line of rails in connection with the Great Northern and the Manchester, Sheffield, and Lincolnshire Railways runs close to the side of the wharf, so that the fish can be loaded into the trucks with the greatest facility.

The scene on the wharf every day is a busy one, and the quantity of fish displayed there makes one marvel at the prices frequently obtained for it by the salesmen. Cod are sold by the score of twenty fish, and they, with ling and holibut, are disposed of by ordinary bidding; but trawl-fish are here, as elsewhere, sold by Dutch auction. A lot of turbot, perhaps, is to be sold—the salesman's bell is rung, and the stentorian voice of the auctioneer is heard calling out, "Now then, turbot buyers, turbot buyers, turbot buyers, come along, ye turbot buyers!" A knot of people collects, and the salesman descants in few words on the quality of the fish; a price is named—no one responds, or indeed is expected to do so, for it begins too high for any dealings; it comes down by degrees until a nod from one of the crowd closes the transaction, and the sale is booked. Then calls may be made for "sole buyers," "plaice buyers," "ling buyers," or "cod buyers," and the work is rapidly got through, for there is no time to be wasted over individual lots where there are so many to be sold, packed, and sent away as soon as possible. A great number of holibuts are brought in by the cod-smacks, and these fish remain only a short time in the dock before they are sold. In the meanwhile they are secured by a line round the tail, and when wanted they are brought alive to the market, where they are familiarly known as "butts."[1]

The packages in which the trawl-fish are stowed have lost much of their significance as denoting any

[1] At Billingsgate turbots are commonly spoken of as "butts."

particular capacity. Pads and half-pads were once recognized measures, and are still spoken of in some of the markets, although the quantity of fish contained in them is rather uncertain. Ten years ago they were the only packages used by the Hull and Grimsby trawlers. The "pad" consisted of three "pots," and the "half-pad" of two pots of fish. This division of a package into three or two imaginary parts called "pots" was for the convenience of the salesmen and buyers; for instance, if two pads and three half-pads were to be sold, they were offered as twelve pots; fish was said to be worth so much per pot one day, and so much another day. This measurement was also found very convenient by the fishermen, as in case they had not enough prime fish at the end of their packing to fill a half-pad, they still put it into a half-pad basket and called it a pot. At one time pot baskets were used, but they have been long given up. Formerly speculative dealers used to bargain with some of the fishermen to take all their prime fish at so much per pot, and then a pot was to weigh 40 lbs.; but a half-pad (two pots) subsequently came to weigh from 80 lbs. to 120 lbs., the difference being caused by the fish being more or less piled up on the top of the basket. A further change was made by the introduction of wooden boxes called "trunks," and they were used especially for the package of soles, a trunk or box of soles usually containing sixty to seventy pairs, weighing about 100 lbs. Plaice and haddocks are also packed in them, about forty of the latter, when sold for the fresh market, going to the "box." Haddocks for smoking are sold by measure, the contents of a small barrel representing a certain weight of fish. We have before mentioned, when speaking of trawling, the difficulty there used to be in disposing of the enormous numbers of haddocks caught by the North Sea trawlers, and that the fishermen were forbidden to bring in more than a certain quantity of these fish. Such an order is no longer necessary, for since the idea of smoking the haddocks has been carried out quite an important trade in the dried fish has sprung up and continues both at Grimsby and Hull. The introduction of ice for preserving the fish has caused another revolution in the trade and in the working arrangements of the trawlers; of this we shall speak presently when we give some account of the Hull fisheries, Grimsby and Hull having much the same customs in these matters;[1] but we may here mention that in 1872 there were as many as 22,000 tons of ice imported at Grimsby, principally for the use of its fisheries. Besides trawling and line-fishing from Grimsby, there are numerous small craft solely employed in the whelk fishery[2]—in collecting bait for the cod-smacks. These three fisheries are the only ones with which Grimsby is immediately concerned; but in the herring season, the drift-boats occasionally land their fish there when they have been working in the neighbourhood.

There is some shrimping carried on at Cleethorpes, a little southward from Grimsby, but it is only done by hand, a "shove-net" with a spread of 10 feet at the foot and a pocket in the bunt of the net being used. Cleethorpes has also some name for oysters, beds for laying them on being prepared along the shore. They are obtained off the coast near Saltfleet, and are collected by the Colchester men, as well as by those in the neighbourhood. The Cleethorpes beds are all private

---

[1] We are indebted to Mr. R. T. Vivian, of Hull, and Mr. Henry Knott, of Grimsby, for much interesting information on these points.
[2] See Line-fishing, p. 113.

property, the ground being rented from the Lord of the Manor.

Goole stands on the register as the station for six smacks, but they all sail from Grimsby, although the residence of their owner is at the former port.

It is now nearly thirty years since Hull became a trawling station. There were one or two vessels belonging to the port previously; but about 1845 there was a migration thither from Brixham and Ramsgate, and forty trawlers fished from Hull in that year. It was soon after the discovery of the famous Silver Pit; and this led to the systematic prosecution of the North Sea trawl-fishery. The success attending these vessels soon induced other smack-owners to settle at Hull, new vessels were turned out every year, and in 1863 the fleet consisted of nearly 270 trawlers, notwithstanding the fact of a few vessels having left Hull for Grimsby, as already mentioned. Since 1863 there has been a further increase, and the register for 1872 shows 313 smacks averaging 55 tons N.M. These vessels are all deep-sea trawlers, Hull having no connection with the cod fishery which is carried on so successfully from Grimsby. The trawlers are of the same description at both places, the modern vessels being much larger than the old ones, and the ketch-rig is the one generally adopted for them.

Before ice became so generally used as it is at present, the Hull smacks usually fished in fleets and sent their fish in every day by whichever vessel was going home. The custom then was to stay out for six weeks at a time, and there was a constant succession of smacks joining and leaving the fleet. Special carriers were not employed to attend on the Hull smacks, but each vessel in turn performed that service as her period of fishing expired. When she was ready to return to port, she hoisted a flag as a signal to the rest of the fleet, and the smacks then assembled round her, and sent their boats with the fish packed in baskets, and a fish note containing the number of packages and a description of their contents as delivered from each vessel. It was a busy scene, and sometimes difficult work getting the fish on board, the boats crowding alongside and knocking about as the vessel rolled and pitched in the angry waters of the German Ocean; but deep-sea fishermen and trawlers' boats are accustomed to rough work; and unless the weather were very bad, the fish was sooner or later "boarded," and the "flagman" or carrier then crowded all sail for the run home. On arrival at the Hull docks she was placed under a steam-crane and the fish hoisted out, the master handing in his manifest or "pot-list," as it was called, so that each salesman might know what fish was consigned to him, and from which vessels it was sent.

The share system has always been adopted by the Hull trawlers, as at Brixham, Ramsgate, and most other stations. When therefore a smack returned from the North Sea after her six weeks' fishing, there were accounts to settle for that time, and on an appointed day the skipper and his two men (the apprentices not taking part in the division, as they are provided for by the owner) met the salesman and received a detailed account of the proceeds of all the fish that had been sent in. Of the net sum realized the skipper received $\frac{11}{80}$ths and each man $\frac{7}{80}$ths; and from this was deducted for each man one-fifth of the cost of the provisions used on board during the trip. The rest of the money realized went to the vessel; and if the skipper had a share in her, which was frequently the case, then of course he came in for his portion as part owner. The vessel remained in port for a week and then rejoined the fleet. Such was the course of proceeding ten years ago at Hull with most of the smacks. Ice was, however, then coming into general use, and a few smacks had an ice-box fitted up on board and worked independently, running their own "voyages," and landing their fish wherever it was most convenient to do so. Some went to the Dogger, others fished off Sunderland or Hartlepool, and took their fish in every day or two to those markets, to the great indignation of the local fishermen. About this time twenty of the Hull smacks were fitted up as ice-cutters to collect the fish and carry it partly to Hull and partly to London; and these are still kept at work from May to September, the trawlers at that time fishing in fleets of from twenty to fifty vessels. They then stay out for ten or twelve weeks at a time, and at the end of the "fleet" season they all return together. It answers to employ carriers during the summer months, as then the wind is often light, and the regular fishing smacks not having special conveniences for stowing away a very large quantity of fish in ice, might not bring their cargoes to market in good condition. From September to May, however, quite a different system is adopted, and each vessel works by herself, bringing in her own catch. An air-tight compartment is fitted in the hold, called the "ice-box," in which from two to four tons of Norwegian block ice are placed when the smack starts for her trip. As the fish is caught it is stowed away below in bulk, with broken ice between each layer, and this is continued till a good quantity of fish has been collected; then the vessel returns to port, after an absence of perhaps ten or fourteen days. The fish is taken out loose and all sold by weight; pads, pots, and trunks are here unknown, and the buyer finds the packages, those now regularly used being small barrels holding about ten or twelve stone of fish, and called "kits." In these the fish is packed, with a sprinkling of crushed ice[1] between each layer, and an extra quantity at the top, which is covered with straw and tied down. In this state the fish is sent all over the country to the fishmongers, so that from the time it is caught till it comes into the hands of the consumer it is kept in ice. Our ideas of fresh fish, however, will not be quite the same now as they were twenty years ago; a great deal of what comes to our tables has been caught for a week or two, perhaps longer, before we see it; and yet is in a more wholesome condition than much that was frequently called fresh fish in former times. This is doubtless owing to the fish having been put into the ice only a few minutes after it was caught — we might almost say whilst it was alive; for the first thing done on board a trawler when the net has been got in and emptied, is the sorting and putting away such kinds of fish as are marketable. The quantity of ice now imported into Hull is from 16,000 to 20,000 tons annually; and a still larger quantity is landed at Grimsby, as before noticed.

How much is used at the other large stations we have no means of ascertaining; but the quantity must be very large, and — to borrow a term from the geologists — the present may well be called the "Glacial Period" of the fisheries. Ice has, in fact, revolutionized the trade, and at the same time has been

---

[1] Almost every wholesale buyer has a large hand-mill by which he crushes the block ice into small pieces about the size of a marble.

productive of good to all concerned with it. Deep-sea fishermen need not now be afraid of their fish becoming spoiled before it reaches the market; and the supply to the consumer is larger and must be, at all events to some extent, cheaper than would otherwise be the case.

Taking into consideration the loss of time while going to and returning from the fishing grounds, the number of days spent in port after the several voyages, and the interruptions from unfavourable weather, the actual time each of these smacks occupies in fishing does not exceed about nine months in the course of the year; and it is in winter when there is no want of wind that the most profitable trawling is everywhere carried on.

The Second Class boats belonging to the Hull district include numerous small craft, which trawl for shrimps in the Humber, others more or less engaged in line-fishing for mackerel, whiting, and other kinds according to the season, and belonging to Hornsea, Spurn, Withernsea, and other places on the coast northwards, and the small trawlers which work in Bridlington Bay. The last locality has been much trawled over for more than twenty years by large open boats of 8 or 10 tons, using a net with a trawl-beam 18 or 20 feet long. Plaice are the fish principally caught there, and the fishing is carried on more or less throughout the year.

From about Flamborough Head to nearly as far as Holy Island the peculiar boats called "cobles"[1] are in regular use. They vary a good deal in size, but are all built on one principle and with one object—that of readily beaching stern foremost in a surf. The bow is

[1] Pronounced "cobbles."

built with a considerable rise, and is sharp and hollow below; the true keel is continued from the stem for only rather more than half the length of the boat, where it meets what is called the keel plank; this extends to the stern, and has two false keels or runners, one on each side of it, and carried forward so as to overlap the after end of the true keel. The stern is therefore practically flat-bottomed, whilst the bow has the form usual in boats. The result of this construction

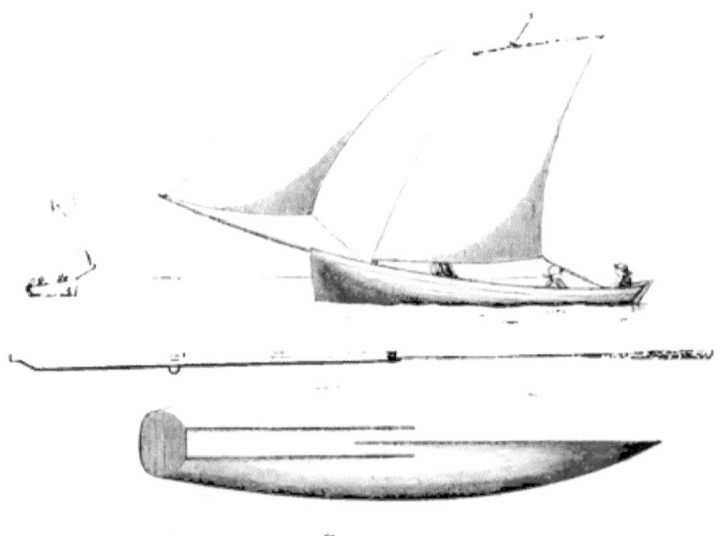

COBLES.

is that the coble can be backed up on the beach with great facility, the flat keel plank and false keels keeping her steady and upright, whilst the hollow bow throws off the waves which may be beating her on the shore. The hauling up and launching are easily managed by the help of an axletree and couple of wheels which are got under the bow and brought far enough aft for the boat to be well balanced on the cross-piece; she is then off the ground and can be readily moved. The only sails carried are a single standing lug and a jib. The difficulty of steering a boat with such a full stern and without the usual run is overcome by making the rudder very deep; and when properly shipped, half of it projects below the bottom of the boat, and it then does its duty. The oars also are of peculiar construction; the blade, which is made of ash, being scarfed to a deal handle, and the oar working with a small iron loop on a single thole-pin. The cobles are clinker built, and the two upper planks tumble in at the quarters, giving the stern a boxed-in appearance. We can say from experience that these boats pull easily, and sail well with the wind at all free; but their low and peculiar shaped sterns make them rather dangerous with a following sea. This has led to some of the larger class of boats being built with a round stern, and these have received the name of "mule cobles." It is for inshore work, however, that the coble build appears most suitable, and for that purpose these quaint-looking craft are in general use along the north-east coast. They are usually painted in stripes of green, yellow, and red; each plank being generally of a different colour from its neighbour.

Besides the boats we have mentioned there is a larger class, called yawls, ranging from 36 to 40 tons N.M., and even larger; they are decked, and in every way are much the same as the Yarmouth luggers. These are employed in the deep-sea herring and longline fisheries, and at certain seasons their rig is altered and they are used as trawlers. Scarborough was the first place on this line of coast to begin trawling, taking precedence of Hull in this respect by about ten years; it has not been so systematically followed up there, however, as at the more southern station, and the Scarborough boats are mostly employed in the various fisheries in turn, as the seasons come round. The herring fishery and that by longlines for cod and haddock give the most important employment; a few mackerel have also been taken by hook along this coast in recent years, but these fish are not in sufficient regular abundance to make it generally worth while to have special nets for catching them. Crab and lobster fishing, however, employ a large number of men at particular seasons. The creel or cage trap, also called a "pot," but of a different shape from those having that name in the West of England, is much used here, as it is very easily worked and is very effective, but it has the disadvantage of catching very small crabs; and the temptation to keep them when thus caught has induced some fishermen in the common interest to use another kind of trap, which permits the escape of the small crabs and lobsters. This is called a "trunk," and is simply an iron ring about 2 feet across, to which is attached a shallow net of 2 inches mesh. Fresh bait is fastened in the centre to a cross-line, and a number of these trunks are then sunk in a suitable place and marked in the usual manner by a cork buoy. Much larger crabs and lobsters are taken by these trunks than by the ordinary creels, but it requires more skill to work them, as there is nothing to prevent the crabs and lobsters from crawling out, and the lobsters are apt to make a sudden spring backwards just as the net is being taken out of the water. The trunks are largely used at Flamborough, but nowhere else along this part of the coast.

Whitby is chiefly interested in the herring and line fisheries, and has only two or three small trawlers.

MIDDLESBORO' TO BERWICK-ON-TWEED.—NUMBER OF BOATS.

Port Letters	Port	Year.	1st Class.	2nd Class.	3rd Class.
M.H.	Middlesboro'	1872	—	55	—
H.L.	Hartlepool, West	,,	1	172	6
S.D.	Sunderland	,,	5	103	—
N.E.	Newcastle-on-Tyne	,,	—	—	1
S.S.S.	Shields, South	,,	—	11	2
S.N.	Shields, North	,,	2	189	6
B.K.	Berwick-on-Tweed	,,	60	599	6

The remaining portion of the English coast is chiefly concerned with the herring fishery and hand and long lining, except in a few places where set-nets are used for catching turbot. There is also a little inshore trawling, but not of much consequence. Between Whitby and Hartlepool lies the picturesque little village of Staithes,[1] long famous for its devotion to the line-fisheries, which by some of the fishermen is still carried on throughout the year, herring fishing occupying others in the season. The fish principally obtained by the line are cod, haddock, holibut, and coalfish or "black jacks"; the last are numerous along the coast and northwards, and we have seen large numbers of them brought on shore here during the time when the herrings were in the neighbourhood. Advantage is taken by the fishermen of the ravenous propensities of the cod and coalfish, when following the shoals of herrings, to obtain a good supply of bait from the well-filled stomachs of these fish; and as soon as the line-boats bring their captives on shore, the fishermen's wives and daughters set to work with their sharp knives, slit open the coalfish and cod with a

[1] We are not quite sure at which of these two ports the Staithes boats are registered.

rapidity which tells of long practice in the work, and in a few minutes a goodly pile of herrings is collected by their side. We have seen as many as twelve full-sized herrings taken from a single coalfish, and they have been in such a condition that they might almost all have been sent to market without exciting any suspicion among the purchasers that they had not been caught in the most orthodox manner. These herrings are professedly saved for bait, but we have no doubt that many of them find their way into the frying pan. Staithes was formerly a great place for cured fish, as the facilities for sending the fish fresh to market were very small before the extension of the railways to the coast. Some cartage is even necessary at the present time, but a much larger proportion of the catches is now sold fresh than formerly. The cured fish is split, salted, and dried on the rocks, and sent away to various markets. An old custom of calling the larger class of fishing boats "fi'men boats" still prevails here; it originated in the fact of these boats each carrying five men in old times, the smaller boats only having three. A larger number of hands, usually seven or eight, are now carried by the yawls. Turbot or "bratt" nets are successfully worked by the Staithes fishermen, although, according to their report, the catches are not nearly as large as they were formerly. This is the general statement along this coast. Assuming the diminution to be real, the explanation of it is not very easy to give, if the circumstances of the case are looked into. The feeling of the fishermen along the north-east coast has been and continues very strong against the trawlers; and, of course, a decrease in the local supply of any kind of fish is there ascribed to the "iniquitous system of trawl-net fishing." The decrease in the supply from the turbot-nets along the coast might possibly be explained by the number of these fish caught by the trawlers; but the diminution is said to have also taken place, and to an enormous extent, in the supply of haddock and cod. Now, the great haddock fishing ground for the trawlers is near the Dogger Bank, and the catches there are as large as they ever were; the number of cod caught in the trawl is utterly insignificant: fifty trawlers would not have caught as many of these fish in a week as the Staithes fishermen say a few of their boats used frequently to catch in a day. But this difficulty is attempted to be got over by saying—and it has been repeated over and over again—that the trawlers destroyed the spawning beds of the cod and haddock, and so caused the diminution. Ten years ago there was not much known on the subject, but M. Sars has since shown that the spawn of these fishes floats, and therefore there can be no destruction of their spawning beds.

It is a remarkable circumstance that nearly thirty years ago turbot became so scarce near North Sunderland, close to Holy Island, that the turbot-nets were given up. At that time trawling in the North Sea was only just beginning from Hull and that part of the coast; and the trawlers have never worked near the place where the decrease of turbot was said to have been greater than even at Staithes. It is evident, then, that we have yet a good deal to learn about what attracts or drives away the fish to or from any particular locality.

Hartlepool and Sunderland are places for shipping rather than fishing boats. At the former port many of the fishermen some years ago gave up their pursuits in order to become pilots, the increasing trade causing a corresponding demand for persons of that description; but the fishermen have again increased, and both drift and line fishing are carried on there as before. Mussels for bait are obtained in some quantity from the beds in the Tees. The deep-sea trawlers land a good deal of fish at West Hartlepool when they are fishing on that part of the coast, as the railway provides very convenient communication with many of the best markets; the smacks, however, do not belong to the town, but come from Hull and Grimsby.

These vessels have also been in the habit of taking some of their fish to Sunderland, where, by breaking down the monopoly of the local fishermen, they raised the storm which in 1863 led to the inquiry into the general condition of the sea fisheries, and the effects of beam-trawling on the supply of fish to the markets. That the inquiry ended in disproving by overwhelming evidence the accuracy of the statements put forward by Mr. Richard Crick, the President of the Fishermen's Committee, and the leader of the assault against the "nefarious practice of trawl-net fishing," was no doubt unexpected by that gentleman; but it may be some consolation to him in his desire for the good of "the takers and the partakers of fish," to find that his gloomy anticipations have not been realized, and that a largely increased fleet of trawlers is now, ten years later, bringing in an enormous supply of fish, though insufficient for the demand, whilst the line-boats are, at all events, not doing worse than they were in 1863, and in many places have increased in number and size.

A few miles north of the Tyne lies the village of Cullercoats, possessing in 1863 a purely fishing population, and sharing with the people of Sunderland and other places along the coast in the anticipation of ruin to be brought about by the increasing numbers of deep-sea trawlers. Our recollection of the visits we made to this little community is a pleasant one, for we found among the fishermen of the place some who, while believing in the mischievous effects of the system of trawling, could discuss the subject with moderation and intelligence, in marked contrast to the manner in which it was treated by the general body of anti-trawlers. The fisheries were the usual ones for herrings and white-fish, and as cobles were the only boats used there, most of the work was done within a few miles of the shore. The line-fishing occupied the men during the greater part of the year, and was the particular method which it was anticipated would suffer from the operations of the trawlers, a few of whom occasionally worked along that coast. The crew of the boats was the same for both kinds of fishing, although the herring cobles were larger than those for the white or line fishing, and consisted of three men, with the addition sometimes of a boy. The herring fishery was conducted in the same manner as on other parts of the coast, but as the boats were small, the fleet of nets was not of very great length. As in these small cobles the single mast was altogether lowered when the nets were in the water, no lantern was hoisted, but a coal or charcoal fire was made in a small brazier standing in a flat iron pan at the bottom of the boat; and this not only answered the purpose of a drift-light, but was useful also for heating the coffee, of which a pannikin was served round in the course of the night.

After a somewhat varied experience of nights spent at sea, we can look back with pleasure to the time when, snugly wrapped in a sail, and lying at the bottom of a herring coble, we have discussed with the Cullercoats fishermen the manners and customs of the finny tribes, the probable influence of weather on their movements, and the evil effect of "marfire," then illuminating the sea around us, and preparing us for what proved to be an unsuccessful night's fishing. For beautiful as is then the appearance of both nets and fish as they are drawn through the water and hauled over the side of the boat (Plate XII.), such a display is not what the fishermen desire; and many more fish are generally caught when the water is dark and the surface broken than in the glassy calm of a fine summer's night. Here, too, we first heard the feeble "cheep" of the herring after it had been shaken from the net, and had joined the dead and dying at the bottom of the boat.

The fishermen of Cullercoats have been fortunate for many years in possessing in the Rev. R. F. Wheeler, the Incumbent of Whitley (a parish extending into the village of Cullercoats), a friend who has taken a deep interest in their pursuits, and whose good offices have in every way secured to him the confidence and respect of his parishioners. To this gentleman we are indebted for an account of the present state of the fisheries at Cullercoats, and we are glad to say it is much more satisfactory than it was expected to be when we were there in 1863. The present prosperity is not, however, entirely due to the ordinary kinds of sea fishing. The herring fishery has been given up to a great extent, owing to the much more profitable employment of the men at that season in the net fishery for salmon in the sea, on their way to the Tyne, which, in consequence of the removal of the several obstructions to the fish, has now become a first-rate river.[1] But the white-fishing is still carried on, the number of cobles has considerably

---

[1] More recent accounts speak of a great decline in the Tyne salmon fishery.

Pl. XII.

HERRING FISHING.
(Northumberland Coast.)

increased, and the average takes per boat are about the same as they used to be. The great want is of mussels for bait; and it is reasonable to conclude that if the supply were more abundant a larger number of line-fish would be caught. The affairs of the Cullercoats fishermen seem to be generally flourishing; the men have been enabled to build themselves good houses, and that has led to improvements in other ways. The fishermen, moreover, have been busy in the construction of a new and very costly breakwater on the south side of their little harbour; it is expected to be completed this winter, and it will probably be followed by a considerable improvement in the size of the fishing boats. No doubt a great deal of the money thus usefully spent has been obtained by the sea fishery for salmon; but what has been gained in that way has not been all extra profit, for the herring fishery has been neglected except by a few boats, and that had always been looked forward to as a productive and profitable fishery during the short time it lasted. We are glad to have been able to obtain trustworthy information about the present condition of Cullercoats, for it is purely a fishing village, within easy reach of railway communication with the markets. Facilities for disposing of the fish are of course of great importance, but only while the supply of fish continues; and from the present very flourishing state of Cullercoats it is clear that the anticipations of ruin in consequence of trawling have not been realized, for it is impossible to credit the salmon fishery with all the improvements of the place. It is one of the curious features of the trawling question that the objection to the system takes the most opposite forms: in some places trawling in shallow water is considered to be so destructive to the young fish that it is said it should not be allowed within a certain number of miles of the shore; but along the north-east coast, including Cullercoats, small trawlers have occasionally worked for soles even in three fathoms water without much objection, and the mischief was said to be only done in deep water where the haddocks, &c., were supposed by some people to spawn; and, we must add, where the line fishermen themselves do their best to catch them whether the fish are spawning or not at the time.

There are numerous fishing villages along the Northumberland coast, but the fisheries are of much the same character at all of them, and cobles are the boats in use everywhere till we come to North Sunderland and Holy Island. There we meet with a distinct class of large sailing boats, which are distinguished from the

KEEL-BOATS (HOLY ISLAND).

cobles by the name of "keel-boats." They are large, powerful craft, but entirely open, and usually carry a single lofty fore-lug, which can be reduced to smaller dimensions by no less than seven rows of reef-points. A mainmast and mainsail on a smaller scale are sometimes also carried, but the boats sail and steer well with only the foresail. These boats are sharp at each end, and are used especially for the herring fishery. They are of much the same style as the Scotch boats, but are somewhat larger than those generally used ten years ago north of the Tweed.

Beyond Holy Island and the dangerous neighbourhood of the Farne Islands the boats and fisheries are essentially Scotch, and the boats of both countries work together on this part of the coast; the fishermen from the Firth of Forth sometimes going as far south as the Tyne for the early herring fishery in May and June, and then devoting a few weeks to the salmon nets. It is only within the last few years that this herring fishery has been attempted in that neighbourhood; but the fish, although selling well in the fresh market, are very small, and not fit for curing. Objection is made to this fishery, on the ground of its probably diminishing the autumn shoals; but judging from what has been going on for some years at Lowestoft, where the autumn fish continue abundant, notwithstanding the destruction of young herrings in the spring, the objection may not be well founded.

Crabs and lobsters are fished for on most parts of this coast, and a few mackerel are sometimes taken in the herring nets.

The line fishermen on the Northumberland coast have an enemy to contend with which seems to be but little known farther south. This is the myxine, a worm-like fish of low organization, and variously called the borer, hag, sucker, or rapper-eel. Numbers of these

T

pests will attack a haddock, cod, or other fish that has been hooked, and, making their way inside in some manner still a subject of doubt, but believed to be through the gill-opening, devour the flesh of the unfortunate victim, and leave nothing but the skin and bones for the fisherman's share. Great destruction is sometimes caused by these borers in summer, which is the season in which they are generally most abundant; and we have heard of even a large holibut having been hauled up on a longline, with nothing but the skeleton left inside the skin. These borers are generally about 10 or 12 inches long, and are most numerous in deep water.

The total number of fishing boats belonging to England and Wales, and standing on the register at the end of 1872, was 15,331. They consisted of

1st Class.		2nd Class.	3rd Class.	Total.
Boats. 2778	Tonnage. 100,332	Boats. 9353	Boats. 3200	15,331

Of these the First Class boats averaged a little more than 36 tons each, and probably about 1400 of them were deep-sea trawlers. The relative importance of the different methods of fishing, as shown either by the supply of fish obtained or the capital invested, will place them in the following order:—

1, trawling; 2, drifting; 3, line-fishing; 4, seaning; 5, set-nets, including all anchored nets; and trawling is entitled to the further distinction of being systematically carried on throughout the year, in any kind of weather except heavy gales and the lightest winds, and by men of whom a very large number entirely abstain from the use of any intoxicating drink.

FISHING STATIONS.

SCOTLAND.

Methods of fishing in use — Partial change from open to decked fishing boats — Advantages of the latter — Fishery Board returns of boats and men in the herring and white fisheries — Board of Trade returns imperfect — **Leith to Kirkcaldy** — Fisheries in the Firth of Forth — Newhaven cod and haddock lines — Dandy-line fishing at Dunbar — Important herring fishery at Eyemouth, North Berwick, Anstruther, &c. — Winter fishery — Seining for sprats — Beam-trawling — Mackerel fishing — Lobsters and crabs — **Dundee to Peterhead** — Herring fishing and longlining — "Finnan haddies" — Steam-tugs at Aberdeen for towing the fishing boats — Advantages of the system — **Banff to Wick** — Extensive drift and line fisheries — Sprat fishing in Beauly Firth — Scottish fishing boats, description of — Increased size and peculiar rig — "Scaith" on the Banff coast — Importance of Wick as a station — Measuring the herrings — Classification of the fish — Scottish Fishery Board — Curing, packing, branding, exportation — Immense number of herrings caught — Winter fishery — Exposed situation of Wick — Fishery harbours — Importance of — Difficulties in constructing them — Drift-nets — Sheep-skin buoys — **Kirkwall to Lerwick** — Orkney fisheries uncertain — Frequent bad weather — Line-fisheries — Dried fish for the Spanish market — Abundance of crabs and lobsters — Orkney fishing boats — Shetland fisheries — Importance of the line-fishery — Herring fishing uncertain — Longlines and handlines — Distant fishing grounds — Cod-smacks — Line-fish salted and dried — Grimsby smacks at Faroe — Discovery of Rockall — Difficulty in fishing there — Cod fishery at Davis' Straits — Shetland boats, Norway yawls — Taaf-net — Whales at Shetland — Industry and enterprise of the Shetlanders — Returns of Shetland cured fish — Markets.

THE fishing population on the coast of Scotland is a numerous one, but, with some exceptions, the stations are small and the people much scattered. The methods of fishing pursued there are much the same as those already noticed on the English coast; the drift and line fisheries, however, far exceed the others in extent and importance, and may be regarded as the characteristic fisheries of the country. Stow-net fishing is, we believe, quite unknown in Scotland; and beam-trawling and seaning—the latter there called "trawling"—are only carried on in a few localities. Set-nets for turbot, skate, and crabs are in frequent use; and the lobster fishery by means of creels is extensively worked, particularly on the rocky northern and western coasts. In the general style and rig of the fishing boats used in Scotland there is a much greater uniformity than on the English coast. This arises in a great measure from the general absence of deep-water harbours, and the consequent restriction in the size of the boats which can be conveniently employed; while the general similarity of the principal fisheries all round the coast does not lead to much variation in the means of conducting them. One very important improvement, however, has been recently made by the introduction of decked fishing boats at many of the stations; the long-standing prejudice against such craft, which has cost the lives of so many fishermen and brought desolation to so many homes, having been at last to some extent overcome. It is difficult to estimate the full value of this change; but, apart from the increased safety to the crews, some idea may be formed of it by a consideration of the fact that when the herring season has been a bad one, the failure has been often in a great measure owing, not to the scarcity of fish, but to the inability of the open boats to face the bad weather so frequent on the Scottish coasts.

In the case of the line-boats, which also go many miles to sea, the advantage of the change must likewise be very great; and the fear of bad weather, which at particular times has made both kinds of fishermen hesitate to risk their lives and property in the open boats, is now giving way before the confidence an increasing number of them feel in being better able to face the gales when they come, and in knowing that the danger of being swamped is reduced to a minimum.

This was practically tested in 1872; and the following interesting information on the subject is given in the Report for that year by the Commissioners of the Scotch Fishery Board :—

"The decked boat undoubtedly costs more than the open boat, but better fishing returns are obtained from it, and of course more safety and comfort to the crew. Thus in the small village of Coldingham, in Eyemouth District, where the boats are nearly all decked, the gains of the crews at the herring fishing of 1872 ranged from 100*l*. to 550*l*. per boat; while in the adjacent village of Burnmouth, where the boats are nearly all open, the gains of the crews ranged only from 60*l*. to 160*l*. per boat; and the Fishery Officer ascertained, from observation and inquiry, that all the decked boats were well fished, while nearly all the open boats were poorly fished; many of the old boats are in consequence to be lengthened and decked, and all the new boats are to be full-decked and larger than those hitherto in use. The first decked boat built in Eyemouth was in 1856. She was 40 feet long and cost 130*l*. In 1872, forty full-decked boats were employed in Eyemouth District, and their average length had increased from 40 feet to 44 and up to 56 feet. Not one of them cost less than 200*l*., several a great deal more."

These forty boats form, however, but a small proportion of the number of fishing boats in the district, and, although a reform was begun so long ago as 1856, the increase of the decked craft has been making but little progress until within the last two or three years. It is remarkable that the objection to the change should have been so persistent in the face of the numerous disasters and the great loss of life which have resulted from the use of open boats. The advantages of decked craft have been publicly and privately pointed out to the fishermen for many years past, but have been met by objections on their part which should be of equal importance now, if they were ever of much value. The logic of increased profits, however, is no doubt convincing, for the Report goes on to say:—

"This improvement in boats is not confined to Eyemouth, but extends over the whole east coast. The Officer at Leith reports that a great change has taken place there in the size and construction of the boats, those recently built being all decked, and having from 42 to 45 feet keel, equal to a length over all of 45 to 48 feet; these boats cost from 250*l.* to 300*l.* each, and the village of Newhaven alone, in the Leith District, had 13 such boats supplied to it within the last eighteen months. At Anstruther, several new first-class boats have been added during the year to the fine fleet of boats in that district. From Buckie, upon the coast of Banffshire, the Officer reports that there are now about 400 boats full-decked in his district; that 64 first and 11 second-class boats were built in it during the year 1872; and that the boat-builders continue to be fully employed. At Lybster, upon the coast of Caithness, 15 new boats were added to the port; 6 having been built in the district of Lybster, 1 at Peterhead, and 8 at Wick, all of them from 38 to 43 feet keel; 8 of these boats were full-decked. At Wick, the boat-building showed more activity than it had done for several years; 37 large herring boats were turned out in 1872 as against 15 of the same class in

1871; of these 37 boats the greater part were full-decked, and in material, finish, and equipment they are stated to be all that could be desired."

Encouraging as these reports are, the change from open to decked boats has hitherto been only a partial one, although it has been begun at many places on the east coast. Few things are more difficult than to induce fishermen generally to work in any other way or by any other means than what they have been accustomed to; and it will probably be some time yet before the advantage of decked boats is universally acknowledged by the Scotch fishermen. There is reason to hope, however, that it will be only a question of time; but the old Norsemen at the Shetlands may well be excused if they are content with the many undoubted good qualities of the open yawls which have long done good service on their dangerous coasts. On the western side of Scotland open boats are, we believe, still almost exclusively used; there is a larger proportion of small boats there than on the eastern side, and the fishermen as a rule do not work so far from land. Still there are numerous boats, especially from the Outer Hebrides and the Campbelton districts, which go far away from their own waters and take part in the herring fishery both on the east coast and in the Irish Sea. These are only the larger boats, and it is impossible to doubt that an advantage would be gained by having them decked.

Among the changes which have been introduced in modern fishing boats, we may mention the adoption in some cases of the composite style of building—that of wooden planking on an iron frame. The lightness and strength resulting from this combination have been well proved in trading vessels of various size; and although the system is undoubtedly of particular advantage in the larger classes, there seems no reason why it should not answer for fishing boats. Steam has also been applied; but, as in the case of trawlers, the experiment has not yet succeeded. We shall probably hear of it again under more favourable circumstances.

The statistics furnished by the Scotch Fishery Board in their Annual Reports, although only relating to the quantities of herring, cod, ling, and hake which are cured, and therefore giving no very definite idea of the total catch around the coast, are still extremely valuable in showing, by the number of boats and men engaged in those fisheries, whether or not there is any indication of failure in the supply of fish. There is frequently considerable fluctuation in the success of the fisheries from year to year, and in the number of boats and men in each district; and the difference between the east and west coast fisheries is sometimes very great; but the general result for the whole coast in 1872 shows a remarkable advance in the extent of the fisheries within the last few years. The following returns, extracted from the Reports of the Fishery Board, show the number of boats and men engaged in the herring and white fisheries in 1862, and after two successive intervals of five years:—

	Boats.	Men.
1862	12,545	41,008
1867	13,502	43,399
1872	15,232	46,178

There was a slight decrease in the number of boats and men in 1872, as compared with those at work in 1871; but the aggregate tonnage of the boats in 1872 was greater than in any previous year. This may be accounted for by the increase at many places in the size of the boats.

The total number of Scotch fishing boats of all classes, and used for all kinds of fishing, as given in the Board of Trade Returns, when compared with the number of boats given by the Fishery Board as engaged in particular fisheries—those for herrings and white-fish—shows a difference of only 1533 boats for the year 1872. This difference should represent the number of boats not engaged in the particular fisheries above mentioned, which are the only ones which come under the notice of the Fishery Board. But an analysis of the two returns shows that they cannot both be right. A difficulty in comparing the details of the two returns meets one at the outset. The whole coast of Scotland is divided by the Fishery Board into districts, varying in extent according to the importance of the fishing stations they include; and the returns they give are for each of those districts. This is an intelligible system; and as each district is superintended by a fishery officer, part of whose duty it is to keep an accurate account of the number of herring and white-fishing boats at work, there should not be much room for error; and from what we know of the working of the system, we believe it to be generally trustworthy. The returns published by the Board of Trade, on the other hand, are collected by the Custom House authorities, and refer to the number of boats registered under the Sea Fisheries Act, 1868, in each Customs district; but those districts vary in size according to the commercial importance of the towns along the coast, and have no relation to the extent of the fisheries. It consequently happens, that a considerable range of coast sometimes has to be accounted for by the officers of a single port; and the returns from outlying villages cannot be obtained with any great accuracy without, in many cases, considerable expense. Thus on the main coast of Scotland, Stornoway, in the Outer Hebrides, is the only Custom House port for registration between Wick on the north-east side and Campbelton on the south-west; and the population along this range of coast is very much scattered, and may be said to be almost dependent on fishing for the means of existence. There is, we believe, an admitted uncertainty about all the boats employed in fishing being included in these returns, and perhaps there has not yet been time enough to ensure the complete working of the Act, some of the provisions of which are sure to be unpopular with a large portion of the fishermen. On the other hand, there are no doubt many boats on different parts of all our coasts which are still on the register, although exempted by the Order in Council of the 18th of June, 1869, they not being usually employed in fishing for purposes of sale; but how many continue thus improperly on the register, and how many boats are absent which should appear in the returns, it is of course impossible for us to ascertain.

Among the several districts into which the coast of Scotland is divided by the Customs and the Fishery Board independently, there are only two whose limits are the same under both, viz. Orkney and Shetland. Now, a comparison of the returns for these two districts, taking them together, shows that there were 2409 boats of all kinds registered by the Customs over and above the number given by the Fishery Board as specially employed there in the herring and white fisheries; yet we find there were registered by the Customs, for the whole of Scotland, only 1533 boats more than the number returned by the Fishery Board for their particular fisheries on the same range of coast.

We cannot attempt to explain the discrepancy; but it is evident that either one or both of the returns must be inaccurate. As we have already pointed out, the special organization of the staff of the Fishery Board is such as should prevent much error in returns of this nature; and it appears likely that there are many more boats than have hitherto been registered by the Customs.

In our sketch of the Scotch fisheries we shall, however, give a continuation of the general returns published by the Board of Trade, as they include every kind of fishing boat, although we have great doubt about the correctness of the figures; as before, we shall only mention the returns for 1872, those for the previous years having evidently included numerous boats which should not have been registered.

LEITH TO KIRKCALDY—NUMBER OF BOATS.

Port Letters.	Port.	Year.	1st Class.	2nd Class.	3rd Class.
L.H.	Leith	1872	137	407	1
B.O.	Bo'ness	,,	—	38	2
A.A.	Alloa	,,	1	—	—
P.E.H.	Perth	,,	—	9	—
K.Y.	Kirkcaldy	,,	135	585	3

These five ports include all the fishing stations north of Berwick-on-Tweed as far as the north-eastern limit of the Firth of Forth. It will be observed that the fisheries within the boundaries of three of them are insignificant, but the others contain some important stations.

The fisheries of the Firth of Forth are more varied than on any other part of the Scotch coast; as besides the almost universal drift-fishery for herrings, and the equally general white-fishing by lines, there is some inshore beam-trawling from Buckhaven and a few other places on the north side; a very considerable sprat fishery is carried on with seans or "trawls" at the higher part of the Firth; oysters are dredged in other parts; and anchored nets are used for the capture of various kinds of ground-fish. The fishermen along its shores are moreover fortunate in being within easy reach of markets for the produce of their labours, and their position in this respect when compared with that of their countrymen on many parts of the west coast is an exceedingly favourable one. Eyemouth, North Berwick, Dunbar, and Newhaven are important among the fishing villages in the Leith District, and are especially interested in the herring and haddock fisheries. Newhaven has long been a thriving fishing station, and its boats, for many years among the best on the coast, are now sharing in the improvements which happily are becoming every day more widely adopted. We need hardly say that the Newhaven fishwives, with their picturesque costumes and their wonderful powers of tongue and work, have been the theme of many a fluent pen; and although the railway has somewhat lightened the labours of these sturdy dames, and the good people of Edinburgh now mostly get their supply of fish from the resident fishmongers, there is still plenty to be done close at home to call forth the energies of the wives and daughters of the fishermen. The oyster beds in the Firth are private property, belonging to the Corporation of Edinburgh and to the Duke of Buccleuch. The fishermen make an annual payment for each dredging boat, and all regulations for working the beds, close-time, &c., are agreed upon and carried out by the fishermen themselves. In the case of the Corporation beds off Newhaven the fishery is under the regulation of the fishermen of that village. Dredges of three sizes are used according to the nature of the ground, and the rings of which the under part of the bag is made up are $1\frac{1}{2}$ inch in diameter in all of them.

The longlines used here are of two kinds—those for haddock and cod. The haddock lines carry from 800 to 1000 hooks each, on snoods 14 inches long and $2\frac{1}{2}$ feet apart, and the baits used are mussels and lugworms. The number of men in a boat depends on her size, and whether the fishing is carried on near or far from land; as the haddocks generally are at no great distance the smaller boats are used for this fishery. There is a considerable trade in smoked haddocks from Eyemouth; the fish are placed for an hour in pickle and then hung for a night in some hardwood smoke. The cod or "great lines" are worked at considerable distances from land, and although on precisely the same principle as the haddock lines, have fewer and larger hooks. They have about six score hooks to a line with the snoods 5 feet long and an interval of $2\frac{1}{2}$ fathoms between them. Small haddock and herrings are here used for baiting them, and cod, ling, skate, holibut, and turbot are the fish taken. The number of lines in a boat varies with the number of men, each of whom has one, and they are all fastened into a string when they are shot, as we have previously described when speaking of longlining from Grimsby.[1] The longlines are mostly used from April to July.

The great herring fishery on this coast is carried on from July to September, and about the end of the season the spawning takes place. It is then the practice at Dunbar and some other places to ground and anchor

[1] See page 137.

the nets so as to catch the fish when they are at the bottom and spawning, and this practice does not appear to have struck the fishermen as open to much objection, although the possible disturbance of herring spawn by a trawler is sufficient to raise the neighbourhood. This ground-fishing is carried on mostly by day. The Dunbar fishermen are also conspicuous among those who use the dandy-line or jigger among the spawning fish; and, in fact, there seems to be no method for catching herrings, no matter what their condition may be, which is not approved by them—except taking the young ones in the sprat seans, and this is only done at the other end of the Firth by another set of fishermen, who cannot avoid it if the sprat fishery is to be worked, as the two kinds of fish are frequently in company.

An important winter herring fishery is also carried on in the Firth of Forth. It is continued more or less through the first three months of the year, but its success depends a good deal on the state of the weather, which at that season is of course very uncertain. These winter herrings are usually ready to spawn at some time in March. Herrings are here counted six score and eight to the hundred, and a very large proportion of the enormous numbers of these fish which are landed in the course of the year on both sides of the Firth do not come into the curer's hands, but are sent to market fresh.

The sprat fishery takes place only at the upper end of the Firth, and at one time was not permitted beyond certain limits. It is carried on from October to February, altogether about three months and a half. The sean or circle net is the only one employed; and there being now no restriction to its use great success attends its working where sprats are abundant. Like all other fisheries, that for sprats is somewhat fluctuating; there does not appear, however, to be any indication of a permanent decrease in the supply; the takes have been very large during the last two seasons, and it is stated in the Report of the Fishery Board in 1872 that the supply in that year was so large it was at one time difficult to obtain as much as one shilling per barrel for the fish.

On the north side of the Firth there are numerous fishing villages coming within the Customs district of Kirkcaldy, which may be taken as nearly corresponding with the Fishery Board's district of Anstruther, the most important station on that side of the Firth. Besides the usual drift and line fisheries, there is some beam-trawling from this district. It is not very important, however, but deserves notice as the only fishery of the kind on the east side of Scotland, with the exception of a little which we understand has recently been attempted on the coast of Kincardineshire. The present style of fishing boat is only adapted for trawling in comparatively shallow water, and the deep water, strong tides, and generally rough bottom along the Scotch coast are not favourable to deep-sea trawling in that part of the North Sea. A steam-trawler from Leith was at work for a short time a few years ago, but did not succeed as she was expected to do; we could not ascertain, however, whether the failure was due to the scarcity of fish or the excessive expense.

Mackerel are found in the Firth about the end of July and in August, but only a few are caught, and those by hook and line; most of the fishermen are then engaged in the all-important herring fishery.

Lobsters are taken in creels, sometimes called trunks; the hoop-net called by the latter title on the Yorkshire coast being here known as a hand-trunk; that was also in use here formerly, but is now generally given up. From twenty to twenty-five creels are used by each boat, and flounders are employed as bait.

Crabs are taken in set-nets, as also are turbot and skate.

DUNDEE TO PETERHEAD—NUMBER OF BOATS.

Port Letters.	Port.	Year.	1st Class.	2nd Class.	3rd Class.
D.E.	Dundee	1872	40	135	26
A.H.	Arbroath	,,	7	146	4
M.E.	Montrose	,,	46	291	19
A.N., or A.	Aberdeen	,,	36	463	2
P.D.	Peterhead	,,	529	277	318

The fisheries along this part of the coast do not require any particular notice, as, although they are of considerable importance, they consist only of those which are carried on in all the other districts, namely, herring fishing and longlining. Haddocks are here perhaps more sought after than the larger white-fish, and the manufacture of "Finnan haddies," begun at the village of Findon, between Stonehaven and Aberdeen, is now carried on at several other places in the neighbourhood. The true Finnan haddies are prepared in the cottages of the fishermen and are smoked over peat fires instead of by the ordinary wood smoke; they thus acquire a peculiar flavour and fetch a higher price than the others, which are properly known as smoked haddocks. It is to be feared, however, that a very large number of the latter are sold in the shops under the more attractive title.

The herring fishery from Aberdeen has been very much developed in recent times, and as will be observed, there is now a large number of fishing boats belonging to the port. Peterhead is, however, the important station on the part of the coast included within the districts here given. In 1871 steam was utilized by the Aberdeen men in a manner which we may hope will be adopted at other places with the same success. Tugs were engaged for the purpose of helping the driftboats to and from their fishing grounds. There can be no doubt that this is a move in the right direction, and the Scotch Fishery Commissioners take a just view of it when they say in their Report for 1871:—"In the absence of direct application of steam to fishing boats, which it may be prognosticated will be introduced before many years have passed, the employment of a steam-tug by the fleet cannot be too much extended. As a resource of modern times it overcomes the hindrances and difficulties of a coast where the tides are rapid and the winds variable and often light; indeed it is impossible too strongly to recommend a force which so easily surmounts these and other obstacles, and, by taking the boats long distances, opens new fishing grounds."

In places like Aberdeen, where there is a large amount of shipping, there are greater facilities for procuring tugs than there would be at the exclusively fishing stations; but as these vessels would only be wanted at the latter stations for two or three months in the year, the expense of chartering many of them for a short season would be likely in many cases to interfere with their profitable employment. Still we may hope to see the system extended, as we fear the present times are not favourable to the direct application of steam to the fishing boats themselves. Such a change as that would, we believe, involve an entire alteration in the size and build of the fishing boats, and great additional expense both in first cost and working. The larger the vessel the more economy there is in the general management; and although we are unwilling to suggest any obstacles to improvements in fishery appliances, we think many difficulties will continue to be found in the direct application of steam to such vessels as are best suited to the Scotch herring fishery. Such a system seemed particularly applicable to deep-sea trawling, where a certain speed is absolutely necessary for work; but the expense has been the great difficulty, and it is now only used in the "carriers" which collect the fish from the different vessels and take it to the market. For this purpose steam is found to answer; but even here it only pays when the vessel is large enough to carry a considerable cargo. Tugs have been used for some time past in towing sailing carriers up the Thames when necessary, and at Yarmouth it is a common thing to see the tugs go out and pick up both trawlers and drift-boats, and bring them into the haven. It is in work of this kind that steam may, we think, be usefully employed; but even in such cases it can be only partially used, for at many of the stations the herring boats congregate in hundreds—Wick, for instance, at times sending forth 1000 or more boats—and it would be very difficult to provide enough towing power to take half of them to sea or bring them back from any distance within the available time.

BANFF TO WICK—NUMBER OF BOATS.

Port Letters.	Port.		Year.	1st Class.	2nd Class.	3rd Class.
B.F.	Banff	..	1872	511	607	9
I.N.S., or I.	Inverness	..	,,	90	1923	355
W.K.	Wick	..	,,	313	1180	24

This portion of the coast, comprising the shores of the Moray Firth continued to their farthest limits eastward and northward, has an essentially fishing population, and includes no less than eight districts according to the divisions made by the Fishery Board. These are Fraserburgh, Banff, Buckie, Findhorn, Cromarty, Helmsdale, Lybster, and Wick. The same drift and line fisheries are carried on in all these districts, but Fraserburgh and Wick are important among the herring stations, while the Buckie men are distinguished for the enterprise and industry with which they prosecute the fishery for cod and ling; not only fishing on their own coast, but going away to Caithness and even the northern islands for that purpose. In the Beauly Firth there is a considerable sprat fishery in winter, subject to the usual fluctuation in the setting-in of the shoals, and the same complaints of catching young herrings in the sprat nets are made here as we have already noticed as occurring in the Firth of Forth.

We have said nothing hitherto of the style of fishing boat generally used on the coast of Scotland, but we may here notice it, especially as in parts of the Moray Firth there are still in use boats of a different build and rig from those in fashion on most parts of the coast of Scotland.

There is little difference at first sight in the appearance above water of the general run of Scotch fishing boats, but there are many distinctions below the waterline, which, however, can hardly be made clear without giving the lines of each local type. The boats are all sharp at both ends and have a great deal of beam, but differ much in depth and in the extent of rise to the floor. Ten years ago the large-class boats at Wick were about 15 tons, 30 feet keel, 34 feet 6 inches over all,

13 feet beam, and 4 feet 9 inches depth of hold. They were, we believe, entirely open boats, except in sometimes having a small covered forecastle; and we do not remember having observed any decked boats among the hundreds of fishing craft which then came under our notice. Since that time there has been a great change for the better; the boats on this part of the coast have been built with 10 or 12 feet more keel, and an increasing number of them are fully decked; while farther south, according to the Report of the Fishery Board previously quoted, the increase in size has been very much greater. The lug-rig (Plate XIII.) is the one universally adopted on the Scotch coast, except on the south-west, where a different style of boat is in partial use. The masting of the Scotch fishing boats, however, is unlike anything we see on the English coast, except near that part of it where the two countries join. The sails consist of two lugs and a jib; the fore-lug is the principal one, and with that alone the boats work exceedingly well; the second lug is smaller, and generally with very little peak, and is set on a mainmast stepped nearly in the centre of the boat. This arrangement of carrying a main-lug instead of a mizen gives a characteristic and peculiar appearance to the Scotch fishing boats, and it cannot fail to strike anyone at all familiar with the different position of the after-sail in English luggers of every kind of build; but although there may be some advantages in the Scotch rig, we can hardly doubt that the handiness and general convenience of a mizen which have led to its use in all our other lug-rigged fishing boats—from the large Yarmouth boats downward—would be equally felt in Scotch waters. The present fashion, however, is so general, and fishermen of any country are so slow in making a

SCOTCH FISHING BOATS.

change from what they have been accustomed to, that it is unlikely an alteration will soon be made in this matter, unless indeed the disadvantage of the present rig should become more apparent to them from a difficulty in lowering the mainmast in the large decked boats now coming into use. The objection which has been made to the use of a mizen on account of the inconvenience of having anything outside the boat when hundreds of boats are going in or out of harbour, or are berthed together at their moorings, will hardly bear consideration, unless we can suppose that Scotch fishermen are incapable of handling a boat with an outrigger or running it in out of the way when it is not wanted. Manx, Cornish, and Irish fishermen have no difficulty in such matters; and during the herring season in the Irish Sea the harbour at Howth may be seen crowded with their fishing boats rigged in this manner. Whether there be fifty or five hundred boats in a fishing harbour they are pretty sure to be crowded together; and there is no practical reason why there should be more difficulty in taking up a berth in one case than in another. The advantage of a mizen if there be a necessity for making short tacks when working in or out of harbour, need not be enlarged upon; and we expect the Scotch fishermen would find much less use for their oars than at present if they could be persuaded to make a change.

On part of the Banff line of coast a boat locally called a "scaith" is in use. It is altogether unlike the rest of the Scotch fishing boats, and if this style of build had been of a recent instead of an old fashion on this coast, it would certainly be supposed to have been taken from the Americans. Although we have seen several of these boats under sail, we have not had an opportunity of examining one of them out of the water, and we are indebted to the *Report on Scotch Fishing Boats*, by Captain Washington (1849), for their actual dimensions and a knowledge of their lines. The midship section is low and broad, with a flat or rather hollow floor; the greatest breadth at the water-line is just three-fifths from the bow, and the lines there and downwards are essentially on the wave principle. There is considerable rake of both stem and stern post, and the boat is entirely open. The dimensions, as given in the Report, are 41 feet over all, 13 feet beam, and 4 feet 9 inches depth of hold. The peculiarity of the "scaith," however, is not confined to her build, as she carries a mizen in addition to the fore and main lugs; and, with poles rigged up to act as bow-lines, she has the quaint appearance represented by the distant boat in Plate XIII.

These boats sail fast, and stand up well to their canvas, but are best adapted for smooth water. The fishermen nevertheless go long distances in them; but we believe they are decreasing in number, and ten years ago we saw comparatively few of them.

Five men are the ordinary crew of a herring boat, except in the winter fishery, when the frequent bad weather makes a larger number desirable, although fewer nets are then used.

Wick is one of the most important herring stations on the east coast, and curing operations are there carried on upon a large scale, although Peterhead and Fraserburgh generally make a more conspicuous figure in the official returns. The method of preparing the fish there, as at the other Scotch stations, is that known as the British White Herring Cure, and consists simply in packing the herrings with a certain proportion of salt in well-made barrels, where they remain until they are required for consumption. The process, however, needs considerable care, and it is considered important that the curing should be commenced as soon as possible after the fish are caught. No time therefore is lost in bringing the fish on shore; and after having been measured in a stamped vessel holding 36 gallons, and known as a "cran," they are at once taken in hand by the gutters, who perform their duties with a marvellous rapidity only to be attained by considerable practice. This part of the work is almost entirely done by women. As soon as the fish have been gutted—and for this purpose it is necessary to make only a small opening near the head—they are placed in large troughs containing salt, where they are well "roused" or stirred up, so that the salt may be applied to their whole surface. The fish are then carefully packed with alternate layers of salt in barrels of regulated size, and after remaining fifteen clear days in the pickle the barrels are filled up as necessary, and finally closed. If, however, they are intended for exportation to a warm country, the barrels are repacked in the same manner as at first.

The cured herrings are separated into four classes, consisting of "Full," or fish having large milt or roe; "Maties,"[1] or fat fish, and with the roe undeveloped;

[1] "Maties" is a corruption of the Dutch *maatjes*, the name applied to herrings in which the roe is small or undeveloped; its signification is doubtful, unless it be derived from *maatje* (*kleine maat*), a small measure. The Dutch separate their herrings into three classes, according to the development or otherwise of the roe; this is the case, at all events, with two of the classes, and if we are correct in our interpretation of *maatjes*, it also holds good for the third. The classes will then stand thus:—"Voll," full of roe; "maatjes," with the roe small or undeveloped; and "ylen," empty or shotten. *Maatjes* are generally fat fish, but herrings are only in that condition when the roes are small. As the breeding season advances the fat is gradually absorbed and the fish become *voll*; and when the spawn has fully matured it is deposited, and the herrings are then called *ylen*, or empty.

"Spent," or shotten, those which have recently spawned; and "Mixed," consisting of inferior and perhaps broken fish. The whole process of curing is carried on under the supervision of the Scotch Fishery Board, or, to speak more correctly, the Board of British White Herring Fishery. This mode of cure is required by Act of Parliament to be carried out under inspection; and if the result of the cure come up to a certain standard of excellence, the curers can have, on payment of fourpence per barrel, a Government brand placed on each barrel so approved. The branding is quite optional on the part of the curer; but in either case the curing must be open to inspection, and barrels of a particular size must be used for packing the fish in. It is one of the anomalies of the system, however, that although it is absolutely forbidden to use barrels of other than a certain size, there is not the slightest restriction as to the quality or condition of the fish to be packed in the barrel, so long as the Government brand is not desired for it. Any refuse fish may be cured and packed, but the barrel must be of a certain size. There are four distinct brands denoting the quality and description of fish cured; but the Crown full brand, given only to "full" fish properly cured, is the one mainly in request. The advantages and disadvantages of the branding system have been often discussed, and we need say nothing more on the well-worn subject, except that it appears to greatly facilitate the sale of "white herrings" in the Continental markets, where there is always a large demand for fish cured in this manner. On the other hand, a Government certificate of the quality of any particular article of commerce is opposed to the policy of free trade now adopted in this country. Branding is, however, still in favour with a majority of the Scotch curers for such fish as they send abroad, and the branding fees for 1872 amounted to 7045*l.*, the largest sum ever received in one year on that account. The total number of barrels of white herrings cured in Scotland in 1872 was 773,859, of which as many as 523,540 were exported to the Continent,—Russia, Germany, Holland, and Belgium being the countries to which they were principally sent; and of this large number exported, 422,731 barrels received the Government brand, and paid the fee of fourpence per barrel.

It is difficult by merely looking at figures to fully realize the enormous number of herrings taken every year on the coast of Scotland alone; but if the low average of 750 fish be allowed for each barrel, we find that no less than 580 millions of herrings were cured in 1872, besides an unknown but undoubtedly very large number disposed of fresh. And when it is remembered that there is no good reason for believing that man takes more than a very small percentage of the herrings around our coasts, any attempt to estimate the number and extent of the shoals only leads one into a state of hopeless bewilderment.

The winter fishery for herrings by the Wick boats was first tried in 1862, and then chiefly for the purpose of obtaining the fish for bait; but the attempt was so successful that the fishery has since been regularly prosecuted, so far as the weather has permitted it. The whole north-east coast of Scotland, however, is very much exposed; and even during the time when the summer fishery is carried on, we hear of serious losses of both life and property by the heavy gales which sometimes spring up with but very little warning. It is painful to think, too, that a good deal of the loss of life has been caused by the absence of easily accessible shelter, and that in attempting to enter such small fishery harbours as have been constructed, both men and boats have sometimes perished within sight of their homes.

The situation of Wick particularly exposes it to the effects of the winter storms, and deep-sea fishing on that coast, whether it be by line or net, is both dangerous and uncertain at that season. It is hardly less so occasionally in summer; for any difficulty there may be in finding shelter under ordinary circumstances is greatly increased by the large number of fishing boats then working from that station.

The construction of a deep-water harbour at Wick is therefore a matter of the greatest importance to the fisheries, and energetic measures have accordingly been taken to carry out the work. But although a large sum of money has been provided for the purpose, partly by the British Fisheries Society, who have a property in the harbour, and partly by advances from the Public Loan Commissioners, the completion of the piers has been seriously retarded; for the terrific force of the waves during some of the winter gales has, time after time, and notably in 1870, destroyed much of the work accomplished during the fine weather, thus affording strong evidence of how valuable would be the shelter if the harbour could be completed and made permanently secure. The work is still in progress, and we may hope that before long all the difficulties will be overcome.

The importance of fishery harbours on this east coast may be judged of by the difficulties it is thought worth while to battle against in their construction; and these may be estimated by the amount of money it has been necessary to raise in order to overcome them. Government help, however, is given to those who will help themselves. The Fishery Board are the administrators of an annual Parliamentary Grant of 3000*l*. for the construction or improvement of fishery harbours and piers in Scotland, and this in the course of years has been distributed over a long list of stations on both coasts, as an *addition* to the funds raised by the local promoters of the works, who have contributed from one-fourth to one-half, and in some cases more, of what has been required. The fishery harbour of Dunbar, at the entrance to the Firth of Forth, and one of the most important herring stations, has cost upwards of 40,000*l*., of which more than half has been raised by the promoters; and at Anstruther Union Harbour — a work, perhaps, of even more consequence, on the opposite side of the Firth—the Board has been for some years contributing towards the very costly piers still in progress. Much injury was caused here by the gales of the winter of 1869–70, by which the expenses of construction were unfortunately greatly increased, and the completion of the work considerably retarded. The injury was so great, and further danger so imminent, that in order to secure the permanence of the remaining work a special grant of 7000*l*. was made by Parliament. We have already spoken of the harbour in course of construction at Wick; the cost of it will far exceed that of any other work of the kind on the coast of Scotland; but it is being carried out without any assistance from the annual Parliamentary Grant; and when completed, it is expected that not only will the herring fishermen along that coast derive great advantage from it, but the line-fishery will also be carried on from Wick on a much larger scale than it is at present. Mussels are not to be obtained there, but a large supply of bait is now procured from the winter herring fishery.

There is nothing to be particularly noticed in the mode of conducting the drift-fishery on the coast of Scotland. The principle on which these nets are worked is the same everywhere, and it has been fully described in previous pages. We may mention, however, that here, as elsewhere, there has been a gradual increase in the size and number of the nets employed, and as larger boats come into use the trains of nets will no doubt be further lengthened. Cotton, as a material for nets, has been generally substituted for hemp; it is lighter and undoubtedly more effective. The buoys used for supporting the drift-nets are, at Wick and many other places, made of sheep-skin. The skin is cut so as to take a globular form when the edges are gathered in, and they are then fastened to a flat circular wooden head, on which a cross piece of wood is nailed, and to this the buoy-rope is made fast. The buoy is inflated through a hole in the flat head, and the small opening is then closed with a plug. Sheep-skin buoys are also frequently used with longlines, but in these a light pole passes through the buoy, and a short wooden nozzle is fastened into the skin so as to provide the means of inflating it.

KIRKWALL TO LERWICK—NUMBER OF BOATS.

Port Letters.	Port.	Year.	1st Class.	2nd Class.	3rd Class.
K.L., or K.	Kirkwall	1872	58	1157	102
L.K.	Lerwick	,,	66	1613	701

These two ports include the several fishing villages in the Orkneys and Shetlands.

The fisheries at the Orkneys have never been of great importance, and for the most part they are carried on by the islanders as an occasional means of livelihood rather than as a regular business. The Orkneys are divided into two groups, commonly known as the northern and southern islands, and this local distinction is to some extent supported by the different character of the principal fishery in each. The northern group of islands is chiefly concerned with the line-fishing, while the herring fishery is the particular occupation of the southerners. The latter not only fish in their own waters, but sometimes join the fleets at Wick and Stornoway. The herring season is from the middle of July to September, and at one time it was carried on in May on the west coast. Herrings are also sometimes caught in winter, and, in fact, are believed to be on the coast throughout the year; but they are very uncertain in their movements, and the fishermen generally are not disposed to devote much of their time to looking for them. As a rule the men are not well off, and for some few years past the increased cultivation of the land has provided them with more certain employment and more regular returns than they would probably have obtained by prosecuting the fisheries. There is no reason to doubt that there are plenty of fish of various kinds on the coast, but they change their localities a good deal, and the Orcadians are not all such thoroughbred fishermen as to follow up their profession under many difficulties. It may be said for them, however, that the rapid tides among the islands and the frequent bad weather are serious difficulties to men who are not well found in boats and gear. Some quantity of herrings are caught near the northern islands, but the principal takes are on the south-east coast, between Stronsa and the Pentland

Skerries. Scapa Flow is also a good fishing ground for both herrings and some kinds of line-fish. The herring fishery generally is subject to great fluctuation, and the number of barrels cured at the Orkneys during the six years, 1867-72, varied between 9000 and 25,000 annually.

In the northern islands the fisheries are principally for cod, ling, saithe or coalfish, and a few tusk; but the last are essentially a northern species, and are not found in any abundance south of the Shetlands. They are quite unknown on the English coast, but are very numerous in the Norwegian seas. They may be roughly described as resembling a very short-bodied ling, but without any division in the dorsal fin. Haddocks, although never very abundant on the Orkney coast, and, as elsewhere, very capricious in their movements, are frequently taken; cod and ling are, however, the most valuable products of the line-fishery, and at one time there was a considerable direct export of the dried fish to the Spanish market, 700 or 800 tons being sent thither annually. It now goes by way of Shetland, various circumstances having in late years interfered with the direct trade.

In Kirkwall Bay very large numbers of young coal-fish or sillocks are taken by the sean, or, as it is there called, the sweep-net; and the same kind of net is used by the poorer fishermen on other parts of the coast, several families perhaps uniting to provide and work it. These young fish are useful for both food and bait, and at times the catches have been so large as to be almost unsaleable.

Lobster fishing at the Orkneys has always been carried on successfully, the rocky nature of the coast being very suitable to the habits of these crustaceans;

this fishery is said, indeed, to have been the only one worked in the islands previous to 1815. The lobsters were formerly taken away in welled-smacks, but are now carried by steamers direct to Aberdeen, and thence by rail to London. They are packed with seaweed in boxes; but it is a question whether they now reach the market in as good condition as when they had no land carriage. Crabs are also abundant, but there is little sale for them, as they will not bear packing on the same plan as is adopted for lobsters. Among the other productions of the Orkneys we may mention the familiar periwinkle, of which a large supply is sent to Billingsgate.

Orkney Fishing Boats.

The Orkney fishing boats are of two descriptions, of which the large class, measuring from 30 to 36 feet in the keel, are used for the herring fishery, and are much the same as the ordinary Scotch fishing boats. The other class are called skiffs, and average about four tons each; these are used for the line-fishery. The latter comprise the bulk of the fishing boats; there are, however, a few smaller ones; and of course, with a population scattered over a number of islands, boats are a necessary means of communication between them, and in many cases they are only occasionally employed for purposes of fishing. The skiffs carry a jib and two large lugs; and these Orkney boats are the only ones we have seen that had their lugsails rigged with booms. The herring boats usually carry five or six men, and the skiffs from two to four, according to the size of the boat. Smacks of small size have been tried before now for the cod and ling fisheries, but they were not found suitable for working the longlines.

We now come to the Shetlands—the northern limit to what may be called the home fisheries. Handlines, longlines, and drift-nets are all used there; but the drift-fishery is comparatively unimportant, if we may judge by the number of barrels of herrings cured. The line-fishery is, in fact, the principal occupation of the Shetlanders; and although they are more or less engaged in cultivating such land as is best available for the purpose, as is also the case with the fishermen of the Orkneys and on many parts of the Scotch coast, fishing is their chief employment, and is followed up with great energy and enterprise while the weather permits it. The herring fishery is carried on in August and September, and principally on the east coast from the Skerries to Balta Sound; but is interfered with by the line-fishing, which is continued during the early part of the drift season. The result of this is that a large proportion of the herrings when taken consists of spent fish, and for this inferior quality there is rarely a good market. The takes of fish fluctuate very much in quantity, and this depends to a large extent on the weather; but the small catches of herrings during the last few years have been mainly due to the increased attention given by the fishermen to the more profitable fishery by the lines. Herring-bait is very valuable for this purpose, and it is unfortunate that it can only be procured just at the close of the line season. It is said that very many years ago herrings were fished for in winter, but it has long been given up, and even in the autumn the drift-fishery is a very uncertain one on the Shetland coast.

The line-fishery is also subject to a good deal of fluctuation, especially as regards the cod, which, not only at the Shetlands but also at the Faroe Islands and Iceland, become abundant or scarce in successive years without any apparent reason. The fish particularly sought after by the liners are cod, ling, tusk, and saithe. The last is taken by handlines near the coast, and usually close to the surface at the edge of a tideway; the bait being mussels or fish. Saithe are particularly abundant about Balta Sound and Dunrossness. Cod are also only caught by the handlines, fitted in the same manner as those used in the North Sea fishery by the Grimsby men. Most of the cod are taken at some distance from the land, and there are particular banks which have long been famous for their general productiveness. Of these the Foula Bank, between Foul Island and the mainland of Zetland, is a favourite resort. Farther north is the great Faroe Bank lying about south-south-west of that group of islands, and still farther is the Iceland ground. For these fisheries large vessels are of course required; and in 1872 there were 66 cod-smacks, averaging 44 tons, and carrying about fourteen men each, sent out from Shetland. The fishing season is from April to

September, and during that period the smacks make two or three trips. Welled vessels are not needed for this work, as all the fish are cured; they are split and salted as soon as they are caught, and on the vessel's return to Lerwick the fish are washed and dried in the open air. They undergo no packing, but are exported in bulk. These smacks are not the property of the fishermen, but are fitted out by the curers, the men receiving half the catch, or its equivalent, after all expenses are paid; they are also provided with bread by the owners. At the close of the deep-sea cod-fishery the Shetland smacks are laid up for the winter, and their crews find some other employment; but the winter days are too short and the weather frequently too stormy for much fishing to be done on the coast.

Under the head of "Line-fishing"[1] we mentioned that many of the Grimsby cod-smacks went northwards in April, at the end of the longline season on the Dogger. These vessels then work near the Orkneys and Shetlands as well as on the Faroe and Iceland banks, and almost all the fish they catch is landed either at Kirkwall or Lerwick—most of it at the latter port, where it is bought by the curers and treated in the same manner as that brought home by their own smacks. The Returns published by the Scotch Fishery Board of the dried fish of different kinds cured at Shetland in each year, therefore include the cod which are caught by the Grimsby vessels at the northern stations as well as those which are obtained from the same grounds by the Shetland smacks, and the ling, tusk, and saithe taken by the open boats nearer home. The proportion of fish caught by the English vessels is very difficult to ascertain, but it must vary year by year in accordance not

[1] Page 145.

only with the number of strange vessels, but with the relative success of the deep-sea and home fisheries.

Among the places occasionally visited by a few English and Shetland smacks in search of cod is the very uncertain ground at Rockall. This bank lies about 300 miles west of the Outer Hebrides, and is marked above water by a single roughly conical rock about 30 feet high, with a smaller one, usually uncovered, at a distance of less than a hundred fathoms north of it. There is more than 20 fathoms water close to the rock, and the 50-fathom line of soundings is nowhere so much as a mile away. From this the bank gradually slopes for about 20 miles in a direction a little east of north, and about 35 miles west of south before the 100-fathom line is passed; and the width of the bank within these soundings is from 20 to 25 miles. The fishery, however, is not carried on in a depth of more than about 50 fathoms, and therefore must be very near the rock. The very limited extent of ground on which the fish are found, the danger of keeping near the rock in bad weather, and the difficulty in finding it again when, as sometimes happens, the vessels are blown away, all combine to prevent regular fishing at Rockall; and there is further discouragement in the fact that except quite at the early part of the season the fishery is not likely to be successful, and even then there is often a great scarcity on the ground. Still good work has been done there at times, and stories are told of gigantic cod, six feet in length, having been caught there when the bank first came into notice. The locality has probably been long resorted to by the cod at particular seasons, and we have no evidence that the fish are not there throughout the winter, when there is no deep-sea line-fishing carried on.

Rockall had been seen on several occasions, but its

position was not known with certainty till 1840, when it was ascertained by Mr. T. Harvey Martin and others of the 'Endymion' frigate. The bank has since been carefully surveyed. The Dutch were, we believe, the first persons to work on this bank; it was then tried by the English, and is still fished occasionally by the Shetlanders, and by the Grimsby smacks when on their way to the Faroe Islands.

Another fishing ground still more to the westward has also been visited, but with only occasional success. It having been reported that cod were abundant in Davis' Straits, Mr. Hay, of Lerwick, sent some of his vessels there in 1846, and had a very successful season; the three following years also proved to be very good, but 1850, 1851, and 1852 were very bad seasons, and no more attempts were made until 1862. An interval of ten years had then passed without the fish having been disturbed, and there had been plenty of time for restocking if the failure had been due to overfishing. But the cod were as scarce then as they were in 1852; and the fishery in Davis' Straits was accordingly given up.

The really important fishery in the home waters at the Shetlands is that for ling and tusk. It is carried on entirely by longlines worked from open boats, which have a crew of six men each. The share of line belonging to each man consists of twelve "strings," with ten hooks to a string; the hooks are fastened to snoods a foot and a half long and three fathoms apart, and the bait is always some kind of fish—"pelticks" or young coalfish being commonly employed. The season for this fishery, which is carried on with great success, particularly on the north-east coast, is from May to the middle of August, the same as for the home cod-fishing. The boats used with the longlines are open yawls—the true "Norway skiffs"; they are like whaleboats, about 20 feet on the keel, 28 feet over all, and 8 feet beam. One large lug is the only sail carried, but six oars can be used when necessary. These boats are wonderfully handled by the fishermen, and go long distances to sea; but, good as they may be, they are hardly fit to contend with the very bad weather so frequent there in winter. They are called "haaf" or deep-sea boats.

SHETLAND YAWL.

A smaller class of boats of the same description, but usually carrying only three men, is used for the saithe fishery inshore.

On some parts of the west coast, cod and ling are fished for near the land in February and March, but this fishery is only a partial one, and many of the fish then caught are very small. A few haddocks are also sometimes taken at the Shetlands, but there are fewer of these fish than even at the Orkneys.

There is generally plenty of bait to be procured, although not always of the very best kinds. Buckies or whelks, however, are tolerably abundant, and are caught by the attraction of a cod's head; very large mussels are obtained at the northern extremity of Lerwick Harbour, a broad, many-toothed grapnel or double rake being used for collecting them; and, as previously mentioned, young coalfish are commonly used as fish-bait. These fish are taken in vast numbers along the shore by means of a large "taaf" or hoop-net, and sufficient oil is obtained from their livers to make it worth exporting. Besides the fisheries we have noticed, the capture of the leading or caa'ing whale frequently takes place. These animals appear in herds on the coast; and, when they enter any of the bays, can by a little dexterous manœuvring be driven on shore and killed. This kind of sport is of course of uncertain occurrence, but it is sufficiently frequent to make it worth while for the fishermen to be always prepared for it. A small herd of these whales was killed near Lerwick when we were there in 1864, and very large captures have sometimes been made.

Lobster fishing has not been attended with much success at these islands, and the supply of oysters is not sufficiently large to attract much attention.

There is a great deal in the Shetlanders and their pursuits which at once distinguishes them as a body from all other fishermen of the United Kingdom. Norsemen by descent, they retain all the characteristic daring and powers of endurance which gave their forefathers an honourable name in years long gone by. For Arctic work, whether it be whaling or exploration,

Shetlanders are regularly sought after as a necessary portion of the crews; while at their island home their instinctive occupation is one which exposes them to all the worst perils of the sea, and which are braved by them in boats whose good qualities and national origin alike tend to give confidence in their well-doing. The stern aspect of the Shetlands suggests a hardy race of inhabitants, for there is apparently little to be obtained from agriculture for the support of those whose lot it is to dwell there. In a barren and treeless region, and so far north that the summer nights have no darkness, and the winter days but little light—the supposed *Ultima Thule* of the ancients—where, but for the genial influence of the warm Atlantic currents, the country would be frozen through the long winter months far more completely than is now the case, what would be the condition of the Shetlanders if they were not an energetic race, and ready to take every opportunity of gathering in the only harvest on which they can depend, that from their deep and dangerous seas? Were it not for their fisheries, so actively followed up along their rocky shores and many miles away from land, these islanders must long ere this have become a degenerate and poverty-stricken people, if even they could have existed there at all. But happily they are far from being impoverished; it is true that they are not rich, but they are thriving, and idlers are scarce when there is any work that can be done. There are no more loyal subjects of the Queen than these Shetlanders; but they are proud of their Norse descent, and a greater insult cannot be offered them than to suppose them to be an offshoot from the Scotch. We may say also that from no one else have we met with more readiness to give every kind of information about their methods of working, and to freely discuss every detail of their gear, or less inclination to complain of the bad times which, there as elsewhere, sometimes fall to the lot of the fisherman.

In the following tables, extracted from the published Returns of the Scotch Fishery Board, we give the quantities of Shetland cured herrings and white fish for two periods of six years each, ending respectively in 1862 and 1872. They will give some idea of the fluctuations to which from various causes both kinds of fishery are subject. A barrel of white cured herrings should contain about two hundredweight of actual fish.

	Herrings.	Cod, Ling, &c.			Herrings.	Cod, Ling, &c.	
	brls.	cwts	tons.		brls.	cwts	tons.
1857	17,860	43,625 =	2,181	1867	10,008	43,540 =	2,177
1858	11,926	43,146 =	2,157	1868	1,209	62,649 =	3,132
1859	6,670	60,245 =	3,012	1869	1,775	81,812 =	4,090
1860	10,550	55,960 =	2,798	1870	4,200	95,667 =	4,783
1861	8,164	39,005 =	1,950	1871	1,682	46,394 =	2,319
1862	3,733	51,706 =	2,585	1872	1,801	84,932 =	4,246

The Shetland cured herrings, like those from the eastern coast of Scotland, are principally sent to Prussia; but home markets are found for a great deal of the dried white fish. Spain is the important purchaser of the cod and of a portion of the ling; some is also sent to Australia, but the ling and tusk find a market chiefly at Dublin, Glasgow, and Leith. The saithe are sent to Belfast, Leith, and Dundee.

We may here mention that the enterprising Dutch fishermen frequently work for white fish in the neighbourhood of the Shetlands, and their quaint-looking vessels or "busses" may often be seen at Lerwick.

FISHING STATIONS.

SCOTLAND (*continued*).

Stornoway — Fisheries at the Hebrides — Herring fishery in the Minch — Close-time for herrings — Bad effects of — Inquiry into, and consequent legislation — Curing herrings — Branding disregarded — Irish markets — Longlining — Line-fish generally cured dry — Lobster fishery — Trade in periwinkles — Fishing boats — Returns of cured fish — **Campbelton to Greenock** — Inshore beam-trawling — Lochfyne — Disputes between drift and sean ("trawl") fishermen — Alleged objections to sean-fishing — Prohibition of seaning — Inquiry into the subject by two Commissions, resulting in repeal of prohibition — Recent scarcity of herrings in Lochfyne — Various suggested explanations of it — Peculiar character of Lochfyne — Great depth of water — Situation of the loch favourable for the visits of the herring, but the object of those visits not easily explained — Lochfyne fishing boats — Returns of cured herrings — **Ardrossan to Dumfries** — Ballantrae banks formerly spawning ground for herrings — Set-nets for cod and turbot — Solway fisheries unimportant — Summary of Scotch fisheries and remarks on the fishermen.

STORNOWAY—NUMBER OF BOATS.

Port Letters.	Port.	Year.	1st Class.	2nd Class.	3rd Class.
S.Y.	Stornoway	1872	28	983	55

On the western coasts of Scotland the first station to be noticed is Stornoway in the Outer Hebrides, and an important centre of both herring and white fisheries.

The herring fishery in the Minch—the sea separating the western mainland of Scotland from the Outer Hebrides—is a very valuable one, and as it begins earlier than the regular east coast fishery, boats from Caithness and the neighbouring counties, the Orkneys included, generally take part in it before their own season commences. The herrings are rarely fished for on the Atlantic side of the islands, but they are frequently seen there at some distance from the land by the longline fishermen early in the year. In April the fish are abundant outside a line between Lewis and the north of Scotland. In May the herrings come into the Minch and work their way southwards, but occasionally they enter the Minch south of the islands, and in 1870, in particular, there was a very large fishery inside South Uist and Barra. They generally remain in these waters for some time, and the fishery is carried on far into July or even later.

In 1860 an Act[1] of Parliament was passed by which a close-time was established for herrings on the west coast of Scotland. The Bill was brought in at the instance of some of the curers at Glasgow and other places, principally on the west coast. By this Act herring fishing was entirely prohibited from the 1st of January to the 31st of May on any part of the coast between Ardnamurchan Point and the Mull of Galloway on the south, and from the 1st of January to the 20th of May between Ardnamurchan and Cape Wrath in the extreme north. Not a herring was allowed to be taken during the close season for the purpose of sale, or to be used as bait on the longlines, or to keep the fishermen from starvation; and it appears that this cruel prohibition was to be enforced that the markets might not be supplied with fish which were not always of the best quality, but yet were sufficiently good to command a ready sale, and therefore tended to lower the prices the curers would otherwise have obtained from the proceeds of the comparatively short summer fishing. It was professed that the early fishing broke up the shoals before they entered the Minch, and therefore diminished the supply in June and July, and it was said that many of the fish caught

[1] 23 & 24 Vict., c. 92.

between January and May were unwholesome and unfit for food. But an inquiry into all the circumstances of the case clearly showed that the promoters of the Bill for establishing close-time were the curers alone, who held meetings of their own body and, without consulting the fishermen, pressed forward a measure which sacrificed everyone's interest to their own. It was one of the most unhappy episodes in the history of the Scotch Fisheries; but fortunately the effects of the close-time were soon made known, and after a short experience it was found impossible to enforce a law which brought misery and starvation to the homes of a coast population, many of whom previously could only manage to gain a bare subsistence by hard and unremitting toil. The law remained practically in abeyance for a time, and no prosecutions for infringing it were carried on pending the result of the Report of the Royal Commission in 1862 on Herring Trawling. In 1864 this question of close-time came before the Royal Commission for inquiry into the condition of the Sea Fisheries generally; and such overwhelming evidence of the evil effects of the close-time on the fishermen was brought before the Commissioners, that, in anticipation of their complete Report, they did not hesitate to bring the subject before the Government with the view to some relief being given before the question could be finally disposed of. This resulted in instructions being given not to enforce the law; and in the following Session of Parliament a Bill was passed by which close-time was entirely abolished north of Ardnamurchan Point. This included all the Inner and Outer Hebrides, where the restriction had been so severely felt. South of that part of the coast close-time was continued as before with the exception of

January, which became free to the fishermen. By subsequent legislation (the Sea Fisheries Act, 1868) this close-time has been abolished beyond the three-mile limit, so that at the present time herring fishing is entirely free everywhere around the British Islands except within the three miles of that part of the coast of Scotland which lies between Ardnamurchan Point and the Mull of Galloway. Such local restrictions, however, cannot be justified by anything that is known of the habits of the herring, for the cause of the annual fluctuation in the apparent numbers of these fish has yet to be discovered.

The hardship of the former close-time was felt in various ways by the west-coast fishermen. It was established for a time of year when food of any kind was often difficult to procure in some of the islands; and besides the direct advantage the fishermen were in the way of obtaining by catching herrings for the use of themselves and their families, the fish when in the worst condition for the table, and according to the Glasgow curers quite unfit for food, were in the best order for the purpose of bait for cod and ling; and they are known to be one of the most attractive baits which can be shown to those fishes; so that the restriction not only prevented the people from taking herrings for food, but materially interfered with their catching anything else. And whilst this law was in operation, the east-coast[1] fishermen were free to fish when they pleased; it was only on the western side there was any close-time; and hence arose a feeling of being unjustly dealt with, which even among the orderly and peace-loving inha-

[1] A Bill was introduced into Parliament during the past session to establish a weekly close-time for the herring fishery on the Scotch coast generally; but it fortunately did not meet with approval, and was withdrawn.

bitants of the Hebrides was one of the last things it was desirable to encourage. With a few exceptions, however, the people patiently submitted, and bore their privations as they best could. In the course of time their condition became known, and the distress of the Skye fishermen in particular was brought into prominent notice by Mr. T. Frazer, the resident Sheriff of the island, whose impartial testimony to the evil working of the Act contributed largely to the relief which we may hope has now been permanently given.

The herring fishery may now be said to continue almost throughout the year for one purpose or another, and depending on the locality. The general season is usually later at the south of the Minch than about Stornoway and the north, but there is an apparently well-founded belief that the herrings are on that coast throughout the year, although not always so abundant and so near the surface or the shore, as they are at particular times. Curing is chiefly carried on at Stornoway, but a considerable quantity of herrings is sent fresh to Glasgow and Liverpool, special steamers being employed almost daily during the season for their transport. Some of the cured fish go to the Continental markets, and there is a large export of them to Ireland. The curing is necessarily carried on under the inspection of the Scotch Fishery Board, but the Government brand is entirely disregarded on the west coast, and the curers trust to their own names for selling the fish in either the foreign or Irish markets. They allege that the western fish are more delicate than the others, and will not bear the close packing requisite for ensuring the proper weight in each barrel if the brand is desired.

The general season for longlining, by which the cod, ling, and tusk are here exclusively taken, is from

November to July; and the tusk are only caught on the Atlantic side of the outer islands. Various baits are used; in the Minch nothing has been found so attractive as herrings, whilst outside the islands sand-eels, limpets, small haddocks, and conger, are more or less in favour, and conger is considered especially good for this purpose. Cod are taken on various parts of the coast, and have long been successfully fished, particularly on a bank off the Butt of Lewis, and on another large bank in the middle of the Minch.

The line-fish, excepting a small number cured in pickle and barrelled, are shore-cured in the manner we have described as carried out at the Shetlands; and these dried fish, including a considerable quantity of saithe, are almost all, if not entirely, sent to the home and Irish markets.

The only other fishery of any importance on the range of coast included in the Stornoway Customs district is that for lobsters. It is not equally successful in all parts, but appears to have been thriving for many years on the western side of Lewis and Harris. The lobsters are purchased in large numbers and taken away to the English markets.

Crabs are little sought for, but there is some trade in periwinkles, the collection of which provides occupation for those members of the family who do not go away to the other fisheries. Beds of oysters are also found in some of the lochs, and it is not very clear why more attention is not paid to them.

The fishing boats on this part of the west coast are of the ordinary Scotch type, the larger ones carrying two lugs, and the smaller a single one. Decked craft are not in favour, and although there are sometimes serious losses owing to bad weather, the fisheries are not generally carried on so far from the land as on the east coast, and shelter is more easily obtained in case of necessity.

The usual plan of giving a bounty to the herring fishermen, and engaging to take their fish at a fixed price per cran, is adopted by the curers at Stornoway as elsewhere.

The following is a return[1] for the six years ending 1872 of the quantities of fish of all kinds variously cured on shore in the Fishery Board districts of Stornoway, Loch Broom, Loch Carron and Skye, and Fort William :—

	Herrings.	Cod, Ling, &c.	
		Dried.	Wet.
	brls.	cwts.	brls.
1867	115,164	20,381	30
1868	55,529	20,784	110
1869	70,212	26,681	150
1870	135,120	16,623	160
1871	62,108	19,094	83
1872	40,446	18,782	255

It will be observed that the fluctuations are considerable; in the herring fishery they are partly due to weather, but a great deal depends on the number of strange boats which may be attracted or not to the western waters. In 1872 there was a decrease of upwards of 200 boats from the number of the previous year, and the weather generally was very unsettled. With regard to the white fish, a varying quantity was cured wet, as is the usual practice at Buckie and other places on the east coast; shore-cured fish being for the most part prepared at the northern islands and the Outer Hebrides.

[1] Taken from the Annual Reports of the Scotch Board of Fisheries, Appendix No. 2, Herring Fishery, and Appendix No. 2, Cod and Ling Fishery.

The fisheries we have just mentioned are carried on more or less all along the west coast, in some places more attention being given to one kind than to another. Among the islands near the coast, herring fishing is perhaps less prosecuted than farther out, and the generally poor fishermen do their best to get a living by line-fishing and lobster catching.

The taaf-net, previously noticed at the Shetlands, is also used in Skye, and considerable numbers of young coalfish or saithe are taken by it. The hoop is about 4 feet in diameter, and the depth about $2\frac{1}{2}$ feet; it is suspended from the end of a long pole, and is worked by hand from the rocks.

CAMPBELTON TO GREENOCK—NUMBER OF BOATS.

Port Letters.	Port.	Year.	1st Class.	2nd Class.	3rd Class.
C.N.	Campbelton	1872	11	277	1
G.W.	Glasgow	,,	10	42	27
P.G.W.	Port Glasgow	,,	--	27	17
G.K.	Greenock	,,	22	1687	337

This section of the coast includes the numerous fishing places in Cantire, Arran, and Bute, with the various lochs in the neighbourhood, the Clyde, and part of the Ayrshire shore. The fisheries are here of a more varied character than on the more northern part of the west coast, but the herring fishery is the one of most importance. At Campbelton we once more meet with beam-trawling, but it is not of the deep-sea kind, and the produce consists principally of flounders, with a few soles. It is carried on close to the shore in a few fathoms of water after the herring season has finished, and the boats employed are half-decked smacks about 20 or 25 tons. The same kind of fishing is worked at the mouth of the Clyde and on some small banks outside.

There is some handline fishing for whiting and haddock near the land, and longlines are worked in the deeper parts of the Firth for cod, ling, and turbot. The latter fishery was very much crippled by the Act enforcing a close-time for herrings, and thus preventing the line fishermen from obtaining the most attractive bait. Trammels or set-nets are also used in some parts of the Firth of Clyde for catching hake, cod, and various other fishes.

Campbelton, the Kyles of Bute, and Lochfyne were for some years the seat of an active struggle between two sets of fishermen, both engaged in catching herrings, but by very different methods. The usual mode of drifting for herrings, as followed in deep water all round our coasts, had been for an unknown length of time the only recognized method in the localities we have mentioned, as it still is practically on other parts of the Scotch coast. But about the year 1838 an innovation was made by the introduction of the sean or circle-net, in Scotland known as the "trawl."[1] It is the same kind of net as is used in Cornwall for the capture of pilchards, and on other parts of the coast for various kinds of fish. It is most effective when used near the shore, and the enclosed fish can then be easily taken into the boats or hauled up on the beach. When the fish are in convenient localities a very large number may be enclosed at once, and a boatload or more of herrings obtained after only an hour or two of work. The difference between the two methods is very great;

---

[1] The beam-trawl and the herring-trawl have been so much confused together by writers on the fisheries, that to prevent further misunderstanding we shall here speak of the latter net as the *sean-trawl*.

Y

for although both sets of fishermen may work in a particular locality where they think the fish are likely to be found, in the one case the sean-trawl is the active agent, enclosing the herrings in a body—in the other it depends upon the movements of each individual fish whether it happen to come in contact with the drift-net and be meshed, or perhaps unconsciously to swim away from the danger. As drift-fishing can be effectively carried on in any depth of water not less than that of the net, and at any distance from the shore, there is obviously a much wider scope for its operation than there can be for the sean-trawl, whose work is most efficiently performed when the foot of the net can touch the bottom. The drift men may therefore frequently have a chance of success when sean-trawlers have none; on the other hand, when the fish come very close to the shore there may be occasions when the produce of a sean-trawl is very far in excess of the result of a night's drift-fishing in the immediate neighbourhood. But these heavy catches of herrings by a different kind of net from that in ordinary use were not likely to be made without some complaint, and a long list of charges was brought against the sean-trawlers. They were accused of catching all sizes of fish,—those which were too small to be stopped by the drift-nets and those too large to be meshed in them—the "mother fish," as some of the fishermen called them; it was said that they sometimes made such enormous hauls that only a portion of the catch could be saved; they broke up the shoals and frightened them away; they intercepted them at the entrance to Lochfyne and prevented the drift fishermen up the loch from getting any sport; they damaged the drift-nets when they came in their way; and finally, they lowered the price of herrings to a very considerable extent. As if these offences were not sufficient, many of the curers added to the cry, and said that herrings caught by the sean-trawl were not fit to be cured, for they did not bleed at the gills like those taken by the drift-nets, and, further, that the markets were sometimes so glutted by the large takes of fish, and prices fluctuated so much from day to day, that the buyers did not know what to be at.

The result of these several complaints was that in 1851 an Act[1] was passed to put an end to sean-trawling for herrings on the coast of Scotland; but it not proving effective, more stringent measures were brought to bear on the fishermen in 1860[2] and 1861,[3] and fishing by the sean-trawl was completely suppressed. So strong a feeling existed, however, among a large body of the fishermen and others that the complaints against sean-trawling were unjust and the prohibition injurious to the interests of the public as well as to the fishermen immediately affected by it, that in 1862 a Royal Commission was appointed to especially inquire into the subject; and in September, 1864, the question was independently considered by two of the members of the general Sea Fisheries Commission, the third Commissioner being purposely absent from the second inquiry as he had taken part in the proceedings of the previous one.

The conclusions arrived at by both Commissions were decidedly adverse to the opponents of sean-trawling, and were to the effect that the fishing in Lochfyne had suffered no diminution by that method of working; on the contrary, it had been steadily progressive, when the periods of comparison were made sufficiently long to correct the annual fluctuations, which are always considerable in this as in all other herring fisheries. They

---

[1] 14 & 15 Vict., c. 26. [2] 23 & 24 Vict., c. 92. [3] 24 & 25 Vict., c. 72.

say [1]—"The selected years of bad fishing, brought as proofs that trawling was destroying the fishery, have, when examined, no application to the question, as an equal number of years of quite as bad fishing are found in every decennial period before the system of (sean) trawling had been discovered. . . . . (Sean) trawling for herring has been an important means of cheapening fish to the consumer, by the large and sudden takes, and has thrown into the market an abundant supply of wholesome fresh fish at prices which enable the poor to enjoy them without having to come into competition with the curer. It is this circumstance which, in our opinion, has produced the demand for repressive legislation, for the gains of the drift-net fishermen are much affected by the sudden and great captures of the (sean) trawler, who, working with less capital and with a more productive kind of labour, is able to undersell the drift-net fishermen, and to derange the market for the curers."

It happened that in 1860, the last year of sean-trawling before its entire suppression, the fishery in Lochfyne was the largest ever known there; in 1861 it fell off, but in 1862 it was again very large, and that was followed by fluctuations as before, although the drift-men then had it all their own way. In the meantime the recommendations of the two Commissions were embodied in an Act passed in 1867,[2] by which any kind of herring net with what was then the legal mesh was permitted; and by the Sea Fisheries Act, 1868, that last restriction as to mesh was removed, and the fishermen were allowed to fish with any kind of net they liked. It is impossible, however, to make people con-

[1] Report of the Royal Sea Fisheries Commissioners, p. 43 (1866).
[2] 30 & 31 Vict., c. 52.

tented by Act of Parliament; and although the two kinds of net have since been used indiscriminately by many of the fishermen, a strong feeling has continued in many quarters against the sean-trawl, and has been greatly increased by the unusual scarcity of fish in Lochfyne during the season of 1873. Various explanations of this failure have been suggested, as we learn from the Secretary to the Board of Fisheries, who has kindly furnished us with some interesting information on the subject. First among the causes locally assigned for the great scarcity of herrings in the loch is sean-trawling; and considering the strong feeling the drift fishermen and many of the curers have long had against that method of fishing, it is not surprising that they should again take the opportunity of raising their voices against what sometimes injuriously affects their interests, although to the material advantage of the general public. Then it is stated with quite as much, if not more, apparent reason that the great increase of late years in the length and depth of the drift-nets has materially added to the impediments which those nets have always presented to the passage of the fish in their attempts to enter the loch. To these suggestions it may be replied that, although drift-nets have been used in all parts of Lochfyne for years and years long past, the fisheries there have been very variable—there have been very good years, and very bad ones; and if it be supposed that the latter have been due to the barriers of nets nightly floating in the loch, how are we to account for there having been very successful fisheries under the same circumstances? In such deep water as there is in almost all parts of Lochfyne it is very difficult to believe that such addition as has been made to the depth of the nets can have prevented the passage of the fish up the loch.

If the herrings always kept near the surface, then, undoubtedly, the drift-nets would present barriers formidable in proportion to their numbers. That the herrings do not generally come near the surface during the day is, of course, a matter of universal experience; and the floating nets are only used at night.

As we have previously mentioned, sean-trawls can be only effectively used in water not deeper than that of the net; and the depth of the sean-trawl at the bunt or deepest part may be taken as not exceeding that of a drift-net. They are therefore used as much as possible in shoal water, where the drift-nets cannot come without danger of getting foul. The sean-trawls have their upper edge always at the surface, and their foot should be so near the ground as to prevent the escape of the fish in that direction. The superficial extent of water in Lochfyne in which these nets can be effectively worked must therefore be quite insignificant compared with that in which the drift-nets can be and are used; and if the latter barriers have no perceptible effect in keeping the herrings out of Lochfyne, it appears incredible that nets used in a certain few localities alongshore should be able to accomplish it. Sean-trawls, however, are sometimes used in deep water as circle-nets, but with much less effect than where they can touch the ground, as the herrings, when alarmed, strike downwards and have a good chance of escape. How soon the fish may thus become frightened as the circle of netting is slowly and silently contracted around them is of course very uncertain; but it is clear that it cannot be very early in the process, or it would never be worth while for the fishermen to attempt to work the nets in deep water. The time at which the fish are evidently disturbed is when the net is so nearly hauled in that the bunt can be brought under the herrings, and they are thus raised near the surface, and all means of escape cut off below. This is in accordance with our observation of "trawling" or seaning in Lochfyne and elsewhere, and we cannot think the disturbance of the fish outside the net can be very great, as we have seen a second successful shot made close to the same spot in Lochfyne immediately after the first one had been completed. On the Cornish coast the same mode of fishing is adopted for catching the pilchard, a fish whose habit of swimming in shoals and coming to the surface at certain times closely resembles that of the herring. There, however, sean after sean is shot into the same shoal of fish if it be a large one; and the particular object of dread to the fishermen used to be the encroachment of the drift-nets, now guarded against, however, by special enactment. What would the Lochfyne drift fishermen say to being obliged to keep at a certain distance from where sean-trawling was going on? Yet the sole reason for the similar regulation being enforced in Cornwall is that the seaners may make as large hauls as possible when the fish come within their reach, and so be enabled to increase the supply to the public.

The following extract from the Report for 1871 by the Commissioners for the Herring Fishery, Scotland, points to the conclusion that the movements of the herrings in Lochfyne are independent of both drift and trawl nets:—

"In Inverary district the fishing was also unproductive. The fishermen there had anticipated an abundant season, as at the end of June and beginning of July a fine regular fishing had been got by drift-nets in every part of Lochfyne. About the 17th of June there were 150 boats using (sean) trawl-nets, and only

81 using drift-nets, but by the end of July there were 364 boats using drift-nets, and only 102 using (sean) trawl-nets. At this period the drift-net boats were having fair success, but the (sean) trawl-boats not; yet while the fishing was thus chiefly in the hands of drift-net fishermen, it fell off quite unexpectedly."

With these facts before us—and they are by no means novel ones—it is difficult to believe that either sean-trawl or drift-nets can have much effect on the movements of the herrings in or into Lochfyne. Had the proportion of sean-trawl to drift-nets at the beginning and end of the fishery of 1871 been reversed, it might, and probably would, have been said by many that the evil effect of sean-trawling was unmistakably shown by the sudden disappearance of the fish; but under the actual circumstances it would have been as reasonable to condemn drift-net fishing. That such has been done by some few people appears to show that hasty conclusions on the subject may be drawn by any-one, and that the fishermen of Lochfyne have as much to learn about the habits of the herrings as those who have been catching these fish for the last forty or fifty years all round our coasts, and yet cannot tell whence they come or what influences their movements.

Other suggestions, however, have been made to account for the recent failure in Lochfyne. It is said that the excessive wetness of the season has caused a great drainage of fresh water from the hills into the loch—that this water, objectionable in itself, has been made further injurious by the guano and artificial manures applied to the land, and which in rainy seasons are washed into the loch; and that besides the direct influence of this water in keeping the fish away, it also affects them indirectly by poisoning the food otherwise likely to attract them. We may add, finally, that the Volunteer artillery practice is believed to scare away the fish. We can venture no opinion on the value of these suggestions, for they can only be tested by careful observations on the spot, and during successive years.

The various explanations, however, that have been given of the recent scarcity, point rather to speculation on the subject than to any ascertained facts; but whatever may have been the cause or causes of the small catch of herrings in Lochfyne[1] in 1873, there seems to be no doubt about the takes of fish there having been diminishing during the last four years. It remains to be seen whether the result of the next season's fishing bears out any of the explanations hitherto given.

As it is unusual to find a regular fishery of so essentially a deep-sea character as that for herrings within such narrow limits as those of Lochfyne, it may be desirable to give a short notice of the locality; and the general conditions under which the two kinds of net are there worked will then be better understood.

The three important stations in Lochfyne are Inverary, almost at the northern extremity, Ardrishaig, about 18 miles south of it, and Tarbert, 10 miles lower down and 6 or 7 miles from the entrance to the loch. Just above Ardrishaig the loch suddenly narrows, and is further contracted at this part by Otter Point, which projects a considerable distance across and forms the lower boundary of what is called the Upper Loch. This portion of Lochfyne is only from 1 to 2 miles wide

---

[1] It appears by the Report of the Fishery Board, published since the above was written, that the great decrease was in the Rothesay district, outside of, and at the entrance to, Lochfyne.

for the whole distance to Inverary. The lower part of the loch varies from 4 to 5 miles in width. There is deep water from one end of the loch to the other, but the depth is very irregular throughout, and, roughly speaking, ranges from 20 fathoms to as much as 100 fathoms, or even more, near the entrance. There is plenty of water therefore for the fish to pass to the extreme end of the loch without the necessity for their coming in contact with any of the nets used there; but if anything would be likely to obstruct their course, it would be the hundreds of trains of drift-nets which are set across the loch, rather than the sean-trawls which, except on rare occasions, only make a semicircular sweep from the shore, and whose headline or backrope is always at the surface.

At Otter Point, by far the most contracted part of the loch, there is some shoal water suitable for sean-trawling on both the north and south sides; but between the Point and the opposite shore—the passage by which the herrings would enter the Upper Loch—there is a depth of 29 fathoms; and supposing the whole space between the two shores to be by any possible chance covered with sean-trawls, there would be at least 20 fathoms of water below the nets for the unobstructed passage of the fish. It would appear extremely improbable therefore that, even at the narrowest part of the loch, the sean-trawlers could materially interfere with the passage of the herrings into the upper waters.

We have given these details about Lochfyne because that particular locality has long been famous for its herrings; it has the same essential character of a long fissure or opening in the land as is found in the other lochs on the west coast; but the abundance in which herrings are usually met with in Lochfyne and the neighbouring inland waters appears to be due to their situation at the head of the Firth of Clyde. It is not very easy to say where the fish caught in June, at the beginning of the summer season, come from; probably many fish remain in the loch throughout the year, but later there is no doubt that the shoals enter the Firth on its western side and proceed northwards to its head. Continuing in the same direction, their course would lead them into Lochfyne and the Kyles of Bute, and at times into Lochlong and Gareloch.[1]

It is a matter of wide experience that the movements of herrings are very capricious; the general body of the fish—the shoals which successively appear on a particular part of the coast, may be found in one year filling every creek and bay; in the next they may not come very near the land, and the inshore fishery may be a failure. This applies equally to the pilchards on the Cornish coast. It can hardly therefore be surprising that the herring fishery in the narrow inland waters of Lochfyne should be very uncertain, and that the shoals of fish should not always penetrate to its farthest extremity. No doubt a certain number of fish spawn there and perhaps remain in the loch throughout the year; but the general opinion among the fishermen is that the shoals which come in during the season leave it again and go southwards, some of them to the spawning ground of Ballantrae, which was said to have been much resorted to for that purpose in former times, although less frequented in later years. Full fish, however, are generally numerous in Lochfyne during August or September, and, of course, when

[1] There were large fisheries off Greenock in 1867 and 1868, and the seantrawls were extensively used there in both years.

they are ripe, spawning must take place wherever the fish may happen to be at the time. But, although there are a very few places around our coasts which are or were known to be spawning grounds, we are in complete ignorance of where that process takes place with most of the herrings, and whether it is not as often far out at sea as it is near the land.

The boats used in the Lochfyne drift-fishery are small cutters or smacks like those we have noticed at Campbelton; and open skiffs, carrying one lug and a jib, are employed for the other fisheries.

Lochfyne Fishing Boats.

The Fishery Board Returns of the herrings cured on the west coast, and particularly at the stations within the districts now under notice, give a very imperfect idea of the actual numbers of fish caught there in recent years. A large and increasing proportion of the annual takes of fish is now sent to the fresh market, and numerous fast steamers are employed in bringing cargoes of herrings to the most convenient railways, by which they are quickly distributed to the large inland towns, where they are sold as fresh fish; the slight sprinkling of salt given to them before shipment being easily got rid of when they reach the market. The Glasgow and Greenock curing trade has been much deranged in consequence; the curing returns from those ports have very much fallen off; and when, as is occasionally the case, an increase is shown there, it is generally due to large catches of fish in Gareloch or at the mouth of the Clyde.

ARDROSSAN TO DUMFRIES — NUMBER OF BOATS.

Port Letters.	Port.	Year.	1st Class.	2nd Class.	3rd Class.
A.D.	Ardrossan	1872	7	178	1
T.N.	Troon	,,	1	50	4
A.R.	Ayr	,,	3	160	10
S.R.	Stranraer	,,	6	163	9
W.N.	Wigton ..	,,	—	19	73
D.S.	Dumfries..	,,	—	93	5

The fisheries on this remaining part of the Scotch coast are not on a very large scale, or of much importance. At the northern stations both drift and scan-trawls are used for catching herrings; but the fishermen there work the drift-nets mostly in Lochfyne and the neighbourhood, and there is not much done on their own coast with the exception of a little scan-trawling and looking after the white fish. We have previously mentioned the banks off Ballantrae as formerly recognized spawning ground for herrings. These banks are about 3 or 4 miles off the land, and a considerable herring fishery was carried on by anchoring the nets at the bottom where the fish were spawning. After a time this was given up, for it was found that the presence of the herrings on the banks attracted large numbers of cod and turbot from the deeper water, and trammels were then set for these more valuable fish. The principal bank is from 8 to 10 miles long, and from 3 to 5 miles broad. The nets used for cod have meshes $3\frac{1}{4}$ inches from knot to knot, and are 4 feet deep and 40 fathoms long; and the turbot nets are $3\frac{1}{2}$ feet deep, 50 fathoms long, and with a 7-inch mesh. Besides these nets for catching cod and turbot, longlines are employed for the same purpose, and herring bait is attractive to both kinds of fish, as well as to the coalfish, which is here also taken in great numbers.

The reputed capacity the cod and turbot on this coast have for gorging herrings is beyond anything we have either seen or heard of elsewhere; and without vouching for the accuracy of the statements, or guaranteeing the size of the fish swallowed, we may mention that one fisherman in his evidence before the Commissioners said he had often taken 15 or 16 herrings from the stomach of a turbot, and another had found from 30 to 35 herrings inside one codfish! Longlines are generally used for the white fish, and are set 8 or 10 miles off the land.

There is very little requiring notice south of Ballantrae till we come to the Solway, and there the fisheries are much the same as already described in Morecambe Bay—shrimping and trawling for flounders, with a little inshore line-fishing for codling.

It will be seen from the notice we have now given of the Scotch sea fisheries that, if not of a very varied nature, they are still important of their kind. The drift-fishery for herrings and the line-fishery for cod, ling, and coalfish, are generally conspicuous, and on a very large portion of the coast are practically those to which the fishermen devote all their energies. On the east coast the herring fishery attracts the attention of almost everyone during the two or three months through which it lasts in summer; and the particular mode of cure to which a large proportion of the herrings is there subjected gives employment to thousands of persons on shore who know nothing of, nor take any part in the capture of the fish. In the northern islands and on the west coast the line-fishing becomes more prominent, although the herring fishery is also largely worked in some places. With the exception of the large cod-smacks, going almost entirely from Shetland to the northern banks, the Scotch fishing boats are not adapted for long-continued deep-sea working, and their catches, whether of herrings or white fish, are as a rule brought in every day. At the end of 1872 there were 16,765 fishing boats standing on the Scotch register; they consisted of the following in the three classes:—

1st Class.		2nd Class.	3rd Class.	Total.
Boats.	Tonnage.	Boats.	Boats.	
2120	35,934	12,510	2135	16,765

The first-class boats, or those of 15 tons and upwards, barely average 17 tons, although 66 large cod-smacks are included among them; and this low average is almost entirely due to the absence in Scotland of deep-sea trawlers, which make such a conspicuous figure on the English register, and raise the average of the first-class fishing boats of England and Wales so high as 36 tons.

Of the Scotch fishermen we may say that as a body they are enterprising and industrious, confident in their own resources if not interfered with, but not more exempt than other people from the prejudices against anything which may appear, however slightly, to affect their particular interests. With very few exceptions they are coast fishermen; for, although they often go far out to sea in the exercise of their calling, they do not remain there for days and weeks at a time as is the lot of those who are engaged in some of the deep-sea fisheries on the English coast. It might perhaps be considered an insult if we were to inquire how many of the Scotch fishermen are teetotallers when on shore; but however attractive the national drink may be to them, it does not prevent money being generally saved, or the fisheries being carried on with energy whenever there is a chance of doing so.

The recent publication of the Scotch Board of Fisheries' Report for 1873 enables us to add a few words more about the fisheries for that year.

The herring fishery is stated to have been the largest on record, "alike in cure, in export, and in branding." 939,233 barrels were cured; 668,008 barrels exported; and 435,274 barrels branded. The brand fees amounted to 7254*l*. 11*s*. 6*d*., exceeding by more than 200*l*. the sum received in 1872, when, for the first time, that source of income reached 7000*l*. The fishery was not uniformly good at all the stations, but varied on both the east and west coasts. The only complaint appears to have been that a larger proportion than usual of small fish was taken, and especially on the east coast.

There was also an increase in the number of cod and ling taken; and it is satisfactory to note that this was not produced by fish caught at Iceland and Faroe by the Shetland fishermen, but was the result chiefly of more successful work on the home grounds near the

Shetlands, Orkneys, and Hebrides. There were 15,095 fishing boats with crews of 45,594 men and boys in 1873, showing a decrease of 137 boats and 584 fishermen compared with 1872, but with an increase of 23,035*l.* in the estimated value of boats, nets, and lines.

FISHING STATIONS.

ISLE OF MAN.

Castletown, Douglas, and Ramsey.— Herring fishery on the west, south, and east coasts — Large herrings near the Calf — Spawning ground in Douglas Bay — Mackerel fishery — Deep-sea trawling — Ling-lining, season for — Manx fishing boats — Number of crew — Shares — Industry of the Manxmen.

NUMBER OF BOATS.

Port Letters.	Port.	Year.	1st Class.	2nd Class.	3rd Class.
Ce.Tn., or C.T.	Castletown				
D.O.S., or D.O., or P.L.	Douglas	1872	227	82	66
R.Y.	Ramsey				

The statistics of the Manx fisheries were formerly included among the returns made by the Scottish Fishery Board; but since the passing of the Sea Fisheries Act, 1868, the Isle of Man has been recognised as an independent division, including the above-mentioned ports.

The herring fishery stations in the island are Castletown, Port St. Mary, and Port Erin, in the district of Castletown; and Peel, in the Douglas division. There are no drift boats actually belonging to Douglas or Ramsey, and the chief occupation of the fishermen of those two ports is with the handlines and longlines. Douglas, however, owns a few trawlers, and groundseans are also in use there. The important fishery in the Isle of Man, as in Scotland, is that for herrings. It is entirely carried on with drift-nets, and usually commences early in June. The fish are at first mostly taken at a little north of Peel, on the western side of the island, and thence southwards to the Calf of Man as the season advances. It is continued along this part of the coast and a little south of the Calf until the end of September, when the fish are said to spawn on the rough ground in the latter neighbourhood. The principal herring fishery is therefore confined to the southern half of the western side of the island, and it is not very easy to explain in a satisfactory manner why it should be so. In October, however, herrings are found in the neighbourhood of Douglas, where there seems to be no doubt of their spawning. These herrings are described as being of a different class from those caught off the Calf, and are supposed by the fishermen to come from the north-east to what is considered as suitable spawning ground. The opinion held by many persons, that each district in the island has its own particular fish, is probably correct within certain limits; but it must not be forgotten that the large herrings taken off the Calf are caught towards the end of the season, when all the fishing is in that neighbourhood, and the herrings on the western side generally may be expected to have attained their full development, which is nowhere the case at the beginning of the season. Indeed, a close-time,[1] ending early in June—the time when most of the boats now begin work—has been advocated by many of the fishermen to prevent the small fish being taken, as is sometimes done in the latter part of May. Although it appears likely therefore that all the fish

[1] By an old Act of Tynwald herring fishing was prohibited between the 1st of January and the 5th of July within nine miles of the island; but the law does not appear to have been enforced for a long time; and the Isle of Man being included among the "British Islands" to which the Sea Fisheries Act, 1868, applies, the local regulations cease to have any force.

caught between Peel and the Calf of Man belong to the same general shoals, come whence they may, there is every reason to think that the herrings which appear and spawn in Douglas Bay are, from their smaller size even at a later period, distinct from those found on the west and south of the island, and which are systematically fished for during the principal portion of the Manx herring season. As the fishery on the eastern side is only where the herrings visit certain parts of Douglas Bay, apparently for the purpose of spawning, the plan of grounding the nets is necessarily adopted; and however objectionable such a practice may be theoretically, the capture of these spawning fish has not been shown to have any effect on subsequent fisheries. As soon as the drift season has come to an end at the Isle of Man the Manx boats proceed to the Irish coast and take part in the herring fishery there in November and December.

There is very little curing done in the island, and almost all the herrings caught on the Manx coast are sent to Liverpool or Wales, the fish usually receiving a slight sprinkling of salt, just sufficient to preserve them till they reach the market. They are generally shipped in sailing vessels from Castletown.

There is no regular mackerel fishery by drift-nets on the Manx coast, but a few of these fish are taken with the herrings on the west side during June, July, and August. The Manx fishermen, however, are an enterprising and industrious race, and before the commencement of their home herring season many of them take their boats to the mackerel fishery at the south of Ireland, and by steady attention to their work succeed in earning a good deal of money if the season prove favourable. In some years considerable numbers of

MANX FISHING BOATS.

mackerel are taken in Douglas Bay by the sean as well as by hook and line. Here also there is some good trawling ground for the few smacks belonging to Douglas; and it is likewise worked occasionally by the Liverpool trawlers, although their usual fishing ground is nearer the English coast.

Line-fishing is more or less carried on throughout the year, except during the herring season. As soon as that fishery is over longlining is begun with the small boats in what is called the "low sea" fishery, not far from the land; this is continued towards the end of January, when the large fishing boats are brought into use, and the lines are shot in deep water at some distance from the island. Cod are the fish specially taken by these lines, the larger ones in deep water, and whelks or buckies are the bait in general use. There is also good handline fishing in Douglas Bay for whiting, and a few haddocks are taken on different parts of the coast, but they are said to have never been generally abundant. Conger fishing occupies a few boats between the end of the longline fishing season in April and the beginning of the herring fishery, and a few lobsters are taken in various places, but that also is not an important fishery.

The Manx fishing boats used for the drift and other deep-sea fishing are fine, substantial, and useful craft (Plate XIV.). They are from 38 to 47 feet on the keel, 12 to 14 feet beam, and 7 to 8 feet deep; they have a round stern and are all half-decked, but can be completely decked over when necessary. Forty or fifty years ago they were rigged as cutters, but the advantage of a mizen, especially when drift-fishing, was so evident in the Mount's Bay boats which came every year to the Irish Sea, that the Manxmen made an alteration in their rig, and on the strength of the additional sail being a lug they henceforth called their fishing boats "luggers," although, strictly speaking, they are dandy-rigged. The mainmast is always lowered as soon as the train of nets has been shot, unless it happen to be very calm weather. A further improvement has taken place by a gradual increase in the size of the boats; most of the old ones, as they became unserviceable or were sold (in many cases to the Irish fishermen), having been replaced by new ones, larger and better in every way. Cotton nets, made by beautiful machinery in the island, have long superseded those of flax which were formerly in general use; the change has been advantageous in many ways; for besides being more effective in securing the fish, the cotton lasts very much longer than the flax when used for fishing nets, and does not require barking so frequently, thus saving time, trouble, and expense. The cost of new nets, whether made of cotton or flax, was very much the same a few years ago, but we cannot say what it may be now when cotton is so much in demand not only for nets but also for lines, and all kinds of fishing gear have become more expensive.

The drift boats carry seven men each, and are generally the property of the fishermen; the proceeds of the fishing being divided into shares, of which ten are given to the nets; and as each fisherman provides a portion of this essential part of the fit out, he shares accordingly. Then the boat takes two and a half shares, and each man one share; the cost of food and carting the nets to and from the boat is provided for by another share and a half, making a total of twenty-one shares into which the proceeds of the week's fishing are divided.

The Manxmen are a thriving set of people, and are a good example of what may be done by fishermen who work hard, are enterprising and thrifty. For many years past habits of sobriety have been general amongst them, and the effects have appeared in their having better houses and a generally improved condition; whilst their surplus money has been put into the savings bank, or profitably employed in providing better boats and gear. The change has been gradual but steady; and they have been indebted for it to no exceptional circumstances of a constant abundance of fish on their coasts, or freedom from the dangers or difficulties to which all seagoing fishermen are liable; for they have been subject to years of scarcity like other people, and their fishing grounds are in as stormy seas as will be found on any part of our coasts. The improvement is the more striking from the apparent association of these islanders with their less thrifty Irish neighbours, implied by their former use of flaxen nets, and the still general employment of the Irish expression, a "mease of herrings," equivalent to 500 fish.

FISHING STATIONS.

IRELAND.

General decline in the number of fishing boats and fishermen — Discrepancy in the returns by different authorities — Small proportion of regular fishermen — Decline of the fisheries on the west and north coasts — East coast fisheries improving — General emigration from the west — Exposed coast and bad weather, obstacles to fishing there — Continued distress said to be the result of the famine in 1846 — Little apparent prospect of improvement — Loans recommended by the fishery inspectors — Questionable advantage of the system — Fishing only a small part of the occupation of many of the fishermen — Unwillingness of the thriving Irish people to help the fishermen — Mr. Whitworth's offer of help — **Dublin to Waterford** — Prosperity of the Dublin trawlers — Scarcity of crews — Agreements — Trawling grounds in the Irish Sea — Objection to the trawlers by line fishermen — Restrictions on trawling — Skerries wherry — Disappearance and temporary return of haddocks — Fishing yawls — Season for herring fishery — Fish mostly sent to England — Arklow fisheries — Wexford herring cots — Trawling at Waterford — Extraordinary regulations — Nymph Bank a productive fishing ground — Native fishermen and strangers — Frequent abundance of pilchards — Hake, sprats.

THE condition of the Irish sea fisheries, as represented by the number of boats and men engaged in them, contrasts very unfavourably with what we find in either England or Scotland. It is equally unsatisfactory whether we compare their general state in 1872 with that in previous years, or inquire how much occupation they give to the fishing boats now on the register.

The statistics of the number of boats and men employed in these fisheries are collected independently by the Customs for the Board of Trade, under whose direction they appear in the Annual Statement by the Registrar-General of Shipping; and by the Coastguard, who procure the requisite information for the Inspectors of Irish Fisheries, by whom they are published in their Annual Report. The returns are given by the two departments according to their independent districts, those by the Customs under the heading of the different ports, nineteen in number, on the same system as in England and Scotland; and those by the Coastguard for the thirty districts into which, for their own regular duties, they divide the coast. In both cases the returns include every description of boat used by professional fishermen; and although, in consequence of the limits of the districts under the two systems being unlike, it is impossible to compare them in detail, we might reasonably expect to find the totals in close agreement. This, however, is not the case. The discrepancy between them is so great that it is difficult to know whether either is approximately correct; for while we have no more reason to place complete confidence in the Customs returns for Ireland than, as we have previously said, we could in the case of England or Scotland, we are hardly prepared to consider the Coastguard returns as entirely trustworthy, although the Inspectors of Irish Fisheries state in their Report for 1872 that from the particular directions given to the Coastguard, theirs are likely to be the more correct.

It should be mentioned, however, with respect to the latter, that there are long stretches of coast on the western side of the island which are unguarded—that is, not patrolled by the Coastguard, who, therefore, not having all the boats and men of these districts constantly under their notice, can only obtain information about them by special visits to the localities, and often at an expense quite out of proportion to the value of the results. The same difficulties are met with by the Customs, and it may be even to a greater extent;

and the probable consequence is that neither set of returns can be regarded as strictly correct.

The difference between them in the number of fishing boats is as much as 536, as may be seen in the following comparative account of the three classes;—

	1st Class.	2nd Class.	3rd Class.	Total.
Customs	386	3589	4475	8450 [1]
Coastguard	372	3091	4451	7914 [2]
Difference	14	498	24	536

The Inspectors further divide each of these classes of fishing boats into three groups, according as the boats are solely employed for fishing, mostly, or only occasionally so; and those persons who have been accustomed to associate fishing boats with the idea of regular fishing will probably be somewhat startled to find the Inspectors reporting that of the total of 7914 boats, 6116 or more than three-fourths, with crews of 22,747 men, do not on an average fish altogether a month in the year. This is said to be owing to the exposed character of some portions of the coast, particularly on the north and west, where even good-sized and well-found boats would be often unable to work; to the want of suitable boats in many places, and the deficiency of gear; the distance from markets and difficulties of transport.

During the eleven months when these boats are not

---

[1] This return is taken from that issued by the Registrar-General of Shipping, who receives his information from the Customs; but the Customs return, as published in the Appendix to the Inspector's Report for the same year, gives 8534 boats, showing a difference of 84 between the two totals professedly obtained from the same source.

[2] The correctness of this return is also open to doubt, as in the Clifden Coastguard district there is said to have been in 1872 an *increase* of 119 boats, with a *decrease* of 756 men and boys since 1871.

employed in fishing, they are engaged in collecting seaweed, and in the transport of goods, turf, manure, and passengers; so that their crews are not necessarily idle, and in many cases fishing might be carried on by them more constantly if other occupations were not found more attractive, or considered of greater importance.

The real business of sea-fishing on the Irish coast may therefore be considered as being represented by the number of boats solely or mostly engaged in fishing; and, according to the Inspectors, these did not, in 1872, exceed 1800 belonging to the three registered classes, and with total crews of 8564 men and boys.

According to a statement of the number of fishing boats and men in 1846 and subsequent years, given in the Inspectors' Report for 1872, it appears that there has been almost a continuous annual decrease under both heads. It is stated that in 1846 there were 19,883 boats of various kinds, and 113,073 fishermen[1] and boys, while in 1872 the numbers given are 7914 boats and 31,311 men and boys; the boats having therefore been diminished by three-fifths, and the fishermen by nearly three-fourths during the twenty-six years. This decline dates from the commencement of the famine in 1846, and some of the districts appear to have never recovered from its desolating effects. We need hardly say, however, that emigration has carried away many thousands of men who were formerly counted as fishermen, and especially from that portion of the coast population which only fished occasionally; and we may add that the Reports sent in by the Inspecting Commanders of

---

[1] According to the return furnished by the Irish Fishery Commissioners in 1864 to the Royal Sea Fisheries Commissioners, the number of fishermen in 1846 was 93,073. See *Rep. Roy. Sea Fish. Com.*, p. 15 (1866).

the Coastguard speak of the feeling in favour of emigration being still so strong in certain districts, that, even if the men could find constant employment in fishing at home, they would not remain there were they provided with the means of leaving the country. Under these circumstances we must not look forward to any early improvement in the Irish sea fisheries generally, although there are now many important aids to their development which did not exist in former times. Among these we may mention greater facilities, both by rail and steamers, for transporting the fish to market, and the increased demand and consequent higher prices paid for the fish. These considerations, of course, are of most importance where a constant supply of fish can be obtained, and therefore do not equally apply to all parts of the Irish coast.

The apparent diminution in the number of Irish fishing boats since 1871, taking the figures given by the Inspectors, is as much as 1185, or more than one-ninth within a year; but an examination of the returns for the two years, 1871 and 1872, shows the decline not to have been uniform around the coast, and that while on the north and west the diminution has been considerable, a general increase has taken place on the eastern and southern portions. There are several reasons why there should be a difference, under any circumstances, between the condition of the fisheries on the two sides of the island. On the east or south all kinds of fish may be obtained according to the season, and with tolerable regularity every year. The weather there does not offer any remarkable impediment to the fisheries being worked; markets are at hand or within easy reach by rail or steamer; and during the herring and mackerel seasons an example of industry, which cannot be without some effect, is set to the native fishermen by many of the Cornish, Manx, Scotch, and at times even French boats, which temporarily leave their own waters for the sake of the fisheries on the Irish coast. With these advantages one is less surprised at there being some increase of the Irish boats and fishermen on that part of the coast than at the numbers being still so small; for the strangers far outnumber the native boats during the most productive periods of the herring and mackerel seasons.

Still it is a hopeful sign that some increase has been made, and it is still more satisfactory to find that the improvement, although small, has been progressive during the last few years. A sensible alteration for the better has also been made in the Irish drift-boats, many of those now in use being purchases from the Cornish and Manx men, while the newly-built craft are of a much better class and description than formerly.

On the west and north these conditions are reversed. What may be called the migratory fishes are very uncertain in their visits there, and even when on the coast, they often do not come near enough to be fished for successfully with the small and ill-found boats which are too commonly the only ones available. The coast also is much exposed; Atlantic storms are felt there in all their fury; and interruptions to the fishing are frequent, and sometimes of long duration, by the bad or unsettled weather. With these disadvantages there are difficulties in the way of transporting the fish to market, except from particular points, and the fishermen are often prevented obtaining a fair price for the produce of their labours, and procuring the means of carrying on their work more effectively.

Under these circumstances it is hardly surprising that the majority of the west population, never accustomed to regard fishing as more than an occasional occupation, should not devote themselves earnestly to the pursuit, or that the tide of emigration should annually carry off so many of those whose relatives and friends have gone before them, and are generally doing well in another country.

There is no reason to believe that, taking one year with another, fish of various excellent kinds are not as abundant around the coast of Ireland now as they ever were; or indeed that a less total quantity of fish is caught than formerly; for it must be remembered that although the diminution of boats and men has been very great, the decrease has been mainly in those districts where the majority of the fishermen had little claim to that title, and who, when other means of support in any way failed them, became unable to keep their boats and fishing gear in such a state as to be of any real service; while in more favoured districts where fishing could be and has been the chief occupation, the use of improved boats and better gear generally has resulted in a greatly increased supply of fish to the market.

The west coast, except at a few places, can never, we believe, become of any importance for its fisheries; and we doubt the expediency of endeavouring to foster such occupations among a population of whom a large proportion have so little heart for that kind of work. We have mentioned that one of the obstacles to profitable fishing on parts of the west coast is the difficulty of getting the fish to market; it is not always that the fish cannot be caught, but few purchasers are to be found for them in the neighbourhood, and in many cases the railway is at some distance. But in regard to markets for fresh fish the west coast of Ireland is not worse off, or even so badly situated, as the Shetlands, the Hebrides, or the greatest part of the west coast of Scotland. What would not the poor fishermen of these districts give for such advantages as are provided by the lines of railway to Donegal Bay, Sligo, Clew Bay, Galway Bay, the Shannon, and Tralee Bay! A glance at the railway maps of the two countries will be sufficient to show that these Scotch fishermen are completely shut out from the fresh markets, and from the other markets also, unless water carriage is available, and that is only partially so when vessels visit a few places on the coast during the herring fishery in the Minch. There is poverty and distress at times among these fishermen, especially on the main coast and the islands in the immediate neighbourhood; but they are generally industrious and energetic when they have a chance of fishing, and do their best to make some provision for the time when no work can be done. We should be very glad if we could feel justified in thinking as much of the majority of the fishermen of Ireland. We have been among them both on many parts of the two coasts, and it was impossible to avoid the conclusion that the greatest obstacles to a general improvement among the Irish fishermen were in the men themselves rather than in the conditions under which they were seeking a livelihood.

We have been told by those who have had long experience of the west coast fishermen that their present depressed state is all owing to the famine in 1846–8. But disastrous as were the effects of that calamitous period, more than a generation has since passed away, not only without improvement in the condition of these people, but with almost a continuous annual diminution in their numbers. If this be their state after twenty-five years, a period in which railways have been largely extended and the general condition of the country improved, there seems little hope of reviving the fisheries on that coast, unless it be by means of strangers, who may perhaps find it worth their while to work there during part of the year. Everything seems to us to point to the probability of the Irish sea fisheries becoming more and more restricted to those parts where they are now being carried on with most success; there we may hope for further improvement, and that native boats will form an increasing proportion of the mixed fleet which annually works on the eastern and southern coasts of the island.

The granting of loans[1] by Government to needy and industrious fishermen for the repair and provision of the necessary boats and gear for working is again strongly advocated by the Inspectors in their Report for 1872; and such a grant was recommended by the Select Committee of the House of Commons on the Sea Coast Fisheries (Ireland) Bill in 1867.

That such loans would be of advantage in many cases, as they have been before, there can be no doubt; and as it is proposed to grant them to those fishermen only who can give satisfactory security for their repayment, there should not be much danger of loss. But independently of the question of whether it should be

---

[1] Our notice of the Irish Fisheries was written before the recent debate in Parliament on the subject of Government loans to the fishermen, which resulted in the decision by a majority of two votes in favour of adopting that system. The arguments in support of Government help were not altogether of a novel or unanswerable character; and there was nothing mentioned during the debate to lead us to modify the opinions we have expressed, or to believe that any real and permanent good will result from thus encouraging the fishermen to look to the Government for help whenever bad times, from whatever cause, may overtake them.

the policy of the Government to lend money to individuals to help carry on their business—a policy that would have a very wide application—there is evidence that advances in the manner proposed have not previously been productive of unmixed good, and that in some instances the money has been applied to other purposes than those for which it was granted.[1]

In discussing the question of the Irish sea fisheries there appears to be a frequent confusion between the idea of developing them as one of the food-producing resources of the country—making them, in fact, one of the industries of the island, and that of treating them as a means of helping the majority of the coast population, the so-called fishermen—for, as has been shown, the real ones are comparatively few—to gain a subsistence. The various appeals for assistance are made on the ground of the poverty of the *fishermen*, but it appears from what the Inspectors say that more than three-fourths of these men do not fish during as much as a month in the year; and this cannot be explained altogether by the want of proper appliances. There are various other occupations which these people are accustomed to, and which there is no reason to think they would give up if they were fitted out with all the fishing gear they could desire. Seaweed cutting, for instance, is not likely to be neglected for the chance of being able to make something by fishing. It would be as reasonable to call the hardy sea-going Shetlanders farmers because they have generally a small bit of ground to cultivate, as to speak of this portion of the Irish people as fishermen. The excellent Society for

[1] See *Appendix to Report of Select Committee on the Sea Coast Fisheries (Ireland) Bill*, p. 264.

bettering the Condition of the Poor appears to us to be the source from which such men should seek assistance, and not from any fund established under the Fisheries Inspectors for the purpose of helping those who, by making fishing their regular occupation, have some claim to the title of fishermen. For we venture to doubt whether the class of which we have been speaking, ignorant as they are of a great deal that is familiar to the professed fishermen with respect either to the best kinds of gear, or to making the most of their surplus fish by curing, are ever likely to rise much above the level at which they now stand. It is not to such men we must look for the development of the Irish sea fisheries; they must first learn to give up their prejudices against modes of fishing to which they are unaccustomed, and take heartily to the work which, in very many cases, is now only a secondary consideration with them.

It has been often asked, and the inquiry will be repeated, whether the patriotic feeling of the Irish people generally should not induce them to show some disposition to take part in helping their needy countrymen? The Inspectors, however, speak strongly of the unwillingness of the landlords and of the opulent portion of the mercantile community to afford any assistance; but add — "Amidst all this indifference it is gratifying to us to be enabled to record an instance — unfortunately the only one — of a generous desire to assist the struggling fishermen. Mr. Benjamin Whitworth, of Manchester, late member for Drogheda, offered this year to give 2000*l.* to this department for their benefit, provided that a further sum of 8000*l.* would be contributed for the purpose. We much apprehend that a sufficient response from even the whole of Ireland cannot be expected so as to enable the noble offer to be availed of."[1]

A year has now elapsed since the proposal was made, but nothing has yet been done in support of it.[2]

Must we then believe that the more wealthy classes in Ireland will do nothing to help even the industriously disposed fishermen on their own coasts, or does their knowledge of the fishing classes or their experience in former years lead them to question the value of such kind of assistance? Annual subscriptions are not called for in this case; but an offer of help has been made to the Irish people if they will only come forward and support it by their own efforts, and thus take some part in the creation of a fund which, it is urged by Irishmen, would be the means of doing incalculable good to one of the poorest classes in their country.

In our notice of the various fishing stations we shall, for the sake of uniformity, continue the returns of fishing boats under the Customs districts, although we think their correctness more open to doubt than those prepared by the Coastguard and published by the Inspectors of Irish Fisheries.

DUBLIN TO WATERFORD—NUMBER OF BOATS.

Port Letters.	Port.	Year.	1st Class.	2nd Class.	3rd Class.
D.	Dublin	1872	156	368	122
W.D.	Wexford	,,	25	228	58
N.S.	New Ross	,,	1	70	25
W.	Waterford	,,	19	179	39

[1] *Report of Inspectors of Irish Fisheries* (1872), p. 7.
[2] Mr. Whitworth has since offered an additional 500*l.* towards making up the fund.

The fisheries on this range of coast are of a varied character, and include some of the most important of the island. Dublin is the head-quarters of the deep-sea trawlers, and now possesses a fleet of nearly fifty smacks, ranging from 30 to 50 tons, N.M., and usually working from that station. The nets used by them are generally about 80 feet in length, and with beams about 44 feet long. Deep-sea trawlers were first worked from Dublin in 1818, some Brixham smacks having been bought for the purpose. Brixham men also came over, and in course of time more vessels were added to the fleet, as the fishing grounds became better known and the profitable character of the fishing was established. The "English boats," as the Dublin trawlers are, we believe, still commonly called, have not always been regarded with favour by the Irish fishermen, and their operations until quite recently have been almost confined to the east coast. The Dublin vessels work all the year round when they can get hands; but the very fine weather usual in June and July is not favourable for trawling, and at that time other occupations are more profitable to the men; so that while in many parts of Ireland fishermen are unable to work for want of boats and tackle, in others boats and nets are obliged to remain idle because there are not sufficient skilled fishermen to manage them. The attractions of the herring fishery carry off a great many of the hands for a time, and in some cases the smacks are themselves used in the drift-fishery during the busy part of the herring season. They are, however, not well suited for that kind of fishing; the size of the vessels is not so objectionable, but their rig is inconvenient for this work, and the inability to lower the mast when "driving" not only makes the vessel very uneasy, but if there is any wind will probably make her drift too fast. There is no doubt that the lug-rig is the one most suitable for drift-boats; the masts are not lofty, and therefore need not be heavily rigged, so that even if they are not lowered when fishing is going on, there is not much weight aloft, and when one or all are got down there is of course less for the wind to act upon, and lighter and more effective nets can be used.

Another and increasing source of interference with trawling during summer is the great demand for men in yachts, and this we hope is leading to the growth of a better class of fishermen; taking the whole year, one employment indirectly helps the other, for it is the men who are sea-going fishermen, and not the amphibious class who merely act as boatmen or do a little hand-lining, who are in request in the yachting season; and when that kind of work is over they return to their fishing and get their living by that means during the winter. There is an inducement therefore to become fishermen that they may be qualified for yachting work during the light weather; while they are secure of employment when that is over. Their familiarity with the fore-and-aft rig of the fishing smacks makes them particularly handy on board either racing or cruising yachts, which now are all, with rare exceptions, rigged in that fashion. It is no doubt hard on the smack-owners that they should not be able to keep their men throughout the year; but they are only liable to be shorthanded at the season when trawling is less likely to be profitable, and they are pretty sure of their crews again when the best fishing can be made. The apprentice system might, we imagine, be here worked with advantage to the boys, the smack-owners, and the country. Some remedy, however, has been attempted by the introduction into the Fisheries (Ireland) Act, 1869, of clauses providing for voluntary agreements between the owners of fishing boats and the crews, with penalties for any breach of such agreements on either side.

The trawl-smacks each have a crew of three men and a boy, and the excellent system of payment by shares is adopted at Dublin as at Brixham, and most other trawling stations. The earnings are divided into eight shares, of which the vessel takes half, and the remaining four are distributed in the proportion of one-and-a-half to the master, one each to the other two men, and half a share to the boy.

The slight change of rig—that from the cutter to the ketch which we have spoken of as having been made in many of the English trawlers, has not been adopted in the Irish vessels; but the size of the latter has not yet been increased to such an extent as to make the alteration especially desirable.

Although trawling has been carried on for many years along this part of the coast, the grounds which have been and are still systematically worked by the Dublin smacks are not very extensive. They lie for the most part within a triangle occupying the space between Dublin and Dundrum Bays and the Isle of Man; but the whole of this ground is not available for trawling purposes, as there are some rough places and a good deal of mud. The fishing grounds consist of an irregular series of patches differing in shape and extent, and these are worked successfully according to the season; the inner grounds—the neighbourhood of the Kish Bank, Skerries Bay, and the Mountain Foot ground—being fished during the colder months. The Isle of Man ground, abounding in soles, and lying in deep water, is usually worked from March to July. In

January many of the smacks go to the coast of Waterford and fish on what is called the Saltee ground, a very productive patch about south-west from the Saltee lightship.

Trawling has been a fertile source of trouble to the Irish Commissioners for many years past, and their souls have been vexed by repeated complaints from line fishermen and others, who alleged that their interests were being ruined by the trawlers in the bays on many parts of the coast. Inquiry after inquiry has been held in the localities where the complaints have been made, with the result of byelaws being enacted, altered or repealed in connection with the exclusion of the trawlers from particular parts in which they were said to destroy the spawn of fish, or interfere with the operations of other kinds of fishermen. As there is no reason for believing that the Commissioners in former years were better acquainted with the spawning habits of the various edible fishes than people are at the present time —and the extent of knowledge on the subject is now extremely limited—we must conclude that the restrictions they imposed were of a tentative character, and for the sake of keeping peace among the fishermen rather than based on any real expectation of increase in the supply of fish. Trawling is still prohibited within the headlands from Ardglass, opposite the Isle of Man, to the southern point of Dublin Bay; but the advantage of this restriction, except in soothing the irritable feelings of the line fishermen, has yet to be proved. The objections made to trawling, however, have not been in all cases so much against the system as to the large smacks which are engaged in that kind of fishing. And some of the difficulties have arisen from the local fishermen not having been able to enjoy an exclusive right of fishing in what they looked upon as their own bays. In one of these bays where the prohibition is still in force, it was proposed by the fishermen of the locality to have it removed; but when they found that if their wishes should be acceded to a right to fish there would be given to anyone who liked to come to the place, the proposal was withdrawn.

Trawling, however, is not confined to the Dublin vessels, but is still carried on by small craft from Balbriggan, and it was so formerly from Skerries; for this method of fishing was in operation on the Irish coast many years before the Dublin fleet of smacks came into existence, and it is only in comparatively recent years that any restrictions to its working have been made.

A peculiar style of fishing boat known as the Skerries Wherry was formerly much used in the district north of Dublin; but in 1864 there were only a very few of them employed in fishing, and we hear that at the present time such vessels of that style as are still afloat are chiefly used for carrying cargo in the coasting trade. As a relic of former times, however, they deserve some notice, and we therefore give a sketch of one we had an opportunity of examining at Balbriggan in 1864, and which was then employed as a trawler.

They are heavy lumbering craft, half-decked or entirely so, and some of them we believe were over 30 tons. These wherries are the only fishing vessels we have seen on any part of our coasts which had the schooner rig; but some of them were in course of time converted into smacks, and that is now the usual rig of the larger fishing boats, except those used for the drift-fishery.

Line-fishing is general along the eastern coast, and longlining is largely carried on in Dublin Bay and northwards. The fishermen at Rush have devoted themselves principally to that kind of work, by which

SKERRIES WHERRY.

they catch cod, ling, haddock, and conger, not only in their neighbourhood, but also during their occasional visits to the western and southern parts of the island. About 1857, both trawlers and line fishermen had their profits materially diminished by the unexpected disappearance of most of the haddocks for which Dublin Bay and the neighbouring coast had long been famous. The scarcity of this favourite fish was of course attributed by the line fishermen solely to the operations of the trawlers, and the latter became more unpopular than ever. It appears, however, that this was not the first occasion on which haddocks had become scarce; and, as on the coast of Scotland and part of the coast of England, they had long previously left their usual grounds for a time without there having been any sound reason for believing the system of trawling could have driven them away. What we now know about the haddock spawn floating at the surface and the young fish being developed under these circumstances, is sufficient to dispose of the charge against the trawlers. The haddocks, however, did not entirely forsake the neighbourhood, but occasionally appeared when they were not expected, and more especially in recent years. In 1872 a very large number was taken during one week, but only a few subsequently; and in answer to a question we recently put to one of the large smack-owners at Dublin, we were informed that the haddocks had "again made their appearance this season in pretty fair abundance on the old fishing grounds."

The smaller boats employed for the line-fishery are of the same style as the Norway yawl, sharp at both ends; and some form of that excellent kind of boat is generally used on many parts of the Irish coast. It was introduced many years ago by Norway ships trading to Ireland, and with some alterations, depending very much on local ideas, continues in great favour. Smacks of from 20 to 30 tons are used for distant fishing.

The most important and profitable fishery on the east and north-east coast to the general body of fishermen is that for herrings, and it attracts, as we have said, a large number of boats from Cornwall, Scotland, and the Isle of Man. The two great stations for this fishery are Howth, at the northern point of Dublin Bay, and Ardglass, a little south of Strangford, and opposite the Isle of Man. The season commences at some time in June, but the boats are not in full work till July. From that time till the end of September, or sometimes far into October, drift-fishing is followed up in some part of the Irish Sea, the boats gradually decreasing in number as the season advances, and many of the Cornishmen leaving in August in order to take part in the pilchard fishing on their own coast.

There is very little curing done in Ireland, although several attempts have been made at Howth, and something is still being done there; but a large proportion of the herrings caught on the east coast is shipped fresh by steamers to England, and finds a ready sale in the inland towns. Any scarcity in the supply of fish in the Irish markets is, therefore, not entirely due to the comparatively small extent of the Irish fisheries. The wholesale buyers can do a more profitable business by sending their purchases across the Channel, even with the additional cost of transport, than by selling the fish in Ireland; and this applies, not only to herrings and mackerel, but also, though to a less extent, to other kinds of sea fish. At the same time cured fish of various kinds are imported from Scotland and our North American Colonies; there were 24,000 barrels of Scotch-cured herrings sent to Ireland in 1872, and double that number in 1871.

At Arklow, which is included in the Dublin Customs district, there is an important oyster fishery, the beds mostly lying in 10 or 12 fathoms water, at varying distances from the shore, and extending almost continuously to the Wexford banks. Large numbers of the oysters obtained here are carried away to be laid down at Beaumaris and on the beds at the mouth of the Thames. The herring fishery from Arklow begins in June, but only lasts a short time; and the boats then go away north and fish in company with the mixed fleet between Dublin and Ardglass. In October, however, herrings are again on this part of the coast, and the fishery is continued with more or less success till nearly the end of the year. The boats used here are luggers and small smacks, the latter being principally employed for the oyster fishery.

Some inshore beam-trawling is carried on from Courtown, a little south of Arklow, as well as at Wexford, and the large Dublin trawlers work at certain seasons on this part of the coast. Herrings appear to be found in the neighbourhood of Wexford more continuously than farther north, and are to be met with there more or less from May to Christmas. The fishery, however, is on a very small scale.

The boats used at Wexford for the herring fishery are of a very peculiar style. They are called "cots,"

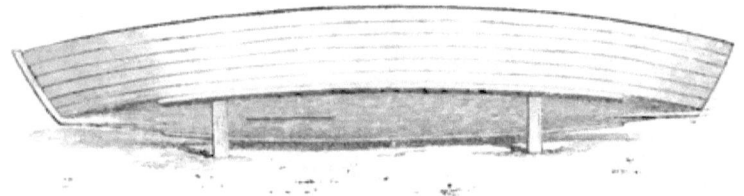

WEXFORD HERRING COT ON SHORE.

and are entirely flat-bottomed, with the exception of a small bit of keel at each end, and what may be called a bilge-piece or false keel running for some distance on each side, between the floor and the planking. Their peculiarities will be seen in the accompanying illustrations, representing one of these cots out of the water and tilted for the purpose of being cleaned, and another under sail. Their usual length is about 30 feet over all, and with 7½ or 8 feet beam. A centre-board, with a depth of 5 feet below the floor, is lowered when the boat is on a wind; and the sails consist of three sprit-

WEXFORD HERRING COT—UNDER SAIL.

sails and a jib. These boats are well suited for working their way over the shoals within and without Wexford Harbour.

The fisheries here are not altogether very important, although including trawling, dredging, drifting and line-fishing. There are no local restrictions to trawling, except that it is prohibited where drift-fishing is being carried on.

Waterford Harbour lies at the junction of the Customs districts of New Ross and Waterford, the eastern side of it being, we believe, in the New Ross division. It is well situated for a fishing station, especially for sea-going craft. There are productive grounds off the coast for both line fishermen and trawlers, and there seems to be generally a fair supply of sea fish within the headlands. The salmon fishery, however, occupies the attention of many of the local fishermen during the season, and it is when that is over that the sea fish are principally sought for.

Some of the difficulties in dealing with the Irish sea fisheries have been well exemplified at Waterford. Trawling has long been carried on there by small boats of 2 or 3 tons, within the harbour, but great hostility has been shown towards any attempts on the part of large vessels to work within the headlands, and violence has been resorted to by the native population in order to put a stop to their proceedings. The difficulty in getting local crews for the large vessels led to English fishermen being employed; but the strong feeling against them induced them sooner or later to return to their own country. The complaints of the small trawlers of the manner in which the large vessels with their bigger nets destroyed the spawn and young fish, as was alleged, resulted in a very remarkable byelaw being made by the former Commissioners of Irish Sea Fisheries, by which fishing boats of *more* than 5 tons measurement were forbidden to trawl within a line drawn between certain points on the two sides of the harbour. Within those limits the right of trawling was reserved for small boats — no matter how small, but for none larger than 5 tons. We must presume that the Commissioners in this instance silently ignored the alleged cause of complaint, and legislated against what was the real one, although it was perhaps not expressed in words—namely, the competition of large trawls with small ones. In fact, for the sake of quieting the turbulent portion of the fishermen, the others were, to a great extent, kept out of their way. As the large trawlers draw 8 or 9 feet water, it is clear that they could not work in the shoal places where the young fish are mostly found. The privilege of doing the particular mischief complained of was therefore reserved to the small boats, which being able to trawl in 3 or 4 feet water, were most capable of exercising it. If the protection of the young fish were intended, it is certainly remarkable that a byelaw should have been made so well adapted to continue their destruction.

We understand, however, that an alteration of the byelaw has been made this year (1873), and that the prohibition now applies to trawlers of more than 10 tons. We hope therefore better counsels are beginning to prevail, and that, in time, if any restriction at all be considered necessary, it will be to the small boats instead of to the large ones.

Dunmore, on the south side of Waterford Harbour, and just within the entrance, is the station for the deep-sea trawlers; and in 1873 there were eleven smacks working from that town. They fish on the Saltee ground, to which we have previously referred, and in the outer part of the harbour; they also work on the Nymph Bank,[1] which lies some 30 or 40 miles off the land, and extends for a considerable distance in a south-westerly direction. There are difficulties, however, in working with trawlers on this ground on account of its distance, unless some organization for sending the fish to market be adopted; and anything like fishing companies seems to have as little chance of success in Ireland as elsewhere. There appears to be a good supply of fish on this ground, but we understand there is some danger of the trawl-nets being damaged by scattered rocks in some parts of it. Taking the bank generally, it is no doubt capable of being

---

[1] Mr. Fraser mentions that in 1726 a proposal was made by Mr. William Doyle, Hydrographer, for supplying the large English markets "with fish preserved in well-boats, from the southern coast of Ireland, and, particularly, from a fishing ground he states he had discovered, unto which he gave the name of Nymph Bank, from a vessel called the 'Nymph,' which he employed in the examination of this fishing ground."—*Review of Domestic Fisheries*, p. 4. 1818.

profitably worked by both trawlers and line fishermen; but for the latter, larger boats are required than are usually employed on the south coast.

Trawling was carried on for a time in 1864 in the open part of Waterford Harbour by means of a steamer, and good catches of fish were made; but the jealousy of the native fishermen was excited, and it resulted in their cutting away the vessel's net early one morning, and in the steamer being afterwards given up. It was intended to use this vessel as a carrier to bring in the fish caught by some large trawlers which were being purchased for working on the Nymph Bank; but the development of that fishery was interfered with by the very fishermen who might have taken part in working it to advantage. It can hardly be a matter of surprise that strangers should be unwilling to remain in a neighbourhood where, as in this case, natives of the locality met with such treatment. A better feeling, however, appears to be gaining ground; and recent reports of the extension of trawling by large vessels on parts of the Irish coast, where a few years ago it was difficult to work with them, lead to the hope that the "mine of wealth" which we hear so much of as being unworked in Irish waters will gradually become developed, and, we trust, by native industry.

Hake and sprats periodically visit Waterford Harbour, besides the choicer kinds of fish, and we were told at Dunmore that "the sea was sometimes dry with pilchards" along that part of the coast, although at that time (1864) no attempt was made to catch them.

Sprats are taken in fixed bag-nets[1] near Passage on the Waterford river.

---

[1] See Bag-nets, p. 166.

FISHING STATIONS.

IRELAND (continued).

Youghal to Tralee — Decline of the Dungarvan fisheries — Trammel-fishing at Ring — The hammer-trawl — The otter-trawl — Kinsale mackerel fishery — Idle habits of the Kinsale fishermen — Fishing Company unsuccessful — Transport of mackerel to England — French fishing boats — Attempted establishment of a pilchard fishery — Objections to it by the fishermen — Kinsale hookers — Bantry Bay a good trawling ground — General fisheries imperfectly worked — Dingle Bay very productive of fish — Royal Irish Fisheries Company formerly successful — Removal of restrictions on trawling — Line and drift fisheries — "Curraghs," or canvas canoes — Dingle fishermen generally industrious — **Limerick to Sligo** — Galway fisheries not fully worked — Difficulties caused by the Claddagh fishermen — Good trawling ground — Systematic search for spawn under the direction of the Fisheries Inspectors — Herring fishery — "Claddagh law" — Other fisheries — Galway hookers — Bofin Island — Fishing Company unsuccessful — Boat harbour now being constructed — Oyster fishery in Clew Bay — Line-fishing on the outer coast — Donegal Bay — Sprat fishery at Inver — Accidents from whales — Herring fishery only near the shore — Line, trawl, and trammel fisheries — Haddock plentiful off the coast, but scarce in the bay — Fisheries probably capable of extension, but fishermen generally very poor — **Londonderry to Drogheda** — Fisheries for the most part unimportant — Fishing boats, yawls — Line-fishing at Rush — Ardglass a large station — Summary and analysis of Irish fisheries — Their uncertain prospects.

YOUGHAL TO TRALEE—NUMBER OF BOATS.

Port Letters.	Port.	Year.	1st Class.	2nd Class.	3rd Class.
Y.	Youghal ..	1872	3	17	33
C.	Cork ..	,,	61	361	398
S.	Skibbereen	,,	11	247	507
T.	Tralee	,,	11	183	434

The only place which has been of any consequence between Waterford and Cork is Dungarvan, but its importance as a fishery station has diminished in a remarkable manner during the last few years. It is one of those places which suffered much from the famine; but in 1864 the fishing interests there were sufficiently strong to make a good show with their complaints before the Royal Commissioners against the fishermen of Ring, a village nearer the entrance to the harbour. The latter were largely engaged in trammel-fishing as well as in trawling, and, it was said, interfered with the Dungarvan men, who worked chiefly with lines, by setting the trammels in their way.

Within the last few years fishing from Dungarvan has practically come to an end; some of the fishermen have emigrated, others have gone to sea, and some, we fear, have moved to the poor-house; while the Ring men continue to follow their own particular modes of fishing without anyone to complain of them. The Irish Inspectors partly attribute the disappearance of the Dungarvan fishermen to the fact of their having possessed no land to fall back upon in times of scarcity. Other causes, however, must, we think, have had greater influence on the fortunes of Dungarvan; and we cannot believe that a town which at one time was of some celebrity as a fishing port can have fallen into its present state of decay, so far as its fisheries are concerned, mainly because the fishermen attended to nothing but their legitimate occupation.

Trammel-fishing is worked to some extent by the fishermen at Ring for the capture of hake, which are generally abundant along this coast at certain seasons. The longlines are also used, and fish-bait is obtained for them by trawling, although mussels are to be had in great abundance.

Seans are used along this south coast for the capture of mackerel and sprats.

The kind of trawl in use here is the one we have

THE HAMMER AND OTTER-TRAWLS

spoken of[1] as the "pole- or hammer-trawl," an old-fashioned contrivance only suited for work in smooth water along shore. It is called the "hammer-trawl," from a peculiarity in part of its gear. A general idea of this kind of trawl is given in Plate XV., but we are unable now to say what were the exact measurements of the net we had an opportunity of examining. The body of the net is of a conical form, with a square mouth, and the cod terminates in an opening as in the ordinary beam-trawl. This is of course closed when the net is at work. The mouth of the trawl is kept open by means of a long wing or "sleeve" of netting on each side, gradually tapering towards its free extremity, which is fastened by its upper and lower edges to an instrument called a "hammer." This consists of a stout flattened bar of iron (*a*) having a wooden upright in the centre, and the end of the net is fastened to the top of this and to one end of the iron bar or shoe. The tow-rope is made fast by a short bridle in a corresponding manner on the opposite side of the upright. The hammers, one in front of each of the wings, serve to keep the ends of the ground-rope at the bottom, and move over the ground in the same way as the iron heads in the beam-trawl. The wings and mouth of the net are corked along their upper margin or back-rope, and weighted with lead on the lower edge or ground-rope. When the trawl is used it is towed along by a rope or warp from each wing, leading on board through a block at the end of a pole 25 or 30 feet long, which is rigged out on each side of the trawl-boat; this arrangement keeping the wings so far separated that the water can act with facility in extending them and so opening the mouth of the net.

[1] See Trawling, p. 52.

The otter-trawl is constructed on much the same principle as regards the shape of the net, but the well-known otter-boards, kite-like in their action, are substituted for the hammers, and no poles are required; a single warp with a bridle to the two wings being all that is necessary. The application of otter-boards to the trawl—in fact, the invention so far of the otter-trawl, originated, we were informed in Ireland, with Mr. Musgrave. This trawl is much used by yachtsmen, and is very suitable for vessels not solely employed in fishing, as there is no trouble with a heavy beam, and the net can be stowed away in a small compass when it is not in use. We have not had much opportunity of working with this trawl, but so far as our experience has enabled us to judge of its merits, it appears to be very efficient in fine weather, and can be shot without much difficulty when there is plenty of light for the fishermen to see what they are about. It is under such conditions that the otter-trawl is used by yachtsmen; but regular deep-sea trawlers work both by night and day, and in almost all kinds of weather; and we can readily believe there is some force in their objection to this particular form of trawl when they say that the otter-boards will not keep on the ground when there is any sea on.

Another *possible* objection, and one supported by the result of our short experience of this net, is that more chance of escape is given by it to round-fish than is the case with the beam-trawl. In the latter the beam and upper front edge of the net are considerably in advance of the ground-rope, so that fish when disturbed by that rope cannot escape upwards; but in the otter-trawl the upper margin of the net is just over the ground-rope, and there is very little to prevent many kinds of fish from escaping over the top of it. This of course would not affect the capture of flat-fish, which seek safety in the ground.

Shooting the net is done over the stern, and the otter-boards (as we have seen) are lowered one over each quarter; as soon as they begin to diverge the bridle is slacked away carefully, the vessel having some way on her so as to ensure a proper resistance to the boards and make them open out the mouth of the net before it reaches the ground. The spans composing the bridle are proportionately much longer in the otter-trawl than in the beam-trawl, so as to allow the wings of the net to spread out and make a wide sweep over the ground; and a short pole or stick is lashed across between the two ropes at a few feet from the shackle joining them to the trawl-warp, to prevent the spans twisting together.

Proceeding westward we come to Ballycottin Bay and Queenstown in the Cork district. Line-fishing is carried on to some extent there, and seans, trammels, and trawls are also used, but there is nothing in these fisheries requiring special notice.

Kinsale was at one time famous for its line fishermen, and the Kinsale hookers stood high as sea-going fishing boats. It is now the chief station for the mackerel fishery, and at that season is the resort of boats from other parts of Ireland, as well as from Scotland, the Isle of Man, and Cornwall. The fishery, which is with drift-nets, begins early in March, and is carried on till about the end of June; and, as is the case with the herring fishery on the east coast, the strange boats capture by far the larger proportion of the fish. During the last few years many French boats have taken part in this mackerel fishery, but their captures are cured on board, and form no part of the fish which is landed at Kinsale.

We should be glad if we could commend the Kinsale fishermen for their industry, but it is difficult to do so when we have ourselves seen almost all their boats lying idle in the harbour in the midst of the mackerel season, whilst Manx boats were bringing in their cargoes of fish. On inquiring the reason for this, we heard that the Kinsale boats had had large takes of mackerel two days before, and the men had since been occupied in "drinking their money." We then went among the fishermen, and after a little conversation here and there about what sort of fishing they were making, ascertained that a good many mackerel had been lately caught, and the boats were going out again soon. A little tobacco is generally very effective in opening a fisherman's heart, but in more than one instance at Kinsale our inquiries were interrupted by a request for "the price of a glass of whisky." The almost irresistible attraction of whisky to these men when they have any money to spend is unfortunately not a matter for question; but better reports of them have been given recently, and it is to be hoped that examples of temperance and industry among themselves will not be without effect on the rest of the fishermen.

Kinsale suffered with other places during the famine years, but it is said the fisheries there were in a declining state before that time. There are, we believe, very few of the large boats now belonging to the fishermen; the owners being fish salesmen, and others who engage the men to fish for them, and would keep them constantly employed if they were willing to be so. The South of Ireland Fishing Company worked for a few years at Kinsale, but has now added one more to the numerous fishing companies which have proved unsuccessful. The boats formerly used by this company are now in private hands.

A great step in the development of the mackerel fishery has been made during the last few years by establishing a system of steamers for the transport to England of the fish landed at Kinsale; many of these vessels besides sailing carriers having been in regular work during the seasons; so that with these facilities for disposing of the captures there has been a great inducement to carry on the fishery with as much vigour as possible. The fish thus transmitted are packed with ice in boxes containing six score each, or what is called a "hundred" according to fishermen's counting in the case of mackerel. According to the Inspectors' Reports there were about 60,000 boxes, equal to 6000 tons, of mackerel sold at Kinsale in 1872, and a larger number in 1871 and 1870. This was the produce of native boats and strangers, but not including the French fishing boats; the French being in the habit of curing their fish on board, and Kinsale not being one of the Irish ports at which, by the *Declaration annexed to the Convention of November* 11, 1867,[1] French fishermen are allowed to land their fish.

The efforts to establish a regular fishery for pilchards on the Irish coast have not been attended with much success. These fish appear sometimes in very large numbers on the south and south-west of the island, but they are not in more favour with the Irish people than they are generally in England, except in the west, where, as everyone knows, they are in great request in the home market and for exportation to the Mediterranean. An objection to catching pilchards is also made by the

[1] 31 & 32 Vict., cap. 45, p. 357.

Irish fishermen on account of the oiliness of the fish which they say injures their nets, but this is a very trifling difficulty, and can be easily removed by the use of the proper materials for preserving them, as in Cornwall. The fact of such an objection having been made, however, shows that something more than money is required to induce these fishermen to work heartily at the fisheries within their reach. A good deal of ignorance and prejudice has to be overcome; and credit is due to the Irish Inspectors for their endeavours to deal with the first by ascertaining and giving instructions about the manner in which the Cornishmen fish for and cure the pilchard; but we have less hope of their being able to persuade the Irish generally that the pilchard is as desirable an article of food as it is considered in Cornwall.

The Kinsale hookers were at one time famous among Irish fishing smacks; they were from 30 to 40 feet over all, with good beam and a great depth of body, and well calculated for knocking about in the rough weather to which they were often exposed; but a faster and more generally useful style of boat has been introduced of late years.

Seans, trammels, and lines are used more or less along this coast, and hake with various kinds of ordinary line-fish are taken. Herrings also appear in considerable numbers at times, and are captured with the sean.

The general fisheries in and about Bantry Bay have been declining for many years, and there was a considerable diminution in the number of boats and fishermen in 1872 compared with the returns for the previous year. This is said to be mainly due to the emigration which has been actively going on from this part of the island. Bantry Bay is one of those localities to which the visits of the herrings and other so-called migratory fishes are very uncertain, and even when they enter the bay they do not always approach those parts of it where they can be easily taken with the sean, which is here the favourite mode of catching them. Drift-nets are, however, also used for herrings, but not specially for mackerel. The hake are mostly caught with trammels, and a great number of these nets were formerly in use. Many parts of the bay are available for trawling on, but the bottom generally is not of the best description, a good deal of it being soft ground. Good takes of soles, however, are sometimes made, with a moderate proportion of other kinds of trawl-fish. The trawlers have not been more fortunate in escaping opposition in Bantry Bay than elsewhere, and the conflicting interests of the trawlers and trammel-fishers led to the issue of a byelaw by the Commissioners in 1858, by which the trawlers are still excluded from a certain portion of ground at the head of the bay. This restriction, however, is not of very great importance, as the largest quantity of fish is usually to be obtained nearer the entrance. The trawlers are also forbidden to work between sunset and sunrise, and this may be a hardship to them at certain times of the year. Trawling in Bantry Bay has not been carried on with regularity, but there were six large trawlers fishing there in 1873, and there is no doubt room for more. There is also plenty to be done there by line fishermen, if they were properly fitted out and would keep steadily at the work. Some little lobster-fishing is carried on in the rocky neighbourhood of Glengariff, that beautiful little deep-water harbour at the head of the bay.

Kenmare estuary also affords plenty of room for fishing of various kinds, and is one of the localities which the Inspectors have lately freed from all restrictions against trawling. The usual kinds of fishing are more or less worked there.

The fisheries of Dingle Bay have been the subject of many official inquiries, in consequence of the complaints made, especially by the fishermen of Anascaul, of the operations of the trawlers from Dingle, some miles nearer the sea. There is no doubt that Dingle Bay is a good locality for both trawl and line fish, and occasionally for herrings. Trawling was introduced there in 1848 by the Royal Irish Fisheries Company, under the management of Mr. William Andrews, a gentleman well known for his practical acquaintance with the Irish sea fisheries and his continued efforts to improve and develop them. This company worked successfully in Dingle Bay for a few years, and much good was accomplished besides by showing the fishermen what could be done by systematic work if advantage were taken of proper methods and appliances for carrying on the fishing.

The proceedings of the company, however, were on a very small scale, disturbances in the country at that time having interfered with the calling up of the capital; and when, after a few years, power was sought to carry out the original terms of the charter, it was thought desirable by the Board of Trade that the limited liability principle should be applied to the enterprise, and a change was then made in the management and constitution of the company, ending unfortunately in its total collapse. The first period of the company's existence, however, so far as it was then constituted, was very successful; and although with only 1000*l.* capital to commence with, the stock and plant after a lapse of seven years were valued at 3000*l.*

Trawling has before now been restricted to certain parts of the bay, but the whole of the ground is now free; many portions of it, however, are too rough for that mode of fishing. It has been more or less followed up during a great part of the year in recent times, and there is no reason to think that any injury to the general fisheries has been caused by it. Trawling can only be carried on satisfactorily within the headlands of this bay, as the water outside is very deep, and there is usually a heavy Atlantic roll setting in.

Line-fishing is extensively practised, and many cod, ling, and other descriptions of fish are taken there either by handlines or longlines. It has been said that large numbers of soles used to be caught by the Anascaul fishermen on their spilliards, using the lugworm as a bait; but although there seems to be no question about soles having been taken by this method, there is very great doubt about the numbers alleged to have been so captured. We have known these fish to have been caught with a hook on the English coast, but it is a very rare occurrence.

Drift-nets are used in Dingle Bay for herrings, and these fish together with mackerel and scad are also taken with seans, generally worked as circle-nets, and not hauled in on the shore.

The boats largely used at Dingle some years ago were heavy open craft commonly known as "sprit-boats"; they carried two spritsails and a jib, and had a crew of six or seven men each. The number of these boats, however, has been very much reduced, and they will doubtless altogether disappear under the influence of this improving age. Another class of boats of very peculiar build here attracts attention. These are the "curraghs," or canvas canoes. They have only been in use at Dingle, so far as we can learn, for about twenty-five years, but are of longer standing on the coast between Dingle and the Clare side of Galway Bay.

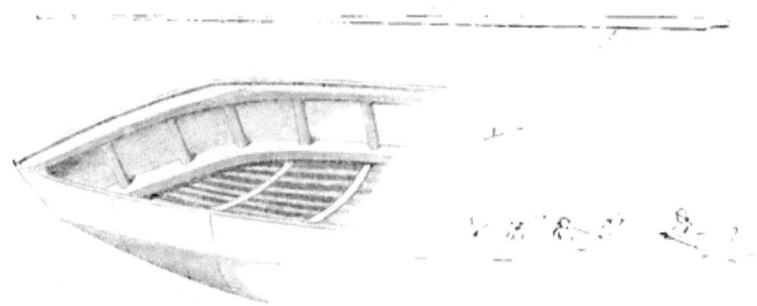

"CURRAGH," OR CANVAS CANOE.

The construction of these curraghs is very simple, consisting of a light frame for the top sides, strengthened by a keelson curved slightly upwards at each end so as to form what may be called the stem and stern-post, which are fitted to the lower part of the frame. The ribs are simply pieces of cask-hoop cut to such a length as to give the requisite curve to the bottom, and outside these are nailed long narrow battens to serve as flooring. Such is the skeleton of the curragh; and as a substitute for planking, the whole outer surface is covered with tarred canvas nailed on in pieces about a couple of feet wide, and extending from one gunwale round to the other. Thwarts are then fixed in the usual manner. The general length of these canoes is about 20 feet, with a breadth of nearly 4 feet. Four men form the crew of one of these frail craft, each man having a pair of small light oars with very narrow blades, working on single thole-pins, which in each case passes through a small triangular piece of wood nailed to the oar at a proper distance from the handle. A small lugsail is carried when a fair wind can be had. The curraghs float like bubbles on the water, and would be likely to be blown away but for the great command over them gained by the use of the four pairs of oars, and the weight of a good crew to give them some hold on the water. We have found by experience in them that even in fine weather the raised bow makes it a little difficult to keep a straight course when there is any head wind; but they are admirably handled by the fishermen, and when properly trimmed and each man has his oars at work, they will go through an almost incredible amount of bad weather.

CURRAGH.

These canoes cost about 5l. each, and a couple of men will turn them over and carry them on their heads without any difficulty whatever. They are used for the line-fishing, and for that purpose are often taken well out to sea.

The Dingle men are as a rule steady and industrious, well used to the sea, and more worthy of the name of fishermen than many who are called so elsewhere on the Irish coast. There, then, we may hope for an improvement and a further development of the fisheries which it has been proved can be worked with advantage in the bay.

On the north side of the Dingle peninsula lies Brandan Bay, in which trawling has been prohibited since 1860. The fisheries are unimportant along this part of the west coast, and consist chiefly of trammel and line fishing, with oyster dredging in a few places. Emigration has diminished the number of the fishermen, and those who still remain at home devote only a small proportion of their time to such occupations.

LIMERICK TO SLIGO — NUMBER OF BOATS.

Port Letters.	Port.	Year.	1st Class.	2nd Class.	3rd Class.
L.	Limerick	1872	—	—	79
G.	Galway	,,	10	635	880
W.T.	Westport	,,	2	34	881
B.A.	Ballina	,,	—	1	191
S.O.	Sligo	,,	1	191	396

The next division of which we need speak is that of Galway. It comprises a large extent of wild coast broken up into innumerable creeks and islands, with a scattered population for the most part in a state of great poverty, and, except in Galway Bay, carrying on but little fishing besides what they can occasionally do with their lines.

The fisheries in Galway Bay have hardly received the attention which there is every reason to think they deserve; and unfortunately the locality has been notorious for the lawless proceedings of a section of the fishermen who for many years virtually decided when and how the fisheries should be carried on. It is impossible to speak of the Galway Bay fisheries without mentioning the Claddagh men. This community is formed of the fishing part of the population of the town of Galway, and occupies a distinct quarter of it known as the Claddagh. Here they have lived for many generations as a separate people, marrying only among themselves, carrying on the fisheries according to their own ideas of times and methods, and seeking too often by violence and intimidation to enforce "Claddagh law" upon the other fishermen of the bay. Although a terror to the district in matters relating to the sea fisheries, they have not been without the sympathy of many of the neighbouring magistrates and gentry for what they considered their grievances. The chief one, we need hardly say, was the presence of trawlers in the bay, who were very successful in their fishing when they could work without molestation; but the Claddagh men thought proper to attack them with volleys of stones, and carried their violence so far that the smack-owners were obliged to lay up their vessels.

A byelaw, made several years ago, and still in force, prohibits trawling on a considerable piece of ground at the head of the bay, and this regulation practically keeps the trawlers to water of not less than 10 fathoms; but there is fine trawling ground westward from the boundary line, in water ranging from 10 to 30 fathoms. The fish appear to frequent the higher part of the bay during the summer, but there is no part of the year in which trawling may not be successfully worked somewhere or other inside the Arran Islands; and there is also a patch of ground in deeper water beyond them that can be fished with advantage for a short time in summer when the weather is fine. Trawling is also prohibited in the bay within three miles of drift-fishing.

The general feeling among the Claddagh men against trawling has been of long standing; and although it was partially allayed in 1853, when a subscription was got up for the purpose of fitting out many of the Claddagh boats with trawls, the objection to that mode of fishing became as strong as ever when their gear began to wear out; and violence was again resorted to in order to put a stop to the trawling by the large smacks, which did not belong to the Claddagh fishermen. It is needless to recount the various disturbances which have taken place in later years, more than once requiring the presence of a gunboat to protect the trawlers; but although the population of the Claddagh has been rapidly diminishing, the same spirit seems to continue; and in the Annual Report (1872) by the Coastguard to the Inspectors of Fisheries we are sorry to find it again stated that "conflicts have taken place between Claddagh fishermen and trawlers, the reason assigned being that the mode of capture practised by the latter destroys the spawn and young fry." The Inspectors themselves report [1] that the conduct of the Claddagh men on this last occasion was so bad, "that after an investigation by a very large bench of magistrates, a number of them were returned for trial at the assizes."

In consequence of the difficulty in arriving at any satisfactory conclusion from the evidence of the Claddagh men against the trawlers, the latter having declared that their lives would be endangered if they ventured into court to defend themselves, it was determined by the Inspectors to carry out a systematic examination of the bay with the object of ascertaining whether spawn was ever brought up in the trawl, and to what extent the young fry were destroyed. Two trawl-boats were gratuitously provided by the smack-

[1] *Report of Inspectors* for 1872, p. 8.

owners, and the experiments were entrusted to Lieutenant Drew, R.N., the Inspecting Commander of the Coastguard at Galway, a gentleman whose experience in scientific exploration of the sea and dredging should make him, as the Inspectors say, well qualified for the task. The experiments were to be continued throughout the year, and if carefully carried out should produce some valuable results. The reports have not yet been published.[1]

There were six large trawlers at work in Galway Bay in 1873, but there is room for a much larger number to fish in; and Galway having the advantage of direct railway communication with Dublin, great facilities are provided for sending the fish to a market where it would be tolerably sure to realize a fair price.

The most important fishery in the bay, so far as the native fishermen are concerned, is that for herrings. There is some fluctuation in the supply of these fish, but there is rarely a complete failure, and in some seasons the herrings are abundant. "Claddagh law" often interferes with full advantage being taken of the shoals which come into the bay, there being a superstitious feeling against beginning the fishery before St. John's Day, the 24th of June. The men from the other villages in the bay sometimes venture out earlier, but it is not good for them if the Claddagh men discover it. The fish may be swarming along their shores, but until the self-constituted rulers of the fishery allow it, not a herring may be caught. It is also considered by these people to be unlucky to fish every day. We are told, however, that from one cause and another the

---

[1] In the recently-published Report of the Inspectors it is stated that these experiments have been suspended in consequence of the removal of the officer to another district.

Claddagh men are fast diminishing in number, and are now even more deeply sunk in poverty than has been their general condition for many years past; and it can hardly be a matter of regret to those who wish to see Irish fishermen and fisheries improving that a community which has for so long a time been a stumbling-block at Galway, and a bad example to other fishermen, should be gradually becoming less powerful for mischief. It is said that a " New Claddagh " is being established in America; and it will surely be a happy thing for Ireland when the old community is quite broken up, and their evil deeds are known only by tradition.

The other fisheries in Galway Bay are for mackerel, sprats, and line-fish of many excellent kinds. Sprats are taken by seans, and mackerel by seans and line; drift-nets would also be used for the mackerel if the fishermen had the means of providing them. Line-fishing was extensively carried on in former times, and there is no want of cod, ling, whiting, and other hook-fish at the present time in the bay; but boats and fishermen have alike diminished, and line-fishing has fallen off in proportion.

The Galway hookers have long been famous, and are of a peculiar build, unlike any other Irish fishing boats. The large class hookers, about 15 tons, are half-decked, from 30 to 35 feet over all, and with about 10 feet beam; the stern-post has a moderate rake, and the stem a large gripe. The depth of hold is not nearly as great in proportion as in the Kinsale boats, and the topsides tumble in for a great portion of their length very much in the American style, giving them a very peculiar appearance.

They are smack-rigged, and the sails are made of Bandle linen covered with a mixture of Stockholm tar and butter, or, when such materials are too costly, with coal-tar and hog's lard. These hookers are excellent

GALWAY AND KINSALE HOOKERS.

craft and sail well. Their crews vary from four to six men, according to the size of the boat, but most of the boats now used are small ones. Besides these there are numerous rowing boats, which are employed for many other purposes than fishing. Cutting and carrying seaweed give a great deal of occupation to the fishermen, and will no doubt always be looked upon as an important means of helping them to gain a livelihood.

On the Clare side of the bay are artificial beds of oysters, the property of persons who have laid them down to fatten.

From Galway to Westport there is not a great deal of fishing, but much more could be carried on with advantage if the fishermen were supplied with the necessary lines and nets. Cod, ling, and haddock abound on this coast in winter, the cod and ling remaining till about the end of April, and the haddock for a month or six weeks later. An association under the name of the Inisbofin Fishing Company (Limited) was formed a few years ago for the purpose of purchasing the fish caught by the men at Bofin Island and in that neighbourhood; but, as with many other fishing companies which have had a short existence, there appears to have been in this case a want of practical knowledge of what could be done. There was undoubtedly an abundance of fish on the coast, but the means of catching it were very limited; and as the company did not profess to do more than purchase, it is not very surprising that the concern should have come to an end after a short experience. The head-quarters of this company were at Belfast, although the intended scene of its operations was far away on the other side of the island. The affairs of the company were wound up in 1872.

An endeavour to construct a boat harbour at Bofin is now being made, and its completion will be a great boon to the fishermen, who are almost without protection for their boats on one of the most exposed parts of the coast. We may reasonably hope it will be followed by an improvement in the fishery there, for the inhabitants have little inducement to devote much of their time to other occupations, and there is no doubt about there being plenty of fish within their reach.

Clew Bay is chiefly notable for its oyster fishery, dredging being extensively carried on among the numerous islands at its eastern end, and a considerable portion of foreshore has been licensed for the purposes of cultivation, but hitherto, we believe, without much advantage.

There is also an oyster fishery in Blacksod Bay, and line-fishing for cod, ling, and haddock is more or less carried on all along the coast towards Sligo. Belmullet is a good locality for this kind of fishing, but the fishermen there have been very much reduced in numbers.

There is very little requiring notice on the northern coast of Mayo or in Sligo Bay; the fisheries are mostly by line, but there are shoals of herrings sometimes on this part of the coast, and good captures have been made. In Donegal Bay there has been some indication of an improvement in the fisheries during the last few years, and herrings which at one time seemed to have almost deserted the locality have again been caught there in large numbers. One of the principal and most regular fisheries there is that for sprats, having its head-quarters in Inver Bay. It begins at about the end of July and usually lasts for three months. Sprats are taken by seans worked as circle-nets, and not hauled on shore. These nets are about 140 yards long, made up of two long wings, and a bunt of small mesh; they belong to the fishermen, who contribute a share each of everything required to make them complete and ready for use. Row-boats of 3 or 4 tons with crews of seven or eight hands each are used in this fishery, and when working by day in clear water they do not like to go into a depth of more than 9 or 10 fathoms, so that the foot of the net may touch the ground; but for night fishing or in muddy water they can go into greater depths. Whales are common in Donegal Bay during the sprat season, and are rather dreaded by the fishermen, as accidents have happened before now from their coming up among the boats and capsizing them. These no doubt are rorquals or fin-whales, a large species frequently entering deep bays and estuaries in pursuit of shoals of fish; they are dangerous and difficult to kill, as they at once make for open water when attacked, and they are not worth very much when by any chance they are captured. We have seen them quite at the head of Bantry Bay.

Herrings have been abundant in Donegal Bay in particular years; they come at the same time as the sprats, and drift-fishing and seaning are sometimes carried on together in the same immediate locality without causing the ill-feeling which has been so strongly shown under similar circumstances in Lochfyne. There is also a small winter herring fishery in the beginning of the year; and, as on the Scotch coast, the fish taken at the two seasons appear to belong to different broods, the one spawning early in September and the other in February. The visits of the herring to the different parts of Donegal Bay are very capricious, but a more regular fishery might probably be obtained if the fishermen were more generally able to use drift-nets, and could work in the open part of the bay. At present they look out for the herrings near the shore in order to catch them with the sean, and there are many places where they have only an occasional opportunity of using that kind of net. If the herrings find their way with tolerable regularity so far up as Inver and the head of the bay, although varying in numbers from year to year, it does not seem unreasonable to expect that they might be caught by systematic drift-net fishing in the thirty miles of open water through which they must pass on their way in from the sea; but to carry this out properly would require better boats and more nets than the fishermen have the means of providing. Mackerel are taken by hook, but are only fished for with nets when they come within reach of the sean; and although there must often be little doubt about their being in the bay, they do not always approach those parts of it where they can be caught by the method now adopted.

Trawling is carried on only by a few small craft, but a greater stimulus to this mode of fishing has been lately given by the removal of some of the restrictions to it in the bay.

Hake are taken here in trammels as well as by the hook.

The chief fishing on the northern coast of the bay as well as outside at Teelin and away northwards, is by longlines and handlines, but especially the former. Turbot and the best kinds of round-fish are taken in some numbers according to the season. It is worthy of note that haddocks are plentiful on the outer coast although they have been very scarce for some years in Donegal Bay. They disappeared from there rather suddenly, and it is not contended in this case that trawling was the cause of it; for although some years ago that mode of fishing met with so much objection that the Commissioners were induced to prohibit it, the haddocks were abundant for some little time after all trawling had ceased. Whiting are sometimes in vast numbers in the bay. It is very difficult to speak with any degree of certainty of the capabilities of Donegal Bay as a fishing ground; the poverty and doubtless to some extent the ignorance of the fishermen have interfered with justice being done to its fisheries; but there is abundant evidence that even under the present adverse circumstances a great quantity of fish of various kinds is taken. Yet the fishermen continue to live merely from hand to mouth, and subscriptions to provide some of them with what is requisite for their fishing seem to have done them little permanent good.

The boats used on this coast for line-fishing are four-oared yawls.

LONDONDERRY TO DROGHEDA—NUMBER OF BOATS.

Port Letters.	Port.	Year.	1st Class.	2nd Class.	3rd Class.
L.Y.	Londonderry	1872	7	444	183
C.E.	Coleraine	,,	—	120	40
B.	Belfast	,,	43	198	45
N.	Newry	,,	35	194	148
D.K.	Dundalk	,,	—	43	4
D.A.	Drogheda	,,	1	46	12

The fisheries on the remaining portion of the Irish coast, although of a varied description, are not of great importance. Line-fishing predominates in the north, with a little drifting for herrings; and a few small trawlers work in Loughs Swilly and Foyle, and on the adjoining coast. Cod and glassen or coalfish are caught by the lines, and much more might be done with this fishing if the boats employed were more fitted for open-sea work. The class of boats in general use are those we have spoken of as a modification of the Norway yawl. They are very good for ordinary coast work, but are not the most suitable for going a long distance from the land; for no excellence of design or construction will compensate for the inherent defects of an entirely open boat where the fishermen are liable to bad weather and a heavy sea with but little warning. The result is that the fishing is often put a stop to on the most favourable grounds because the boats cannot venture out. In the following cut we have given a representation of one of these yawls, which we had an opportunity of closely examining and sailing in at Moville near the entrance to Lough Foyle. The

IRISH FISHING YAWL.

largest of these yawls is about 24 feet on the keel with 6 feet beam, and they carry two spritsails and sometimes a jib. Good well-shaped oars are used with them, and they row and sail well, although a little tender down to a certain point. Drifting for herrings goes on within the lough, and there are several oyster beds, both public and private, which give employment to the fishermen in winter. The ready communication by steamer with England and Scotland provides the means of sending away soles and such other fish as may be in demand there. All restrictions to trawling in the loughs on the north and north-east coasts are now removed, and the result has been such as to encourage the Inspectors to continue the repeal of prohibitions in other places.

Belfast Lough presents no points of difference in respect to its fisheries from what is done farther north; but there is some increase in the number of small trawlers working there.

At Strangford and Carlingford there are oyster beds of considerable extent, and the herring fishery off the coast is important, but it is mostly carried on by strange boats. Ardglass, however, has several good boats, and is the principal station for landing the fish at; thence it is sent by steamers to Ardrossan. Greencastle, near Dundrum Bay, has obtained some celebrity for its boats, some reputed improvement by altering the proportions having been made there on the Norway yawl; and Greencastle yawls are the type of the northern Irish line-boats, such as we have already particularly noticed at Moville. In the Drogheda district cod, ling, and conger are fished for to some extent, and especially by the people at Rush, who are rather conspicuous among their neighbours for the energy with which they work at the line-fishing, as well as for their practice of curing the white fish. There is a little trawling with small craft from Balbriggan and one or two other places; but the great trawl-fishery on this part of the coast is carried on, as we have before described, by the large smacks from the adjoining district of Dublin.

From the sketch we have now given of the present state of the Irish sea fisheries it will be seen that all the usual methods of fishing are more or less followed up around the island, and only require proper development to ensure much larger takes of fish than are now obtained. Deep-water trawling, the herring fishery on the east coast, and the mackerel fishery on the south are, however, the only ones of any great importance; and the large number of strange boats annually taking part in the two last shows that there is an abundant supply of fish to encourage more systematic work from the native fishermen. The following is the classified return of Irish fishing boats for 1872, according to the published Statement of the Registrar-General of Shipping:—

1st Class.		2nd Class.	3rd Class.	Total.
Boats. 386	Tonnage. 9121	Boats. 3589	Boats. 4175	8150

The first-class boats, consisting of trawlers, large line-boats, and some drift-boats, give an average of 23 tons, but if the trawlers were excluded, the average size would be considerably less. Taking the other classes into consideration, we find the second averaging less than 4 tons, and the third under 2 tons. All three classes are represented in the number of boats regularly employed in fishing; but it must be remembered that these, the true fishing boats, do not amount to one-fourth of the number passing under that name on the register.

Of the prospects of the Irish sea fisheries generally it is difficult to form an opinion. No one doubts the capacity for hard and excellent work of various kinds in the class to which the fishermen belong. This capacity is shown as soon as they leave their own country; but at home they are too often subject to disturbing influences, and are too familiar with improvident habits for us to believe that any amount of assistance would do permanent good to them as a body; or would lead to what we must all desire to see—the Irish sea fisheries being properly worked by Irish fishermen.

The Report for 1873 of the Inspectors of Irish Fisheries lately published is not very cheering so far as it relates to the sea fisheries. Unfortunately a difference again appears between the returns of the number of fishing boats and fishermen as given by the Customs and the Coastguard. Taking the latter as probably the more correct of the two, we find there were 7181 fishing boats of various kinds and 29,307 fishermen, showing a decrease since 1872 of 733 boats and 2004 in the number of the men. Of the entire number of boats and men thus given it is stated that "not more than about 1934 vessels and boats can be considered as devoted almost exclusively to fishing, and about 8548 men and boys." It is satisfactory, however, to find that even these small numbers are larger than were recorded in 1872; and although a great decrease is shown in the general return, the diminution has been entirely among that portion of the fishing population with whom fishing is only an occasional occupation.

The Kinsale mackerel fishery was a successful one, the produce having been 120,000 boxes, exactly double that of 1872, although, in consequence of a dispute between the united body of fishermen and the buyers, all fishing was stopped for eight days during the best part of the season. The herring fishery was not so good as in the previous year; and no progress appears to have been made in the pilchard fishery. Line-fish are said to have kept at a greater distance than usual from the land, but doubts about the correctness of this are expressed by some of the Coastguard in their divisional reports. Trawlers are gradually increasing.

FISHERY REGULATIONS.

WITH the exception of a local Act[1] relating to the management of the sean fishery for pilchards at St. Ives, and the Act[2] establishing close-time for herrings on part of the west coast of Scotland, the only regulations which now affect the working of the sea fisheries of Great Britain are those embodied in the Sea Fisheries Act, 1868,[3] and in the Order in Council of the 18th of June, 1869,[4] relating to the lettering, numbering, and registration of sea-fishing boats under that Act. These regulations, unless otherwise mentioned, apply to the whole of the British Islands, and therefore include Ireland; but the Fisheries (Ireland) Act, 1869,[5] gives the Inspectors of Irish Fisheries power to make byelaws in addition for that country, or to alter, amend, or repeal them when they think it expedient or necessary to do so, subject to the approval of the Lord Lieutenant in Council, and an appeal to him in Council.

The Sea Fisheries Act, 1868, for carrying into effect a Convention between England and France, and for amending the laws relating to British sea fisheries, came into force in this country on the 1st of February, 1869, and applies to the whole of the British Islands except in the case of oyster fisheries, a subject which has been largely discussed by other writers, and has therefore been only incidentally noticed in the present work.

The British Islands are thus defined in Section 5 :—
" The term '*British* Islands' includes the United

[1] 4 & 5 Vict., c. 57. [2] 28 & 29 Vict., c. 22. [3] 31 & 32 Vict., c. 45.
[4] See Appendix. [5] 32 & 33 Vict., c. 92.

Kingdom of *Great Britain* and Ireland, the *Isle of Man*, the Islands of *Guernsey*, *Jersey*, *Alderney* and *Sark*, and their dependencies; and the terms ' *Great Britain* and *Ireland*,' and ' United Kingdom,' as used in the First Schedule[1] to this Act, shall be construed to mean the ' *British* Islands,' as herein defined."

Besides those portions of the Act which relate to the carrying out of the Convention, and to the formation, protection and regulation of oyster and mussel fisheries, provision is made by Section 68 for the better protection of the sean fisheries on the greater portion of the coast of Cornwall. These regulations we have already given at page 195.

The regulations in the Sea Fisheries Act, 1868, which affect the practical working of the sea fisheries in general, and with which it is important that our fishermen should be specially acquainted, are those relating to the lettering, numbering and registration of fishing boats, as published in the Order in Council before referred to; and the following Articles of the Convention:—

Article I. (part).

" British fishermen shall enjoy the exclusive right of fishing within the distance of three miles from low-water mark, along the whole extent of the coasts of the British Islands; . . . .

" The distance of three miles fixed as the general limit for the exclusive right of fishing upon the coasts of the two countries shall, with respect to bays, the mouths of which do not exceed ten miles in width, be measured from a straight line drawn from headland to headland.

---

[1] Containing the Convention.

" The miles mentioned in the present Convention are geographical miles, whereof sixty make a degree of latitude.

Article X.

" Fishing of all kinds, by whatever means and at all seasons, may be carried on in the seas lying beyond the fishery limits which have been fixed for the two countries, with the exception of that for oysters, as hereinafter expressed.

Article XI.

" From the 16th of June to the 31st of August inclusive, fishing for oysters is prohibited outside the fishery limits which have been fixed for the two countries, between a line drawn from the North Foreland light to Dunkirk, and a line drawn from the Land's End to Ushant.

" During the same period and in the same part of the channel no boat shall have on board any oyster dredge, unless the same be tied up and sealed by the Customs authorities of one of the two countries in such a manner as to prevent its being made use of.

Article XII.

" No boat shall anchor between sunset and sunrise on grounds where drift-net fishing is actually going on.

" This prohibition shall not apply to anchorings which may take place in consequence of accidents, or any other compulsory circumstances; but in such case the master of the boat thus obliged to anchor shall hoist, so that it shall be seen from a distance, two lights placed horizontally about 3 feet (1 mètre French) apart, and shall keep those lights up all the time the boat shall remain at anchor.

Article XIII.

"Boats fishing with drift nets shall carry on one of their masts two lights, one over the other, 3 feet (1 mètre French) apart.

"These lights shall be kept up during all the time their nets shall be in the sea between sunset and sunrise.

Article XIV.

"Subject to the exceptions or additions mentioned in the two preceding Articles, the fishing boats of the two countries shall conform to the general rules respecting lights which have been adopted by the two countries.

Article XV.

"Trawl boats shall not commence fishing at a less distance than three miles from any boat fishing with drift nets.

"If trawl boats have already shot their nets, they must not come nearer to boats fishing with drift nets than the distance above mentioned.

Article XVI.

"No boat fishing with drift nets shall shoot its nets so near to any other boat which has already shot its nets on the fishing ground as to interfere with its operations.

Article XVII.

"No decked boat fishing with drift nets shall shoot its nets at a less distance than a quarter of a mile from any undecked boat which is already engaged in fishing.

Article XVIII.

"If the spot where fishing is going on should be so near to the fishery limits of one of the two countries that the boats of the other country would, by observing the regulations prescribed by Articles XV., XVI., and XVII. preceding, be prevented from taking part in the fishery, such boats shall be at liberty to shoot their nets at a less distance than that so prescribed; but in such case the fishermen shall be responsible for any damage or losses which may be caused by the drifting of their boats.

Article XIX.

"Nets shall not be set or anchored in any place where drift-net fishing is actually going on.

Article XX.

"No one shall make fast or hold on his boat to the nets, buoys, floats, or any part of the fishing tackle belonging to another boat.

"No person shall hook or lift up the nets, lines, or other fishing implements belonging to another person.

Article XXI.

"Where nets of different boats get foul of each other, the master of one boat shall not cut the nets of another boat except by mutual consent, and unless it be found impossible to clear them by other means.

Article XXII.

"All fishing boats, all rigging gear and other appurtenances of fishing boats, all nets, buoys, floats, or other fishing implements whatsoever, found or picked up at sea, shall, as soon as possible, be delivered to the Receiver of Wreck if the article saved be taken into the United Kingdom, and to the Commissary of Marine if the article saved be taken into France.

"The Receiver of Wreck or the Commissary of Marine, as the case may be, shall restore the articles saved to the owners thereof, or to their representatives.

"These functionaries shall fix the amount which the owners shall pay to the salvors."

Penalties of detention, fine, or imprisonment are provided for any infraction of these regulations, according to the nature and extent of the offence committed.

As we have previously mentioned, the Inspectors of Irish Fisheries have power to make byelaws for the regulation of all the fisheries in their own waters, but Section 67 of the Sea Fisheries Act, 1868, also empowers them "from time to time to lay before Her Majesty in Council byelaws for the purpose of restricting or regulating the dredging for oysters on any oyster bed or banks situate within the distance of twenty miles measured from a straight line drawn from the eastern point of *Lambay Island* to *Carnsore Point* on the coast of *Ireland*, outside of the exclusive fishery limits of the *British* Islands, and all such byelaws shall apply equally to all boats and persons on whom they may be binding."

Such byelaws may be approved, revoked, or altered by Order in Council.

"Every such Order shall be binding on all *British* sea-fishing boats, and on any other sea-fishing boats in that behalf specified in the Order, and on the crews of such boats."

The Convention between England and France, embodied in the Sea Fisheries Act, 1868, and now brought into operation in this country, has not, we believe, been carried out by the French Government up to the present time, no day having yet been fixed by them for its taking effect. As regards French fishermen, therefore, the Convention of 1839 appears to be still in force. But we have done our part in giving effect to the new Convention by passing the Sea Fisheries Act, 1868, and naming a day (Feb. 1, 1869) for its coming into force. The regulations contained in that Convention have been practically adopted as the law of this country; and by Section 4 of the Act they will continue so notwithstanding the determination at any time of the Convention.

Under the Sea Fisheries Act, 1868, our fishermen have been freed from all restrictions in respect to methods of fishing, times and seasons, and dimensions or weight of gear, the only exceptions, so far as we can understand, being in the case of the oyster fisheries, the sean fishery at St. Ives before mentioned, and the close-time for herrings within the 3-mile limit on part of the west coast of Scotland. With regard to this close-time law it has been contended that it is not at all affected by the Sea Fisheries Act, 1868; but this appears to us to be incorrect. Among the various Acts mentioned in the Second Schedule of that Act, as being in part or entirely repealed by it, is the close-time Act (28 & 29 Vict., c. 22), of which the repeal is said to be "in part; namely, so much as is inconsistent with this Act"—the Sea Fisheries Act. Now Article X. of the Convention, which forms a part of the latter Act, says—"Fishing of all kinds, by whatever means and at all seasons, may be carried on in the seas lying beyond the fishery limits which have been fixed for the two countries, with the exception of that for oysters, as hereinafter expressed."

It appears to us that close-time for herrings beyond the 3-mile limit is inconsistent with this Article, and is therefore abolished; and we have reason to believe that such was the intention in passing the Act, and that it is so understood at the Board of Trade.

The laws affecting our sea fisheries at the present time, with the exceptions above noticed, relate only to interference with the working of drift and certain sean fisheries, to the maintenance of order among the fishermen, and to the registration and marking of fishing boats of all kinds.

APPENDIX.

REGULATIONS for the LETTERING, NUMBERING, and REGISTERING of BRITISH SEA FISHING BOATS, under PART II. of the SEA FISHERIES ACT, 1868 (31 & 32 Victoria, Chapter 45).

NOTE.—*The Regulations approved by Her Majesty in Council on the 4th day of February 1869 are REVOKED by the Order in Council of the 18th day of June 1869, and the following Regulations are now in force.*

1. The following Regulations shall be in future observed by owners and masters of all British boats or vessels hailing from or belonging to any port or place in the United Kingdom, the islands of Guernsey, Jersey, Alderney, Sark, or Man, of whatever size, and however propelled or navigated, which find any portion of their ordinary employment in sea fishing, or oyster or mussel dredging, for purposes of sale; subject, however, to the following qualifications:

(1.) Yachts, vessels, or boats not usually employed in fishing or dredging for purposes of sale shall not be subject to the following Regulations when they are not so employed:

(2.) If a boat or vessel employed in fishing or dredging for purposes of sale is also used as a pilot boat, and is marked and numbered as such, under any laws or regulations governing such pilot boat, such boat or vessel shall not be subject to the following Regulations:

(3.) Boats employed in the pilchard seyn fishery on the coasts of Cornwall shall, if otherwise duly marked to the satisfaction of the Officers of Customs or Coast Guard, be exempt from the necessity of having letters and numbers painted on their sails, bows, or sterns as required by the following Regulations.

2. Every sea fishing vessel or boat, whether registered under any other Act or not, shall, except as hereinbefore provided for, be lettered, numbered, and have a Certificate of Registry, and shall for that purpose be entered or registered in a Register of Sea Fishing Boats to be kept at the principal office of Customs in each collectorship. Application, as hereafter prescribed, for letters, numbers, and Certificates of Registry shall be made by all owners of fishing boats to the Officer of Coast Guard or Fishery Officer in charge of the Station at or near the place where the boat may for the time being be employed. In any case where a boat belongs to a place situated at a distance from a Coast Guard Station, such application may be delivered to the principal Officer of Customs or to any Fishery Officer at the creek or station at or nearest to the place to which the boat belongs, or at which she may be temporarily employed in fishing. And such application, upon being received by any such Officer, shall be forthwith forwarded to the Collector of Customs of the Port in which the place to which the boat belongs is situated, who, upon the receipt of such application, shall cause the boat to be registered and numbered, and grant the Certificate of such Registry, and forward the same to the Officer through whom the application was received, who is to deliver such Certificate to the applicant.

3. The port or place at which any British vessel or boat is registered under the provisions of "The Merchant Shipping Act, 1854" (17 & 18 Vict. c. 104) shall be considered the port or place to which she belongs.

4. In Scotland the Officers of the Board of British White Herring Fishery shall assist the Officers of Customs and of Coast Guard in the performance of the duties imposed by these Regulations; and shall, in places where there are no Coast Guard, themselves discharge the duties hereby imposed upon the Coast Guard.

5. If, in the opinion of the Collector of the Port to which any boats belong, or of the Inspecting Commander or Divisional Officer of the District, it is desirable, from local circumstances or otherwise, that the mode of application prescribed in the second article of these Regulations should be partially modified or altered, such Collector, Inspecting Commander, or Divisional

APPENDIX.

Officer shall make a special report to the Board of Trade, setting forth the reasons for and particulars of such modification or alteration.

6. There shall be series of numbers and distinguishing letters for the boats belonging to each collectorship of Customs. The following shall be the distinguishing letters:—

Name of Collectorship.	Distinguishing Letters.	Name of Collectorship.	Distinguishing Letters.
ENGLAND AND THE CHANNEL ISLANDS.		ENGLAND AND THE CHANNEL ISLANDS – continued.	
Aberystwith	A.B.	Harwich	H.H.
Barnstaple	B.E.	Hayle	H.E. or S.S.
Beaumaris	B.S.		
Berwick-on-Tweed	B.K.		
Bideford	B.D.	Hull	H.
Boston, Lincolnshire	B.N.	Ipswich	I.H.
Bridgewater	B.R.	Jersey	J.
Bridport	B.T.	Lancaster	L.R.
Bristol	B.L.	Littlehampton	L.I.
Cardiff	C.F.	Liverpool	L.L.
Cardigan	C.A.	Llanelly	L.A.
Carlisle	C.L.	London	L.O.
Carnarvon	C.O.	Lowestoft	L.T.
Castletown, Isle of Man	Ce. Tn. or C.T.	Lyme, Dorset	L.E.
		Lynn, Norfolk	L.N.
		Maldon, Essex	M.N.
Chepstow	C.W.	Maryport	M.T.
Chester	C.H.	Middlesborough	M.H.
Colchester	C.K.	Milford	M.
Cowes, Isle of Wight	C.S.	Newcastle-on-Tyne	N.E.
Dartmouth	D.H.	Newhaven, Sussex	N.N.
Deal	D.L.	Newport, Monmouth	N.T.
Douglas, Isle of Man	D.O.S. or D.O. or P.L.	Padstow	P.W.
		Penzance	P.Z.
		Plymouth	P.H.
		Poole, Dorset	P.E.
		Portsmouth	P.
Dover	D.R.	Preston	P.N.
Exeter	E.	Ramsey, Isle of Man	R.Y.
Falmouth	F.H.	Ramsgate	R. or R.E.
Faversham	F.M. or F.		
		Rochester	R.R.
Fleetwood	F.D.	Runcorn	R.N.
Folkestone	F.E.	Rye, Sussex	R.X.
Fowey	F.Y.	Scarborough	S.H.
Gainsborough	G.A.	Scilly	S.C.
Gloucester	G.R.	Shoreham	S.M.
Goole	G.E.	Southampton	S.U.
Grimsby	G.Y.	Shields, North	S.N.
Guernsey	G.U.	Shields, South	S.S.S.
Hartlepool, West	H.L.	Stockton	S.T.

408 APPENDIX.

Name of Collectorship.	Distinguishing Letters.	Name of Collectorship.	Distinguishing Letters.
ENGLAND AND THE CHANNEL ISLANDS—*continued.*		SCOTLAND—*continued.*	
Sunderland	S.D.	Leith	L.H.
Swansea	S.A.	Lerwick, Shetland	L.K.
Teignmouth	T.H.	Montrose	M.E.
Truro	T.O.	Perth	P.E.H.
Wells, Norfolk	W.S.	Peterhead	P.D.
Weymouth	W.H.	Port Glasgow	P.G.W.
Whitby	W.Y.	Stornoway	S.Y.
Whitehaven	W.A.	Stranraer	S.R.
Wisbeach	W.I.	Troon	T.N.
Woodbridge	W.E.	Wick	W.K.
Workington	W.O.	Wigtown	W.N.
Yarmouth, Norfolk	Y.H.		
SCOTLAND.		IRELAND.	
Aberdeen	A.N. or A.	Ballina	B.A.
		Belfast	B.
Alloa	A.A.	Coleraine	C.E.
Arbroath	A.H.	Cork	C.
Ardrossan	A.D.	Drogheda	D.A.
Ayr	A.R.	Dublin	D.
Banff	B.F.	Dundalk	D.K.
Borrowstoness	B.O.	Galway	G.
Campbelton	C.N.	Limerick	L.
Dumfries	D.S.	Londonderry	L.Y.
Dundee	D.E.	New Ross	N.S.
Glasgow	G.W.	Newry	N.
Grangemouth	G.H.	Skibbereen	S.
Granton, Edinburgh	G.N.	Sligo	S.O.
Greenock	G.K.	Tralee	T.
Inverness	I.N.S. or I.	Waterford	W.
		Westport, Ireland	W.T.
Kirkcaldy	K.Y.	Wexford	W.D.
Kirkwall	K.L. or K.	Youghal	Y.

7. For purposes of numbering, lettering, and registration, boats shall be divided into three classes, as follows:—

    1st class:—Boats of 15 tons burthen and upwards:

    2nd class:—Boats of less than 15 tons burthen, navigated otherwise than by oars only:

    3rd class:—Boats navigated by oars only:

Provided that the officer to whom the application to register is made may, if he think proper, place any small boat occasionally navigated or propelled by sail in the third instead of the second class.

8. For boats of the above classes the positions and dimensions of the letters and numbers shall be as follows:—

1st class:—For the hulls, 18 inches in height, and 2½ inches in breadth, and for the sails one-third larger every way:

2nd class:—For the hulls, 10 inches in height, and 1¾ inches in breadth, and for the sails one-third larger in every way:

3rd class:—Three inches at least in height, and half an inch in breadth:

Provided that in boats that have a "bend piece" or "rubbing streak" the letters and numbers shall be as high as the space above the "bend piece" or "rubbing streak" will admit. In boats where the space between the gunwale and water-line is not sufficient in size for the prescribed letters and numbers, the letters and numbers shall be as high as the size of the boats will admit.

9. In boats of the 1st and 3rd class the number will follow, and in those of the 2nd class precede, the distinguishing letter or letters.

10. When vessels carry, or have attached to them, small boats as tenders or otherwise, such boats must be marked with the same numbers and letters as the vessels to which they belong. Such numbers and letters may be of the size appropriate to the class to which the boat would belong according to its own size and means of propulsion, but in position and precedence according to the class of the vessel to which the boat is attached.

11. In sailing boats, and boats navigated by the occasional use of sails, the letters and numbers shall be placed on each bow, three or four inches below the gunwale, and on each side of the mainsail, except for lug-sail boats, in which the letters and numbers may be placed on the foresail or mizen instead of the mainsail. For boats of the third class, the letters and numbers shall be placed on the outside of the stern of the boat immediately under the name. On the hulls all letters and numbers shall be painted in white oil colour on a black ground; and on sails, in black oil colour on white or grey sails, and in white oil colour on tanned or black sails. Except in the case of vessels only occasionally engaged in fishing for purposes of sale, hereinafter in the thirteenth article of these Regulations specially

provided for, the letters and numbers of sails shall be painted on each side of the cloth forming the substance of the sail, and not upon any cloth or other thing sewn or otherwise attached to it; and shall be placed on each side of the centre cloth or cloths of the mainsail, clear of and immediately above the close reef, and so as to be at all times conspicuous whether the sail be reefed or not.

12. All boats of whatever class shall have their names, and those of the ports to which they belong, painted in white oil colour on a black ground on the outside of the sterns, in letters which shall be at least 3 inches in height and $\frac{1}{2}$ an inch in breadth.

13. In the case of any vessel or boat only occasionally engaged in fishing for purposes of sale, and not usually so employed, the letters and numbers prescribed by these Regulations may be temporarily affixed, by pieces of canvas or board attached to the mainsail and bows, but of the same dimensions as those specified in the eighth article of these Regulations.

14. The letters, numbers, and names placed on boats and on their sails shall not be effaced, covered, or concealed in any manner whatsoever.

15. All the buoys, barrels, and principal floats of each net, and all other implements of fishery, shall be marked with the same letters and numbers as the boats to which they belong, so as to be easily distinguished. The owners may further distinguish them by any private marks they think proper. Provided that this Regulation shall not apply in the case of boats employed,

(1) in the Scotch herring fishery;
(2) in the drift net and seyn fisheries in Cornwall;
(3) in such other drift net and seyn fisheries (if any) as the Board of Trade may direct.

In the above-mentioned cases it will be held sufficient that the nets and buoys be numbered, so as to identify their true owners; but in all cases of doubt it will devolve upon the masters of buoys and nets to satisfy Sea Fishery Officers (as defined by the eighth section of the Sea Fisheries Act, 1868) that the said buoys and nets properly form part of the trains of the boat with which they may be found, or that they belong to the fishermen of other boats temporarily fishing in it.

16. The owner and master of any boat not having all its nets, buoys, and other implements duly marked in the manner above directed, shall be liable to a penalty not exceeding five pounds.

17. A register of sea fishing boats, in the form contained in Table A hereto annexed, shall be kept by the Collector of Customs at each collectorship, which shall contain the date of registry, name of the vessel or boat, and of the port or place to which she belongs, names of owner and master, description of her rig and of her ordinary mode of fishing, her registered number, class, tonnage, and length of keel, and number of crew usually employed.

18. Certificates of Registry in the above register shall be issued by the respective Collectors of Customs, on application being duly made as directed by the second article of these Regulations; and such certificate shall be in the form contained in Table B hereto annexed, and when necessary shall be transmitted to the Officer of Coast Guard or Customs or other Fishery Officer through whom the application may have been transmitted for delivery by such Officer to the owner. The Certificates of Registry shall contain the name of the collectorship and the distinguishing letters, the name and description of boat, the name of the owner and master, the registered number and class, and the date of entry.

19. All applications for letters, numbers, and registration of fishing boats must be in writing, and according to the form contained in Table C hereto annexed, and in duplicate if they are to be forwarded from a distant station as provided by the second article of these Regulations; and the duplicate copy is to be retained and filed by the Officer of Coast Guard or Customs at the station to which the boat belongs.

20. Whenever the owner of any registered vessel or boat proves to the satisfaction of the proper Officer of Customs or Coast Guard or any Fishery Officer that he has lost or been deprived of any Certificate of Registry already granted to him, the proper Officer may cause a copy of such Certificate of Registry to be made out and delivered to such owner; and such copy, duly certified by the proper Officer, shall have all the effect of the original.

21. Once in every year the owner of every boat shall submit

his Certificate of Registry for examination, either at the head office in each collectorship or at the station through which it was originally obtained, and the proper Officer shall sign his name on the back of the said Certificate, together with the date of examination, as a record of its authenticity and correctness.

22. In the first week of every year each Officer of Customs or of Coast Guard and each Fishery Officer shall forward to the Collector of Customs of the district a list, showing the numbers and classes of all boats whose Certificates of Registry have been presented for examination and endorsed in the preceding year; and a notation of all inspections of Certificates shall be made in the Register against the name of each boat. On a change of ownership, or on removal to another collectorship, of any boat registered under these Regulations, a fresh Certificate of Registry must be applied for, and the former Certificate be given up, in order that the same, together with the former Registry, may be cancelled; and on a change of Master due notice shall be given of such change, which shall be duly noted in the Register, and be endorsed on the Certificate of Registry. A failure on the part of the owner of any boat to comply with these Regulations shall subject the owner and master to the same penalties that they would have incurred if the Certificate of Registry had never been applied for.

23. If any boat required to be registered, lettered, and numbered in pursuance of these Regulations, and not being so registered, lettered, and numbered, in the manner prescribed, is used as a fishing boat, the owner and the master shall each be liable to a penalty not exceeding twenty pounds. Any Sea Fishery Officer may seize and detain such boat, and prevent it from going to sea and from sea fishing until it is duly registered, lettered, and numbered, and may for that purpose, if it is at sea, take it back into the nearest or most convenient British port. Such boat shall not be entitled to any of the privileges or advantages of a British Sea Fishing Boat, but all obligations, liabilities, and penalties with reference to such boat shall be the same as if it had been duly registered.

24. The master of every boat registered under these Regulations shall have on board his boat at all times the Certificate

of Registry hereby required to be obtained; and any master not having such Certificate shall, in the absence of any reasonable cause for the same (proof whereof shall lie on him), be liable, together with his boat and crew, to be taken by any Sea Fishery Officer, without warrant, summons, or other process, into the nearest or most convenient port, and there to be ordered by the Court, on any proceeding in a summary matter, to pay a penalty not exceeding twenty pounds. Provided that the masters of boats employed in the pilchard fishery in Cornwall, or in such other fishery (if any) as the Board of Trade shall direct, shall be exempt from this Regulation.

25. After registration no change shall be made in the name of any Sea Fishing Boat.

TABLE A.

SEA FISHERIES ACT, 1868, 31 & 32 VICT., CAP. 15.

Port of ―――――

Registry of Vessels and Boats engaged in Fishing.

Date of Registry.	Name of Vessel.	Port or Place to which belonging.	Name of Owner.	Name of Master.	Description		Registered No.				Size.		No. of Crew usually employed.		Remarks.
					Of Vessel or Boat, how rigged, what Sails used, &c.	Ordinary Mode of Fishing.	1st Class.	2nd Class.	3rd Class.	Tonnage.	Length of Keel.		Men.	Boys.	

TABLE B.

Sea Fisheries Act, 1868,
31 & 32 Vict., Cap. 45.

Port of

Certificate of Registry

of , named
of
Owner
Master
Registered No.   of   Class
Signature of }
Registering Officer }
Date

TABLE C.

Sea Fisheries Act, 1868,
31 & 32 Vict., Cap. 45.

Application to Register a Vessel or Boat.

Port of , Letter

The
Port or place to }
which belonging }
Owner
Master
Description of vessel or }
  boat, how rigged, what }
  sails used, &c. }
Mode of fishing
Tonnage
Length of keel
No. of men   } usually employed.
No. of boys   }
Signature of applicant
Residence

INDEX.

A.

ABERDEEN herring fishery, 289
——, steam tugs at, 289
Access to markets in Ireland and Scotland compared, 351
Action of the trawl, 74
Acts relating to Cornish pilchard-seaning, 188, 195
Advantages of storing live cod, 152
Agreements between trawl-owners and fishermen, 358
Alleged injury to spawn by trawlers, 32
—— waste of fish by deep-sea trawlers, 203
Allman's evidence on floating spawn, 27
—— experiments with herring spawn, 46
Anstruther Union Harbour, 299
"Appearance of fish," 112
—— ——, Mr. Mitchell's remarks on, 113
Approach to land of spawning and fat herrings, 40
—— —— spawning and half-grown mackerel, 41
—— —— spawning and fat pilchards, 41
—— —— sprats in all conditions, 41
Ardglass, herring fishery at, 362, 393
Arklow, fisheries at, 363
—— oyster beds, 363

B.

BAG-NETS, 161
—— in Bridgewater Bay, 186
—— near Waterford, 166, 368
——, small fish caught in, 186
Bait, few kinds of, 4
Ballantrae, set-nets at, 334
——, spawning ground at, 331, 333
Bandle linen for sails, 386
Banff coast, boats used on, 293
Bantry Bay, fisheries in, 376
—— ——, trawling in, 377

Barking, its decline as a fishing station, 226
——, its long connection with the sea fisheries, 226
—— pattern of trawl-head, 56, 201
Barking the sails, 70
Barking supposed to have originated deep-sea trawling, 200
Barnstaple Bay, trawling in, 186
Beachmen at Yarmouth, 239
Beam-trawl, the, 54
——, uncertain origin of, 53
Beam-trawling in the Firth of Forth, 287
—— probably long practised inshore, 201
Belfast Lough, fisheries in, 393
Belmullet, line-fisheries at, 389
Best kinds of fish mostly caught by the trawl, 86
Bideford, ground-seans at, 187
Billingsgate formerly the only large market, 19
—— mainly supplied from the North Sea, 84
——, increase of water carriage to, 225
"Black jacks," 265
"Blind-hauling," 160
Bloaters, curing of, 242
Blowsers, 192
Branding fees, 297
—— —— in 1873, 326
—— of white herrings, 296
—— system, advantages of, 296
—— ——, objections to, 296
Bratt-nets, 174
Bridgewater Bay, fisheries in, 186
Brighton drift-boats used for trawling, 221
——, fisheries at, 220
—— fishing boats, increase in size of, 220
—— Log-boats, 220
' Brimming,' 114
"British White Herring Cure," 294
Brixham fish formerly sent away by carts, 209

2 E

418

INDEX.

Brixham fish sent away by rail, 209
—— fishermen at Ramsgate, 222
—— fishing ground long worked over, 92
—— long famous for its fisheries, 200
—— smacks, cost of, 210
—— ——, crews of, 210
—— ——, size of, 65
—— said to be the mother-port of trawling, 200
—— trawlers at Tenby, 208
—— —— in the North Sea, 208
—— —— in the time of Elizabeth, 202
—— —— settled at other stations, 205
—— ——, number of, in 1852, 205
—— ——, number of, in 1865, 206
—— trawl-fishery increasing, 92
—— trawling, Mr. Barry's reports on, 201
—— ——, present condition of, 203
—— —— grounds, 208
—— —— grounds, small extent of, 93
Buckie fishermen, enterprise of, 291
Buckies, mode of fishing for, 310
Bulter (see Longline.)
Buoy or dan to longline, 138
Buoys or bowls to drift-net, 102
Burnham fishing boats, 186

C.

Caa'ing whales at Shetland, 310
Calms and gales stop trawling, 83
Campbelton, beam-trawling at, 320
"Capstan-men," 106
Carlingford, fisheries at, 393
Carriers, Mr. Hewett's, 245
"Cast off seizings," 110
Catching herrings on Sunday, 214
Channel Islands, fisheries at, 213
—— ——, lobsters and crabs at, 217
"Cheep" of the herring, 270
Chesil Beach, sean-fishing at, 159, 212
Circle-net fishing, 326
Claddagh, the, 382
—— fishermen, decrease of, 386
—— ——, violence of, 383
"Claddagh law," 385
Classification of fishing boats misleading, 179
Cleethorpes, oyster beds at, 256
——, shrimping at, 256
Clew Bay, oyster fishery in, 388
Close-time Act for herrings, 403

Close-time for herrings at the Isle of Man, 339 note
—— for sea fish unnecessary, 46
Clovelly, fisheries at, 187
Cobles, description of, 261
——, where used, 261
Cod family, probable spawning habits of, 30
—— fishery at the Shetlands, 305
—— fishing by handlines, 145
—— —— by longlines, 137
—— ——, seasons for, 144, 145
—— in Grimsby fish-dock, 150
—— smacks at Barking, 226
—— —— at Grimsby, 251
—— —— increasing in number, 148
—— ——, bait used in, 142
—— ——, expenses of, 142
—— ——, how long at sea, 144
—— ——, number of crew in, 141
—— ——, wages to crew of, 141
——, spawning of, 28
Collecting fish from the North Sea fleet, 258
Columbia Market, objections to, 20
Condition of trawl-fish affected by bad weather, 85
Conger fishing at Guernsey, 215
Consumption of spawn by the public, 33
Continued productiveness of Yarmouth fishery, 37
Convention, Articles of, 398
Cork district, fisheries in, 373
Cornish coast, various fisheries on, 187
—— drift-boats, classes of, 197
—— ——, cost of, 197
—— fisheries, importance of, 187
—— line-fisheries, 197
Costermongers, fish sold by, 17
Couch's description of the whitebait, 124
Couch on the spawning of the pilchard, 31, 132
"Cran," contents of a, 295
Credit given to fishermen, 23
Cromer crab-boats, 247
—— Knoll a good fishing ground, 144
——, crab and lobster fishery at, 247
——, regulations among the fishermen at, 248
Cullercoats, fisheries at, 269
——, herring fishery at, 270
——, present condition of fishermen at, 270
Cured fish exported to Australia, 312
—— —— Germany, 297, 312

Cured fish exported to Ireland, 312, 317
—— —— Mediterranean, 193, 244
—— —— Spain, 302, 312
—— —— imported to Ireland, 363
Curing bloaters, 242
—— herrings at Yarmouth, 241
—— pilchards in Cornwall, 193
—— supervised by Scotch Fishery Board, 296
—— white herrings, 294
Curraghs, or canvas canoes, 379
——, cost of, 381
Custom House, returns of boats obtained through, 180

D.

DANDY bridle, 65, 79
Dandy-line or jigger, description of, 153
——, probable derivation of the name, 154
——, where used, 153
—— fishing at Dunbar, 286
Dandy-wink, 67, 71
"Darwen salmon," 183
Davis' Straits, cod fishery in, 308
Decked and open boats, comparative gains of, 277
—— fishing boats coming into use, 276
—— fishing boats, advantage of, 276
Deep-sea trawling, uncertain origin of, 201
Deep water in Silver Pit, 84
Depth of water for deep-sea trawling, 83
Destruction of herrings by cod and ling, 35
—— of herrings by gannets, 35
Difference between fishermen's and Admiralty soundings, 85
Dimensions of seans at St. Ives, 189
Dingle Bay, drift-fishing in, 379
—— ——, trawling in, 378
Dogfish, 80
—— in Morecambe Bay, 183
——, injury caused by, 109, 144
Donegal Bay, capabilities of fishing in, 391
—— ——, disappearance of haddocks from, 391
—— ——, fisheries in, 389
—— ——, herring fishery in, 390
—— ——, sprat fishery in, 389
—— ——, whales in, 389
Drift-boats, best rig for, 357
——, temporarily rigged for trawling, 69, 217

Drift-nets, description of, 100
——, explanation of the name, 98
——, how mounted, 101
——, how the fish are caught by, 98
——, materials used for, 100
DRIFT-NET FISHING, 97
—— —— by Brighton boats, 224
—— ——, commencement of, unknown, 97
—— —— on the coast of Scotland, 300
—— ——, probable antiquity of, 97
—— ——, usually at night, 99
Drogheda district, fisheries of, 394
Dublin trawlers, 356
—— ——, crews of, 358
—— ——, rig of, 358
—— ——, scarcity of crews for, 357
Dunbar, dandy-line fishing at, 286
—— Harbour, cost of, 299
Dungarvan fisheries, decline of, 369
Dunmore, trawling from, 367
Dutch auction, trawl-fish sold by, 209
—— trawling, 53

E.

EARLY capture of large cod, 38
Emigration of Irish fishermen, 347
Enemies of the herring, 36
England and Wales, number of fishing boats in, 274
English fisheries, relative importance of, 274
Escape from the beam-trawl difficult, 76
Evidence required of spawn being buried, 46
Exhaustion of an open-sea line-fishery by overfishing impossible, 148
Export of pilchards dependent on the sean-fishery, 196
Eyemouth, smoked haddocks at, 285

F.

FALMOUTH oyster fishery, 198
Faroe cod-bank, 305
Ferry-boats at Yarmouth, 239
Fi'men boats, 266
"Finnan haddies," mode of curing, 288
—— ——, where made, 288
Firth of Clyde, fisheries of, 320
—— of Forth, fisheries of, 283
—— ——, oyster beds in, 284
Fish business by telegraph, 19, 209
—— carried by rail from Harwich, 234
—— on Irish coasts not decreased, 350

Fish spawn not taken in the trawl, 33
—— supposed to come inshore in order to spawn, 39
Fisheries, condition of, 10
Fishermen's fathom, 190
Fishermen, independent habits of, 9
—— indisposed to alter their mode of fishing, 5
Fishery harbours on east coast of Scotland, 298
FISHERY REGULATIONS, 397
Fishing boats at Banff, 293
—— —— Brighton, 220
—— —— Brixham, 64, 210
—— —— Burnham, 186
—— —— Cromer, 247
—— —— Dingle, 379
—— —— Flamborough, 261
—— —— Galway, 386
—— —— Greencastle, 394
—— —— Grimsby, 252
—— —— Guernsey, 213
—— —— Holy Island, 272
—— —— Isle of Man, 341
—— —— Leigh, 228
—— —— Lochfyne, 332
—— —— Morecambe Bay, 182
—— —— Mount's Bay, 196
—— —— Orkney, 303
—— —— St. Ives, 191
—— —— Shetland, 309
—— —— Skerries, 360
—— —— Tenby, 184
—— —— Torbay, 211
—— —— Wexford, 364
—— —— Wick, 291
—— —— Yarmouth, 102
Fishing boats, Board of Trade returns of, 178, 281
—— ——, classification of, 179
—— ——, distribution of (see Fishing Stations).
—— ——, general increase of, 21
—— ——, increased expenditure on, 22
—— ——, larger size of, 26
Fishing every day unlucky, 385

FISHING STATIONS—ENGLAND.
  Carlisle to Runcorn, 180-183
  Beaumaris to Cardiff, 183-185
  Bristol to Padstow, 185-187
  Hayle to Fowey, 187-198

FISHING STATIONS—ENGLAND—(cont.):
  Plymouth to Weymouth, 198-212
  Channel Islands, 212-219
  Poole to Newhaven, 219-221
  Rye to Ramsgate, 221-223
  Faversham to Colchester, 223-229
  Harwich to Boston, 230-250
  Grimsby to Whitby, 250-264
  Middlesboro' to Berwick-on-Tweed, 265-274

SCOTLAND.
  Leith to Kirkcaldy, 283-288
  Dundee to Peterhead, 288-290
  Banff to Wick, 290-300
  Kirkwall to Lerwick, 300-312
  Stornoway, 313-320
  Campbelton to Greenock, 320-333
  Ardrossan to Dumfries, 333-337

ISLE OF MAN.
  Castletown to Ramsey, 338-343

IRELAND.
  Dublin to Waterford, 355-368
  Youghal to Tralee, 369-382
  Limerick to Sligo, 382-392
  Londonderry to Drogheda, 392-394

Flax nets superseded by cotton ones, 342
Fleetwood as a trawling station, 184
Folkestone, trawling at, 223
Foreign markets for pilchards, 193.
—— —— for white herrings, 297
—— —— for Yarmouth herrings, 244
French fishing boats at Kinsale, 373
—— trawl, 57, 58, 60, 61
—— trawl-heads, 56
Froude's mention of Brixham trawlers in the time of Elizabeth, 202
Full herrings in demand for curing, 34
Full pilchards caught far from land, 131

G.

GALWAY BAY, herring fishery in, 385
—— ——, oyster beds in, 387
—— ——, restriction to trawling in, 383
—— ——, search for spawn in, 384
—— ——, trawlers in, 385
—— fisheries neglected, 382
—— hookers, 386
Glasgow curing trade fallen off, 333

"Gorings" of trawl-net, 60
Gorleston, Mr. Hewett's establishment at, 244
Government loans to Irish fishermen, 352
"Great lines" for cod, 285
Greencastle yawls, 394
Grey mullet fishing at Jersey, 218
Grimsby, advantageous situation of, 250
——, cod-smacks at, 252
——, importation of ice at, 256
——, increase of trawlers at, 251, 252
——, quantity of fish landed at, 254
——, selling the fish at, 254
——, whelk-boats at, 256
—— cod-chest, 149
—— cod-smacks at Shetland, 306
—— fish-dock, 253
—— fish-market, 254
Ground-rope, 58
——, chains on, 60
——, materials for, 59
——, proper working of, 75
Ground-sean, 159
Ground-seans at Bideford, 187
Ground suitable for trawling, 75
Grounds frequented for cod fishing, 144
Growth of fish probably long continued, 37
Guernsey, disappearance of herrings from, 214
——, fisheries at, 213
——, line-fishing at, 215
——, mackerel fishing at, 213
——, pilchard fishing at, 214
——, trammel-nets at, 216
——, trawl-nets at, 216
—— drift-boats, 213
—— famous for congers, 215
Gun-firing, alleged effect of, on fish, 115, 329
Günther's description of the herring, 125
Gutting the herrings in Scotland, 295

H.

HABITS of fish when disturbed, 75
Haddock lines, 285
Haddocks, scarcity of, at Dublin Bay, 361
—— ——, at Shetland, 310
——, spawning of, 28
—— near the Dogger Bank, 267
—— rarely caught by the Brixham trawlers, 90

Hammer-trawl, the, 52, 371
Hampshire coast, fisheries on, 220
Handline, description of, 146
—— fishing for cod, 147
Hand-trunk for lobster fishing, 287
Harbour grant to Scotland, 299
Hartlepool fishermen, 267
Harwich, history of, as a fishing station, 231
——, storing live cod at, 232
——, welled-smacks at, 231
—— cod-chest, 233
—— fisheries, Mr. Groom's account of, 231
—— railway fish traffic, 234
Hauling in drift-nets, 110
—— —— longlines, 139
Heaving up the trawl, 79
Hebrides, curing white fish at the, 318
——, longlining at the, 318
——, lobster fishing at the, 318
——, open boats at the, 318
——, returns of cured fish at the, 319
Herring brand disregarded, 317
—— close-time Act, 314, 403
—— close-time Act, bad effects of, 314, 316
—— close-time Act, partial repeal of, 315, 316, 403
—— close-time unjustifiable, 316
—— fishery in the Irish Sea, 362
—— —— at the Isle of Man, 338
—— —— at Shetland
—— season on the English coast, 118, 121
—— —— Irish coast, 120
—— —— Manx coast, 120
—— —— Scotch coast, 118, 119
—— spawn not injured by disturbance, 46
"Herring-trawl," 321
Herring trawling, alleged objections to, 322
—— ——, disputes about, 322
—— ——, prohibition of, 323
—— ——, prohibition of, repealed, 324
—— ——, Report on, 324
—— ——, Royal Commission on, 323
—— —— in Lochfyne, 321
Herrings, capricious movements of, 214, 331
——, classification of, by the curers, 295
——, disappearance of, from Guernsey, 214
——, enormous numbers of, caught, 297
——, a "last" of, 241
——, regular appearance of, 117
——, spawning of, 30

422 INDEX.

Herrings, two distinct arrivals of, 117
—— caught by the dandy-line, 154
—— devoured by birds, 35, 36
—— —— by fishes, 36, 266, 334
—— resident in our seas, 123
—— sent fresh from Ireland to England, 363
—— spawning in Douglas Bay, 340
—— —— near the land, 123
Hewett and Co.'s fish steamers, 225
"High-dried" herrings, 243
Hog-boats at Brighton, 220
Hogshead of pilchards, average contents of, 194
Hoisting in the fish, 80
Holibuts at Grimsby, 254
Holy Island, fishing boats at, 272
Hookers, 153
"Huers," duties of, 191
Hull, commencement of trawling at, 257
——, importation of ice at, 260
——, increase of trawlers at, 257
——, sale of fish at, 260
——, use of ice by trawlers at, 259
Humber, fisheries in the, 261
"Hundred" of herrings, 241, 286
—— of mackerel, 241
Huxley's evidence on floating spawn, 27

I.

Ice, effect of, on the supply of fish, 18
——, whence obtained, 245
Ice-box, 259
Ice-cutters, 259
Ice for packing the fish at Brixham, 210
—— imported at Grimsby, 256
—— in the fish trade, general advantage of, 261
—— on board trawlers, introduction of, by Mr. S. Hewett, 244
—— used by fishmongers, 16
Icing the fish, flavour affected by, 18, 246
Inaccurate reports on Brixham trawling, 204
Increase of North Sea trawling, 95
—— of trawlers at Brixham, 206, 207
—— —— Grimsby, 252
—— —— Hull, 257
—— —— Plymouth, 199
—— —— Ramsgate, 222
Increased cost of fishing gear, 15
Inisbofin, boat harbour at, 388
—— Fishing Company, 388

Injury to harbours by bad weather, 298, 299
Inquiry by Royal Commission at Brixham, 206
Inshore cod-fishing, 147
—— trawling on Irish coast, 359
—— —— on Lancashire coast, 181
Interference of drift-boats with seaning, 195
Irish fisheries, aids to their development, 348
—— ——, bad condition of, 344
—— ——, uncertain prospects of, 395
—— ——, various methods of working, 394
—— —— improving on the east coast, 348
—— —— Report for 1873, 395
—— fishermen, effect of the famine on, 347, 351
—— ——, emigration of, 347
—— ——, gradual decrease of, 347, 395
—— ——, help offered to, by Mr. B. Whitworth, 354
—— ——, small number of, 347
—— ——, unwillingness of the Irish people to help, 354
—— ——, various occupations of, 347
—— fishing boats, decrease of, in 1873, 395
—— fishing boats, statistics of, 344
—— fishing yawls, 362, 392
—— Sea, trawling grounds in the, 358
Isle of Man, fisheries at the, 338
—— ——, large herrings at the, 339
—— ——, line-fishing at the, 341

J.

Jersey, fisheries at, 217
——, grey mullet at, 218
—— men at the Newfoundland fishery, 219

K.

Keel-boats, 272
Keer-drag, description of, 219
Kenmare Bay, fisheries in, 378
Kettle-net, action of, 168
——, danger from, to navigation, 169
——, description of, 167
——, fish caught by, 167
——, interference of, with seaning, 169
——, where used, 167
Killing the cod for market, 151
Kinsale fish exports, 375

INDEX. 423

Kinsale fishermen, habits of, 374
—— hookers, 376
—— mackerel fishery, 373, 396
Kirkwall Bay, sean-fishing in, 302

L.

LARGE cod on newly worked ground, 38
Large supply of fish by the trawl, 86
"Last of herrings," 241
Leach's herring, 249
Leigh, shrimpers at, 226
Length of fleet of herring-nets, 101
—— of mackerel-nets, 111
Line-fish, local scarcity of, 24
Line-fisheries important at Shetland, 334
—— in the Irish Sea, 360
LINE-FISHING, antiquity of, 136
——, two principal methods of, 136
—— at Guernsey, 216
—— in Torbay, 211
—— boats, rig of, 153
Line-haddocks comparatively few, 89
Live bait for sea-fishing, 4
"Live cod," 152
—— —— no longer stored in the Thames, 224
Live plaice, 91
Liverpool an old trawling station, 181
Lobster fishing at the Channel Islands, 217
—— —— at Flamborough, 264
—— —— at the Hebrides, 318
—— —— at the Orkneys, 302
—— —— by creels, 287
—— —— by pots, 218, 264
—— —— by trunks, 264
Lochfyne, deep water in, 330
——, description of, 329
——, fishing stations on, 329
——, net-fishing in, 325
——, scarcity of herrings in, 325
——, spawning ground in, 331
——, "trawling" in, 321
—— fishery in 1871, 327
—— fisheries, suggested causes of failure of, 328
—— fishing boats, 332
London trawlers in the North Sea, 224
Longlines, buoys to, 139, 300
——, description of, 137
——, fish caught by, 137, 141, 285, 308
——, number of hooks on, 138

Longlines, various names given to, 137
Longlining at the Shetlands, 308
—— from Grimsby, 137
——, season for, 144
Looking for fish, 112
"Look on" drift-net, 109
Loss of fishing boats on coast of Scotland, 297
Loss of trawlers in the North Sea, 84
Loughs Swilly and Foyle, fisheries in, 392
Lowestoft, fisheries at, 234
——, increase of fisheries at, 234
——, number of fishing boats at, 235
—— autumn herring fishery, 122
—— midsummer herring fishery, 122
—— spring herring fishery, 121
Lug-rig general in Scotch fishing boats, 292
Luminous water unfavourable for drift-fishing, 115

M.

MACKEREL, a "hundred" of, 241
——, approach of, inshore, 41
——, spawning of, 29
—— drift-nets, 111, 213
—— fishing by drift-nets, 111, 127, 129, 213, 220, 222
—— —— by hook, 153, 210
—— —— by kettle-net, 167, 222
—— —— by sean, 129, 212, 221
—— in the Firth of Forth, 287
—— on the Manx coast, 129, 340
—— season on the English coast, 127
—— on the Irish coast, 129
Malm's observations on spawning, 30
Manilla hemp for trawl-nets, 7, 70
Manship on the origin of Yarmouth, 236
Manx fishermen, improved condition of, 343
——, shares amongst, 342
—— —— at the south of Ireland, 340
—— fishing boats, 341
—— ——, crews of, 342
"Marfire," 114
Markets for Shetland cured fish, 312
"Maties," probable meaning of the name, 295 *note*
"Mease" of herrings, 343
Mesh of drift-net for herrings, 104

Mesh of drift-net for mackerel, 111
—— of drift-net for pilchards, 111
—— of stow-net, 165
—— of trammel-net, 175
—— of trawl-net, 65
Minch, herring season in the, 313
——, line-fishing in the, 318
"Mingle," 164
Mode of measuring the size of mesh, 101 *note*
Moray Firth, fisheries of, 291
Morecambe Bay famous for shrimps, 181
—— —— shrimp trawling, 182
More haddocks caught than could be sold, 89
Motive instincts of animals, 132
Mount's Bay boats, cost of, 197
—— —— boats, crews of, 197
—— —— boats, description of, 196
Mumbles, oyster-perches at, 185
Mussel beds in the Tees, 268
—— fishing in Lerwick Harbour, 310
—— scorps in the Wash, 250
Myxine or borer, injury caused by, 273

N.

NAVAL RESERVE, fishermen in, 8
Nets made by machinery, 6, 100, 312
"New Claddagh" in America, 386
Newhaven, fisheries at, 284
Noise, effect of, on fish, 115
Northumberland coast, early herring fishery on, 273
North Sunderland, disappearance of turbot from, 266
Norway skiffs, 309
Number of trawlers on English coast, 96
Nymph Bank, discovery of, 367 *note*
—— ——, large boats required for, 368
—— ——, situation of, 367
—— —— a good fishing ground, 367

O.

OBSTACLES to fishing on west coast of Ireland, 349
"Offal" fish sent inland, 13
Old theory of migration of herrings, 117
Old trawling grounds still productive, 91
Orkney, fisheries at, 301
——, herring season at, 301

Orkney, line-fishing at, 302
—— dried fish, export of, 302
—— fishing boats, 303
Otter-trawl, 52, 372
——, invention of, 372
——, objections to, 372
——, possible escape of fish from, 372
——, shooting the, 373
Over-supply of haddocks formerly, 89
Oyster beds in the Firth of Forth, 284
—— dredging at Milford, 183
—— fishery at Arklow, 363
—— —— at Falmouth, 198
Oystermouth or Mumbles, dredging from, 185
Oyster-perches at Mumbles, 185
Oysters laid down at Beaumaris, 183

P.

PACKAGES for trawl-fish, 254
Packing herrings at Yarmouth, 243
—— lobsters for the market, 305
—— pilchards at St. Ives, 193
Pads, pots, and trunks of fish, 255
"Parejas," 52
Pegwell Bay, shrimp fishery at, 223
Periwinkles from the Hebrides, 318
—— from the Orkneys, 303
Phosphorescent light in the sea, 114, 270
Pilchard drift-nets, 111
—— fishery almost confined to Cornwall, 187
—— fishing in Cornwall, 130, 157, 188
—— —— at Guernsey, 214
—— —— on the Irish coast, 375
—— oil, quantity obtained, 194
—— ——, use made of, 194
—— seaning at St. Ives, 157, 188
—— —— on south coast of Cornwall, 194
——, seans. different sizes of, 194
—— season on the Cornish coast, 130
Pilchards, large catch of, 194
——, method of curing, 193
——, mode of packing, 193
——, spawning of, 31, 132
——, table of exports of, 196
——, where do they spawn? 131
—— come inshore after spawning, 41
—— come inshore when ready to spawn, 41
—— on the Irish coast, 130, 368, 375
—— on the northern coast of Cornwall, 188

"Pit seasons," 95
Plaice, abundance of, in the North Sea, 91
———, demand for, 17, 91
———, spawning of, 30
——— and haddocks, large catches of, 88
Pleuronectidæ, spawning of, 30
Plymouth, drift-fish landed at, 200
———, fisheries at, 200
———, fish sent from, 199
———, former low price of fish at, 199
——— trawlers, 199
——— trawling grounds, 93, 200
Pole-trawl, 52, 371
Poole Harbour, shrimping in, 219
Port Letters, 180, 407
Position of fish in a tideway, 74
Possibility of increasing the supply of fish, 49
Prejudice against trawled haddocks, 89
Preparation of cotton nets, 100
Prime and offal fish, 15
Proportion of herrings caught to those uncaught, 35
——— of prime to offal fish, 87
Protection of Cornish sean-fisheries, 195
——— of young crabs and lobsters, 248
Puncturing the air-bladder, 139

Q.

QUANTITY of fish caught by a trawler, 16, 83
——— of fish landed at Grimsby, 253
——— of ice imported at Grimsby, 256
——— of ice imported at Hull, 260
——— of whelks used in a cod-smack, 143
Quick delivery of fish necessary, 66, 246, 255

R.

RAILWAY, completion of, to Grimsby, 252
———, fish carriage by, 11
Railways, effect of their extension, 12, 19
Ramsgate, Brixham fishermen at, 222
———, number of trawlers at, 222
———, progress of, as a trawling station, 222
——— trawling grounds, 222
Rate of speed for trawling, 70, 75
Red mullet at Guernsey, 216
Registration of fishing boats, 405
——— of fishing boats imperfect, 178, 282

Regulations for lighting drift-boats, 108, 400
Resistance of trawl, 77
Restrictions on Irish trawling, 359
Ring, fisheries at, 370
Rockall, deep water around, 307
———, difficulty of fishing at, 307
———, large cod at, 307
———, position of, 307
———, uncertainty of finding fish at, 307
Round-fish in trawl more liable to injury than flat-fish, 86
Royal Irish Fisheries Company, 378
Royal Navy, fishermen's objections to, 7
Ruffled water best for drift-fishing, 112
Rye Bay, trawling in, 222

S.

ST. IVES, arrangement for working seans at, 191
——— ———, description of seans at, 190
——— ———, sean-boats used at, 191
——— ———, working the sean at, 157, 192
——— ——— Bay, seaning stations in, 189
——— ——— famous for its sean-fishery, 188
Sale of cod at Grimsby, 254
Sand-eel as bait, 5, 217
——— seans at Guernsey, 217
Sars' discoveries about fish spawn, 28
"Scaith," build and rig of, 294
Scarborough, early trawling at, 263
——— yawls, 263
Scarcity of turbot on north-east coast of England, 266
Scotch coast divided into fishery districts, 281
——— fisheries, importance of, 334
——— Fisheries Report for 1873, 336
——— fishermen, industry of, 335
——— fishing boats, composite build of, 279
——— ———, cost of, 278
——— ———, general build of, 291
——— ———, general rig of, 292
——— ———, peculiarity in the rig of, 292
——— ———, size of, 291
——— herring boat, crew of, 294
——— "trawl," 51 note
Scotland, general fisheries of, 275
Scudding pole, 110
"Scudding the fish," 110
Sea Fisheries Act, 1868, 397, 403

Sean, the, 157
———, ground or foot, 159
——— stop, 157
——— tuck, 158
———, working the, 157
——— boats at St. Ives, 191
——— fishery at Brighton, 221
——— ——— at the Chesil Beach, 159, 212
SEAN-FISHING, 156
———, long practice of, 156
———, supposed introduction of, 156
Seaning ground at St. Ives, 189
——— regulations at St. Ives, 189
Seans, classes of, 156
———, general description of, 157
"Sean-trawling," 321 *note*
Seasons for drift-fishing, 116
Selling the fish at Grimsby, 254
SET-NETS, 173
———, description of, 173
———, fish caught by, 174
——— sometimes called trammels, 173
Share system with trawlers, 210, 246, 258
Sheep-skin buoys, 300
Shetland, bait used at, 310
———, cured fish at, 306
———, fisheries at, 304
———, fishing grounds at, 305
———, fish-oil made at, 310
———, whaling at, 310
——— cod-smacks, 305
——— cured fish, returns of, 312
——— yawls, 309
Shetlanders a hardy race, 311
——— proud of their Norse descent, 311
Shooting the drift-nets, 106
——— the longlines, 138
——— the beam-trawl, 71
——— the otter-trawl, 373
Shrimping in Bridgewater Bay, 186
——— at Cleethorpes, 256
——— at Pegwell Bay, 223
Shrimping ground in the Thames, 228
Shrimp-nets used in the Thames, 227
Shrimps sent from Leigh, 229
Shrimp trawling in Morecambe Bay, 181
——— ——— in the Thames, 229
——— ——— in the Wash, 250
Silver Pit, discovery of, 94
——— ——— very productive in hard winters, 95
Skerries wherry, 360

Slapton Cellars once a curing place for pilchards, 212
Sligo Bay, fisheries in, 389
Small cod caught inshore, 147
——— fish baits to large ones, 38
——— herrings far from the land, 40
——— proportion of dead fish in the trawl, 87
——— ——— of ground trawled over, 47
Smoked haddocks at Eyemouth, 285
——— ———, trade in, 89, 286
Solent, stow-boating in the, 219
Soles caught by spilliards, 379
——— from the Norfolk coast, 90
——— in the Silver Pit, 95
——— mostly sent to Billingsgate, 99
——— on clean sandy ground, 90
Solway, fisheries in the, 334
Sound, transmission of, 115
Spanish trawl, 52
Spawn, enemies to, 37
——— drifted into bays, 43
——— ——— out of bays, 43
——— eaten by fishes, 32, 37
Spawning habits of sea fish, 26
Spawning of the cod, 28
——— Gadidæ, 29
——— haddock, 28
——— herring, 30
——— mackerel, 29
——— pilchard, 31
——— plaice, 30
——— Pleuronectidæ, 30
——— sprat, 133
Spawning plaice on the Doggerbank, 42
——— season of herrings, 119, 120
——— ——— of mackerel, 128
——— ——— of sprats, 133
Spilliard or spiller (see Longline).
Sprat fishery in Beauly Firth, 291
——— ——— in the Firth of Forth, 286
——— ——— at Inver, 389
——— ——— at Passage, 166, 368
——— ——— at Plymouth, 200
——— ——— at Ramsgate, 135
——— ——— in the Solent, 219
——— ——— in the Thames, 161, 223
——— ——— in Torbay, 211
——— ——— in the Wash, 161, 249
Sprats, drift-fishing for, 134, 135
———, periodical appearance of, 133
———, season for fishing, 133
———, spawning time of, 133

Sprats in all conditions come inshore, 11
—— sold by the bushel, 164
—— —— for manure, 165
Sprit-boats at Dingle, 379
Staithes, cured fish at, 266
——, line-fisheries at, 265
Start Bay, fisheries in, 211
Statistics of Scotch fishermen and boats, 280
Steam applied to fishing boats, 280, 290
—— carrying-vessels, 225
—— Cutter Fish-carrying Company, 225 note
—— trawlers expensive to work, 225
—— tugs at Aberdeen, 289
—— —— in the Thames, 290
—— —— at Yarmouth, 290
Steering the trawler, 73
"Stems" in St. Ives Bay, 189
Stop-sean, 157, 158, 190
Storing live cod, 149, 232
Stornoway, fisheries at, 313
——, fresh herrings sent from, 217
Stow-boating, season for, 164
—— on the Thames, 161, 229
Stow-net, description of, 161
——, kind of fish caught by, 161
——, large takes of fish by, 165
——, where used, 161
——, working the, 163
Strain on drift-nets, 112
Strangford, oyster beds at, 393
Substances mistaken for fish spawn, 32
Sucker, borer, or bag, 273
Sunderland, inquiry at, into complaints of fishermen, 268
——, outcry at, against trawlers, 268
——, trawl-fish landed at, 268
Supply of fish, evidence of increase in, 12
—— —— difficult to be ascertained, 11
—— —— at coast towns, 13
Swansea Bay, fisheries in, 185
"Swills," 239
Swinden's account of Yarmouth, 236
"Swing-rope," 107

T.

Taaf-net, 310, 320
Takes of fish by trawlers, 24
Teelin, line-fishery at, 391
Tenby, trawling season at, 184

Tenby, various fisheries at, 184
—— as a trawling station, 184
—— fishing boats, 184
—— ground worked by Brixham trawlers, 184
—— trawling ground, 184
Thames, fisheries of the, 223
—— shrimp-boats, 228
—— shrimp-net, 227
Tides suitable for trawling, 70
Time occupied in fishing by trawlers, 264
Tolls at Billingsgate, 11
Torbay, fisheries east of, 212
—— fisheries, 210
—— hookers, 210
Train, fleet, or drift of nets, 101
Trammel-fishing at Guernsey, 176, 216
Trammel-net, action of, 175
——, derivation of the name, 175 note
——, description of, 174
——, for red mullet, 176
Trammel or Set Nets, 173
Trawl-beam, 54
Trawl-bridle, 65
Trawlers and liners, 144
—— charged with destroying fish spawn, 32
—— fishing in fleets, 259
—— to keep three miles from drift-boats, 109, 400
—— working throughout the year, 274
Trawl-fish, classification of, 15
—— sent to Billingsgate, 224
—— sold by weight, 260
—— stowed in bulk with ice, 259
Trawl fishermen shipping in yachts, 357
Trawl-heads, description of, 55
——, Barking pattern, 56, 201
——, Brixham pattern, 56, 201
——, French, 57
——, use of, 55
——, weight of, 56
Trawling, 51
——, derivation of the name, 51
—— for hake, 78
—— grounds in the Channel, 93
—— —— in the Irish Sea, 358
—— —— in the North Sea, 94
—— —— on the Welsh coast, 183
—— —— still productive, 203
—— stations, 54
—— ——, Bantry Bay, 377
—— ——, Barking, 225

Trawling stations, Brixham, 200
———, Carnarvon, 183
———, Dingle, 378
———, Douglas, 341
———, Dover, 222
———, Dublin, 356
———, Fleetwood, 181
———, Galway, 383
———, Grimsby, 252
———, Hull, 257
———, Liverpool, 181
———, Lowestoft, 235
———, Plymouth, 199
———, Ramsgate, 222
———, Scarborough, 263
———, Tenby, 184
———, Waterford, 366
———, Yarmouth, 244
Trawl-net, action of, 74
———, back, 58
———, belly, 58
———, bosom, 58
———, cod-line, 61
———, cod or purse, 60
———, cost of, 70
———, flapper, 62
———, gorings or wings, 60
———, materials for, 70
———, pockets, 61
———, use of, 64
———, proportions of, 64
———, rubbing pieces, 61
———, size of mesh, 65
———, square of, 58
———, wear of, 69
Trawl vessels, crews of, 210, 246
——— ———, improvements in, 65
——— ———, present and former cost of, 69, 210
——— ———, rig of, 66, 67, 69, 220, 247, 252, 257, 320, 358, 360
——— ———, size of, 66, 199, 252, 257, 356
——— warp, 65
Trim-net, description of, 165
———, fish caught by, 165
———, where used, 165, 250
Trim-tram net at Harwich, 233
Trot (see Longline).
Trotting for whelks, 142
Trunk-fishing for lobsters, 264
Tuck-seam, 158
"Tumbling-net," 176

Turbot formerly supplied by the Dutch fishermen, 90
——— in the Channel, 90
——— near the Wolf Rock, 90
——— on the Dutch coast, 90
Tusk found only in northern seas, 302
Twine drift-nets, how made, 102

V.

VARIED produce of trawl-fishing, 80
Vomerine teeth of the herring, 126
Voracity of the coalfish, 266
——— of the cod and turbot, 334

W.

"WASH" of whelks, 143
Wash, fisheries in the, 249
———, mussel-scorps in the, 250
———, sprat fishing in the, 249
———, trim-nets in the, 165, 250
Waste caused by every method of fishing, 43
"Waterburn," 114
Waterford Harbour, fisheries at, 365
——— ———, objections to trawling in, 366
——— ———, plenty of fish in, 368
——— ———, steam trawling in, 368
——— ———, trawling in, 366
Weather suitable for trawling, 82
Weirs in Swansea Bay, 170
———, complaints against, 170
———, construction of, 170
———, fish taken by, 172
Welled-smacks, construction of, 140
———, cost of, 141
———, fish kept alive in, 140
———, the idea of, taken from the Dutch, 231 note
———, when first used in England, 139
Welled-smacks at Grimsby, 149, 251
——— ——— at Harwich, 139, 232
Welsh fisheries generally unimportant, 183
——— mining and quarrying more attractive than fishing, 184
——— trawling grounds fished by English boats, 183
"West End fish," 152
Wexford fisheries, 365
——— herring cots, 364
Weymouth Bay, trawling in, 212

Whales in Donegal Bay, 389
—— at Shetland, 310
Whelks, as bait for cod, 138
——, how kept alive, 143
——, measurement of, 143
——, methods of catching, 142, 143, 310
——, quantity used by each cod-smack, 143
——, where procured, 142
Where do fish spawn? 39
Whitebait, 124
——, as described by Yarrell and Couch, 125
—— and herring, their specific characters compared, 125, 126
—— net, 166
"White herrings," branding of, 296
—— ——, classification of, 295
—— ——, method of curing, 294
—— ——, packing, 295
—— ——, where exported, 297
Whiting in Donegal Bay, 391
—— on the coast of Devon, 81
Wholesale purchase of fish, 15
Why do fish approach the land? 40
Wick an important station, 294
—— winter herring fishery, 297
—— Harbour, construction of, 298, 299
Wink, 198
——, dandy, 67, 71
Winter herring fishery in Scotland, 286, 297
—— herrings for bait, 297
—— the best trawling season, 83
Working the trawl, 70

Y.

YARMOUTH, curing herrings at, 241
——, landing the fish at, 239
——, payment of fishermen at, 241
——, smoking herrings at, 242
——, Swinden's account of, 236
——, trawling at, 244
—— drift-boats used as trawlers, 246
—— "ferry-boats," 239
—— fishery, antiquity of, 236
—— —— in the sixth century, 97
—— Haven, difficulty in entering, 238
—— herrings, mode of packing, 243
—— herring season, 237
—— luggers, crews of, 105
—— ——, description of, 104
—— smoke-room, 242
—— trawlers, crews of, 246
—— wholesale fish-market, 239
Yarrell on the spawning time of the sprat, 133
Yarrell's description of the whitebait, 125
Yorkshire coast, fisheries on, 264
Young fish at all distances from the land, 44
—— —— caught by shrimpers, 44
—— —— caught by trawlers, 45
—— —— in bays, probably not spawned there, 44
—— —— inshore, 42
Young fry, early destruction of, 37

THE END.

LONDON: PRINTED BY EDWARD STANFORD, 6, 7, & 8, CHARING CROSS, S.W.

SELECTED LIST OF BOOKS

PUBLISHED BY

EDWARD STANFORD,

6, 7, & 8, CHARING CROSS, LONDON, S.W.

ADDERLEY (Sir C. B.).—COLONIAL POLICY and HISTORY— REVIEW of "The COLONIAL POLICY of LORD J. RUSSELL'S ADMINISTRATION, BY EARL GREY, 1853," and of SUBSEQUENT COLONIAL HISTORY. By the Rt. Hon. Sir C. B. Adderley, K.C.M.G., M.P. Demy 8vo, cloth, 9s.

ANSTIE.—THE COAL FIELDS OF GLOUCESTERSHIRE and SOMERSETSHIRE, AND THEIR RESOURCES. By John Anstie, B.A., Fellow of the Geological Society of London, Associate of the Institute of Civil Engineers, Civil and Mining Engineer, &c. With Tables and Sections. Imperial 8vo, cloth, 6s.

BIRCH.—EXAMPLES of LABOURERS' COTTAGES, with PLANS for IMPROVING the DWELLINGS of the POOR in LARGE TOWNS. By John Birch, Architect, Author of 'Designs for Dwellings of the Labouring Classes,' to which was awarded the Medal and Premium of the Society of Arts. Imperial 8vo, cloth, illustrated, 3s. 6d.

BROWNE (W. A., LL.D.).—The MERCHANT'S HANDBOOK. A Book of Reference for the use of those engaged in Domestic and Foreign Commerce. Second Edition. Demy 12mo, cloth, 5s.

This work affords full and reliable information from official sources of the currencies and moneys of account, and the weights and measures of all the great commercial countries in the world.

EDWARDS (H. Sutherland).—The GERMANS in FRANCE. Notes on the Method and Conduct of the Invasion; the Relations between Invaders and Invaded; and the Modern Usages of War. By H. Sutherland Edwards. Crown 8vo, cloth, 10s. 6d.

HANDBOOK to GOVERNMENT SITUATIONS: Showing the MODE of APPOINTMENT and RATES of PAY, and containing the most RECENT REGULATIONS for OPEN COMPETITIONS for the HOME and INDIAN CIVIL SERVICES, the ENGINEERING COLLEGE, the FOREST SERVICE, and for ARMY EXAMINATIONS. With Examination Papers, and Specimens of handwriting extracted from the Reports of the Civil Service Commissioners. Fourth Edition. Crown 8vo, cloth, 3s. 6d.

HULL.—COAL FIELDS of GREAT BRITAIN: their History, Structure, and Resources; with Notices of the Coal Fields of other parts of the World. By Edward Hull, M.A., F.R.S., Director of the Geological Survey of Ireland, Professor of Geology in the Royal College of Science, Dublin, &c. With Maps and Illustrations. Third Edition, revised and enlarged, embodying the Reports of the Royal Coal Commission. Demy 8vo, cloth, 16s.

JENKINSON'S PRACTICAL GUIDE to the ISLE OF MAN. Containing Introduction — Population — Table of Distances — Heights of Mountains — Charges for Porters and Conveyances — How to Spend a Flying Visit to the Isle of Man — Voyage round the Island — Hotel Tariffs — Coaches, &c. — Douglas, Castletown, Peel, and Ramsay Sections — A Walk round the Island — Index, &c. Also, Chapters on Local Names — Mineralogy — Civil History — Ecclesiastical History — Geology — Botany — Zoology — Agriculture — Commerce — And Sea Trout-fishing. With Map. Fcap. 8vo, cloth, 5s.

—— **SMALLER PRACTICAL GUIDE to the ISLE OF MAN.** Containing Distances — Heights of Mountains — Charges for Porters and Conveyances — How to Spend a Flying Visit — Voyage round the Island, &c. With Map. Fcap. 8vo, 2s.

—— **PRACTICAL GUIDE to the ENGLISH LAKE DISTRICT.** With Nine Maps and Three Views. Contents:— Introduction — How to Spend a Flying Visit to the Lakes — A Fourteen Days' Pedestrian Tour — Charges for Conveyances, Ponies, and Guides — Heights of Mountains, Lakes, Tarns, and Passes — Local Names — Meteorology, Geology, and Botany.

WINDERMERE, LANGDALE, GRASMERE, CONISTON, KESWICK, BUTTERMERE, WASTWATER, and ULLSWATER SECTIONS, containing full Information and Instructions respecting Walks, Drives, Boating, Ascents, Excursions, &c. Third Edition. Fcap. 8vo, cloth, 6s.

*** The SECTIONS separately: KESWICK — WINDERMERE and LANGDALE — CONISTON, BUTTERMERE, and WASTWATER — GRASMERE and ULLSWATER. With Maps, price 1s. 6d. each.

—— **EIGHTEEN-PENNY GUIDE to the ENGLISH LAKE DISTRICT.** Containing Charges for Conveyances, Ponies, and Guides — Heights of Passes, Mountains, Lakes, and Tarns: with Information and Instructions respecting Walks, Drives, Boating, Ascents, Excursions, &c. Fcap. 8vo, with Map, 1s. 6d.

RAMSAY.— PHYSICAL GEOLOGY and GEOGRAPHY of GREAT Britain. By A. C. RAMSAY, LL.D., F.R.S., &c., Director-General of the Geological Surveys of the United Kingdom. Fourth Edition, considerably enlarged, and illustrated with NUMEROUS SECTIONS and a GEOLOGICAL MAP of GREAT BRITAIN, printed in Colours. Post 8vo, cloth, 7s. 6d.

"This edition has been partly re-written, and contains much new matter. . . . . The preliminary sketch of the different formations, and of the phenomena connected with the metamorphism of rocks, has been much enlarged; and many long and important paragraphs have been added in the chapters on the physical structure of England and Scotland — partly on subjects connected with the coal question, partly on the glacial epoch, partly on the union of Britain with the Continent at various epochs, and the migrations of animals hither; and on many other subjects. An entire new chapter has been added on the origin of the river courses of Britain; and large additions have been made to the earlier brief account of soils, and the economic products of the various geological formations. There are also many new illustrative sections." — *Extract from Preface.*

RUSSELL.— BIARRITZ and the BASQUE COUNTRIES. By Count HENRY RUSSELL, Member of the Geographical and Geological Societies of France, of the Alpine Club, and Société Ramond, Author of 'Pau and the Pyrenees,' &c. Crown 8vo, with a Map, 6s.

STAINBANK (H. E.).— COFFEE in NATAL, its CULTURE and PREPARATION. By H. E. STAINBANK, Manager of the Natal Coffee Works, Umgeni, Natal. In Two Parts, with an Appendix and 24 Diagrams. Crown 8vo, cloth, 2s.

www.ingramcontent.com/pod-product-compliance
Lightning Source LLC
Chambersburg PA
CBHW051857300426
44117CB00006B/432